THE POLITICS OF ETHNIC SURVIVAL

THE POLITICS OF ETHNIC SURVIVAL: GERMANS IN PRAGUE, 1861-1914

GARY B. COHEN

PRINCETON UNIVERSITY PRESS
PRINCETON, NEW JERSEY

For my parents,
and my friends in Prague

TABLE OF CONTENTS

MAPS, TABLES, AND PLATES

ACKNOWLEDGMENTS

I have incurred many debts in completing this study, more than I can properly acknowledge here. A number of individuals and institutions, however, provided assistance without which the project would not have been possible. Three historians, in particular, offered vital guidance in the formative stages of the work. Carl E. Schorske supervised the doctoral dissertation in which I first began to study the Prague Germans, and he brought to the task his unique understanding of German liberal culture in old Austria. Then and since he has been a patient and perceptive critic as well as loyal counselor. John R. Gillis first guided me in the study of social history, and he provided valuable suggestions on early drafts of the study. During my researches in Prague, Jan Havránek led me to sources and gave generously of his time and deep knowledge of Czech political and social history. At the end of the project, Docent Havránek and his colleagues in the Archive of the Charles University provided vital aid in collecting and preparing illustrations for inclusion in the book.

Others also contributed significantly. Robert A. Kann helped on many points of Austrian political and legal history, and Christoph Stölzl shared his knowledge of the history of Bohemian Jewry and the Czech-German conflict. At crucial junctures Myron Gutmann, David Hammack, William Jordan, Arno Mayer, Mary Jo Nye, and Robert Nye offered needed advice and encouragement. In the final stages, David Levy and Henry Tobias assisted with problems of presentation and style, and James J. Sheehan and H. Gordon Skilling each thoughtfully commented on the whole study. Roy Davis sorted out my untutored notions of cartography and drew the maps which appear here. Valli Powell merits special thanks for managing to type the whole manuscript with so much skill, patience, and good cheer. At Princeton University Press I benefited from the great experience of its associate director and editor, R. Miriam Brokaw, who shepherded the manuscript through the process of publication.

(xiii)

A number of foundations and universities have generously supported my work on this study. A graduate fellowship from the Danforth Foundation and an exchange fellowship to Czechoslovakia sponsored by the International Research and Exchanges Board (IREX) and the Czech Ministry of Education made possible the initial research and writing. Princeton University supported subsequent research and writing with a faculty research grant and a Shelby Cullom Davis Post-doctoral Fellowship in the Department of History. The Research Council of the University of Oklahoma at Norman undertook the costs of preparing the final manuscript. The Leo Baeck Institute in New York graciously gave me permission to use a number of unpublished memoirs, photographs, and rare periodicals in its rich collections.

I am deeply grateful to all who have helped along the way. If the results do not always fulfill their confidence, the shortcomings are my own.

A NOTE ON PLACE NAMES AND
CZECH REFERENCES

Except for instances where there are generally recognized English equivalents, the Czech designations will be used in this study for all place names in the Bohemian Lands to conform with current usage in atlases, Czech histories, and publications of the Czechoslovak government. Where the Czech place names have changed since World War I, the pre-1914 designations will be used to avoid anachronisms. For readers more accustomed to the German names, those will be given along with the Czech the first time a place is mentioned.

Czech-language sources will be cited in Czech only to avoid cluttering the footnotes. The list of sources provides English translations of the Czech titles for all items cited.

ABBREVIATIONS

AHMP   Archiv hlavního města Prahy [Archive of the Capital City Prague]

APA   Archiv pražského arcibiskupství [Archive of the Prague Archbishopric]

AUK   Archiv University Karlovy [Archive of the Charles University, Prague]

AVA   Allgemeines Verwaltungsarchiv [General Administrative Archive, Vienna]

AŽM   Archiv židovského muzea [Archive of the State Jewish Museum, Prague]

ČM   Fond českého místodržitelství [Files of the Bohemian Governor's Office]

ČSČH   *Československý časopis historický* [Czechoslovak Historical Journal]

HHStA   Haus-, Hof-, und Staatsarchiv [House, Court, and State Archive, Vienna]

IB   Informationsbüroakten, Ministerium des Äussern [Documents of the Intelligence Section, Ministry of Foreign Affairs, Vienna]

LBI   Leo Baeck Institute Library and Archive, New York

M   Morning edition of newspapers with several editions daily

MCR   Manuscript census return

MI-Praes,   Ministerium des Innern-Praesidialakten,
MV/R   Ministerstvo vnitra-Rakousko [Documents of the presidium of the Cisleithanian Ministry of the Interior]

PM   Presidium českého místodržitelství [Presidium of the Bohemian Governor's Office]

PMT   Tajný spisy presidia českého místodržitelství [Secret files of the presidium of the Bohemian Governor's Office]

PP   Fond pražského policejního ředitelství [Files of the Prague Police Directorate]

SÚA   Státní ústřední archiv [Central State Archive, Prague]

UC-I   Documents from the Archive of the German Foreign Office filmed at Whaddon Hall for the University of California, series I

VGDB   Verein für Geschichte der Deutschen in Böhmen [Society for the History of the Germans in Bohemia]

ŽNOP   Židovská náboženská obec Prahy [Jewish Religious Community of Prague]

THE POLITICS OF ETHNIC SURVIVAL

In 1892 the Czech nationalists who dominated the Prague board of aldermen decided to replace the city's bilingual Czech-German street signs with exclusively Czech ones. Leaders of the local German minority heatedly protested the action, but in the end the Austrian imperial authorities upheld the decision of the aldermen. Much more was at stake than merely whether the municipality would insist on the name "Celetná" for what Germans called "Zeltnergasse" or "Kaprová" for "Karpfengasse." In the view of a professor at the German University of Prague, the affair of the street signs was only one more of many humiliations suffered by the city's once powerful German community:[1]

> Whoever has grown up in Prague and has memories will readily grant that this is a symptom of the general situation of the Germans in the Bohemian capital. Decades ago it was a German city, where only the lowest classes of the population dared express themselves in Czech. . . . Now the times are long since gone when every educated Prager naturally spoke German, when it would have been unheard of for any army officer to speak in Czech.
>
> While previously great capital was exclusively in the hands of the Germans, Czech banks have also come into existence in recent years. Whoever strolls through the streets of Prague with observant eyes will be able to confirm that elegance and taste are by no means a privilege of the German ladies, and there is already a Czech *jeunesse dorée*. . . . In short, one will see in general a prodigious growth of the Czech nation, and the initiated will realize that it is not only prodigious but also powerful.

Contemporaries as well as subsequent observers of modern East-Central Europe have given more attention to the rise of the Czech majority than to the decline of the Germans. At the time German community leaders as well as their Czech counterparts understood the processes by which the Czech population grew, a Czech middle

---

[1] Ottokar Weber, "Prag," *Deutsche Arbeit*, VIII (1909), pp. 325-26.

class arose, and the Czech language gained in respect. They com-
prehended less well, however, why the once dominant Germans
lost in numbers and how they adjusted to the accompanying loss
of power and position. Subsequently, historians, political scientists,
and sociologists have often remarked the decline of German groups
in Prague and many other cities along the frontier between Ger-
manic and non-Germanic cultures, but they have made little study
of the internal evolution of these once powerful groups.

Historians and social scientists interested in ethnicity have generally neglected declining upper-strata minorities.[2] Compelling reasons have focused their attention on lower-strata minorities and
subordinate groups in general: the frequency of their presence,
the economic and political deprivation they have suffered, and the
sometimes valiant efforts to improve their situations. General social
development and the advance of majority rights in the modern
world, in fact, have frequently caused the decline of dominant
ethnic minorities, but too often historians have simply relegated
such groups to the categories of historical failures or "dying classes."
Forces deemed more "progressive" have received primary attention. Similarly, many sociologists have assumed that the injustices
suffered by subordinate groups present more urgent problems for
understanding and solution than do declining upper-strata minorities.

Yet declining upper-strata groups deserve closer study, for they
too contribute to the general evolution of societies. Their stubborn
defense of old bastions of political and economic power has, of
course, caused much social conflict in the modern world, but their
determination to survive has also produced creative forms of social
and political adaptation which have shaped the lives of minority
and majority alike. Moreover, emerging majority groups, whether
Finns throwing off the dominance of Swedish-speaking upper
classes in Finland or Czechs and Slovenes displacing German-speakers in the old Habsburg Monarchy, have generally defined their
group values and social relations not in isolation but in a dialectical

---

[2] The social science literature on ethnic minorities is enormous. The following are
representative of work from the 1960s and 1970s: Fredrik Barth, ed., *Ethnic Groups
and Boundaries* (Boston, 1969); Cynthia H. Enloe, *Ethnic Conflict and Political Devel-
opment* (Boston, 1973); Milton J. Esman, ed., *Ethnic Conflict in the Western World*
(Ithaca and London, 1977); Nathan Glazer and Daniel P. Moynihan, ed., *Ethnicity:
Theory and Experience* (Cambridge, Mass., 1975); Milton M. Gordon, *Assimilation in
American Life* (New York, 1964); R. A. Schermerhorn, *Comparative Ethnic Relations:
A Framework for Theory and Research* (New York, 1970); and George E. Simpson and
J. Milton Yinger, *Racial and Cultural Minorities*, 4th ed. (New York, 1972).

relationship with the old dominant minorities.[3] Subordinate ethnic groups have pushed aside ruling minorities sufficiently often in the nineteenth and twentieth centuries to make both halves of the relationship deserving of study.

In the modern world, upper-strata ethnic minorities have arisen most commonly where weak and economically less developed peoples have been subject to external domination. Although the phenomenon is most obvious in the cases of European colonization of the Third World, similar ethnic stratification has appeared in underdeveloped areas of Europe and North America as well. Here, though, economic, cultural, and racial differences between dominant and subordinate groups have tended to be narrower than in the Third World, and ruling linguistic or culture groups have often included indigenous as well as foreign elements. In Europe, ethnic stratification has appeared most frequently in peripheral segments of larger states and in those regions which have experienced retarded or abortive state-building. Celtic groups in Wales, Scotland, and Brittany have experienced ethnic subordination just as many French-speakers in Quebec see their province as having been colonized by Anglo-Canadians and Americans.[4] In the eighteenth century, French-speaking elements achieved ascendancy over the Flemish in what are now Belgium and Luxembourg. In a larger process, lasting through the late middle ages and early modern era, German-speaking groups reached out from the German states and the Austrian core of the Habsburg lands to establish dominance over the Baltic peoples and Slavs of East-Central Europe.

Examining the decline of the German elites can contribute much to understanding of the Habsburg Monarchy and the successor states in the nineteenth and early twentieth centuries. Conflict between the dominant German and Magyar elements and between them and the various subject peoples became decisive factors in the political life of the Monarchy in the nineteenth century. Rising ethnic consciousness and competition for power and economic ad-

[3] See Fredrik Barth, "Introduction," in Barth, ed., *Ethnic Groups*, pp. 9-16; and Michael Hechter, "Towards a Theory of Ethnic Change," *Politics and Society*, II (1971), pp. 41-44.

[4] Hechter compares ethnic stratification in the peripheries of European states to conditions in the Third World in *Politics and Society*, II, pp. 33-34. See also Hechter, *Internal Colonialism: The Celtic Fringe in British National Development, 1536-1966* (Berkeley, Calif., 1975). On Quebec see Henry Milner and Sheilagh H. Milner, *The Decolonization of Quebec* (Toronto, 1973).

vantage spawned vigorous political movements among the various
ethnic groups, each of which demanded autonomy or self-deter-
mination for itself within its home area. These "national" loyalties
became so strong by the end of the century that contemporaries
typically spoke of "national" differences and "nationalities" rather
than of "ethnicity" or some other term that we might use to indicate
merely cultural and social distinctions. Political conflict among the
various ethnic groups has been a major theme in the historiography
of the Habsburg Monarchy, but as yet there is little understanding
of the actual development of popular ethnic identities for either
the dominant or subject groups or of the relation of ethnicity to
class, status, and religion in determining basic social cleavages.

Until recently scholars have generally neglected the social history
of ethnic differences in the Monarchy. Historians have conventionally assigned a central role to nationality conflicts in explaining
the Monarchy's growing instability in the late nineteenth century
and its ultimate demise in 1918, but older studies focused almost
exclusively on ministerial and parliamentary politics, party development, and the intellectual bases of nationalist ideologies.[5] The
two finest studies of the Czech-German conflict, for instance, the
works of Elizabeth Wiskemann and Hermann Münch, date back
more than thirty years; both concentrate on politics and lack sociological depth and precision.[6] Since the early 1960s Polish, Czech,
Slovak, Magyar, and Slovene scholars have begun to study the history of social structures and popular culture in their countries,
using approaches like those of Western European and American
social historians. Yet historians in the successor states have dealt
primarily with the development of their own peoples and have

[5] For examples see Hugo Hantsch, *Die Nationalitätenfrage im alten Österreich* (Vi-
enna, 1955); idem, *Die Geschichte Österreichs*, 2nd ed., 2 vols. (Graz, 1947); Robert
A. Kann, *Das Nationalitätenproblem der Habsburgermonarchie*, 2nd ed., 2 vols. (Graz
and Cologne, 1964); C. A. Macartney, *The Habsburg Empire* (New York, 1969);
Berthold Sutter, *Die Badenischen Sprachenverordnungen von 1897*, 2 vols. (Graz and
Cologne, 1960-65); Joachim Remak, "The Healthy Invalid: How Doomed the Habsburg Empire," *Journal of Modern History*, XLI (1969), pp. 127-43; and the symposium,
"The Nationality Problem in the Habsburg Monarchy in the Nineteenth Century:
a Critical Appraisal," in *Austrian History Yearbook*, III (1967). For a review of literature
on the Czechs under the Monarchy in the nineteenth century, see G. B. Cohen,
"Recent Research on Czech Nation-Building," *Journal of Modern History*, LI (1979),
pp. 760-72.

[6] Elizabeth Wiskemann, *Czechs and Germans* (1st ed., New York, 1938; 2nd ed.,
New York, 1967); Hermann Münch, *Böhmische Tragödie* (Braunschweig, Berlin, and
Hamburg, 1949).

slighted inter-group relations.[7] The social history of the now vanished German minorities has evoked little scholarly interest in either
the eastern bloc or Austria and West Germany.[8]

To explain properly the evolution of the nationality conflicts or
Habsburg politics as a whole, we must look more closely at the
social history of ethnic and national identification and the relationships between ethnic solidarity and social bonds based on class,
economic interest, and geographic origin. As long ago as 1948,
A.J.P. Taylor warned against simply equating language with national loyalty in the nineteenth century; many peasants may have
lacked real ethnic or national consciousness and townspeople could
expediently adopt the language which was locally dominant.[9] Still,
little has been done to examine systematically the strength and
character of popular identification with the various national movements at each stage in their development.

Our inadequate knowledge of popular ethnic identification
makes understanding of the Monarchy's politics at the end of the
nineteenth century particularly problematic. In the 1880s and
1890s new mass-based political formations, some grounded narrowly on class or economic interests and others combining nationalist goals with specific economic demands, arose to compete with
the old nationalist parties. A complex crosshatching of ethnic and
class cleavages came to mark public life. Much of the older non-
Marxist literature assumes that ethnic loyalties in the populace generally overrode class interests and split most of the class-based
movements: to the end of the Monarchy, in this view, the struggle
of the subject nationalities against the Germans and Magyars dom-

[7] The articles published in the Western-language journal of the Hungarian Acad-
emy of Sciences, *Acta Historica* (Budapest), are representative of the best recent
Hungarian work. See *Acta Poloniae Historica* (Warsaw) and the articles by Stefan
Kieniewicz and J. Leskiewicz in Keith Hitchins, ed., *Studies in East European Social
History*, I (Leiden, 1977), for recent studies in Polish social history. *Historica* (Prague),
the Western-language journal of the Czechoslovak Academy of Sciences publishes
Czech and Slovak studies. For a review of Czech works, see G. B. Cohen in *Journal
of Modern History*, LI, pp. 760-72.

[8] What has been written on the Germans of the Bohemian Lands in West Germany
is best represented by the monograph series of the Collegium Carolinum published
by Oldenbourg and the articles in *Bohemia: Jahrbuch des Collegium Carolinum* (Munich
and Vienna). Sudeten German traditions are represented by Emil Franzel, *Sudetendeutsche Geschichte*, 2d ed. (Augsburg, 1962), and Josef Mühlberger, *Zwei Völker in
Böhmen* (Munich, 1973).

[9] A.J.P. Taylor, *The Habsburg Monarchy, 1909-1918* (London, 1948; repr., New
York, 1965), p. 264.

inated domestic politics.[10] Other perspectives give greater emphasis to the conflict of class and economic interests. In a revisionist interpretation, Istvan Deak, for example, has argued that the Monarchy in its last half century had no dominant nationalities, only powerful classes, interest groups, and institutions. For Deak, the "nationality conflict" in Hungary was really between the Magyar upper class and Magyar as well as non-Magyar lower classes. The Austrian half of the Monarchy saw a struggle between the elites of various nationalities, each of which in turn faced growing lower-class challenges at the turn of the century.[11] Polish, Czech, Slovak, and Magyar historians have assigned even greater importance to class conflict in the Marxist-Leninist interpretations which they have generally followed since 1948, but they have been hard put to explain how the desires of peasants and workers for national emancipation sometimes engendered solidarity with bourgeois nationalists.[12]

The role of religion and race in the development of ethnic identities in nineteenth-century Austria is no better understood than that of class and economic interests. Some scholars have argued that as each people developed a nationalist movement and revolted against the liberal centralist constitution of the 1860s, some elements in every movement turned against Jews as an easy target for their group anxieties and as a symbol of the system they now rejected.[13] There is much evidence for this view, to be sure, in the anti-Semitism and racism of extremists in nearly all nationalist

[10] This is most obvious in older works such as Taylor, *The Habsburg Monarchy*, R. W. Seton-Watson, *A History of the Czechs and Slovaks* (London, 1943), and S. Harrison Thomson, *Czechoslovakia in European History* (Princeton, N.J., 1st ed., 1943; 2d ed. rev., 1953), although J.F.N. Bradley, *Czechoslovakia: A Short History* (Edinburgh, 1971), expresses a similar view.

[11] Istvan Deak, "Comments," *Austrian History Yearbook*, III (1967), pt. 1, pp. 303-05. For the sake of simplicity, I shall use "Austria" to refer to all the territories of the western half of the Habsburg Monarchy, i.e., the non-Hungarian portions, which were represented in the Reichsrat after 1867. In contexts where this might be confused with the Habsburg Hereditary Lands of Upper and Lower Austria, the geographic designation "Cisleithania" will be used.

[12] The Marxist-Leninist orthodoxy followed by Czech historians in the 1950s and early 1960s is represented well by Oldřich Říha and Július Mésáros, ed., *Přehled československých dějin*, II (Prague, 1960), especially pp. 802-06, 1001-06. For views representative of Magyar historiography in the 1960s, see the chapters by Peter Hanák in Ervin Pamlényi, ed., *Die Geschichte Ungarns* (Budapest, 1971), pp. 337-498.

[13] See, for example, Hannah Arendt, *The Origins of Totalitarianism*, 2d ed. (Cleveland and New York, 1958), pp. 42-45. For further discussion of this issue see below, Chapter 4, pp. 175-77.

camps and in the concurrent beginnings of Jewish nationalism in Austria. Yet much of the populace apparently failed to respond to religious or racial appeals, and there is no precise knowledge of which elements actually made religion or race integral to their sense of social and political identity. Clearly, study of parliamentary politics, the statements of party leaders, and the polemics of nationalist ideologues cannot by itself explain the connections between popular ethnic identities and class or religion and race. This task requires systematic analysis of popular mentalities and grass-roots group formation for all peoples of the Monarchy.

The relation of ethnic identity to politics, class, and religion and the development of ethnic group solidarities in the Habsburg Monarchy can be traced only through a series of micro-studies. In the long run these issues need to be addressed for the Monarchy as a whole, but by their nature they require in-depth knowledge of popular experience in a number of individual localities. As yet, though, there have been no systematic studies of the development of ethnic identification and social relations between the groups in any of the mixed communities in the Austrian half of the Monarchy.[14]

Close examination of a declining German minority in a single locality can contribute much to understanding Austrian politics and society in the late nineteenth century, as well as the more general phenomena of ethnic stratification and ethnic change. In each of the cities and towns where once dominant German-speakers faced decline, the loss of political, numerical, and economic strength forced them to define a group identity and to establish a separate group life if they were to survive as a distinct segment of the population. To maintain group solidarity, they had to confront all the problems of conflicting class and economic interests as well as differences of religion or geographic origin, and they had to balance these with their continuing claims to power and status. No one declining minority group can be considered representative of all, but what is truly unique in the experience of a minority in one

[14] The only recent major social histories of Austrian urban populations in the late nineteenth century are William H. Hubbard, "A Social History of Graz, Austria, 1861-1914" (unpubl. Ph.D. dissertation, Columbia University, 1973), and Monika Glettler, *Die Wiener Tschechen um 1900* (Munich and Vienna, 1972). Neither addresses the development of ethnic identity. For a study of group identity and solidarity among a German minority elsewhere in East-Central Europe, see Anders H. Henriksson, "The Riga German Community: Social Change and the Nationality Question 1860-1905" (unpubl. Ph.D. dissertation, University of Toronto, 1978).

locality can be isolated by internal analysis and by comparison with what may be known of others.

The German minority of Prague is an obvious choice for study among the many German groups which experienced decline in late nineteenth-century Austria. Prague's German-speaking middle and upper strata suffered sharp losses in power and numbers after 1861. German-speakers had dominated government and society in the historic capital of Bohemia from the Thirty Years' War to the end of the 1850s, but Czechs won a majority of the city council in the early 1860s and controlled nearly all of local government by the mid-1880s. If the census returns can be trusted, German-speakers accounted for more than one-third of the citizens in 1857, but by 1910 they comprised only seven percent of the population in the city and inner suburbs.[15] As the Germans declined and as the Czechs won dominance, Prague became one of the principal flashpoints in the larger conflict between Germans and Czechs in Austria.

Ethnic conflict in Prague, in fact, exerted a powerful influence elsewhere in the Monarchy. The contention in Prague contributed much to the tone and substance of Czech-German disputes throughout Bohemia and Moravia. Czech leaders elsewhere often defined ethnic interests in light of the situation in Prague, and many politicians in the solidly German borderlands of Bohemia closely followed developments in the provincial capital, whether or not they actually supported the Prague Germans. Imperial officials in Vienna also paid close attention to the Czech-German conflict in Prague.

In addition, Prague offers special opportunities for examining the place of religion and of race in the development of ethnic identities. Catholics accounted for over ninety-five percent of the Christian population throughout the nineteenth century, but since the tenth century Jews had also been recorded in the city. In 1900 they numbered some 26,342, nearly seven percent of the civilian population of Prague and the inner suburbs.[16] Jews who desired full civil equality with non-Jews openly identified with either Germans or Czechs, and at various times both of the latter groups debated the question of how much Jewish participation they wanted in their social and political life. Like the Czech-German conflict

---

[15] See Chapters 1 and 3 below for discussion of the population trends.

[16] The 1900 statistics derive from Jan Srb, ed., *Sčítání lidu v král. hlav. městě Praze a obce sousedních provedené 31. prosince 1900*, 3 vols. (Prague, 1902-08), I, pp. 88-96. For territorial definitions of Prague and the suburbs, see Chapter 3, note 14.

itself, the role of Jews in Czech and German group relations in Prague evoked considerable interest elsewhere in Austria among both Jews and non-Jews.

The history of Germans in Prague is also better documented than that of many other European minority groups which have disappeared in the upheavals of the twentieth century. Dispersion of populations and the liquidation of political, social, and cultural organizations at the end of World War II have made it difficult to study most of the old German minorities of East-Central Europe, and unpublished private papers are scarce for the vanished Germans of Prague. On the other hand, the bitterness of the ethnic conflict there before World War I, the large bureaucratic and educational establishments of a capital city, and the Germans' own stubborn pretensions to social and cultural distinction have resulted in a rich legacy of official documents, published memoirs, newspapers, pamphlets, and realistic novels which reveal much about Czech-German relations.

This study will examine the Prague Germans' responses to their loss of power and of numbers in the city. By analyzing the development of group loyalties in the population, we can see the relations between ethnicity and social, economic, and political differences. The overall political relations between Germans and Czechs in Bohemia and Moravia and among all the major ethnic groups of Austria must be viewed as crucial elements in the context of the Prague Germans' social experience. Nonetheless, the primary purpose here is to understand how Germans in Prague adapted in their everyday life to the loss of power and position, not to explain the general development of the nationality conflict at the level of constitutional and legislative politics.

We need to establish at the outset what questions are essential to understanding the social experience of a declining upper-strata minority, and we must articulate the concepts and distinctions that can give order to the inquiry. The great range of possible relationships between the development of ethnicity and social, economic, and political cleavages in a population complicate the historian's task in studying any ethnic group. We must first of all be clear as to where even to look among the range of a population's values, social relations, and everyday activities for the elements of experience which bind them together as an ethnic group and which they themselves perceive to link them. For this the large body of sociological and anthropological work on ethnicity offers useful analytic concepts and models of behavior. In drawing assistance from the other social sciences, the historian does not assume as primary task the derivation or validation of general theories of ethnic group behavior. Nonetheless, insofar as a social history of a group like the Prague Germans offers the special perspective of a declining upper-strata minority and an understanding of ethnic change, it may have unmistakable implications for theories of ethnicity which have often lacked both these dimensions.

An ethnic group is united, above all, by a consciousness of shared identity, and the social history of any group must describe and explain the development of that group identity. Most social scientists would agree that an ethnic group is a body of persons which perceives itself and is perceived by others to be distinguished from the rest of the population by certain shared cultural characteristics: language, religion, traditional customs, shared history, or geographical origin.[17] The traits that actually come to define an ethnic group vary enormously from one group to another, depending on circumstances. Moreover, the characteristics which define a particular group may themselves change over time.

Individual ethnic loyalties as well as group identities must be considered as continually in flux, and it is the historian's task to explain how both develop. Some groups, of course, transmit the defining cultural traits almost exclusively through birth and upbringing in the group, and individual identification follows largely from lineage or race. In many other cases, however, birth and upbringing do not irrevocably determine an individual's ethnic identity.[18] Individuals may choose to adopt or abandon the distinguishing cultural traits and embrace or renounce the social relationships which unite the group. If others in the group and the surrounding society accept these decisions, the individuals will have succeeded in changing their ethnic identity.

If ethnic identity is often mutable for individuals as well as whole groups, we need to examine closely how and why individuals in Prague established a German identity and were perceived as mem-

---

[17] Cf. Barth in Barth, ed., *Ethnic Groups*, pp. 10-11; Enloe, *Ethnic Conflict*, pp. 15-17; Gordon, *Assimilation*, pp. 23-24; and Michael Hechter, "The Political Economy of Ethnic Change," *American Journal of Sociology*, LXXIX (1974), p. 1151.

[18] See Talcott Parsons, "Some Theoretical Considerations on the Nature and Trends of Change of Ethnicity," in Glazer and Moynihan, ed., *Ethnicity*, pp. 57-88; and Donald L. Horowitz, "Ethnic Identity," in Glazer and Moynihan, ed., *Ethnicity*, pp. 113-14.

bers of a distinct German group in the city. Ethnicity is ascribed to a group on the basis of shared cultural traits; it is not simply determined by the special social and economic functions that the members may perform in the larger society. In the mixed communities of East-Central Europe in the nineteenth century, members of the German-speaking middle and upper strata were not perceived as Germans merely because many performed special roles as wholesale merchants, insurance brokers, jewelers, and physicians. They were viewed as Germans by themselves and by others because they differed from the surrounding population in their preference for German language, education, and high culture and because they consciously identified with the values and interests of other Germans in Central and East-Central Europe. Germans and non-Germans alike perceived these traits as setting them apart from the rest of the population. Whatever the origins of the defining cultural characteristics, they actually come to distinguish groups in society because individuals articulate group identities on the basis of those traits and subjectively attach social meaning to them.[19]

While ethnicity is essentially an ascribed cultural identity, the specific roles that group members play in society may directly affect their ethnic loyalties. The special interests of a group and the impact on it of general social and economic development can motivate efforts to articulate, maintain, or abandon an ethnic identity. As a consequence, considerations of class, economics, or political goals often strongly influence individuals' decisions to identify with one group or another. Where an ethnic group is defending particular political and economic advantages or combatting deprivation, acceptance in the group may depend on support for certain economic or class interests or for a given political viewpoint. These considerations may have crucial importance in encouraging some individuals to identify with an ethnic group while discouraging or even excluding others. Economic interest, class, and ideology may become integral elements in a group's identity, and ethnic solidarity will then not easily cross occupational, class, or ideological lines.[20]

The development of class and political considerations as part of ethnic identification may follow a special course among declining upper-strata minorities. We shall see a strong and not surprising tendency among the Prague Germans, from the beginnings of the Czech challenge, to identify themselves as a social and political elite

[19] See Barth in Barth, ed., *Ethnic Groups*, pp. 10-11; and Enloe, *Ethnic Conflict*, p. 16.

[20] Cf. Gordon, *Assimilation*, pp. 51-54.

group. To defend their threatened position, Germans from the outset made acceptance into their group life contingent on support for the social and political arrangements which formerly gave them dominance. Later these same strictures provoked increasing contention within the German minority as Czech strength grew and as German groupings arose which claimed to be German but differed in social and political outlook.

The possible connections between ethnic identity and specific social and economic interests oblige the historian to look closely at what concerns actually lie behind a group's assertion of a distinct cultural identity and its demands for cultural rights. Ethnic conflicts in the nineteenth and twentieth centuries have often focused on rights of language, religion, or some other single cultural factor as the critical issue in dispute. Like many other minorities in East-Central Europe, the Prague Germans tended to treat language ostensibly as the principal group-defining characteristic. They generally made linguistic rights the principal given aim of their political action, even when they were really disputing larger issues of power, status, and group welfare.[21]

As we trace the development of German group identification in Prague in the late nineteenth century, we must also examine the patterns of social interaction which distinguished or separated Germans from non-Germans in everyday life. Often the articulation or persistence of a conscious group identity itself depends on some degree of functional or even spatial separation of the group from others in day-to-day social relations. The anthropologist Fredrik Barth argues persuasively that in general "ethnic identity implies a series of constraints on the kinds of roles an individual is allowed to play and the partners he may choose for different kinds of transactions."[22] These constraints can govern whom members of a group choose as friends, whom they marry, where they reside, what jobs they take, and with whom they do business or spend leisure time. Whatever the balance of social and economic advantages that accrue from membership in an ethnic group, inclusion in the social

---

[21] Aristide Zolberg argues that culture can be a dependent factor in relation to the political ideas and structures of some ethnic groups in "The Making of Flemings and Walloons," *Journal of Interdisciplinary History*, V (1974-75), pp. 180-81. See also the discussions of what actually divides French and English Canadians in Richard D. Basham, *Crisis in Blanc and White: Urbanization and Ethnic Identity in French Canada* (Cambridge, Mass., 1978), pp. 77-85, and Catholics and Protestants in Northern Ireland in Chester L. Hunt and Lewis Walker, *Ethnic Dynamics: Patterns of Intergroup Relations in Various Societies* (Homewood, Ill., 1974), pp. 24-36.

[22] Barth in Barth, ed., *Ethnic Groups*, pp. 16-17.

relationships which set that group apart can in itself influence individuals to retain their ethnic identity. In Prague, as we shall see, those who might have identified with the German minority but found themselves excluded from German group relationships were those who exchanged German identities for Czech in greatest numbers. Knowing this, both German and Czech leaders at times tried to alter the social boundaries separating the two groups in order to advance their respective interests.

The social boundaries which demarcate ethnic groups in everyday life vary from one group to another according to circumstances and change over time. At one point a given group may be distinguished by occupational specialization, lineal descent, and rigid endogamy, while another in the same society may persist primarily by means of separate networks of friendship and residential segregation.[23] Fifty or one hundred years later, economic and political development may have broken down some boundaries while stimulating the creation of new ones.

The social constraints which separate groups are usually limited in modern societies, and ethnic groups are seldom totally isolated from each other. In Northern Ireland today, for instance, Protestants and Catholics may still work side by side or shop in the same stores despite the intensity of the political conflict. In nineteenth-century Austria, contemporary observers spoke frequently of occupational specialization, endogamy, and commercial boycotts separating the ethnic groups in mixed populations, but we have little precise knowledge of the actual distinctions anywhere.

Some of the most important keys to interpreting the evolution of ethnic identities and the social boundaries between groups lie in the connections between ethnicity and the larger processes of modern societal development, and we need to explore those linkages as well to understand the social history of any ethnic group. General social, economic, and political development can alter the relative power, status, and prosperity of various ethnic groups in a society and cause individuals to increase their commitment to ethnic group interests or to change their group affiliation. Although modernization has often directly affected the degree of ethnic consciousness and conflict in developing and advanced societies, we cannot assume that ethnic differences always evolve in the same general manner and direction.

Social scientists now recognize that ethnic cleavages can increase

---

[23] Cf. Parsons in Glazer and Moynihan, ed., *Ethnicity*, p. 65.

as well as diminish in developing and advanced societies. Through the early 1960s many scholars assumed that in the modern world advanced differentiation of social and economic functions, mass political participation, and mass communications generally promoted broader national integration and eroded ethnic differences. When ethnic consciousness did flare up in advancing societies, social scientists conventionally argued that it represented a revival of age-old or "primordial" attachments to a distinctive traditional culture or separate lineage.[24] This interpretation viewed heightened ethnicity largely as a transitory, atavistic response to unwanted social development or group deprivation and assumed that modernization would lead to increasing social and cultural integration in all countries, the triumph of the "melting pot" in American terms.[25] Yet a growing accumulation of evidence argues for a contrary view.

Ethnic conflict in the Third World and the intensification of ethnic loyalties in many advanced industrial societies have forced a general rethinking of theories of ethnic change since the early 1960s.[26] In developing societies, ethnic consciousness has often increased among groups which welcomed modernity and were beginning to experience it. Many, like the Czech nationalists in nineteenth-century Austria, have used ethnicity to channel the forces of social and economic change, not simply to impede or reverse them. Moreover, if members of an ethnic group themselves can shape the content of their group identity, the concept of primordial attachments to a received cultural heritage may explain little of the contemporary expression of ethnicity. Indeed, ethnic loyalties have

[24] For influential statements of some of the older views, see Karl W. Deutsch, *Nationalism and Social Communication* (Cambridge, Mass., 1st ed., 1953; 2d ed., 1966), and Edward Shils, "Primordial, Personal, Sacred, and Civil Ties," *British Journal of Sociology*, VIII (1957), pp. 130-45. For general critiques see Hechter in *Politics and Society*, II, pp. 32-33, and in *American Journal of Sociology*, LXXIX, pp. 1153-55; Walker Connor, "Ethnonationalism in the First World," in Esman, ed., *Ethnic Conflict*, pp. 19-21; Enloe, *Ethnic Conflict*, pp. 3-20; and Arend Lijphart, "Political Theories and the Explanation of Ethnic Conflict in the Western World: Falsified Predictions and Plausible Postdictions," in Esman, ed., pp. 47-48.

[25] See the review and critique of the "melting pot" theories in Gordon, *Assimilation*, pp. 3-18, 84-131.

[26] The transition in thinking about the relations between ethnic change and modern nation-building can be seen in the influential essay of Clifford Geertz, "The Integrative Revolution: Primordial Sentiments and Civil Politics in the New States," in Geertz, ed., *Old Societies and New States: The Quest for Modernity in Asia and Africa* (New York and London, 1963), pp. 105-57. The abandonment of the "melting pot" view of American society was heralded by Nathan Glazer and Daniel P. Moynihan, *Beyond the Melting Pot* (Cambridge, Mass., 1963).

often strengthened in advanced societies as the real cultural differences between groups diminished and social interaction increased. In light of this, social scientists have had to elaborate more plastic notions of ethnic change to explain how ethnic consciousness and group conflict can develop in various ways in response to uneven social, economic, and political development in the modern world.[27] A group's own explanations for its behavior may be deceiving, for a declining ethnic minority such as the Prague Germans may claim that its identity, group values, and social solidarity represent prized historical legacies even when they are to a great extent new creations. To understand the experience of such a group we need to distinguish those innovations and establish what new conditions in the group's environment elicited them.

This study will trace the social history of the Prague Germans as they declined between 1861 and World War I. To understand the Germans' response to their loss of dominance in the city, we need to examine not only the development of their collective values and goals but also the evolution of their group identity, the social boundaries between Germans and Czechs, and the criteria for participation in German group relations. Although the primary concern will be with the German minority's social experience, their political action also merits attention.

Social histories of ethnic groups in developing and advanced societies can no more exclude political activity than political histories of ethnic conflict can ignore the social bases and limits of ethnic movements. The affirmation of an ethnic identity may depend fundamentally on the social and economic advantages reaped by those who share a group's defining cultural traits, but whatever the ultimate bases of group differences, ethnicity becomes a matter of conscious concern through political processes. In the modern world individuals most often develop their awareness of ethnic differences and articulate commitments to ethnic group goals through the conventional political mechanisms of mobilizing groups,

[27] For examples see Enloe, *Ethnic Conflict;* Hechter in *Politics and Society,* II, pp. 21-45, and in *American Journal of Sociology,* LXXIX, pp. 1151-78; idem, *Internal Colonialism;* Talcott Parsons, Donald L. Horowitz, and Daniel Bell in Glazer and Moynihan, ed., *Ethnicity,* pp. 53-83, 111-40, 141-76; Chung-Do Hah and Jeffrey Martin, "Toward a Synthesis of Conflict and Integration Theories of Nationalism," *World Politics,* XXVII (1975), pp. 361-86; and Arend Lijphart in Esman, ed., *Ethnic Conflict,* pp. 46-64.

defining group interests, and contending for power, status, and civil rights.[28] The efforts of a declining upper-strata minority to preserve a distinct identity and to insure group survival are as much a matter of political action as are the struggles of lower-strata groups to end oppression. In this light a social history of Prague's German minority must examine both how and why Germans themselves mobilized to define a group identity and to maintain social solidarity amidst an ever more powerful Czech majority.

The German protests over the change in the Prague street signs may seem petty to outsiders, but such issues had great significance for both sides in the ethnic conflict. Germans and Czechs often attached as much importance to the symbols of group power and prestige as to the substance. In a situation where the two groups lived together on close terms, it was a long series of political contests over both the tokens and reality of group interests that actually forced many in the city to define and articulate loyalties to one side or the other. In the end the outcomes of those contests and the political processes of rallying support for the German cause crucially affected the survival of the German minority as a distinct group in Prague.

[28] See Milton J. Esman, "Perspectives on Ethnic Conflict in Industrialized Societies," in Esman, ed., *Ethnic Conflict*, pp. 373-77; Geertz in Geertz, ed., pp. 120-27; Lijphart in Esman, ed., pp. 46-64; and Zolberg in *Journal of Interdisciplinary History*, V, pp. 179-236 passim.

CHAPTER ONE

From Bohemians to Czechs and Germans

In the late nineteenth century, leaders of Prague's German community developed elaborate historical justifications for their presence in the city and their insistence on political and social recognition. This was part of a larger effort to cultivate a strong German identity and to stem the group's decline. German spokesmen contrasted the unpleasant realities of life as a beleaguered minority to a golden age before 1861 when all the wealthiest, most powerful, and influential in the city were Germans and a majority of the population spoke German.[1] German leaders still saw their group as a social and economic elite. As a minority of less than ten percent of the population, however, they had to bow to the economic and numerical strength of the Czech bourgeoisie and to Czech control of the municipal government and Prague's parliamentary representation.

Such visions of a glorious past, in fact, were largely illusory. Caught up in the emotions of ethnic conflict, both the Germans and their Czech adversaries projected sharp *fin-de-siècle* distinctions between two consciously defined and socially separate ethnic groups back to an era when they had not actually existed. At mid-century many of the city's residents, if not a majority, spoke primarily German, but few had any individual or group identity as Germans. As will be seen, two separate ethnic groups emerged only gradually out of a previously less differentiated population. The process of ethnic differentiation in the 1840s and 1850s must be understood to explain much of the Prague Germans' subsequent experience as a minority group.

[1] For examples see Ottokar Weber in *Deutsche Arbeit*, VIII, pp. 325-26; and Julius Lippert, "Prag, die deutsche Stadt," *Deutsche Arbeit*, VIII (1909), pp. 332-48.

Ethnic Identity in Prague before 1848

Prague in the 1830s and 1840s was typical of the major administrative and commercial centers in Austria's German-Slavic border
provinces: German-speaking elements enjoyed political, social, and
economic hegemony over the local Slavic population. Prague, the
capital of Bohemia, was much like Brno (Brünn) and Olomouc
(Olmütz) in Moravia, Opava (Troppau) in Silesia, and Ljubljana
(Laibach) and Maribor (Marburg) in Carniola: each had a substantial German-speaking population despite the large majority of
Slavic peasants in the immediate hinterland. There are no comprehensive statistics to measure this with precision before the 1860s;
Austria took its first reliable modern census in 1869. The only
general population statistics published for Prague before 1848
claimed 66,046 Germans and 36,687 Czechs among the Christian
population in the four historic quarters of the Old Town (Staré
Město), New Town (Nové město), Malá strana (Ger., Kleinseite), and
Hradčany in 1846. In addition, over 6,400 Jews resided in the
ghetto of Josefov and the adjoining sections of the Old Town (see
Map I).[2] The reliability of these statistics is highly questionable since
the Prague law professor who compiled them simply took the principal language used in each parish by the Catholic clergy to indicate
the overall composition of the Christian residents. Quite justifiably,
Czech nationalist critics argued in rebuttal that this often amounted
to counting as German anyone who spoke the German language
at all.[3] The Czechs offered no statistics of their own, but it is in-
disputable that aristocrats, state officials, army officers, higher
clergy, professionals, the wealthier merchants, and manufacturers
in Prague were overwhelmingly German-speaking. They were educated exclusively in German and conducted their business and
professional affairs in German.

Through the 1850s the majority of Prague's residents probably
spoke something of both German and Czech. Only the very highest
strata of the German-speaking elements failed to learn any Czech.[4]

---

[2] Georg Norbert Schnabel, *Tafeln zur Statistik von Böhmen* (Prague, 1848), table 8.
Schnabel counted 1,828,105 Germans and 2,577,399 Slavs in all of Bohemia. On
the history of Austrian censuses, see Wilhelm Hecke, "Die Methode and Technik
der öster. Volkszählungen," *Statistische Monatsschrift der öster. Statistischen Central-Commission*, N.F., XVII (1912), pp. 466-474.

[3] Karel Havlíček-Borovský, *Politické spisy*, 3 vols. (Prague, 1900-03), I, pp. 293-
301.

[4] See the accounts by Jakub Malý, *Naše znovuzrození* (Prague, 1880), I, pp. 92-93;

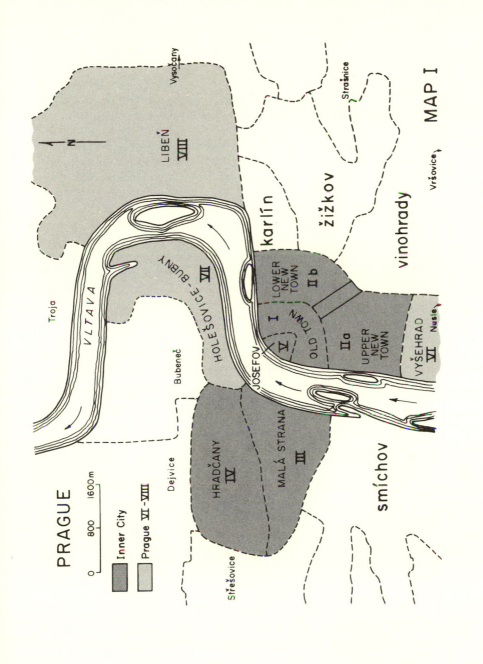

PRAGUE

Inner City
Prague VI - VIII

0   800   1600m

PRAGUE

Střešovice

Dejvice

Bubeneč

Troja

VLTAVA

HOLEŠOVICE - BUBNY
VII

N

LIBEŇ
VIII

Vysočany

karlín

JOSEFOV
V

OLD TOWN
I

LOWER NEW TOWN
II b

žižkov

Strašnice

HRADČANY
IV

MALÁ STRANA
III

UPPER NEW TOWN
II a

VYŠEHRAD
VI

Nusle

vinohrady

Vršovice

smíchov

MAP I

One cannot establish a precise level in the social hierarchy above which German-speaking predominated; too much depended on individual circumstances. The laboring, poorer artisanal, and small shopkeeping strata were predominantly Czech-speaking; but only the humblest had so little contact with German-speakers that they learned no German. The Jewish population showed a strong preference for German, but in the 1840s and 1850s most also knew some Czech and *Mauscheldeutsch*, the regional Jewish dialect.

The central administrative and economic functions which Prague served in Bohemia largely accounted for the social preeminence of German-speakers in the city and the numerical strength they enjoyed before 1861. Prague had been the capital of the Bohemian state since its beginnings around the year 900. Although political control shifted to Vienna after the Habsburg imperial forces defeated the Bohemian Estates at White Mountain in 1620, Prague retained thereafter a vital position as administrative, judicial, and ecclesiastical center for the kingdom of Bohemia.[5] The Habsburgs' deliberate Germanization of government, education, and the Catholic hierarchy in Bohemia after the Thirty Years' War led naturally to the growth of a large German-speaking bureaucratic and professional elite in Prague.

The city's centuries-old functions as a commercial entrepôt also contributed to the steady growth of the German-speaking middle and upper strata before 1861. Situated in the center of Bohemia, Prague occupied the largest expanse of open, flat or gently sloping land on the banks of the Vltava (Moldau) along its whole middle and lower courses.[6] In the nineteenth century much of the trade of the fertile central Bohemian agricultural lands focused on the city, and Prague also served as a major entrepôt in the movement of goods from Austria's Alpine provinces, Bohemia, and Moravia to the Elbe and on down to Hamburg. Since German-speaking

Fritz Mauthner, *Erinnerungen, I: Prager Jugendjahre* (Munich, 1918), pp. 123-125; and Naděžda Melniková-Papoušková, *Praha před sto lety* (Prague, 1935), pp. 38-48.

[5] See Josef Janáček, ed., *Dějiny Prahy* (Prague, 1964), passim, on the early history of the city. Ernest Denis, *La Bohême depuis la Montagne Blanche*, 2 vols. (Paris, 1903) remains the classic account of the consequences of the Habsburg victory in the Thirty Years' War. For more recent surveys, see R. W. Seton-Watson, *A History of the Czechs and Slovaks* (London, 1943); S. Harrison Thomson, *Czechoslovakia in European History*, 1st ed. (Princeton, 1943); and Josef Macek, ed., *Přehled československých dějin*, I (Prague, 1958).

[6] See the detailed geographical analysis by Ctibor Votrubec, *Praha: Zeměpis velkoměsta* (Prague, 1965), and the briefer work by Julie Moscheles, "Prague, a geographical sketch of the town," *Geografiska Annaler*, II (1920), pp. 67-79.

elements controlled most of the important commerce and credit institutions in the western half of the Habsburg Monarchy before the 1860s, Prague's rich trade supported a sizable German-speaking mercantile group.

The beginnings of industrial development in Prague in the late eighteenth and early nineteenth centuries also contributed to the formation of the German-speaking upper strata. Prague, Vienna, and Budapest were the only cities in the Habsburg Monarchy to reach 100,000 in population by the mid-nineteenth century, and this must be attributed to the strength of early industrialization along with the commercial and administrative functions. Textiles, brewing, distilling, milling, sugar refining, simple chemical production, and leather working comprised the largest manufacturing branches in Prague in the late eighteenth century. All grew significantly in the next fifty years, particularly textile production, where the rapid growth of cotton spinning and calico printing gave rise to the first mechanized production in the city.[7] By the 1840s the machine-building industry had begun to develop. At first connected with food processing and textiles, machine manufacture grew in the next three decades to be the single largest industrial branch in the city's economy.

As in the larger commercial enterprises, German served as the lingua franca for industrialists in the western half of the Habsburg Monarchy for most of the nineteenth century. Until the 1860s most of the entrepreneurs for the textile, sugar-refining, and machine-building industries in Prague were German-speakers who came from Germany and Switzerland, from other Bohemian towns, or from the Austrian and Bohemian ghettoes.[8] Czech-speakers, on the other hand, accounted for most of the millers, brewers, soapmakers, and some of the raw sugar processors, who were all closely tied to the Czech agrarian population of central Bohemia.[9]

---

[7] See F. W. Carter, "The Industrial Development of Prague 1800-1850," *Slavonic and East European Review*, LI (1973), pp. 243-275, for an analysis of the early growth in light of recent theories of economic development and urban growth. For more general discussions, see Jaroslav Purš, "The Industrial Revolution in the Czech Lands," *Historica*, II (1960), pp. 183-272, and Pavla Horská, "K otázce vzniku průmyslové revoluce v ČSR," *Československý časopis historický* [Hereafter *ČSČH*], II (1954), pp. 669-702.

[8] See Herbert Matis, *Österreichs Wirtschaft 1848-1913* (Berlin, 1972), pp. 64-82, and Josef Mentschl, "Das österreichische Unternehmertum," in A. Wandruszka et al., ed., *Die Habsburgermonarchie 1848-1918*, I (Vienna, 1973), pp. 250-260.

[9] See the discussion of Prague's early industrial entrepreneurship in Melnikova-Papoušková, pp. 38-39; Richard Rudolph, *Banking and Industrialization in Austria-*

The German-speaking middle and upper strata of Prague at mid-century thus arose out of the strong Germanizing forces at work there and whatever immigration came from the German areas of Austria and the German states. Since migration was relatively limited before the onset of full-scale industrialization, the processes of Germanization primarily accounted for the formation of the German-speaking population.[10] The high frequency of non-German and especially Czech names among the German-speaking element throughout the nineteenth century testified clearly to the diverse origins. Those of the Czech-speaking population who retained close ties of kinship to the Czech people of the Bohemian and Moravian countryside could attribute their language, culture, and any group identity they had to family descent and to communal heritage. For the German-speakers, however, their language and Austro-German acculturation followed basically from the rank in Bohemian society they occupied or to which they aspired. All those who made their way into the more prosperous commercial or manufacturing strata, the professions, or the bureaucracy had to adopt the German language, Austro-German culture, and Catholicism if they lacked one or the other. This did not involve, however, the adoption of a specific German ethnic identity before the 1850s.[11]

Status and occupation separated German-speakers from their Czech neighbors in Prague. Beyond the sometimes great differences in status and means, the great majority of German-speakers had frequent and close contacts with the Czech-speaking population. Before mid-century few German-speakers were set apart by endogamy or had any sense of belonging to a distinct German group defined essentially by language or culture. Only some of the tiny German Protestant colony in the city saw themselves as part

---

Hungary (Cambridge, 1976), pp. 39-65; and Theodor Mayer, "Zur Geschichte der nationalen Verhältnisse in Prag," in *Aus Sozial- und Wirtschaftsgeschichte: Gedächtnisschrift für Georg von Below* (Stuttgart, 1928), pp. 267-68.

[10] See Mayer in *Aus Sozial- und Wirtschaftsgeschichte*, pp. 254-78, who used the records for the granting of formal citizenship in Prague from the late seventeenth century to the late eighteenth to examine the role of immigration in shaping the composition of the city's population.

[11] See Philipp Knoll, *Beiträge zur heimischen Zeitgeschichte* (Prague, 1900), pp. 231-33; and Melniková-Papoušková, p. 46. In Hungary's more rigid corporate society, German minorities before the mid-nineteenth century were more sharply set apart than in the western half of the Monarchy because of occupational restrictions in the towns or separate, homogeneous settlements on the land. See E. V. Windisch, "Die Entstehung der Voraussetzungen für die deutsche Nationalitätenbewegung in Ungarn in der zweiten Hälfte des 19. Jahrhunderts," *Acta Historica Hungaricae*, XI (1965), pp. 3-56.

of a closed descent group consciously distinguished as Germans.[12]

Under such circumstances one can hardly describe Prague as a German city in the early nineteenth century.[13] The distinguished economist Friedrich von Wieser was one of the few Prague Germans who later would admit this openly:[14]

> Prague was no German city before 1848. Perhaps it might have become one if the revival of the Czech nation had not intervened. Prague like all of Austria in the *Vormärz* stood under German leadership. . . . The ruling classes were exclusively German. The Czech who obtained an education was trained to be a German and added to the strength of the German "society" which, based on the Czech substratum, presided over the city and passed for the whole city to the outside world.

Even speaking of a German upper stratum as if it possessed a specific German self-identity distorts the actual situation. The great preponderance of the German-speaking population, like many of the Czech-speakers before 1848, lacked any conscious identity as a distinct ethnic or national group. When intellectuals who led the Czech national movement spoke of stamping out "national indifference," they were describing the efforts needed to cultivate national consciousness in the Czech-speaking population during the first half of the nineteenth century.[15] When representatives of all the German-speaking communities of Bohemia convened in Teplice (Teplitz) in August 1848, one of the Prague delegates had to explain with some embarrassment that it was as impossible to count the Germans in Prague precisely as it was "even to tell whether they were Germans or not."[16]

It is essential to distinguish between mere German-speakers and Germans possessing a conscious ethnic identity. The self-image of the higher strata in Prague and indeed in all of Bohemia and

[12] Protestants never accounted for more than four percent of the entire German population in the late nineteenth century. See Chapter 3.

[13] As recent a work as Berthold Sutter's *Die Badenischen Sprachenverordnungen von 1897* (Graz and Cologne, 1960), I, p. 32, describes Prague in 1848 as a "German city."

[14] Friedrich Frh. von Wieser, *Die Deutsche Steuerleistung und der öffentliche Haushalt in Böhmen* (Leipzig, 1904), p. 57.

[15] The Czech philosopher Emanuel Rádl in *Der Kampf zwischen Tschechen und Deutschen* (Liberec, 1928), pp. 27-29, 50-51, 122-23, argued that a national consciousness had to be developed on both sides in the nineteenth century.

[16] *Stenographischer Bericht über die Verhandlungen der am 28. August in Teplitz im Namen deutscher Städte, Gemeinden, und konstitutioneller Vereine Böhmens zusammengekommenen Vertrauensmänner* (Litoměřice, n. d.), pp. 48-49.

Moravia in the early nineteenth century had a supra-national, cosmopolitan hue. Prague's German-speakers felt attached to monarch and to territory, not to nation; they were Bohemians and Austrians, not Germans.[17] A society which was still largely ordered by estates had little place for national identification; Czech-German linguistic and cultural differences largely followed status differences. The German-speaking elements in the Bohemian capital developed no significant German nationalist tendencies comparable to the Czech in the 1840s. Indeed, what liberal political and intellectual sentiment arose among them took the form of a Bohemian patriotism that desired to further the interests of all the people in the kingdom, their greater political autonomy, and the development of both German and Czech cultures.[18]

The Czech nationalist intelligentsia provided the impetus for differentiating the inhabitants of Prague and other cities with mixed Czech- and German-speaking populations into distinct Czech and German social groupings. In the 1830s and 1840s, the Czech nationalists mobilized ever larger numbers of followers, who identified with the Czech nation and wanted rights as Czechs in state and society. This not only diminished the flow of recruits from the lower strata into the German-speaking urban elites but also produced increasing competition for positions of political and economic power in all three lands of the Bohemian Crown: Bohemia, Moravia, and Silesia.[19] In the process of defending themselves against the Czech challenge, the German-speaking middle and upper strata transformed themselves from Bohemians to Germans.

The Impetus for Change: The Czech National Movement and the Revolution of 1848

Scholars, professionals, and small businessmen led the Czech national movement in the 1830s and 1840s. They proposed a total reconstitution of society in the Bohemian Lands to abolish cor-

[17] See the judicious assessment by Melniková-Papoušková, pp. 38-39, and Gustav C. Laube, "Gedenkrede auf Philipp Knoll," in Knoll, *Beiträge*, x-xi.

[18] On *Bohemismus*, see William M. Johnston, *The Austrian Mind* (Berkeley, 1972), pp. 276-79; Hellmut Diwald, "Bernard Bolzano und der Bohemismus," in Diwald, ed., *Lebendiger Geist: Hans Joachim Schoeps zum 50. Geburtstag* (Leiden, 1959), pp. 91-115; idem, "Deutschböhmen, die Deutschen Prags und das tschechische Wiedererwachen" *Zeitschrift für Religions-und Geistesgeschichte*, X (1958), pp. 124-141. Bernard Bolzano, *Über das Verhältnis der beiden Volksstämme in Böhmen* (Vienna, 1849), expresses many of the movement's central ideas.

[19] See the perceptive comments in Friedrich Frh. von Wieser, p. 57.

porate privilege and to allow Czechs to move freely into positions of political and economic leadership without having to accept Germanization.[20] Formally these liberal nationalists demanded no more than civil equality of Czechs and Germans in a freely competitive, individualist society and the equal provision of all administrative, judicial, and educational services in Czech and German. Yet the Czech nation-builders envisioned as their ultimate goal the creation of a fully articulated Czech national society that would enjoy dominance in the Bohemian Lands by virtue of its numerical preponderance. While Czech nationalists wanted to maintain the protective umbrella of a large multinational state in East-Central Europe, they considered the dominance of German-speakers over Czechs in the Bohemian Lands as iniquitous and intolerable.

By the 1830s and 1840s the Czech movement had begun to convert political and cultural ideals into social realities. During the preceding half century, linguists, historians, writers, and clergy revitalized the Czech language and literature. They worked among Czech-speaking peasants, artisans, and shopkeepers to develop a consciousness of their membership in a distinct Czech nation and of their inheritance of rich national traditions. In the last two decades of the Francisco-Metternichian regime, the Royal Bohemian Historian František Palacký (1798-1876), his son-in-law František L. Rieger (1818-1903), the journalists Karel Havlíček-Borovský (1821-1856) and František Brauner (1810-1880), and their colleagues labored to root out national indifference or "Bohemianism" wherever they persisted in the Czech-speaking population, particularly in Prague and other cities where Germanizing tendencies remained strong.

Once Czech identity was established, the Czech nation-builders began to mobilize their following into social and cultural organizations and to create a Czech public life. Nation-building required social change as much as cultural and political development, and Czechs needed to seek new patterns of association with other Czechs in both public and private affairs to solidify Czech identification in the populace and to give substance to the movement's vision of

[20] For western language surveys of the Czech national movement, see Ernest Denis, *La Bohême depuis la Montagne Blanche*; Hermann Münch, *Böhmische Tragödie* (Braunschweig, Berlin, and Hamburg, 1949); Seton-Watson, and S. H. Thomson. The most important Czech surveys are Kamil Krofta, *Dějiny československé* (Prague, 1946); Josef Kočí, *Naše národní obrození* (Prague, 1960); Macek, ed., *Přehled československých dějin*, I; Oldřich Říha, ed., *Přehled československých dějin*, II (Prague, 1960); and Jozef Butvin and Jan Havránek, *Dějiny československa*, III (Prague, 1968).

a new, distinct Czech society. The increasing numbers of well-educated but underemployed sons of artisanal and lesser burgher families common to much of Western and Central Europe in this era supplied the Czech movement with additional leadership, and the Czech intelligentsia gradually extended and refined their social and economic appeals to win over an ever broader mass following.[21]

In the late 1830s the Czech leaders began to address the specific needs of the shopkeepers, small masters, and handicraft workers in Prague and in the other larger Bohemian cities. In part this only extended the earlier appeals to the more prosperous Czech peasants and small-town traders who wanted release from the persisting elements of seigneurial privilege, guild regulations, and the power of the German-speaking elites in Bohemia. In the cities the poorer masters and workers found themselves trapped by the forces of the craft guilds, developing industry and commercial entrepreneurship, the municipal corporations, and the absolutist state bureaucracy. All of these forces could be viewed as German-dominated and hence alien to the Czech nation. Czech national identity and group solidarity offered the urban lower middle and working strata protection from the alien oppressors and assistance for social and material improvement. The appeal to the urban lower strata, however, had its risks for the Czech national movement. As elsewhere in Europe, the urban poor in the Bohemian Lands were a politically volatile element attracted to a radical democracy that could easily come into conflict with the moderate liberalism and defense of property of the Czech agrarian and small-town elements. Indeed, the Czech national movement split over these differences in 1848 and again after 1863.[22]

The economic conditions of the 1840s added weight to the Czech nationalists' social appeals. The Bohemian Lands, together with most of Central Europe, experienced a severe crisis compounded

[21] On the early leadership of the Czech national movement, see Miroslav Hroch, *Die Vorkämpfer der nationalen Bewegung bei den kleinen Völkern Europas* (Prague, 1968) [*Acta Universitatis Carolinae Philosophica et Historica Monographia*, XXIV], pp. 41-61; idem, "The Social Composition of the Czech Patriots in Bohemia, 1827-1848," in *The Czech Renascence of the Nineteenth Century*, Peter Brock and H. Gordon Skilling, ed. (Toronto, 1970), pp. 33-52; and Macek, ed., *Přehled*, I, pp. 680-694. On the oversupply of intellectuals throughout Europe see the analysis by Lenore O'Boyle, "The Problem of an Excess of Educated Men in Western Europe, 1800-1850," *Journal of Modern History*, XLII (1970), pp. 471-495.

[22] See Macek, ed., *Přehled*, I, pp. 664-76, 680-82; Karel Kosík, *Česká radikalní democracie* (Prague, 1958), pp. 52-311; and Jan Novotný, *František Cyril Kampelík* (Prague, 1975), passim.

of crop failures, the onset of industrialization, and a general business depression. Rising food prices, industrial competition, and declining demand particularly beset artisans in spinning and weaving. Moreover, the skilled workers in the new cotton-spinning, weaving, and calico-printing factories in Prague found that each new mechanical improvement cost the jobs of various workers. When the depresssion set in, peasants, factory workers, and many craft producers faced severe decline or total loss of income.[23]

Czech nationalists believed they had to establish an independent Czech social life in Prague and the other central Bohemian cities to stop the Germanization of upwardly mobile elements and to build a Czech society. In 1840 the Czech journal *Květy* pointed out the importance of group social and cultural activities in the nationalists' program:[24]

> Of course, if we look around Prague for clubs, salons, and balls where Czech social life has blossomed, we look in vain. Except for the pubs and dancehalls . . . the native tongue up to now has not been heard in public and social situations as much as it should be in Prague, that grandfather of Czech glory, the heart of the kingdom of Bohemia. . . . We assert, however, that without that social life, a complete revitalization, enrichment, and propagation of the language are impossible and cannot be imagined.

The new Czech clubs, balls, artistic and literary salons, and reading societies did not merely reflect the movement's rising respectability or serve only as instruments for attaining political goals.[25] The new groups made it possible for Czechs to act in social affairs as part of the Czech nation, to associate with other Czechs apart from German-speaking society, and to win social honors independently.

The efforts in the forties to create a Czech social life in Prague registered their greatest achievement in 1846. After considerable official delay, Rieger, Palacký, and the great Slovak Slavicist Pavel Josef Šafařík (1795-1861) finally succeeded in organizing the Burghers' Club (*Měšťanská beseda, Bürgerresource*), a Czech liberal

---

[23] On the effects of the depression, see Macek, ed., *Přehled*, I, pp. 665-672, 674-676; Janáček, ed., *Dějiny Prahy*, pp. 430-34; and E. Wolfgramm, "Der böhmische Vormärz, im besonderen die böhmischen Arbeitsunruhen des Jahres 1844 in ihren sozialen und politischen Zusammenhängen," in Karl Obermann and J. V. Polišenský, ed., *Aus 500 Jahren deutsch-tschechoslowakischen Geschichte* (Berlin, 1958), pp. 171-222.

[24] Quoted in Melniková-Papoušková, pp. 305-06.

[25] Stanley Z. Pech, *The Czech Revolution of 1848* (Chapel Hill, 1969), pp. 27-29, offers the conventional interpretation of the social and cultural organizations.

nationalist equivalent to Vienna's Juridical-Political Reading Society. Here the budding Czech middle class could gather, ostensibly for purposes of general sociability and self-improvement, but unofficially also for the discussion of public affairs.

Palacký, Rieger, and Havlíček had won only limited organized popular support in Prague by the end of February 1848 when news of the Parisian revolution arrived. Many might identify with the Czech nation, but as yet only a small number were ready to reorder their social affairs to separate themselves from the existing Bohemian social order.[26] Moreover, the rapid decline of Czech nationalist activity in Prague and in the other Bohemian cities in the period of the reaction after 1848 demonstrated how weak the commitment to belonging to a separate Czech society had actually been.

Members of Prague's German-speaking middle and upper strata began to develop a German identity comparable to the Czech only during the revolutionary upheavals of 1848. The near collapse of the Habsburg central authority, the rapid unfolding throughout Central Europe of a liberal movement for German national unification, and a great increase in the Czech movement's militancy— all worked to persuade German-speakers in Bohemia that they too had a national identity. This was a natural enough development in the solidly German-speaking border areas of Bohemia contiguous to Saxony and Bavaria, but the relatively complacent German-speaking elite of Prague needed the shock of direct Czech threats to their power and position before any visible group began to think of themselves as a separate people and act accordingly. Not only did they, in effect, begin to accept the Czech argument that two distinct peoples inhabited Bohemia, but some of the now consciously German elements avowedly copied patterns established by the Czechs. One liberal German preached to his colleagues at the Teplice meeting of Bohemian Germans in August 1848, "Let us learn from the Czechs, learn from them to be zealous, resolute, and disciplined; we can confidently take their associations as a model."[27]

Aggressive action by Czech nationalists during the April-June phase of the 1848 upheaval elicited the first overt expression of a distinct German identity in Prague. In the initial March phase Ger-

[26] Jakub Malý, *Naše znovuzrození*, pp. 90-91, asserts that only members of the "middle estate" of shopkeepers and artisan masters were extensively mobilized before 1848.

[27] From a speech by Uffo Horn of Trutnov (Trautenau), *Stenographischer Bericht . . . Teplitz*, p. 11.

man-speaking liberal elements had joined with the moderate Czech nationalists in demanding constitutional government and broader civil rights.[28] The Czech-dominated provisional National Committee, however, developed into a de facto Bohemian government after the first week in April and espoused Czech national political and educational goals. The National Committee's actions helped to galvanize German sentiment throughout Austria, and in Vienna in early April a group of Germans from the Bohemian Lands founded the "Association of Germans from Bohemia, Moravia, and Silesia for the Preservation of their Nationality." The Association fought the National Committee's efforts to unify the Bohemian Lands and win parity for the Czech language in Bohemia's secondary and higher schools.[29]

An invitation from the Frankfurt Parliament to send delegates to discuss German unification precipitated the first organized German political activity in Prague. On April 18 the Czech members of the National Committee followed Palacký's lead in refusing to participate in the Frankfurt Parliament. The next day, a group of young middle-class liberals with German national sentiments organized a "Constitutional Society" to oppose the National Committee. This was the first clear sign of a genuine German group consciousness in Prague, and the organizers hoped that the new group would serve as a forum for the participation of all Bohemian Germans in the unification of the German states. Nonetheless, many of Prague's German-speaking upper strata continued to oppose any action that might subvert the unity of the Habsburg Empire or needlessly provoke the Czech nationalists, and the Constitutional Society found itself severely limited in strength and effectiveness.

Little is known about the political behavior of most of Prague's German-speakers in 1848. Inaction, of course, leaves few documents.[30] Even the exact composition of the Constitutional Society

[28] On the events of 1848 in the Bohemian Lands, see the solid work of Pech, *The Czech Revolution of 1848*; the classic Czech account by Karel Kazbunda, *České hnutí roku 1848* (Prague, 1929); and the more recent study by Arnošt Klima, *Revoluce 1848 v českých zemích* (Prague, 1974). Friedrich Prinz, *Prag und Wien 1848* (Munich, 1968), compares the political and social developments in the two cities while Josef V. Polišenský, *Revoluce a kontrarevoluce v Rakousku 1848* (Prague, 1975), sheds new light on the counterrevolutionary forces.

[29] See the radical German nationalist account by Josef Pfitzner, "Die Wahlen in die Frankfurter Nationalversammlung und der Sudetenraum," *Zeitschrift für sudetendeutsche Geschichte*, V (1941-42), pp. 205-07.

[30] Although distorted by an extreme German nationalism and anti-Semitism, the

is unknown, but the founders apparently comprised primarily university graduates who espoused radical liberal nationalist views. Many of those who subsequently joined, however, had a more conservative outlook, and the Constitutional Society formally supported a moderate *Grossdeutsch* nationalism which it hoped would be compatible with Habsburg dynastic interests.[31]

Even this exceeded by far what most of Prague's still strongly conservative German-speaking merchants and professionals could accept. Anti-German tirades in the Czech press, the rise of mass unrest during April and May, and the radicalization of the Viennese revolution in mid-May only heightened the German-speakers' general fears and their inhibitions against expressions of nationalist sentiments. Claiming the danger of anti-German violence, the Constitutional Society finally decided not to participate in elections for the Frankfurt Parliament, and only three persons in Prague cast ballots.[32] In view of the persisting weakness of German national sentiment in the Bohemian capital, the Constitutional Society's decision not to support the elections may have saved it the greater embarrassment of an only slightly larger turnout.

Only limited liberal German national feeling developed in Prague in the early phases of the 1848 upheavals, and that waned as the political and social conservatism of the German-speaking elements strengthened in the late spring and early summer. The public ceremonies that inaugurated the Slavic Congress in mid-June led to violence by Czech workers and radical students. Bombardment of the city and the bloody repression of the June uprising by the Habsburg military commander Prince Windischgrätz ended the revolution in Prague. Windischgrätz immediately dissolved the National Committee and all radical political groups and established a new absolutist regime in Bohemia. Most of the other voluntary political associations in the province disappeared within the following year and a half.

The June uprising confirmed the conservatism of many of the German-speaking burghers, and under the reaction they enthu-

---

articles of Josef Pfitzner, "Zur nationalen Politik der Sudetendeutschen in den Jahren 1848-1849," *Jahrbuch des Vereines für die Geschichte der Deutschen in Bohmen*, III (1930-33), pp. 210-43, and in *Zeitschrift für sudetendeutsche Geschichte*, V, pp. 199-240, summarize what is known about German politics in Prague in 1848-49.

[31] One such relatively conservative member was the prosperous merchant Richard Ritter von Dotzauer. See Edmund Schebek, *Richard Ritter von Dotzauer* (Prague, 1895), pp. 52-53.

[32] See Pech, *The Czech Revolution*, pp. 93-94.

siastically supported a return to pre-1848 conditions and the crushing of liberal Czech nationalism as well as social radicalism. The more moderate members of the Constitutional Society left the group with Windischgrätz's victory in June.[33] The remaining radical writers and professionals tried as long as possible to maintain contact with German national groups elsewhere in Bohemia and Saxony. Members of the Society attended the Teplice meeting of all the German national groups in Bohemia in August 1848, where they had to deal with the embarrassing questions of why citizens of Prague had done so little for the German cause.[34]

Few in Prague manifested any German national sentiment in the darkest years of reaction. Besides the Constitutional Society, German students in the Prague university managed to found a "reading and discussion hall" (*Lese- und Redehalle*) in November 1848 to counterbalance the pro-Czech Academic Reading Society.[35] In the spring of 1849 a new wave of repression under the government of Prince Felix zu Schwarzenberg forced the Constitutional Society, now called the German Club, to dissolve as a political association and to become a reading society for self-improvement and general sociability, a "casino" in contemporary parlance.[36] This feeble German casino provided the only German alternative to the Czech-dominated Burghers' Club through the 1850s.

The reaction, in fact, saw a general ebbing of German national sentiment in Bohemia. Liberal nationalism declined even in the solidly German-speaking borderlands after the collapse of the Frankfurt Parliament.[37] Members of the old conservative German-speaking upper strata regained political power and social influence. Men such as Prague's new mayor, the publisher and property owner Andreas von Haase, naturally opposed the Czech nationalists' political aims and insisted on the supremacy of the German language

[33] See Pfitzner in *Jahrbuch VGDB*, III, pp. 221-24.

[34] See Polišenský, *Revoluce a kontrarevoluce*, pp. 206-09, and *Stenographische Protokolle . . . Teplitz*, p. 19.

[35] See Gustav Laube in Knoll, *Beiträge*, x-xi, on the lack of German national sentiment in Prague in the early 1850s and the founding of the *Lese- und Redehalle*.

[36] Richard Klier, *Das Deutschtum Prags in der Vergangenheit* (Karlsbad-Drahowitz and Leipzig, 1936), p. 63, and Pfitzner, in *Jahrbuch VGDB*, III, pp. 231-33. Hans Lades, *Die Tschechen und die deutsche Frage* (Erlangen, 1938), p. 151, asserts that the small German casino dissolved completely in 1852. The small casino, however, seems to have maintained a shadowy, informal existence until the founding of the new "large" casino in 1862. See Schebek, *Dotzauer*, p. 117.

[37] See the colorful description by František Palacký's son Jan published anonymously in *Böhmische Skizzen* (Litomyšl, 1860), pp. 34, 45-46.

and of the German-speaking elite in Austria. Yet these conservative burghers lacked any positive commitment to a Great German or even an Austro-German nationalism; they were Bohemians and Austrians loyal to the Habsburgs. The upheavals of 1848 had given birth to a distinct German identity comparable to the Czech in Prague and in the other cities with mixed populations.[38] But to judge from the lack of overt manifestations in the succeeding decade, the reaction drove most of those in Prague who had begun to identify as Germans either into silence or back to their traditional identification as Austrians or Bohemians.

The Revival of Bohemian Society under the Bach Absolutism

Counterrevolution encouraged the revival of the old Bohemian loyalties in Prague after 1848. The revitalized absolutist regime invoked rigid press censorship and denied freedom of association in order to contract public life and to depoliticize the population much as Francis I and Metternich had done after 1815. This powerfully affected the processes of ethnic differentiation in the Prague population. Czech nationalist leaders complained of renewed Germanizing tendencies among Czech-speakers, but the decades of efforts in the Czech national revival had succeeded in propagating widely at least an awareness of belonging to a separate Czech nation. Few German-speakers in Prague had as yet adopted such a self-identity. Neither cultural heritage nor family descent gave the German-speakers any conscious identity as part of an ethnic or national group; they could most readily acquire it through experience in their wider social, cultural, and political life. Status, occupation, and religion, not purely ethnic Czech-German differences, still primarily determined group formation for all residents of Prague; and Czech- and German-speakers continued to live together on close terms. Any reordering of individual and group interrelations to make the Czech-German difference a fundamental cleavage could only begin in the public sphere of collective action for political, cultural, and social purposes.[39] Czech nationalist leaders had realized this in the 1830s and 1840s. By sharply reducing the sphere

[38] On Brno and Plzeň, see Jaroslav Dřímal and Václav Peša, ed., *Dějiny města Brna*, I (Brno, 1969), pp. 221-27; and Václav Čepelák, ed., *Dějiny Plzně*, II (Plzeň, 1967), pp. 73-76.

[39] For a discussion of the middle-class distinction between public and private affairs in nineteenth-century Europe, see Jürgen Habermas, *Strukturwandel der Öffentlichkeit* (Neuwied, 1972), pp. 60-75.

of public life and quelling both Czech and German associational activity, the neo-absolutist regime of Emperor Francis Joseph and his interior minister Alexander Bach stopped and even partly reversed the process of ethnic differentiation among the residents of Prague.

Here the evidence of manifest behavior and expressions of sentiment must bear the major burden of the argument. Obviously, not all social attitudes can be determined from simple, overt expressions, particularly under a repressive political system. Yet to delineate the mentality of any large group which left few personal documents, the historian has little choice but to infer values and attitudes from concrete acts. Conscious ethnic identification and the ordering of social relationships along ethnic lines are distinct phenomena, but social behavior can show how seriously people take their group identity as well as indicate the boundaries between groups in everyday life.[40]

While the reaction nearly wiped out expressions of German national identity in Prague, it also caused the desertion of many adherents from the Czech cause. The early phases of the reaction reversed most of the Czech advances of the 1840s; Czech-language instruction ceased in those of Prague's primary and secondary schools which had introduced it, and Germanization revived among upwardly mobile Czechs. All public offices down to the lowliest state pawnshop conducted all their affairs in German once again, and a number of private businesses resumed the use of German.[41]

Czech leaders could not prevent the renewal of Germanizing pressures in Prague. The revolution had split the nationalist leadership into liberal and radical factions, and the reaction laid both prostrate. Dr. Servác Heller (1845-1922), a Czech journalist and politician, later sharply etched the Prague of his early childhood:[42]

> In Prague all who adhered to fashion Germanized, for German was in vogue. All who set store by official favor became Germans, for the all-powerful absolutist government was of German stock and tendencies. . . . In the 1850s Prague again gave the impression of being a German city as it had before 1848, that is, not a totally unalloyed German city, but German in so far as it appeared

[40] See the discussion of the importance of social boundaries between ethnic groups for articulating and maintaining group identities in the Introduction, pp. 14-15.

[41] See the detailed description in Servác Heller, *Z minulé doby našeho života národního, kulturního, a politického*, 5 vols. (Prague, 1916-23), II, pp. 47-49; and Jakub Malý, *Naše znovuzrození*, III, p. 61.

[42] Heller, *Z minulé doby*, II, pp. 116-17.

as if only the common people, as if only so many of the lower classes, servants, laborers, petty craftsmen, and smaller traders were of Czech nationality. All the others then, in particular the larger and greater merchants, entrepreneurs, and proprietors of extensive industries, the more prosperous burghers, officials in all categories, lawyers, notaries, etc., belonged to the German nationality.

Other recollections confirm Heller's observations, but there is little statistical data available to determine precisely the linguistic habits of the various social strata.[43] As of October 1857, the Imperial Administrative Statistical Bureau, using simple linguistic and religious criteria, counted 40,216 Czechs, 24,000 Germans, and 7,706 Jews among the 71,922 native residents of Prague's four historic quarters and the ghetto.[44] Yet one cannot apply indiscriminately to this period the late nineteenth-century equation of linguistic preference with national identity. Speaking German made the conservative mayor Andreas von Haase no more an adherent of the German nation than it did members of František Palacký's own household, who spoke German until 1860.[45]

When controls on associational activity began to relax in the mid-1850s, the Czech nationalist leaders set to work again to build their Czech society. As before, they were convinced that their success depended on disproving the popular adage that "you won't get far with Czech" (S češtinou nedojde se daleko). Czech nationalists had to persuade peasant farmers and the urban lower middle strata that they would have greater opportunities for social and economic advancement in a Czech society than as German-speakers in a German-dominated society. The Czech movement benefited from the strong elements of Czech identification that remained from before 1848 in the Bohemian countryside, the small towns, and the poorer districts of Prague; and leaders could draw on the experience in directing larger masses of people gained in the revolution. Further, the double-edged sword of rapid economic development in the 1850s provided both financial resources and social tensions which

[43] See Malý, Naše znovuzrození, I, pp. 90-91, and Jan Palacký, Böhmische Skizzen, pp. 45-46, 62-65, for accounts similar to Heller's.

[44] Tafeln zur Statistik der österreichischen Monarchie, N. F., III (1855-57), 1. Heft, pp. 10, 48-49. The total resident population in the city was 142,588.

[45] Jan Palacký, "Intimní vzpomínky na Fr. Palackého," in Památník na oslavy stých narozením Františka Palackého (Prague, 1898), pp. 126-29. The historian's father-in-law was a wealthy Prague lawyer and landowner, and German was apparently the mother tongue of Palacký's wife.

could be exploited for the renewed expansion of the Czech national movement. This time no revolutionary upheaval and reaction intervened to cause a reversal.

From the mid-1850s on, Czech nationalism won strong support from the prosperous farmers of medium and large holdings in central Bohemia. Aristocrats had fewer great estates here than in southern Bohemia. The compensatory payments for the abolition of the old hereditary labor obligations caused the gradual disappearance of many smallholders in central Bohemia and consolidation of their plots into larger peasant holdings.[46] Intermediate and larger landowners profited from the boom of the early and mid-1850s by expanding sugar-beet cultivation and adopting more intensive methods. To aid agricultural development the neo-absolutist regime permitted the spread of local chapters of the Patriotic Economic Society, which discussed agricultural problems and circulated Czech pamphlets and periodicals on agricultural and technical subjects. As the agrarian improvement movement grew, Czech nationalist farmers and intellectuals injected an increasingly bold Czech nationalist element.[47] In succeeding decades a politically vocal Czech agrarian middle class arose out of the self-help societies and the agricultural prosperity that continued until the 1880s.[48]

In the late 1850s Czech agrarian leaders also helped to initiate self-improvement and mutual-aid societies to assist Czech craftsmen and small businessmen in their struggles with the more powerful alien economic forces, be they Austro-German, Jewish, or foreign. The Czech nationalist movement appealed especially to small- and medium-sized traders and businessmen and to skilled workers who felt unfairly consigned to inferior positions relative to greater Austrian entrepreneurial interests outside the Czech nation.[49] The final emancipation of the peasants, the beginnings of

---

[46] See Christoph Stölzl, *Die Ära Bach in Böhmen* (Munich and Vienna, 1971), pp. 29-35, and Ríha, ed., *Přehled*, II, pp. 159-80. Stölzl's fine study serves as the principal basis for the outline here of the revival of the Czech movement in the 1850s.

[47] See Stölzl's treatment in *Die Ära Bach*, pp. 41-55.

[48] There are no local studies of the rise of Czech nationalist sentiments among the independent farmers or of the functioning of the mutual aid societies. Stölzl, *Die Ära Bach*, pp. 92-99, treats the rise of the Czech savings and loan societies from the top down. See also Čeněk Klier, *České spořitelnictví v zemích koruny české do roku 1906* (Prague, 1908), and for the subsequent but parallel German Bohemian development, Heinrich Rauchberg, *Die deutschen Sparkassen in Böhmen* (Prague, 1906). For an insightful overview of Czech agrarian politics in this era, see Peter Heumos, *Agrarische Interessen und nationale Politik in Böhmen 1848-1889* (Wiesbaden, 1979).

[49] On the progressive economic policies of the neo-absolutist regime, see Herbert

industrialization, sharp business fluctuations, and, most importantly, the shift from a corporate to a class society—all combined
to set the members of the old middle estate adrift economically and
socially. The historian Christoph Stölzl has argued persuasively that
the Czech national movement, with its ideology of social integration
and mutual-aid societies, provided craftsmen, shopkeepers, and
middling farmers with functional substitutes for the guarantees of
status and security under the old corporate society.[50] Both Czech
moderates and radicals rejected corporate restrictions on economic
freedom and development, but they trod a narrow path between
their commitment to a free, achievement-oriented society and their
hostility to great entrepreneurial interests alien to the nation. Czech
nationalists tried to avoid the potential conflict between their liberalism and nationalism by advocating national economic solidarity
and cooperative efforts to assist small Czech entrepreneurs to compete with non-Czechs in an otherwise free market.[51]

Czech nationalists established cooperative and educational societies after the mid-1850s wherever the police authorities would
permit. As before 1848, these organizations served the larger purposes of mobilizing popular participation in the national movement
and creating a distinct Czech social and political life. These seem-
ingly modest groups provided the foundation for the rapid development of Czech political action in cities and towns throughout
the Czech-speaking two-thirds of Bohemia at the end of the fifties
when the imperial government lifted the general restrictions on
public life.

Matis, *Österreichs Wirtschaft*, pp. 30-63; idem, "Leitlinien der öster. Wirtschaftspolitik,"
in Wandruszka, ed., *Habsburgermonarchie*, I, pp. 29-38; and Hans Rosenberg's comparative treatment in *Die Weltwirtschaftskrisis von 1857-1859* (Stuttgart and Berlin,
1934) [*Vierteljahrschrift für Sozial- und Wirtschaftsgeschichte*, Beiheft 30], pp. 13-32.

[50] Stölzl, *Die Ära Bach*, pp. 120-46. Stölzl is more successful in explaining the social
raisonnement of what emerged as the petit-bourgeois radical wing of the Czech
national movement than the more classically Mancunian and socially conservative
wing identified with Palacký, Rieger, and the Old Czech Party. For an introduction
to the economic thought of the latter see F. L. Rieger, *Průmysl a postup výroby
jeho v pusobení svém ke blahobytu a svobodě lidu zvláště pracujícího* (Litomyšl, 1860),
passim; and Valentin Urfus, "Průmyslový liberalismus a české měšťanstvo v
období národního obrození," *Právněhistorické studie*, X (1964), pp. 5-32.

[51] See Novotný, *Kampelík*, pp. 176-80, on the rationale and function of the cooperative efforts among the Czech small producers and commercial entrepreneurs.
For characteristic Czech nationalist attacks on the privileges of guilds, see *Posel z
Prahy*, I (1857), no. 1, pp. 17-25, 116-27; II (1858), no. 1, pp. 117-23, no. 4, pp.
132-38.

The Beginnings of Ethnic Division

The forces of general economic and political development in the Habsburg Monarchy in the late 1850s made possible a new flowering of the Czech national movement and impelled Bohemia's German-speaking elites to develop a new consciousness of their own group interests. The economic crisis of 1857 and the ensuing brief depression exacerbated all the social and political tensions in the Monarchy engendered by economic development earlier in the decade. Lower-class elements and conservative aristocrats demanded a halt to further economic liberalization.[52] In cities with mixed German-Slavic populations, such as Prague, the economic crisis caused increasing political and social polarization between the German-speaking elites and the Slavic lower classes. On the one hand, new economic hardships provided grist for the mill of the Czech nationalists in their appeals to the urban lower-middle and working strata. German-speaking entrepreneurs and professionals, on the other hand, responded with demands for greater influence over the state's economic policies, new financial concessions for large firms, and additional protective tariffs on industrial goods. Even before the near collapse of state finances and military defeat in 1859 brought down the neo-absolutist regime, the Habsburg authorities had to permit an efflorescence of new voluntary associations for economic, educational, and social purposes. The state budget could ill afford additional security forces, and, having encouraged economic development, the government had little choice but to accept the formation of groups to deal with the consequences.

Czech nationalists made impressive advances in building a Czech social life among Prague's lower middle strata in the late 1850s. Rieger and his colleagues made the Burghers' Club, which had survived the revolution, and the Manufacturing Society (*Průmyslová jednota, Gewerbeverein*), founded in 1829, the focal points for a slowly growing Czech middle-class society. The Burghers' Club remained officially bilingual from its founding until 1882, and its general social functions even attracted a significant German-speaking element in the early 1850s, when Czech nationalist connotations were weakest. Still, moderate Czech nationalists retained control, and later in the 1850s the Club sponsored annual Czech balls in op-

---

[52] On the economic and political effects of the crisis, see Rosenberg, *Weltwirtschaftskrisis*, passim; Helmut Böhme, *Deutschlands Weg zur Grossmacht* (Cologne and Berlin, 1967), pp. 83-90; and Stölzl, *Die Ära Bach*, pp. 104-09.

position to the exclusively German-speaking New Year's events.[53] When the first open elections were held in 1861, Czech political initiatives emanated from the ranks of Czech retailers, lawyers, physicians, and small manufacturers who had assembled in the Burghers' Club over the previous decade.

The Manufacturing Society complemented the social functions of the Burghers' Club in the economic sphere. As a sounding board for Czech petit-bourgeois interests in Prague, the Society served as a counterweight to the official Chambers of Trade and Manufacture which were dominated by German-speakers. Aristocrats and entrepreneurs had originally founded the Society to encourage the general development of manufacture, industry, and trade in Bohemia. The reduction of membership fees in 1841 opened the group to Czech-speaking small producers and artisan masters, and after the mid-1850s it had a Czech majority.[54] Although the Society continued to favor general economic development, F. L. Rieger and other Czechs such as František Pštross, a tannery owner, arranged for it to sponsor general educational and self-help programs for craftsmen and small traders. The Czech nationalist coloration of these activities was only thinly disguised.

In the late 1850s and early 1860s Czech nationalists also achieved dominance in nearly all of Prague's artisan groups. Czech nationalist sentiments predated 1848 among many of the poorer masters and craft workers, but the artisans had stronger affinities with the radical democratic wing of the Czech movement than the moderate liberals. In the neo-absolutist decade the compulsory craft guilds were officially bilingual and apolitical, but the predominantly Czech Masters' Collegium, a voluntary educational and mutual-aid society, propagated nationalist views until the Bohemian Governor dissolved it in 1854.[55] The surviving records do not permit a systematic ethnic analysis of all the guilds or the craft associations (*Genossenschaften, společenstva*) which replaced them after 1859. Apparently most had both Czech and German-speaking elements in the 1850s,

[53] On the balls see Heller, *Z minulé doby*, III, p. 104. The lists of founding members and benefactors for the Burghers' Club from the 1850s and 1860s include Josef Dotzauer, the father-in-law of Richard Dotzauer, and Adalbert Lanna, a wealthy industrialist closely identified with the German Casino in the 1860s and 1870s; from Archiv hlavního města Prahy (Archive of the Capital City Prague, hereafter AHMP), fond spolků: no. 68, Měšťanská beseda, fasc. 6-3-1878, EXP 18 6/3 78.

[54] See Bedřich Mendl, *Český průmysl před sto lety a počátky Průmyslové jednoty* (Prague, 1934), pp. 63-73, 140-45, and idem, *Vývoj řemesel a obchodu v městech pražských* (Prague, 1947), pp. 65-66.

[55] See Urfus in *Právněhistorické studie*, X, pp. 22-25.

but Czechs generally predominated by the early 1860s.[56] Whatever German-speaking elements were present put up no resistance when Czech nationalists formally began to take over the associations. In fact, religious differences produced conflict where Czech-German cleavages did not. When the craft associations were organized in 1860 and 1861, Christian members of the old tailors', shoemakers', and cobblers' guilds of the inner city opposed merger with their Jewish counterparts in Josefov.[57]

No articulate German national identification or associational activity arose to compete with the Czech among the masters and craft workers of Prague in the late 1850s and early 1860s. German-speaking artisans, who were probably never numerous except in the most prestigious crafts, apparently lived in social isolation from the other German-speakers in the city. After 1861 only a few of the most prosperous artisans, typically goldsmiths, jewelers, bookbinders, and printers, ever appeared in any German organizations.[58] Even in the prestigious trades the great majority of Prague craftsmen belonged to fervently Czech nationalist organizations by the mid-1860s.[59]

In fact, no group with a German identity initiated any efforts to build a community life in Prague comparable to the Czechs' during the neo-absolutist decade. Some of the German-speaking middle and upper strata responded to the economic conditions after 1857 and the weakening of the Bach regime, however, by abandoning conservative Bohemian loyalties and advocating representative government and the abolition of all remaining corporate privileges. Members of the academic community and the more progressive commercial and industrial entrepreneurs began to articulate a liberal ideology and demand power for a middle-class elite based on

[56] To date there is no detailed social history of the Prague artisanate in the 1850s and 1860s. The best source known to me on the membership of the guilds and the successor craft associations is the incomplete collection of registries of masters in AHMP, fond společenstev. A cursory review of these generally showed mixed Czech- and German-speaking groups in the 1850s and early 1860s with the Czechs predominating by the early 1860s.

[57] See *Verhandlungen der Handels- und Gewerbekammer in Prag in den Jahren 1858 bis Ende 1861* (Prague, 1862), proceedings of March 12, 1860; April 4, 1860; Feb. 25, 1861; and March 4, 1861.

[58] See Chapters 4 and 5.

[59] Jan Ev. Vondruška, *Stručný přehled činnosti ústředního spolku Typografická Beseda v Praze 1862-1887* (Prague, 1887), passim, and AHMP, fond společenstev: "Meisterbuch des Gold-, Silber- und Galanteriearbeiter Gremiums Prag, angelegt in 1860-1881," "Pamětní kniha pořádku knihařů pražského," and "Matrika členů společenstva knihařů, ozdobniků, pouzdrařů."

individual achievement, not birth. In the university the Reading Hall of German Students voiced liberal aspirations and grew increasingly concerned about the national exclusiveness that alloyed the liberalism of their Czech fellow students.[60]

The Chambers of Trade and Manufacture of Prague provided the principal forum for the expression of liberal views by elements of the German-speaking upper strata, and the first German community leadership arose out of the Chambers. Characteristically, however, the German-speaking merchants and industrialists in the Chambers at first voiced primarily liberal ideological goals and middle-class interests, not specifically ethnic interests. These German-speakers could not deny that they shared more in common with the German-speaking bourgeoisie throughout Austria than with the Czech peasants and lower middle class in the Bohemian Lands, but they began to organize as a distinct ethnic group and express a German ethnic identity only when they could no longer avoid the challenge of Czech nationalists.

A minority of Czech members sat alongside the German-speakers in the Chambers of Trade and Manufacture during the 1850s, but Czech-German disputes as such did not arise there before 1861. It was characteristic of the Bach regime that the only elective bodies it tolerated throughout the Monarchy were district councils to represent commercial and manufacturing interests and act as quasi-administrative bodies.[61] A complicated restricted suffrage guaranteed the German-speaking bourgeoisie a large majority in the Chambers of Prague, Pardubice, and the surrounding central Bohemian territory until the early eighties. The Czech members elected by small-craft producers and lesser businessmen in the 1850s raised no challenge to the German-speakers' supremacy.[62] At the end of the decade the older, conservative German-speaking leaders in the Chambers were joined by liberal figures such as the

---

[60] On the *Lese- und Redehalle,* see *Festschrift der Lese- und Redehalle der deutschen Studenten in Prag anlässlich des 150. semestrigen Sitzungsfestes 1848-1923* (Prague, 1923), pp. 21-25; Gustav C. Laube, "Die Entstehung der farbentragenden Verbindungen an den Prager Hochschulen," *Deutsche Arbeit,* I (1902), pp. 519-34; and the brief study by Antonín Slavíček, "Dějiny a archiv spolku Lese- und Redehalle der deutschen Studenten in Prag" (unpubl. diploma thesis, Charles University, Prague, 1973), pp. 1-54.

[61] See Ernst Mischler and Josef Ulbrich, ed., *Österreichisches Staatswörterbuch,* 2d ed., 4 vols. (Vienna, 1906-09), II, pp. 687-91, for a summary of the constitutional and legal history of the Austrian Chambers of Trade and Manufacture.

[62] See Josef Gruber, *Die Handels- und Gewerbekammer in Prag in den ersten fünfzig Jahren ihres Bestandes* (Prague, 1900), pp. 62-81, and Schebek, *Dotzauer,* pp. 94-110.

sugar manufacturer Clemens Bachofen von Echt, the bankers Karl Thorsch and Karl Ritter von Zdekauer, the textile manufacturer Maximilian Dormizer, the *Creditanstalt*'s local director Eduard Seutter Ritter von Lötzen, and the publisher Friedrich Tempsky. The liberals pressed for unrestricted industrial development, new credit institutions, and tariffs to favor rapid economic growth. The Czech members tried to protect the interests of small producers and traders, but most could agree with the German-speaking liberals in the support of general economic expansion and the abolition of guild privileges. The peaceable election of the generally respected František Pštross as president in 1858 testified clearly to the lack of national conflict in the Prague Chambers.[63]

Outside the Chambers of Trade and Manufacture, an increasingly assertive Czech public life confronted the German-speaking burghers in the final years of the neo-absolutist era. Whether the German-speakers wished it or not, the Prague population was beginning to divide into separate Czech and German groupings in public affairs. The beginnings of a Czech middle class spearheaded the new Czech public life, and it offered white-collar employees, businessmen, and professionals an alternative to German-speaking connections. Czech national sentiments exerted a simple, strong attraction on Czech-speaking workers, who could not aspire to the ranks of German-speaking society in Prague. Middle-class and lower-middle-class elements, on the other hand, had to choose at one point or another in the late fifties and sixties between Czech and German group affiliations.

Sharp Czech-German distinctions developed first in public affairs and apparently only later in the private sphere of life. Differences in status and occupation, of course, separated many Catholic German-speakers from their Czech-speaking neighbors, but where socioeconomic levels were comparable, they still mingled freely in individual commercial dealings, home life, and even family relations. Legal restrictions on residence and movement kept the private life of the Jewish population sharply separate from both Czech- and German-speaking Christians until the end of the fifties. As will be seen, though, Prague Jews thereafter developed much closer relations with the Czech and German communities in public life than in private affairs.[64] For Catholics, Jews, and many of the few

[63] Gruber, *Handels- und Gewerbekammer*, pp. 72-74.

[64] See Ruth Kestenberg-Gladstein, "The Jews between Czechs and Germans in the Historic Lands, 1848-1918," in *The Jews of Czechoslovakia*, 2 vols. (Philadelphia and New York, 1968-71), I, p. 43, and further discussion below in Chapter 2.

Protestants as well, actually to belong to Czech or German society in Prague in the 1860s required an open affirmation of allegiance to one or the other group and some participation in organized Czech or German group life. As contemporaries realized, neither family descent, residential patterns, nor even linguistic habits sharply separated Czechs and Germans as social groups or gave them conscious ethnic identities.[65]

Social and economic interests generally served as the major influence on the choice between Czech and German loyalties. The existing differences between Czech- and German-speakers made it predictable that most tailors and glovemakers in the Old Town became fervent Czech nationalists while most wholesale commodities brokers, particularly those involved in long-distance trade, established German allegiances. The Germans tended to come from the "haves" in terms of power, wealth, and status or from those who identified closely with these elements. The Czechs generally derived from either the "have-nots" or those who had begun to achieve some means and standing but considered themselves unjustly treated compared to the German-speaking burghers.

Under the circumstances the vagaries of friendships, immediate family connections, career success or failure, and even mere happenstance might determine individual loyalties. Jindřich (Heinrich) Fügner, for instance, was born in 1822 to the bilingual owner of a Prague fabric store and his German-speaking wife. Young Fügner had a German upbringing and in 1855 became general agent in Prague for a large Austrian insurance company. His work brought him into contact with Czech nationalist circles, and the abuse of economic power by the great industrial and commercial interests gradually alienated him from the German-speaking bourgeoisie. By 1860 Fügner had joined the radical wing of the Czech national movement; in late 1861 he helped found the national gymnastics society *Sokol* (Falcon).[66] Similarly, Ottokar Zeithammer, a moderate Czech nationalist leader in the 1860s and 1870s, was the son of a provincial school inspector of strong German convictions. Yet, in

[65] For typical comments see Knoll, *Beiträge*, pp. 231-33; and Mauthner, *Erinnerungen*, I, pp. 123-25.

[66] See Emmanuel Tonner, "Jindřich Fügner," in Josef Müller and Ferdinand Tallowitz, ed., *Památník vydaný na oslavu dvaceti letého trvání . . . Sokola pražského* (Prague, 1883), pp. 3-13, and Othmar Feyl, "Die Entwicklung des Sokolgründers Heinrich Fügner im Lichte seiner Prager Briefe an den Böhmendeutschen Konservativen Joseph Alexander von Helfert in den Jahren 1848 bis 1865," in Hans H. Bielfeldt, ed., *Deutsch-Slawische Wechselseitigkeit in sieben Jahrhunderten* (Berlin, 1956), pp. 511-18, 552, 559.

the words of a friend, the younger Zeithammer "was as fanatic a Czech as all his other relatives were Germans."[67]

For many in Prague, adopting a firm Czech or German identity and establishing primary social connections with one group over the other took place only over a number of years. The differentiation of Prague's population into Czech and German groups, distinct in ethnic identity and social interrelationships, was an evolving process that lasted through the 1860s and 1870s. As long as bilingualism was frequent and Czechs and Germans intermingled extensively in private life, individuals could move with surprising ease from one identity and affiliation to another. One distinguished Prague German journalist later commented about this era, "How many there were who did not really know whether they should count themselves among the Germans or Czechs!"[68] Yet the late 1850s and early 1860s marked a significant turning point, for at this time the Czech-German distinction first emerged as a social reality, and Bohemianism finally ceased to be a real option.

The End of Absolutism and the Transformation of Bohemian Society

The end of the neo-absolutist regime in 1860 and the first new elections in 1861 brought on open conflict between Czechs and Germans for political sway in Prague and in the Bohemian Lands as a whole. The near collapse of Austria's financial institutions in early 1859 and humiliating military defeat by the French and Piedmontese in June and July forced Emperor Francis Joseph finally to accede to liberal demands for constitutional rule and parliamentary institutions.[69] Those who supported liberalization had to organize rapidly in 1860 and 1861 for participation in the representative bodies that were revived or created at all levels of government. In Bohemia Czech nationalists and liberal German-speakers agreed on the need for constitutional rule and freely elected representation at all levels, but the Czechs' aspirations for special political, educational, and social rights in the Bohemian Lands *qua* Czechs soon collided with German liberal presumptions that gen-

---

[67] Sigmund Mayer, *Ein jüdischer Kaufmann 1831 bis 1911* (Leipzig, 1911), p. 154.

[68] Ernst Rychnovsky, *Der Deutsche Turnverein in Prag 1862-1912* (Prag, 1912), p. 2. See also the descriptions of the Prague population in the contemporary guidebooks, Franz Klutschak, *Der Führer durch Prag*, 8th ed. (Prague, 1862), p. 13, and A. Seifug, *Prag und Umgebungen*, 4th ed. (Berlin, 1873), p. 25.

[69] C. A. Macartney neatly summarizes the imperial political, financial, and diplomatic situation in *The Habsburg Empire 1790-1918* (New York, 1969), pp. 493-517.

eral progress in Austria depended on a centralized government and German middle-class dominance.

In Prague, Czech and German public life separated rapidly between 1859 and 1861. At first differences between liberal ideology and conservative, corporatist sentiments caused more basic conflict in political affairs than did Czech-German cleavages, but gradually the latter replaced liberal-conservative disputes as the ultima ratio in middle-class public life. New elections for the municipal board of aldermen in March 1861 caught the evolving process in mid-passage.

By early 1861 distinct Czech and German political formations had emerged for Bohemia as a whole. These were based primarily in the solidly Czech and German regions of the land; in Prague neither the Czech nor German liberals were yet able or willing to oppose independently the remnants of "Bohemian" conservatism. Under Andreas von Haase the conservatives tried to retain their power in local government and organized the deceptively titled "Election Committee of Liberal Friends of the Constitution." Haase and his colleagues supported a few prominent Czech and German liberals as candidates for municipal aldermen such as Palacký, Pštross, and Eduard Seutter, but more conservative figures predominated.

Rieger, Palacký, other moderate Czech nationalists, and the most prominent German liberals—Bachofen von Echt, Seutter, and Maximilian Dormizer—formed an opposing electoral committee under the slogan "Progress toward betterment" (*Pokrok k lepšímu, Fortschritt zum Bessern*).[70] In contrast to Haase's group, the "Progressives" called for institutions truly representative of the whole population and for equal use of Czech and German in public administration and education. Since the Czech liberals were so much better organized than the Germans and could claim considerable voting strength even under the municipality's restrictive three-class franchise, they greatly predominated over Germans on the Progressives'

[70] Heller, *Z minulé doby*, III, pp. 161-65; Vojtěch Kraus, ed., *Dějiny obecní správy Král. hlav. města Prahy za léta 1860-1880* (Prague, 1903), I, pt. 1, pp. 4-5. Haase's newspaper, *Bohemia*, 3 March 1861, published the whole conservative slate. Both Czech and German historians have mistakenly viewed this election as a simple Czech-German contest in light of the board of aldermen that resulted. Miloš Kratochvíl, *O Vývoji městské správy pražské od roku 1848* (Prague, 1936), pp. 60-62, admits that there were Germans and Czechs on both sides but still treats Haase's group as German and the Progressives as Czech. Klier, *Das Deutschtum Prags*, p. 63, describes the 1861 election as the victory of a "federalist Bohemian" slate over the "Austrian centralist" party.

list of candidates for aldermen.[71] The German liberals left no explanation of their own for joining with the Czech nationalists in Prague at the same time that some of them were helping to organize a German liberal campaign committee for all of Bohemia to oppose the Czechs in the forthcoming elections for the Diet.[72] Comments in the Czech press suggest that while they had a German identity, they were primarily concerned with ousting the conservatives from the municipal government. The militantly nationalist *Národní listy* praised the "honest German like Herr Edler Bachofen or Herr Edler Seutter who has his sense of nationality but wants to be just with us" and had joined in the struggle for liberal government against its opponents, who claimed to have no national loyalty.[73] In Prague the German liberals were apparently unprepared to stand alone in trying to end the conservative local regime.

The coalition of Czech and German liberals soundly defeated the conservatives in March 1861, but hopes for Czech-German harmony in local affairs did not long survive the municipal elections. Distaste for Haase and the conservatives among the electorate and the Czech nationalists' organizational work gave the Progressives fifty-two out of the ninety aldermanic seats. Fully seventy-five of the new aldermen identified with the Czech national cause, leaving only fifteen liberal Germans and conservative German-speakers.[74] The aldermen chose from themselves the twenty-four members of the city council, who in turn named the moderate Czech František Pštross as the first mayor of the constitutional era.

Soon after the municipal elections in Prague, the more radical of the new Czech aldermen began pressing nationalist demands. Henceforth the municipal bureaucracy must render all adminis-

---

[71] The Prague municipal franchise divided the voters into three classes based on minimum annual direct tax payments of 100 fl., 20 fl., and 5 fl., respectively. Educated state officials and professionals were exempt from the tax quotas and voted in the second group. Landlords tended to dominate the first group; state employees, professionals, and merchants, the second group; and small businessmen and independent master artisans, the third. See C. Horáček, "Die wirtschaftlichen und sozialen Verhältnisse der Stadt Prag," in *Verfassung und Verwaltungsorganisation der Städte, VI: Österreich* (Leipzig, 1907), pp. 76-79.

[72] The liberal *Tagesbote aus Böhmen*, 11 March 1861, published the German liberal manifesto for the Diet elections and the membership of the election committee, which included Bachofen, Dotzauer, Seutter, and Tempsky from Prague.

[73] *Národní listy*, 12 Jan 1861. On the role of *Národní listy* in Czech politics, see Bruce M. Garver, *The Young Czech Party 1874-1901 and the Emergence of a Multi-Party System* (New Haven and London, 1978), pp. 102-08.

[74] Kratochvíl, *O Vývoji městské správy*, p. 64.

trative services in both Czech and German, all the employees must be fully competent in Czech as well as German, and Czech should be the principal language of instruction for the primary schools operated in all of Prague's parishes. These schools had previously used German as their principal language, but now they would provide parallel classes with German-language instruction only where a minimum number of pupils spoke exclusively German and their parents requested German instruction.[75] Moderate Czechs counseled a less extreme position on the school question, but the radicals won a majority of the aldermen. The German liberals in Prague reacted in consternation to what they now perceived as direct Czech attacks on the social and political position of the local German population.

The German middle and upper strata in Prague were convinced that their power and wealth would be secure as long as Germans or German-speakers dominated economic and political life at the imperial and provincial levels and the government guaranteed Germans everywhere the ability to gain property and education as Germans. The Czech nationalists' increasing strength among the Bohemian peasant farmers and the urban lower middle classes could have only limited effects on the Germans. Indeed, the suffrage systems for the Bohemian Diet and the Austrian Reichsrat, which were more restricted than for the second and third classes in the Prague municipal electorate, guaranteed German liberals majorities in the higher bodies and control over Prague's seats in them until the end of the 1870s.[76]

Nonetheless, Czech dominance in the Prague municipal government after 1861 threatened to do more than merely deprive the Germans of control over local administration. In the view of liberal German aldermen and journalists, the Czech proposals for educational reform would close off public primary education in German for many German children in the city who were bilingual in their early years.[77] The Czech aldermen were primarily concerned

[75] *Tagesbote aus Böhmen*, 11 Sept 1861. Heller, *Z minulé doby*, II, pp. 129-67, and Jan Šafránek, *Školy české: Obraz jejich vývoje a osudů*, 2 vols. (Prague, 1913-18), II, pp. 180-81, offer the standard Czech interpretation.

[76] See Macartney, pp. 513-14, for a brief discussion of the suffrage systems for the Austrian Reichsrat and the provincial diets. In protest against the suffrage systems, the moderate Czech nationalists, the Old Czechs, boycotted the elections to the Bohemian Diet and the Reichsrat between 1863 and 1879. See Stanley Z. Pech, "The Passive Resistance of the Czechs, 1863-1879," *Slavonic and East European Review*, XXXVI (1958), pp. 434-52.

[77] *Tagesbote aus Böhmen*, 12 Sept 1861.

I. City Hall, Old Town, decorated for the visit of Crown Prince Rudolf, 1881

II. Wenceslas Square around 1890

with stopping the Germanization of Czech children, but the German liberals were convinced that the Czech nationalists intended to make it ever more difficult to raise any child in Prague as a German. The Germans paid little heed to the Czech rejoinder that it was primarily the children of artisans and other poor elements, who included few Germans, who attended the parish schools under municipal control. The generally more prosperous German families sent their children to other schools or taught them at home for the first years. The Czech aldermen thought it sufficient that German-language instruction would continue in the intermediate schools (*Hauptschulen*), not attached to the parishes, and at the higher levels.[78]

The Germans' response to the question of the primary schools showed a fear for their very survival as a group in the city. That in itself demonstrated how far the liberal leaders, at least, had come in thinking of themselves as part of a group uniquely distinguished by language, culture, political values, and upbringing—that is, a German ethnic group. In this instance, however, as in many others during succeeding decades, the Germans' influence at higher levels of government won a modification of the city aldermen's decision in their favor. The Bohemian Governor (*Statthalter*), who was responsible to the German liberal ministry of Anton von Schmerling in Vienna, permitted all of the parish primary schools and one lower *Realschule* to use Czech as their principal language of instruction with German-language parallel classes where needed. In addition, the municipality must operate two four-year, German-language primary schools.[79] Yet, despite the partial reversal, the Czechs had served notice that they were intent on denying the German middle class in Prague the deference in political and social affairs that the latter considered its just due.

The Czech actions gave the liberal German burghers in Prague little choice but to follow the Czechs' own lead and to organize their own distinct social and political life. If the Czechs now rejected Germanization as the price for upward mobility and would compete with the German elite for political power and social honors as Czechs, the Germans had best separate their public affairs from the Czechs in order to defend German interests at the provincial and imperial levels and to avoid sharing in the same social hierarchy

---

[78] *Ibid.* The Bohemian German martyrology subsequently adopted an exaggerated version of these events claiming that the Czech proposal would have deprived the Germans of all German-language primary education.

[79] *Tagesbote aus Böhmen*, 2 Oct 1861.

with the Czechs. Conscious now of a German group identity, members of Prague's German upper strata moved slowly to create their own community life. They still found it hard to shake off the complacence bred of their elite origins and of the rising fortunes of the German middle class in Bohemia and Austria as a whole. As the Bohemian governor reported to Schmerling in 1862, the Germans' "spokesmen can be roused out of their passivity only with difficulty and are only moved to action when the ground beneath their feet begins to cave in."[80] When the Germans did begin to build their own community structure, they relied heavily on voluntary associations and consciously followed the models established first by the Czechs:[81]

> As is well known, one should learn from his enemies. If the Czechs simply do not want to be our friends now, well and good, we will learn then to attack them with their own weapons. The Czechs above all have shown us what purposes seemingly harmless associations serve and what can be made of anniversaries and similar observances. Fine, now we can have our own associations and our own celebrations, too.

[80] Quoted in Stölzl, *Die Ära Bach*, p. 154.
[81] *Deutsches Museum* [Leipzig], XII (1861), p. 867. According to the Prague police records, the Prague correspondent at this time was the liberal German journalist Theophil Pisling; Státní ústřední archiv Praha (Central State Archive, Prague, hereafter SÚA Praha), fond pražského policejního ředitelství (Prague police directorate, hereafter PP) 1863-69 P/63/19 Theophil Pisling, Per 163c.

CHAPTER TWO

A German Community Emerges,
1861-1879

German group life emerged in Prague after 1861 with the creation of an elaborate network of voluntary associations. Common language and education, commitment to the special status of Germans in Austria, and a strong need to defend their own local position gave Germans in Prague a basic sense of shared interests. The associational network that they developed made concrete that sense of community in an organized collective life. At the beginning of the 1860s, patterns of family descent and everyday private affairs did not sharply distinguish Germans from Czechs at most levels of society; but the exclusively German organizations for political action, sociability, and self-improvement which now developed allowed their members to express a German identity and to associate with other Germans. In fact, organized German public life helped many who had previously lacked a clear loyalty to define and articulate an ethnic identity. In this regard Paul Leppin, one of the "Prague Circle" of German Jewish writers around World War I, rightly argued that the city lacked a distinct, pure German population defined by descent. There was no German community that resulted from an organic development, "merely a number of associations."[1]

Throughout Germany and Austria in the nineteenth century, middle-class and working-class elements used networks of voluntary associations to conduct their political, social, and cultural affairs, but a declining minority such as the Prague Germans looked to such bodies to perform special functions in building and preserving a community life and in sustaining ethnic identity. The

[1] Paul Leppin in *Das jüdische Prag: Eine Sammelschrift* (Prague, 1917), pp. 5-6.

other bodies in which public life was carried on in Prague—the organs of local government and religious institutions—were either ethnically neutral or increasingly Czech-dominated. To understand the development of the Germans' group life in the city, the formation of their associational network must be viewed against the backdrop of the general patterns of associational activity in Germany and Austria. Only then can we distinguish the activities and structural features that were peculiar to the public life of a once dominant group which now faced inexorable decline.

Voluntary Associations in Central European Society

Middle- and working-class elements in nineteenth-century Germany and Austria established their first collective life as class-conscious groups through the means of voluntary associations. For these purposes a voluntary association was any free, formal combination of individuals established independently of the state for joint purposes other than earning a livelihood.[2] Unlike corporate bodies in the traditional society of estates, membership in a voluntary group depended in theory on individual merit, not on birth or legally defined status. Yet for all their libertarianism and individualism, voluntary associations generally followed the basic social cleavages in their communities and played a crucial role in articulating social hierarchy.

At the end of the eighteenth century, groups of merchants, lawyers, physicians, officials, and independent manufacturers began to meet intermittently in the cafes and public houses of towns in the German states and in the western parts of Austria. In many

---

[2] This definition excludes producers' and consumers' cooperatives, which transcended the classic liberal distinction between public and private affairs that was fundamental to Prague's German community life in the formative decades. For general discussions of the social and ideological bases of voluntary associations in Central Europe, see Georg G. Iggers, "The Political Theory of Voluntary Associations in Early Nineteenth-century German Liberal Thought," in D. B. Robertson, ed., *Voluntary Associations: A Study of Groups in Free Societies* (Richmond, 1966), pp. 141-58, and Thomas Nipperdey, "Verein als soziale Struktur im späten 18. und frühen 19. Jahrhundert," in Hartmut Boockmann et al., *Geschichtswissenschaft und Vereinswesen im 19. Jahrhundert* (Göttingen, 1972), pp. 1-44. See also the fine local studies, Herbert Freudenthal, *Vereine in Hamburg* (Hamburg, 1968); Monika Glettler, *Sokol und Arbeiterturnvereine der Wiener Tschechen bis 1914* (Munich and Vienna, 1970); idem, *Die Wiener Tschechen um 1900* (Munich and Vienna, 1972); Wolfgang Hofmann, *Die Bielefelder Stadtverordneten 1850-1914* (Lübeck and Hamburg, 1964); Wolfgang Meyer, *Das Vereinswesen der Stadt Nürnberg im 19. Jahrhundert* (Nürnberg, 1970); and Heinz Schmitt, *Das Vereinsleben der Stadt Weinheim* (Weinheim, 1963).

areas these gatherings for sociability and discussion of public issues became regular by the 1830s and 1840s. Known variously as reading societies, burghers' clubs, casinos, or *Ressourcen*, these associations functioned outside the guilds and the traditional municipal corporations and came to oppose them in many cases.

The middle-class movements for social and political reform in Central Europe developed out of local voluntary associations as they began to draft petitions for legislation and put forward candidates for public office.[3] In Austria official suspicion of all public gatherings retarded the development of reading societies and casinos until the late 1830s, but by the mid-1840s they were common in the larger cities and towns of the Habsburg Hereditary Lands, Bohemia, and Moravia. Although some groups had conservative political views, most, like the Viennese Juridical-Political Reading Society and the Burghers' Club in Prague, led liberal agitation against the remnants of the corporate society.

In the towns of northwestern and southwestern Germany, where associations could operate more freely, a pattern of stratification characteristic of a class-based society began to appear by the early 1840s even before the full development of an industrial economy. A small middle-class elite organized in a social club or reading society occupied the highest rank. Shopkeepers and master artisans had mutual-aid societies, self-improvement groups, and singing societies at the next level, while brotherhoods of journeymen and other skilled workers rested at the bottom.[4]

Similar patterns began to appear in Austrian cities and towns as absolutist controls weakened after the death of Emperor Francis in 1835. The upheavals of 1848 and the ensuing reaction interrupted their development, but associational activity flowered again at the end of the 1850s, when middle-class notables resumed their efforts to create a liberal social and political order. When intermediate and lower-middle-class elements began to develop specialized groups for self-improvement and amusement, the elite clubs of the notables tried to incorporate the special-purpose groups into networks of associations dependent upon their own

[3] Cf. Habermas, *Strukturwandel*, pp. 48-52.

[4] See Hofmann, *Bielefelder Stadtverordneten*, pp. 30-44, for a description of an almost archetypical case. For a more complex but essentially similar structure, see Freudenthal, *Vereine in Hamburg*, passim. On the early development of workers' associations see the insightful study of Berlin by Frederick D. Marquardt, "A Working Class in Berlin in the 1840's?" in Hans-Ulrich Wehler, ed., *Sozialgeschichte Heute: Festschrift für Hans Rosenberg zum 70. Geburtstag* (Göttingen, 1974), pp. 191-210.

leadership and financial support. In Prague, for instance, the Burghers' Club and later the German Casino often took the initiative themselves in organizing singing societies, gymnastics groups, and associations for continuing education in order to rally lower-middle-class support.

The advent of representative government in Austria after 1860 added to the power of the elite burghers' clubs and casinos over middle-class public affairs. In the larger towns of the Habsburg Hereditary Lands and the Bohemian Lands, burghers' clubs took the lead in proposing slates of liberal candidates and in campaigning for their election.[5] Liberal political associations as such developed only gradually at the local level in Germany and Austria, and when they appeared they typically drew their leadership from the burghers' clubs and met in the same quarters. This took place in Austria only after 1867, when a new law of associations first permitted political bodies.[6]

Grass-roots political organizations, in fact, mattered little to most middle-class notables in the 1860s and early 1870s. Protected by systems of limited suffrage, they generally expected the rest of the middle-class and lower-middle-class elements to defer political decision-making to the social elite of education and property. Despite the expansion of the Austrian suffrage in the 1880s and 1890s, German as well as Czech liberal parties steadfastly relied for their local organization on the elite social clubs, the subsidiary political associations, and volunteer "trusties" (*Vertrauensmänner, duvěrníci*), who provided liaison between the party leadership and the electorate.

Liberal and democratic reformers in Central Europe developed an elaborate rationale in the mid-nineteenth century for the broad political and social functions they accorded to voluntary associations. For the middle classes and lower middle classes at large, clubs and associations offered a mode of sociability which made up in

[5] On the local bases of the parties of notables, see the general discussion for Germany by Thomas Nipperdey, *Die Organisation der deutschen Parteien vor 1918* (Düsseldorf, 1961), pp. 74-85; and for Austria, the general comments by Georg Franz, *Liberalismus: Die Deutschliberale Bewegung in der Habsburgischen Monarchie* (Vienna and Munich, 1955), pp. 145-52, 214-20; Stölzl, *Die Ära Bach*, pp. 142-46; and the descriptions of local experience in Dřímal and Peša, ed., *Dějiny Brna*, II, pp. 15-18, 22-26, 36-41; Čepelák, ed., *Dějiny Plzně*, II, pp. 97-99, 105-21; and for the Czechs in Prague, Janáček, ed., *Dějiny Prahy*, pp. 470-80, 498-99.

[6] On the legal history of voluntary associations in Austria, see Friedrich Tezner, *Österreichisches Vereins- und Versammlungsrecht*, 5th ed. (Vienna, 1913), and idem, "Vereinsrecht," in Mischler and Ulbrich, ed., 2nd ed., IV, pp. 712-22.

part for what was lost, in the seclusion of family life, from the interaction and scrutiny of the local community or broader kin connections, but such bodies were also intended to serve as instruments for the reform of society according to progressive values. These organizations were to be free and open, and participation in them could improve the lot of even the humblest in society:[7]

> The association leads the individual out of a narrow technical regimen as well as out of social isolation and back into the living community; it gives him the sense of being a useful member of a greater whole. . . . The association, which has free activity for educational, cooperative, sociable, and humanitarian purposes as its basis along with the common objectives of work and economy, increases above all the moral and intellectual powers of men for the individual and common good and redounds to enrich and exalt every human endeavor.

Liberals promised that in a free society anyone with talent and energy could win a place in the middle class. Associations could assist in individual social advancement, but liberal spokesmen, at least, did not promise equality of achievement in wealth, power, and prestige. Indeed, once in operation, the liberals' associations often played a vital part in articulating status differences and social hierarchy.

Voluntary associations along with municipal councils and church vestries carried the principal burden of distributing power and social honors in local society. The associations to which one belonged and the honors won in them visibly indicated an individual's status as well as social and political loyalties.[8] Those who could claim respect by virtue of membership in an old, distinguished family or prestigious friendships did not need to win honors in associations to establish their status, but often they turned to the associations to exercise influence over local public affairs.[9] On the other hand,

[7] Ernst von Schwarzer, *Geld und Gut in Neuösterreich* (Vienna, 1857), pp. 76-77.

[8] The pride that members took in their participation in associations is apparent in many nineteenth-century memoirs. See, for example, Moritz Austerlitz, *Aus meinem Leben* (Prague, 1913), in the Leo Baeck Institute Library and Archive, New York, nearly half of which is devoted to his public welfare efforts and activity in associations.

[9] Compare the discussion of status differences in contemporary British voluntary organizations by Thomas Bottomore, "Social Stratification in Voluntary Organizations," in D. V. Glass, ed., *Social Mobility in Britain* (London, 1954), pp. 349-82.

those who were new to a community or who aspired to a higher rank could gain prestige through participation in associations.[10]

Middle-class society in nineteenth-century Central Europe generally awarded power and social honors on the basis of a composite test of occupation, wealth, life-style, and personal cultivation. The middle classes honored individuals' *Bildung und Besitz*, literally "cultivation and property," which presumably reflected individual achievement in a competitive society, not the happenstance of birth.[11] Although wealth was important, it was not the sole arbiter. For most of the second half of the century, the middle class (*Bürgertum* or Cz., *měšťanstvo*) as a functioning grouping extended beyond what we now generally term the bourgeoisie, the owners of commercial and industrial capital. University professors and distinguished physicians, whose only capital was their university degrees, sat as equals with bankers and manufacturers on town councils and on the boards of associations. Provided one had the appropriate values and life-style, higher education or merely the status of self-employment could counterbalance a significant gap in income in the social reckoning. On the other hand, a parvenu entrepreneur would find acceptance difficult if he lived too frugally or too ostentatiously or failed to share essential middle-class social and political ideals. Women for the most part won honors according to their husband's or father's rankings.

Voluntary associations both reflected and helped to define basic social cleavages and status differences in each community. Middle-class notables hoped that the associations they established would integrate diverse groups into a tight structure with clear lines of social and political deference, but they were seldom able to surmount fundamental cultural or class differences in the local population. For instance, in Rhenish towns which divided sharply between Protestant entrepreneurs and professionals with liberal tendencies, on the one hand, and more conservative Catholic shopkeepers and craftsmen, on the other, Protestant liberal and Catholic associations developed in separate networks.[12] In Brno and other

[10] Cf. Freudenthal, *Vereine in Hamburg*, pp. 455-56, and Meyer, *Vereinswesen Nürnberg*, pp. 263-64.

[11] Cf. Ernest K. Bramsted, *Aristocracy and the Middle Classes in Germany*, rev. ed. (Chicago, 1964), pp. 107-19, and Werner Sombart, *Der Bourgeois* (Munich, 1913), pp. 135-69, 212-42.

[12] See Hofmann, *Bielefelder Stadtverordneten*, pp. 39-44, and Helmut Croon, "Das Vordringen der politischen Parteien im Bereich der Kommunalen Selbstverwal-

Austrian cities in the 1860s and early seventies, German middle-class public life split between liberal anti-clerical groups and conservative Catholic associations.[13] In Prague and Plzeň, Czechs and Germans developed separate associational networks.

Class cleavages steadily widened in the public life of Central European cities in the sixties and seventies. Liberal and left liberal leaders tried to win the support of artisans and laborers through cultural and educational societies, but in the industrializing areas many workers gradually severed what ties they had with middle-class groups and formed their own associations with democratic socialist politics.[14] Increasing numbers of craft producers and shop-keepers also rejected the tutelage of the middle-class notables in the two decades of the "Great Depression" after the financial crash of 1873.

While both convenience and ideology recommended voluntary associations as the primary vehicles for middle-class and working-class group life, the habitual suspicion of Central European police authorities for all public gatherings made formal organizations imperative. Nearly all Central European states adopted the principle of freedom of assembly and association as part of liberalization in the 1850s and 1860s, but in many states, including Austria, state officials, conservative politicians, and even some liberal leaders still opposed informal group activity in public affairs. They insisted on formal organization, official registration, and advance notice to the police of all public meetings.[15] The law of November 15, 1867, which regulated associational activity in Austria until 1918, also required all groups to be chartered by the provincial governors and to report the names of their officers and directors to the police. Political associations had to report the names of all members as

tung," in Croon, ed., *Kommunale Selbstverwaltung im Zeitalter der Industrialisierung* (Stuttgart, Berlin, Cologne, and Mainz, 1971), pp. 23-37.

[13] Dřímal and Peša, ed., *Dějiny Brna*, II, pp. 36-38.

[14] See Werner and Conze and Dieter Groh, *Die Arbeiterbewegung in der nationalen Bewegung* (Stuttgart, 1966), pp. 41-54, 114-26; Cyril Horáček, *Počátky českého hnutí dělnického*, 2d ed. [Rozpravy I. třídy České akademie věd a umění, č. 19] (Prague, 1933), pp. 32-80; Zdeněk Šolle, "K počátkům dělnického hnutí v Praze," *ČSČH*, V (1957), pp. 664-87, VI (1958), pp. 266-310, VII (1959), pp. 49-70; Jiří Kořalka, *Vznik socialistického dělnického hnutí na liberecku* (Liberec, 1956), pp. 39-43, 107-26; and Emil Strauss, *Die Entstehung der deutschböhmischen Arbeiterbewegung* (Prague, 1925), pp. 67-96.

[15] See Gustav Kolmer, *Parlament und Verfassung in Österreich*, repr. (Graz, 1972), I, pp. 297-99. The development of the Austrian laws on associations merits further study.

well.[16] The Austrian police regularly exercised their prerogative of sending uniformed agents to meetings to assure that the associations stayed within the limits of their bylaws. The laws of association gave the police considerable discretion regarding which groups could even form and what activities they might undertake, as the early working-class organizations quickly and painfully discovered.[17] Irregular, informal group activities, of course, still went on in pubs, cafes, and private dwellings, but regulations like those in Austria forced all collective action of a planned, continuing character to proceed in formal associations. It was primarily in voluntary associations, then, that a new public life developed in Austria's cities and towns after the late fifties. In Prague, Czech and German liberals alike looked to associations to replace the old "Bohemian" order with new social and political structures.

German associational life in Prague, however, followed its own special course in the succeeding decades. The associations of the growing Czech majority quickly developed the social and political diversity that one would expect in a city of Prague's size and economic development. Czech middle and upper-middle-class elements, the members of the old and new lower middle classes, skilled workers, and laborers all found their way into separate groupings by the mid-1870s. Ideological differences came to the surface as Czech clerical-conservatives, moderate liberals, radical liberals, socialists, and later Christian Socials formed competing bodies. Down to the late 1880s, however, Prague's German organizations showed a uniformity and solidarity which reflected the values and needs of a largely middle- and upper-strata minority which was trying to stave off political, numerical, and economic decline. Throughout the late nineteenth century, the German liberal notables in the city tried to use their network of voluntary associations to make up for what the Germans' loss of power in local government deprived them of, and German group life in Prague remained predominantly middle class in its constituency and resolutely liberal in ideology. As will be seen, German public life in Prague only began to show more diversity when the Prague Germans saw the collapse of the power and influence of German liberal forces in Austria, and even the proudest middle-class Germans realized that Germans

[16] For details of the 1867 law and the provisional ordinances that preceded it, see Tezner in Mischler and Ulbrich, ed., IV, pp. 712-22.

[17] See the vignettes related by Pavla Horská-Vrbová, "Ke vzniku a charakteru tzv. dělnických besed v šedesátých letech 19. století v Praze," ČSČH, V (1957), pp. 116-19.

might not survive as a distinct element in the city without a greater popular base.

The Era of Liberal Dominance in Bohemian German Politics

In the early 1860s liberal, middle-class notables quickly achieved dominance over German politics in Prague and most of the other cities in the Bohemian Lands and in portions of the Habsburg Hereditary Lands. Economic development during the 1850s and popular resentment against the neo-absolutist regime had severely weakened the appeal of the old conservative elites. Moreover, the liberal notables benefited from control over the new middle-class voluntary associations and the deference of lower-middle-class elements. This and the exclusion of workers from the suffrage gave the liberals a strong base of power in the cities and in many of the towns.

The German liberal forces enjoyed particular advantages in Austria at the beginning of the constitutional era. With more than one-third of the population, the Germans constituted the largest single nationality in the western half of the Monarchy, and they were the only group to reside in every province. The emperor's centralist Patent of February 1861, which served as a constitution until 1867, permitted the liberal representatives of the German middle class and their aristocratic allies to devise a limited, multi-class suffrage which gave them control of the Austrian Reichsrat for most of the period until the early 1880s. The Bohemian and Moravian diets were more evenly divided between Czech and German deputies, but with the aid of liberal great landowners the German liberals dominated these bodies as well through most of the sixties and seventies. But for the brief interlude of the conservative Hohenwarth ministry in 1871, the *Verfassungspartei* (Constitutional or Liberal Party) of the German liberals also controlled the Austrian ministerial council from 1861 to 1879.

The German Liberal Party worked to realize its own vision of a free, progressive society in the two decades after 1861. It fought corporate privilege in politics and in the economy and clerical influence over the state and public education. Like their early nineteenth-century British forebears, Austria's German liberals expected to achieve full civil equality but not social or economic equality. They envisioned a new social hierarchy based on individual achievement, to replace the old one of orders and estates. To preserve the historic rights and autonomy of Austria's various lands would only sustain corporate privilege and prolong general backwardness; a centralized state and free commercial and industrial development were the best guarantees of progress. On national questions the German Liberal Party granted that the non-Germanic peoples of Austria were entitled to their own languages and cultures, but insisted that the Germans, particularly the German middle class, had a special civilizing and unifying mission in the Monarchy.[18] On this, of course, the German liberals clashed directly with Czech nationalists, Slovenes, and, to a lesser extent, with the Polish parties. Until the mid-1870s the only German opposition to the Liberal Party in parliament came from the fragmented clerical and conservative factions, which drew their support mainly from aristocrats and from peasant farmers in the Alpine provinces.

In Bohemia the nationality conflict and economic considerations encouraged the concentration of all German political activity under the umbrella of the Liberal Party at the beginning of the constitutional era. The clerical-conservatives might show some strength in rural areas along the southwestern and southern borders of Bohemia that were dominated by great landowners, but most of Bohemia's German population resided in the north in poor mountainous country or in towns undergoing industrialization. The German liberals' championing of economic development and their defense of German interests against the Czechs had a strong appeal to most Germans who met the suffrage requirements.

After 1861 it was hard to support conservative politics in Bohemia without also aiding the Czech national movement. Conservative aristocrats and Catholic prelates tried to maintain their influence in Austrian public affairs by advocating a federal ordering of the Monarchy and the preservation of traditional institutions in the various provinces. These conservative notions accorded well with the doctrine of the historic "state right" (*státní právo, Staatsrecht*) of a united, autonomous government for the Bohemian Lands which Czech nationalists had developed in the 1850s, and in January 1861 the conservative Bohemian nobility formed an alliance with the moderate Czech nationalists.[19] The latter were more liberal than

---

[18] On the ideology of the German Liberal Party, see Richard Charmatz, *Deutschösterreichische Politik* (Leipzig, 1907), pp. 43-156; Karl Eder, *Der Liberalismus in Altösterreich* (Vienna and Munich, 1955), pp. 141-89; and Georg Franz, *Liberalismus*, pp. 227-63, 345-52, 386-91.

[19] On Bohemian state right see Josef Kaloušek, *České státní právo*, 2nd rev. ed. (Prague, 1892); Karel Kramář, *České státní právo* (Prague, 1914); and H. Platz, *Das historische Recht und das österreichisch-ungarische Ausgleichsproblem* (Leipzig, 1930).

the nobility on economic and social questions, but the pact between F. L. Rieger and Count Heinrich (Jindřich) Clam-Martinitz lasted until the early 1890s, when Rieger and his party disappeared from Czech politics.

In view of this alliance, conservative Bohemian Germans whose opposition to Czech nationalism exceeded their dedication to an unchanged political order had little choice but to support the Liberal Party. When German liberal deputies in the Bohemian Diet first organized themselves in the spring of 1861, they were joined by Richard Dotzauer, a relatively conservative Prague merchant, and even by Andreas von Haase. The loosely knit Liberal Party accepted such recruits, but the resulting diversity of views and interests included under the German liberal umbrella led to recurring dissension.[20]

The crash of 1873 and the ensuing depression sparked lower-middle-class revolt against the German liberal notables in the Bohemian Lands as elsewhere in Austria. German industrial workers, who were largely excluded from the liberals' social and political order, had begun to organize independently in the late 1860s.[21] After the crash, the Progressive Party, a German left-liberal splinter group, began to win lower-middle-class support by attacking the Liberal Party leaders for selling out to great capitalist interests.[22] The revolt against the liberal elite affected local as well as parliamentary politics. In Brno, for instance, German lower-middle-class elements founded their own Burghers' Society at the beginning of the depression and forced the German liberal mayor out of office in 1876.[23] The German minorities of Plzeň and Prague, on the

[20] Neither Eder, *Der Liberalismus*, nor Franz, *Liberalismus*, discusses the absorption of conservative German burghers into the movement in the early 1860s or the party's formation at the grass-roots level; likewise, the parliamentary history by Gustav Kolmer, *Parlament und Verfassung in Österreich*, 8 vols. (Vienna, 1902-14), I, pp. 46-132.

[21] See Ludwig Brügel, *Geschichte der österreichischen Sozialdemokratie*, 5 vols. (Vienna, 1922), II, pp. 157-64, and Emil Strauss, *Die Entstehung der deutschböhmischen Arbeiterbewegung* (Prague, 1925), pp. 80-96.

[22] See Diethild Harrington-Müller, *Der Fortschrittsklub im Abgeordnetenhaus des öster. Reichsrats 1873-1910* (Vienna, Graz, and Cologne, 1972), pp. 27-41; and Friedrich Prinz, "Die böhmischen Länder von 1848 bis 1914," in Karl Bosl, ed., *Handbuch*, III, pp. 150-51.

[23] A new Catholic-Patriotic Casino followed in 1879. See Dřímal and Peša, ed., *Dějiny Brna*, II, pp. 36-38. Compare the evolution of liberal-conservative Catholic-radical petty bourgeois divisions in the politics of Graz, William H. Hubbard, "Politics and Society in the Central European City: Graz, Austria, 1861-1918," *Canadian Journal of History*, V (1970), pp. 25-47.

other hand, did not exhibit the same political divisiveness, and maintained unified support for the German liberal leadership through the seventies. Here the potential forces of dissent were weak, and most of the politically active Germans were convinced of the need for unity in the face of growing Czech strength.

The Creation of German Community Life in Prague

Liberal middle-class notables created and dominated the voluntary associations that first gave the Germans a group life in Prague. The first new German organizations arose at the end of the Bach era in response to the Czechs' winning control of a number of social and professional groups which were formerly bilingual. Czech nationalists had previously taken over the Society for the Bohemian Museum, the Royal Bohemian Society for Sciences, the Masters' Collegium, and the Manufacturing Society—with no significant German response.[24] After 1860, however, German notables began to resist the Czech challenge to their position, either by forcing the Czechs out of existing groups or by founding their own exclusively German organizations.

Following the same pattern as municipal politics in Prague, a number of associations which began with both Czech and German members in 1859 and 1860 split along ethnic lines by the end of 1861. Czech-German polarization occurred first in singing societies and gymnastics groups. These associations attracted primarily employees in commerce and craft production, shopkeepers, and university students. Some of the most zealous Czech nationalists could be found among these elements, and students were prominent among the few in Prague who expressed a German identity through the 1850s. In 1859 Germans founded the "Magic Flute" society dedicated to German song, but from the start it had Czech as well as German members. Over the next two years the Czech contingent grew to dominate the group. Finally, in May 1861, a number of German members seceded to found a new German society, "Flute."[25]

Similarly, a single gymnastics hall served both Czech- and German-speakers in Prague through the 1840s and 1850s. Czech gym-

---

[24] Cf. Laube in Knoll, *Beiträge*, xii, and Rychnovsky, *Der deutsche Turnverein*, pp. 3-4.

[25] On the German groups see Franz Mathé, ed., *Geschichte des Deutschen Männergesang-Vereins in Prag* (Prague, 1886), and Klier, *Das Deutschtum Prags*, p. 62. On the Czech groups see Heller, *Z minulé doby*, III, pp. 152-53.

nasts assumed that they would be able to join the gymnastics society that a young German lawyer and several commercial employees began to organize in July 1861. By this time, however, deep enmity had developed between Czechs and Germans in municipal and provincial politics, and the organizers of the new society insisted on a German *Turnverein*, with German as its sole official language.[26] The German group found a rich and influential patron in Eduard Seutter Ritter von Lötzen, one of the German liberals elected as alderman on the Progressive ticket. Seutter had participated in the Constitutional Society in 1848; as Prague manager for the Credit-anstalt, the great Vienna-based bank, he epitomized Austria's German entrepreneurial element.[27] Under the leadership of Jindřich Fügner and a young philosophy instructor, Miroslav Tyrš, the Czech gymnasts responded to the German action in late 1861 by organizing the first Czech nationalist gymnastics group, the Prague *Sokol*.

The division of professional organizations into separate Czech and German groups followed as Czech nationalism gained adherents at higher levels of Prague society. The Germans' strength in the learned professions and their resistance to internal Czechification of the existing associations forced Czech physicians and lawyers to secede and found their own groups. Thus, in late 1862, a group of young Czech physicians led by the great physiologist Jan Purkyně established the Association of Czech Physicians (*Spolek českých lékařů*) to compete with the predominantly German Society of Practicing Physicians.[28] The Czech Jurists' Union (*Právnická jednota*) followed in 1864. On the other hand, *Merkur*, the principal association of retail businessmen and their employees, continued to include both Czech and German members until 1867. Through most of the 1860s, common business concerns apparently drew Prague's retailers together more strongly than Czech-German differences divided them, and their daily commercial dealings went on regardless of ethnic distinctions among the customers, employees, and competitors. By 1867, however, Czech members had

[26] Rychnovsky, *Turnverein*, pp. 9-10.

[27] I have been unable to substantiate the assertion of Josef Müller in "Vznik a záložení pražské tělocvičné jednoty Sokola," in Müller and F. Tallowitz, ed., *Památník výdaný na oslavu dvacetiletého trvání . . . Sokola pražského* (Prague, 1883), pp. 44-52, that Seutter made exclusion of Czechs a condition for his support of the group. Rychnovsky, *Turnverein*, pp. 9-12, indicates that the group's German character was established at the very beginning of the planning.

[28] Otakar Matoušek, "Purkyňovská leta spolku a časopisu českých lékařů," *Časopis českých lékařů*, XCI (1952), pp. 58-62, 87-93.

gained a majority in *Merkur*, and a number of German commercial employees led by an officer of the Creditanstalt, withdrew in protest.[29] Merchants from Prague's German liberal elite assisted this group in founding a new German Merchants' Club (*Deutscher Kaufmännischer Verein*), and Richard Dotzauer served as the first president.

While the developments in politics, in the associations for general sociability and amusement, and in the various professional bodies led to the separation of Germans and Czechs in Prague in the 1860s, they continued to mingle in other areas of public life. Separate Czech and German systems of primary and secondary education developed in the sixties and seventies, but Czechs could attend German schools and vice versa.[30] The small numbers of Czech and German Protestants in the city had separate churches, but a single system of parishes continued to serve all Catholics in Prague, regardless of ethnic or political differences. Similarly, the Austrian Ministry of Religion and Instruction authorized a single Jewish community organization to serve all Jews in Prague and in each of the suburbs.[31] A number of the oldest voluntary associations in the Bohemian capital, particularly charities connected to the Catholic Church or to the Jewish religious establishments and to independent charitable, artistic, and musical groups, also escaped the Czech-German division of public affairs. Here, endowments, connections to the religious bodies, or merely strong traditions worked against Czech-German polarization. Old bodies, such as the Archduchess Sophie Academy and the Society of the Arts, also showed the persistence of some "Bohemian" sentiments among the nobility, higher clergy, and among some of the highest bourgeois strata who supported them.[32] These bodies stand out in sharp relief, however, against the rest of organized group life for middle-class,

---

[29] SÚA Praha, PP 1888-92 V/24/23 Deutscher Kaufmännischer Verein: ad N2265pp, police report on the founding of the German Merchants' Club, 29 June 1867.

[30] On Czech-German relations in the Prague schools see Chapter 3 below and Gary B. Cohen, "The Prague Germans 1861-1914: The Problems of Ethnic Survival" (Ph.D. dissertation, Princeton University, 1975), pp. 551-73.

[31] See the discussion of Czech-German relations in the churches and synagogues in Chapter 5 below.

[32] Klier, *Das Deutschtum Prags*, pp. 61-62; AHMP fond spolků, Sophien-Akademie: miscellaneous papers, and spolkový katastr: protocols for the various Catholic charitable groups. In the late 1880s the Czech members dropped out of the Sophien-Akademie, which was involved in musical activities, but most of the older Catholic charitable groups remained bi-national, although predominantly Czech, until 1918.

lower-middle-class, and laboring elements in Prague, which divided sharply into separate Czech and German spheres after the early 1860s.

The German associations which developed in the sixties and seventies functioned as part of a tightly integrated network. The sharing of leaders and intertwining of memberships bound them together, and at the head of the whole structure stood the German Casino, a large general-purpose social club. The Casino provided the other groups with direction and financial support as well as with rooms for meetings.

Prague's German liberal notables had considerable difficulty at first in organizing the Casino. Confident and intensely proud, they found it hard in 1860 and 1861 to unite and discipline themselves to meet the new Czech challenge. In December 1861, a local German journalist, Theophil Pisling, complained that "up to now the establishment of a German Casino, for which there have been efforts for over a year, has foundered time and again because of the disunity and lack of political discipline which unfortunately reigns among our Germans. . . ."[33] The emerging liberal elite found it hard to agree on leadership within its own ranks, but after much discussion the Casino was finally organized in June 1862. Still, problems continued, and six months later Pisling wrote, "Something truly significant could grow around the Casino were it not for the old failing of the Germans, everyone wants to command, none to obey."[34]

The identity of the founders and early directors of the German Casino indicates what elements rose to the top of the nascent German community. The fifty-five who underwrote the founding of the Casino were, above all, prosperous; and each contributed the sum of 100 fl.[35] They included many of those already prominent in the German Liberal Party in Bohemia: the publisher Heinrich Mercy, the lawyer Dr. Moriz Raudnitz, Richard Dotzauer, Eduard Seutter von Lötzen, and a gifted young lawyer from Česká lípa (Böhmisch Leipa), Franz Schmeykal (1828-1894). Dotzauer chaired the initial organizational meetings, but as the first president the Casino Association chose Schmeykal, who was rapidly emerging as

---

[33] *Deutsches Museum*, XI (1861), p. 869.

[34] *Ibid.*, XIII (1863), p. 20.

[35] See Anton Kiemann, *Die ersten vierzig Jahre des Vereines Deutsches Kasino in Prag 1862-1902* (Prague, 1902), p. 8. 100 Austrian gulden (fl.) equaled at par value in gold U.S. $50.

leader of the German deputies in the Bohemian Diet.[36] Schmeykal presided over the Casino for thirty-two years until his death.

The directors of the German Casino in the sixties and seventies were primarily lawyers, wealthy merchants, manufacturers, professors, and a few state officials. Virtually all were either self-employed or respected tenured employees of the state.[37] All enjoyed relatively high standards of living, and each possessed some capital, either in goods and property or in university degrees and professional status attained in a society which reserved higher education for the few. In contrast to the Czech Burghers' Club and Manufacturing Society, the leadership of the German Casino included no master craftsmen or shopkeepers. The small businessmen and more prosperous masters in Prague who considered themselves Germans might join the Casino as members, but they won no high honors there.

Between 1862 and the late 1870s, commercial and industrial entrepreneurs increased their role in the Casino's leadership, while state officials nearly disappeared. These changes followed the general evolution of the German middle class in Prague and in Bohemia at large. The abolition of guild privileges at the end of the 1850s and the boom of the sixties and early seventies led to an increase in both the wealth and the social prestige of factory owners and merchants. State officials, on the other hand, had only a small share in Prague's leading German circles at the outset; and their role in local German society declined steadily thereafter. Economic development in the cities of German Bohemia made commerce and industry more attractive to Bohemian Germans than less lucrative government service, where, in any case, they faced increasing Czech competition for positions. The gradual decline in the prestige of state service in the late nineteenth century only strengthened the disinclination of Bohemian Germans, while the sons of Czech peasants and the urban lower middle classes continued to see the expanding bureaucracy as an avenue for achieving some upward mobility.[38]

[36] *Ibid*. Dotzauer's bitterness at not being elected president of the Casino is reported by Schebek, *Dotzauer*, p. 118.

[37] AHMP fond spolků, Deutsches Haus: minutes of the directors' meetings and annual reports for the Verein des Deutschen Casino, 1862-1879.

[38] See Stölzl, *Die Ära Bach*, pp. 116-19; Malý, *Naše znovuzrození*, I, p. 93; and the novelistic treatment in Martin Havel (pseud. of Matej Šimáček), *Ze zápisků phil. studenta F. Kořínka: Pohledy do rodin*, 4 vols. (Prague, 1893-96), I, p. 166. For discussion of the general decline in prestige of the European state bureaucracy, see

The German Casino attracted a membership that was large but still overwhelmingly middle class in character. In addition to the founders, 632 individuals had paid the annual dues of 12 fl. by November 1862; the membership grew to 1,098 by December 1870.[39] In 1879 the Casino had 1,200 members from a total German population in the city and inner suburbs of only 31,000.[40] Individuals from the middle class of property and education comprised the great majority: in 1879 there were over 400 self-employed businessmen; 104 independent manufacturers; 160 lawyers, physicians, and engineers; 80 professors from the university, technical college, and gymnasium faculties; and 60 officers of banks and insurance companies. The Casino included 130 white-collar employees but only 10 master craftsmen and no retail clerks nor any workers (see Table 4/1 in Chapter 4).

The membership of the German Casino grew far beyond a small group of notables who might gather over coffee or beer several times a week to discuss public affairs. The broader membership—almost all adult heads of households—joined out of a sense of civic duty and of desire for social distinction and proximity to the centers of community power. To accommodate the members, their lectures, and their amusements as well as the gatherings of other German associations, the Casino had to find ever larger quarters. In 1873 the German Casino finally purchased a three-story, eighteenth-century palace on the great commercial thoroughfare Na příkopě (Am Graben) in the Lower New Town (see Plate III). Here there was space for a reading room, restaurant, game rooms, several assembly halls, and a garden. The Casino quickly established itself as the locale for all major German group activities in Prague as well as the headquarters for the Liberal Party in Bohemia. For both Germans and Czechs the Casino quickly came to symbolize the German presence in the city.[41]

The German Casino guided the activities of most of the other

Eugene N. Anderson and Pauline R. Anderson, *Political Institutions and Social Change in Continental Europe in the Nineteenth Century* (Berkeley, 1967), pp. 231-37.

[39] Kiemann, *Die ersten vierzig Jahre*, p. 11, and AHMP fond spolků, Deutsches Haus: "Bericht der 9. ordentlicher Generalversammlung, 3 Dec 1870."

[40] AHMP fond spolků, Deutsches Haus: "Mitglieder-Verzeichnis des Vereines des Deutschen Casino, 1879-80."

[41] *Tagesbote aus Böhmen*, 20 and 24 Jan 1868, reported demonstrations by Czech crowds in front of the Casino to protest the Austro-Hungarian Compromise and the visit to Prague of the German liberal Minister of Justice, Eduard Herbst, one of the first of many major Czech demonstrations at the German Casino.

III. German Casino on Na příkopě (ca. 1912)

German associations in Prague until the late 1880s. Even where leading members of the Casino did not actually found the other German groups, they directed most of them once in operation. The same businessmen, industrialists, and bankers who contributed heavily to the Casino also supported most of the more specialized groups, and the Casino Association itself often provided subventions and gifts of books and periodicals.[42]

The Casino's control of virtually all German associational life in Prague made it easy for Schmeykal, Dotzauer, and the other liberal notables around them to monopolize local German politics throughout the sixties and seventies. The liberal leaders established a deferential hierarchy in the associations, which reserved political decision-making for those who also held the highest social honors, and made opposition to them nearly impossible. Under these conditions, ad hoc committees of the Casino's leading members could easily manage the formation of policy and the selection of candidates. Liaison with the German liberal delegations in the Bohemian Diet and in the Reichsrat presented no problems: Franz Schmeykal and the five or six other members of the Casino who normally held seats in one or the other body maintained constant contact.[43] German liberal leaders communicated with their constituents in Prague through the associations and through the local German press, but they were under little pressure actually to consult with the voters or with the general public. In fact, the German Casino had few election cares at all in regard to the Bohemian Diet and the Reichsrat between 1862 and 1879, when the Czech nationalists boycotted most of the elections. The German liberals themselves abstained from Prague's municipal elections after 1870 in all districts except Josefov, rather than engage in hopeless contests with the Czechs.[44]

Although the 1867 law on associations permitted political societies, the German liberals in the Bohemian capital did not bother to establish one until they confronted a crisis in 1869. Czech antagonism to the Austro-Hungarian Compromise of 1867 and Aus-

[42] AHMP fond spolků, Deutsches Haus: minutes of the board of directors, 1864-1918. The collection in the Prague City Archive does not include complete financial records for the Casino, and financial documents for other German organizations and private individuals are all but nonexistent.

[43] The heavy correspondence between Schmeykal and the German liberal parliamentary leader Ernst von Plener makes this clear; Haus, Hof-, und Staatsarchiv, Vienna (Hereafter, HHStA): Nachlass Plener, Kt. 19.

[44] On the Germans' abstention from the aldermanic elections see Knoll, *Beiträge*, pp. 176-77.

tria's German liberal ministry peaked in a series of mass camp meetings (*tábory*) in the autumn of 1868, and the Austrian government responded by declaring a state of emergency in Prague and its environs.[45] In the meantime, conservative politicians and Czech journalists were mounting a sharp attack on the German liberals' anti-clerical educational policies. The German leaders in Prague reacted to the situation by creating a new "Constitutional Society of Germans in Bohemia" (*Verfassungsverein der Deutschen in Böhmen*), which they intended "to propagate knowledge of the modern state based on law and constitution" and "to arouse and strengthen the national consciousness, political life, and undertakings of the German people in Bohemia."[46] To pursue these ends, the organization would hold public meetings in Prague, circulate petitions, and sponsor candidates for public office.

In practice the Constitutional Society did more to reinforce the Prague Germans' existing political system than to change it. The Society functioned essentially as a political subsidiary of the Casino and merely gave the liberal elite an additional forum to propagate its views. Predictably, Franz Schmeykal presided over the new group, and the other directors also came from the Casino's highest echelons.[47] Despite having dues of only one-third the amount for the Casino, the Constitutional Society and its successor after 1882, the German Club, always attracted a much smaller and more exclusive membership than the Casino. Lawyers, merchants, professors, government officials, and physicians accounted for nearly eighty percent of the 107 members at the end of 1869.[48]

The Constitutional Society met regularly for less than three years after its founding. It ceased to function after the fall of the short-lived Hohenwarth ministry in 1871 and the return to power of the German Liberal Party; the leaders of the Casino apparently felt it safe to rely again on the old devices of ad hoc committees and of

---

[45] For an exhaustive discussion of the *tábory*, see Jaroslav Purš, "Tábory v českých zemích v letech 1868-1871," *ČSČH*, VI (1958), pp. 234-65, 446-69, 661-89.

[46] SÚA Praha PP 1900-07 V/15/10 Deutscher Verein: kt. 1966, no. 2 56390, "Statuten," 26 Oct 1869. [Alfred Klaar], *Franz Schmeykal: Eine Gedenkschrift* (Prague, 1894), pp. 37-39, gives the attack on the Liberal Party's educational legislation as the immediate instance for Schmeykal's decision to found the Constitutional Society.

[47] SÚA Praha PP 1900-07 V/15/10: kt. 1966, "Candidatenliste für die Ausschusswahl, 20 Dec 1869." See Appendix II, Table 9 for the members of the first board of directors.

[48] SÚA Praha PP 1900-07 V/15/10: kt. 1966, 5832/pp 3542, "Mitglieder Verzeichnis, 26 Dec 1869."

journalistic appeals to the voters. The Constitutional Society resumed meeting in 1881 only after the Liberal Party had lost control of the Austrian ministerial council.

The financial collapse of 1873 and the severe business slump of the mid-seventies slowed the growth of German associational life in Prague and forced a number of groups to reduce their activities sharply. Understandably, the associations with the greatest concentrations of manufacturers, businessmen, and commercial employees were most strongly affected. Overall investment and production levels continued to rise in Austria during the two decades of the "Great Depression" after 1873, but in the particularly difficult years between 1873 and 1878, bankruptcies, falling prices, and reduced consumer demand greatly increased the cares of merchants and manufacturers and threatened many employees with unemployment.[49] In Prague many Germans in finance, commerce, and industry now found that they lacked the resources of time and money needed to participate in associational life at the accustomed levels. The membership of the German Merchants' Club, for instance, fell from 430 in 1872 to 72 in 1877; and the directors had to suspend the group's activities between 1877 and 1882.[50]

The liberal notables maintained their control over German public life in Prague despite the economic strains of the mid-seventies. Political developments among the Prague Germans did not follow the patterns of more diverse German urban populations in Austria: no radical German opposition to the liberals arose in the Bohemian capital during the 1870s. At the root of this was the fact that German community life developed in Prague with strong limits of class as well as of ideology; lower-middle-class elements had a weak position in the associational network, and there were almost no workers. As will be seen, even outside the organized community, the German lower strata—to describe more generally the pettiest retailers, low-level employees, workers, and their families—were too few and too isolated in Prague to organize on their own before the late 1880s.

The Class Limits of the German Community

The German group life that arose in the liberal voluntary associations embraced few persons outside the middle class of property

[49] On the crash and the character of the depression in Austria, see the detailed account by Matis, Österreichs Wirtschaft, pp. 260-97.

[50] SÚA Praha PP 1888-92 V/24/23 Deutscher Kaufmännischer Verein: NE 10135/

and education and the more respectable lower middle class of small businessmen and white-collar employees. Indeed, the German community of the sixties and seventies did not escape its origins in Prague's German-speaking middle and upper strata of the 1840s and 1850s, and neither aristocrats nor industrial workers really shared in German group life. The German associations expected that their members not only have a German self-identity and support German liberal politics but also that they be *bürgerlich*, middle class, or at least aspire to that class and accept its values.

The leaders of the German Casino did accept the support of small masters and workers when they could get it. Yet, beyond the German Gymnastics Society and several other special-purpose groups, the associational network offered the lower strata little opportunity for participation and for the development of a sense of community with the German middle class. Commercial employees and clerks, who could identify with the higher commercial strata, comprised one-third of the Gymnastics Society, but no German organization in the 1860s and 1870s attracted any sizable number of workers from the crafts or from industry.[51] The Czech nationalists' ideology of social integration offered much more to craftsmen and to laborers than did the liberalism of the German community.

Throughout this era, the great social diversity of Czech public life in Prague contrasted sharply with the narrowness of German group life. There is no way of knowing precisely how many German workers lived in Prague before the 1880 census, but incidental remarks in police reports from the preceding two decades indicate that the work force comprised a few Germans who had either immigrated from German areas or had been Germanized in Prague.[52] Yet neither the Casino nor any body of German craftsmen tried to organize artisans in opposition to the Czech domination of the craft associations.[53] When workers and craftsmen with Ger-

---

7266, 19 Dec 1882, police report of the 18 Dec 1882 meeting, and "Jahresbericht des Deutschen Kaufmännischen Vereines in Prag für das Vereinsjahr 1883."

[51] For a more exact analysis of the membership of the Gymnastics Society, see Chapter 5.

[52] Zdeněk Šolle notes police reports on unidentified "German workers" in Prague in *ČSČH*, V (1957), p. 680, n. 47.

[53] By 1868 German liberal leaders in Prague had written off the craftsmen so completely that they chose to transfer Czech small businessmen from the commercial section of the German-dominated Prague Chambers of Trade and Manufacture to the crafts section as a means of strengthening the German hold on the commercial section. See Gruber, *Handels- und Gewebekammer*, pp. 179-81, 313-15, 582-87.

man sentiments tried once to band together and to build links to the other German associations, the small numbers of German workers in the city, along with the strong class and ideological limits of the organized German community, doomed the effort.

In 1867 a diverse group of weavers, printers, smiths, and white-collar employees in the suburb of Smíchov formed an association for sociability and self-improvement called *Eintracht* (Concord). Smíchov had been the first of Prague's industrial districts. Most of the factory owners at this time were still Germans, and their desire to counterbalance the growing strength of Czech workers' associations in the district provided the real impetus for the founding of Concord.[54] One industrialist sat on the first board of directors, and many of them contributed funds during Concord's first two years.[55] The association's credit union, lecture series, and evening classes on practical and academic subjects quickly won a large following, and 400 persons joined in little over a year.[56] No membership lists survive, but small masters, skilled workers, and white-collar employees apparently comprised a large portion. Concord affirmed its solidarity with the local German liberal establishment by naming Franz Schmeykal an honorary member and by electing professors and industrialists as directors alongside workers. Yet it soon proved impossible to reconcile working-class interests with those of the liberal middle class.

Within a year and a half of Concord's founding, conflicts erupted between workers' desires for social legislation and the liberalism of the other members. In February 1869 the president and eight directors resigned their offices to protest a resolution of the association which supported limitation of working hours in factories. The liberal directors favored self-help, not state intervention in the economy; and one stated pointedly that "a society for continuing education is not a workers' club."[57] For a time the supporters of the

---

[54] SÚA Praha PP 1870-75 V/9/5 Eintracht: ad 27822, "Statuten-Entwurf" (1867) and accompanying police report to the Bohemian Governor, NE 1760/pp, 26 May 1867. On the social and political affairs of the German middle-class elements in Smíchov, see Gustav von Portheim, "Aus meinen Erinnerungen," *Deutsche Arbeit*, VII (1907-08), pp. 714-23.

[55] SÚA Praha PP 1870-75 V/9/5: "Bericht über die Verwaltung und Tätigkeit des Vereines 'Eintracht' in Smichow, 22 September bis 24 Juni 1868." The donors included M. von Portheim, Alexander Richter, Johann Bermüller, and Johann Krumbholz, all industrialists.

[56] SÚA Praha PP 1870-75 V/9/5: police reports on Eintracht, 1867-69.

[57] SÚA Praha PP 1870-75 V/9/5: NE 774 VL, 21 Feb 1869 police report; NE 882 ST, 28 Feb 1869 police report.

resolution and a neutral group prevailed and Concord continued to grow, but more disputes broke out between liberals and working-class radicals later in 1869 and 1870. By September 1870 liberal industrialists, merchants, professors, white-collar employees, and a few master artisans managed to win control of the organization. Thereafter the membership shrank, and the group became merely a middle-class and lower-middle-class educational society. Nothing is known of any further group activities on the part of Concord's former working-class members. For its part, Prague's German liberal elite made no other attempts to create an association for German workers until a new era of ethnic defense began in the early 1880s.

At the other end of the social spectrum, the hereditary nobility also failed to share significantly in German collective life. Even the "constitutional" (*verfassungstreu*) nobility, who were allied with the German Liberal Party, abstained from participation in Prague's German associations. The social distance between the "first society" (*erste Gesellschaft*) of aristocrats and even the highest German middle-class circles in the city remained unbridgeable until the end of the Monarchy. Rohans, Fürstenbergs, Thun-Hohensteins, Thun-Salms, and Waldsteins occasionally attended the great festivities in the Casino or the German opera balls and often contributed to the German theatres and charities, but they did not take part in the everyday activities of the associations. A few upper-middle-class Germans in the Casino attained the petty titles of Ritter or Edler, but in the late 1890s, for instance, Prince Egon zu Fürstenberg was the only aristocrat on the membership lists.[58] Count Oswald Thun-Hohenstein, one of the leaders of the constitutional nobility, lent his name to the German Theatre Society as president from its founding in 1883 until 1913. Yet Thun managed few of the group's affairs and almost never chaired the annual general meetings.[59]

The nobility apparently had no more contact with the middle-class Germans outside the associations than within. The journalist Willy Haas, born in Prague in 1891, later recalled that conservative and liberal aristocrats alike held themselves aloof from the Czech and German burghers of Prague. As far as the middle-class elements were concerned, "the noblemen in their huge, mysterious

[58] AHMP fond spolků, Deutsches Haus: "Namens-Verzeichnis der Mitglieder 1898-99."

[59] SÚA Praha PP 1893-99 V/42/15 Deutscher Theaterverein: police reports of meetings, lists of officers, and annual reports, 1883-96, and PP 1908-15 V/42/9 Deutscher Theaterverein: papers, reports, 1896-1915.

baroque palaces in Malá strana spoke French and belonged to no nation but rather to the Holy Roman Empire, which had not existed for a century."[60] Even though individuals such as Prince Karel Schwarzenberg and Count Oswald Thun had strongly defined Czech or German political loyalties, Central European aristocratic custom dictated that they minimize social interaction with other classes.

Thus while German community life in Prague proved socially and politically too exclusive for workers, it was not exclusive enough for the nobility. Even where workers or noblemen had German loyalties, that allegiance failed to generate any significant social interaction or a general community of interest across the strong class barriers that characterized German collective life in the Bohemian capital from the outset.

Jews in the German Community

The emergent German associational network established social and political criteria that effectively limited participation to middle-class and lower-middle-class liberals, but the German community established no religious or racial bars to exclude Jews. In the 1860s and 1870s growing numbers of Jews who wanted to share in the Christians' public life entered into the German associations on essentially the same basis as non-Jews. To win acceptance, Jews had to speak primarily German, support the German Liberal Party and the German national cause in Austria, and belong to the middle or lower middle class. The Jews had only just been freed from the old discriminatory laws and the ghettoes, and they shared in the German liberals' determination to treat religion as a private matter and to exclude it as a factor from public affairs. For their part, the German associations in Prague admitted Jews without insisting that they fully amalgamate with the Christian population in their private lives and thereby cease to be Jews.[61]

The experience of many centuries in ghettoes surrounded by Gentile populations gave Bohemian Jews an outlook much more

[60] Willy Haas, *Die Literarische Welt* (Munich, 1958), pp. 10-11. See also the biting parody of the nobility by Gustav Meyrink, *Walpurgisnacht* (Leipzig, 1917), pp. 6-8.

[61] I will consider as Jews those who affirmed membership in a Jewish population or religious community and exclude all those who formally renounced any such affiliation. Cf. the definition of Robert A. Kann, "Assimilation and Antisemitism in the German-French Orbit in the Nineteenth and Early Twentieth Century," *Leo Baeck Institute Year Book*, XIV (1969), p. 92.

like the Jews of Germany than those of Poland and western Russia who resided in all-Jewish settlements. The desire to escape the poverty and restrictions of ghetto life provided a strong impetus for Bohemian Jews to adopt the values and life-style of secular, liberal middle-class society. Even before the abolition of the last restrictions on residence and occupation in 1859-1860, Jews in Prague and the larger central Bohemian towns took the lead in commercial and industrial innovation and developed an interest in secular learning.[62] Rich and poor alike, Prague Jews developed a strong identification with the emerging entrepreneurial and professional middle class:[63]

> Of course, they were divided above all into rich and poor; but this difference did not cut so deeply in social terms. . . . There was a certain uniformity of thinking and feeling. It derived primarily from the circumstances that the inhabitants of the ghetto all had the same calling as traders. . . . Moreover, the humblest Jew had the intuitive economic understanding that the difference between large amounts of property and small arises naturally.

Excluded from the Gentile craft guilds in the corporate society, relatively few Bohemian Jews engaged in the traditional handicrafts or identified with small craft producers. In the second half of the nineteenth century, over half of all self-supporting Bohemian Jews engaged in commerce and finance while another 15 to 25 percent were in the professions and state employ.[64] The only statistics available for Prague come from 1900; in that year fully 51 percent of the self-supporting Jews in the city and inner suburbs were self-

[62] For a more thorough discussion of Jewish-German assimilation in Prague, see Gary B. Cohen, "Jews in German Society: Prague, 1860-1914," *Central European History*, X (1977), pp. 28-54. On the general history of the Bohemian Jews in the nineteenth century, see Ruth Kestenberg-Gladstein, "The Jews between Czechs and Germans in the Historic Lands, 1848-1918," in *The Jews of Czechoslovakia*, 2 vols. (Philadelphia and New York, 1968-71), I, pp. 21-71; Christoph Stölzl, "Zur Geschichte der Böhmischen Juden in der Epoche des modernen Nationalismus," *Bohemia: Jahrbuch des Collegium Carolinum*, XIV (1973), pp. 179-221, and XV (1974), pp. 129-57, and Michael A. Riff, "The Assimilation of the Jews of Bohemia and the Rise of Political Anti-Semitism, 1848-1918" (Ph.D. dissertation, University of London, 1974).

[63] Sigmund Mayer, *Ein jüdischer Kaufmann 1831 bis 1911* (Leipzig, 1911), p. 103. On the legal history of Jewish emancipation in Austria, see Johann Scherer, "Juden," in Mischler and Ulbrich, 2nd ed., I, pp. 946-71.

[64] Jan Heřman, "The Evolution of the Jewish Population in Bohemia and Moravia, 1754-1953," paper read at the Sixth World Congress of Jewish Studies, Jerusalem, August, 1973.

employed or independent in the commercial, professional, service, and manufacturing sectors, compared to 27 percent qualified employees in all sectors, 12 percent commercial workers, and only 7 percent workers in manufacturing.[65]

The patterns of migration to Prague before World War I helped to keep the Jewish working class small and facilitated the Jewish residents' rapid adoption of the values and culture of German and Czech society. Largely because of immigration, Prague's Jewish population grew steadily after 1860. In 1869 the Jewish civilian residents of the municipality and the inner suburbs numbered 14,918, or 7.3 percent of the total; in 1880, 19,609, or 7.7 percent.[66] Thereafter, the Jewish population grew at a slower rate than the Gentile, but by 1910 the number of Jews had risen to 27,986.[67] The immigration of Jews to Prague, like that of Catholics and Protestants, came principally from other towns in Bohemia. Unlike that of Berlin, Vienna, and Budapest, Prague's economy attracted few poor Polish and Russian Jews until the upheavals of World War I. In 1900, 94 percent of the Prague Jews were native to the Bohemian Lands, and less than 3 percent had come from Galicia, the Bukovina, Hungary, and Russia.[68]

Jews in Prague and the other larger Bohemian towns looked to full equality with non-Jews in civic life and economic affairs as the way to escape the deprivation and disadvantages of the ghetto life. Religious piety declined sharply among the Prague Jews after 1860, but most retained something of their Jewish religious and cultural heritage as well as a distinct group identity within the confines of domestic life. Throughout Central Europe only a small number of Jews renounced their religion before 1900, and in Prague typically

[65] Heinrich Rauchberg, *Der nationale Besitzstand in Böhmen*, 3 vols. (Leipzig, 1905), II, p. 368.

[66] Jan Srb, ed., *Sčítání lidu v král. hlavní městě Praze a obcech sousedních provedené 31. prosince 1900*, 3 vols. (Prague, 1902-08), I, pp. 88-95. The 1857 statistics on religion counted only the native residents and therefore are not comparable.

[67] *Statistická zpráva král. hl. města Prahy r. 1910* (Prague, 1912), p. 58.

[68] Srb, ed., *Sčítání lidu*, III, p. 750. On the impact made by the arrival of East European refugees during the war, see Felix Weltsch, "The Rise and Fall of the Jewish-German Symbiosis—The Case of Franz Kafka," *LBI Year Book*, I (1956), p. 271, and Hans Tramer, "Prague—City of Three Peoples," *LBI Year Book*, IX (1964), pp. 320-26. Studies of migration for the Bohemian Lands offer few explanations of the absence of East European Jews in Prague. The Bohemian capital did not lie astride any of the major paths from Poland and Russia to North America, and the highly skilled character of the city's industrial work force together with the weakness of textile and clothing manufacture in the late nineteenth century may have deterred East European Jews from settling in Prague.

IV. Staronová synagogue (*Altneuschul*) and Hall of the Jewish Religious
Community, Prague [Leo Baeck Institute]

V. High Synagogue (*Hochsynagoge*)
and Hall of the Jewish
Religious Community, Prague
[Leo Baeck Institute]

no more than ten a year gave it up during the seventies, eighties, and nineties.[69] Moreover, noticeably few Prague Jews married non-Jews before the turn of the century. In 1881, for instance, Prague had 0.5 mixed marriages per 100 homogeneous Jewish unions, compared to 11.8 per 100 in Vienna.[70] In public affairs, on the other hand, Prague Jews, like most of their brethren in the Habsburg Hereditary Lands and Germany, wanted full participation in Gentile society. In civic life the Prague Jews wanted to be considered simply as Germans or Czechs, regardless of their religion, and only after 1900 did any local Jewish group begin to advocate a distinct ethnic identity on a par with the other two.[71]

Between the 1840s and the mid-1880s, the overwhelming majority of Prague Jews adopted the culture of Austria's German middle classes. The large-scale linguistic and cultural Germanization of Bohemian Jews began in the reign of Emperor Joseph II, who established German-language schools for Jews.[72] By 1860 German had almost completely supplanted *Mauscheldeutsch* as the principal language spoken in Bohemia's larger Jewish communities, even though nearly all were in predominantly Czech areas.[73] In Prague and the other cities with large Czech populations, Jewish

[69] See the statistics in *Statistisches Handbüchlein der kgl. Hauptstadt Prag für das Jahr 1878* (Prague, 1880), pp. 128-29, and for 1891, *Österreichisches Städtebuch*, V (Vienna, 1893), pp. 24-25. See further analysis by Cohen in *Central European History*, X, pp. 39-40. Fritz Mauthner, *Erinnerungen, I: Prager Jugendjahre* (Munich, 1918), pp. 95-105; Auguste Hauschner, *Die Familie Lowositz* (Berlin, 1908), pp. 112-19; Arnold Höllriegel (pseud. of Richard A. Bermann), "Die Fahrt auf dem Katarakt" (unpubl. autobiography in the Leo Baeck Institute, New York; used by permission), pp. 5-6; and Hans Kohn, *Living in a World Revolution* (New York, 1964), pp. 36-39, describe the decline in piety.

[70] *Österreichische Statistik*, V, no. 1, pp. 20-21, See further discussion by Cohen in *Central European History*, X, pp. 47-48.

[71] See further discussion in Chapter 6. Hartmut Binder, "Franz Kafka and the Weekly Paper *Selbstwehr*," *LBI Year Book*, XII (1967), pp. 135-48; Stuart Borman, "The Prague Student Zionist Movement, 1896-1914" (Ph.D. dissertation, University of Chicago, 1972); and Oskar K. Rabinowicz, "Czechoslovak Zionism: Analecta to a History," in *The Jews of Czechoslovakia*, II, pp. 1-30, trace the history of Zionism in Prague.

[72] See Ruth Kestenberg-Gladstein, *Neuere Geschichte der Juden in den Böhmischen Ländern*, I (Tübingen, 1969), pp. 357-59, and Guido Kisch, "Linguistic Conditions among Czechoslovak Jewry," in Miroslav Rechcigl, Jr., ed., *Czechoslovakia Past and Present*, 2 vols. (The Hague, 1968), II, pp. 1451-62.

[73] Auguste Hauschner, *Familie Lowositz*, pp. 24-26, and Mauthner, *Erinnerungen*, p. 33, note the efforts by upwardly mobile Jewish families in the 1860s to stamp out the vestiges of *Mauscheldeutsch* in household use. See also Karel Adámek, *Slovo o židech*, rev. ed. (Chrudim, 1900), passim.

residents, particularly those in commerce, also had to know a good amount of Czech. Yet the preeminence of German and German-speakers in government, great commerce, and higher education in Bohemia and Austria as a whole caused most Prague Jews to prefer the German language, German learning, and, where possible, German social connections.[74] The parents of ninety percent of the Jewish pupils in the public primary and secondary schools chose the German institutions over the Czech until after 1900.[75]

Despite the liberal principles of the early Czech nationalists, many elements of Czech politics in the second half of the nineteenth century repelled the Prague Jews and reinforced German allegiances. The alliance of Rieger's Old Czechs with the conservative nobility and Catholic hierarchy obliged moderate Czech nationalists to support reactionary economic legislation and clerical influence over public education. The more radical Czech nationalists who broke away as the "National Liberal" or Young Czech Party in 1874 took a more strongly anti-clerical position, but they tolerated and occasionally joined in lower-middle-class demagoguery which identified the Jews with all the alien forces who oppressed the Czechs in their own land.[76] Here, as elsewhere, elements of a Czech movement which saw itself as basically progressive exploited lower-middle-class antagonism to modernizing forces by translating it into national hatred. Like anti-Semitism in Lower Austria and the German states, the Czech variety found support among shopkeepers, small masters, skilled workers, and peasants for whom Jews epitomized the threatening forces of industrialization and social liberalization. Nonetheless, the willingness of many Jews to ally with German middle-class interests and all the liberal, centralizing forces in Austria in opposition to the Czech national cause provided the principal articulated grounds for Czech animus against Jews. This

---

[74] In the 1830s and 1840s a number of Jewish intellectuals flirted with Bohemianism. See Stölzl in *Bohemia: Jahrbuch*, XIV, pp. 190-210, and Kestenberg-Gladstein in *The Jews of Czechoslovakia*, I, pp. 22-23.

[75] See Cohen in *Central European History*, X, p. 38.

[76] On Czech politics in the late nineteenth century, see Říha, ed., *Přehled*, II, pp. 214-31; R. W. Seton-Watson, *Czechs and Slovaks*, pp. 200-43; and Garver, *The Young Czech Party*, passim. On Czech anti-Semitism see the brief comments of Peter G. J. Pulzer, *The Rise of Political Anti-Semitism in Germany and Austria* (New York, 1964), pp. 138-43, 215, and Riff, "The Assimilation of the Jews of Bohemia," pp. 154-80. Garver, pp. 569-73, minimizes the anti-Semitic strain in the Young Czech movement while Stanley B. Winters, "The Young Czech Party (1874-1914): An Appraisal," *Slavic Review*, XXVIII (1969), p. 434, notes the tolerance of the party leadership for anti-Semitic manifestations.

distinguished Czech anti-Semitism from the racial ideology of the German *völkisch* movement. The resentment of Czech shopkeepers, white-collar employees, artisans, and skilled workers against German and Jewish entrepreneurs erupted in mass violence in Prague and other Bohemian towns in 1843, 1848, 1859, 1861, 1866, and at intervals thereafter until World War I.[77]

In contrast, German liberal public life throughout Austria welcomed Jewish participation. Through the late 1880s the German Liberal Party rejected anti-Semitism, supported anti-clerical legislation, and recruited Jewish votes.[78] In the Bohemian Lands, Jews responded with overwhelming support for the Liberal Party, and in Prague the chief rabbi and lay leaders of the religious community regularly endorsed German liberal candidates until the early 1880s. In the late seventies Czech nationalists managed to win nearly all of the Prague seats in the urban curia of the Bohemian Diet; the exceptions were in the old Jewish quarter of Josefov, which continued to elect Jewish German liberals until 1883. By then the German liberals' loss of power in the Austrian government, the lowering of suffrage requirements, and the desire of poorer Jews to curry favor with the ascendant Czechs gave the seats for Josefov to pro-Czech candidates.[79]

From the inception, the German associational network in Prague accepted Jewish participants. Jewish notables such as the industrialists Maximilian Dormizer and the Portheim family, the physician Dr. Ludwig Tedesco, the lawyer Dr. Moriz Raudnitz, and the journalist David Kuh helped to found the first German organizations in 1848 and at the end of the 1850s. Jewish membership in the German voluntary associations grew steadily in the following two decades. Jews comprised some thirty of the Constitutional Society's 107 members in 1869.[80] In this era Jewish participation in the major

---

[77] See František Roubík, "Drei Beiträge zur Entwicklung der Judenemanzipation in Böhmen," *Jahrbuch der Gesellschaft für Geschichte der Juden in der Čechoslovakischen Republik*, V (1933), pp. 373-84; Riff, "Assimilation of the Jews of Bohemia," pp. 103-10, 156, 173-74; Stölzl, *Kafkas böses Böhmen* (Munich, 1975), pp. 37-40; and idem, in *Bohemia: Jahrbuch*, XV, pp. 129-57. On the violence of the late 1890s see Chapter 6.

[78] See Franz, *Liberalismus*, pp. 186-214, 405-34.

[79] *Bohemia*, 29 June 1883 (morning edition; hereafter, M), commented on the whole 1883 election campaign; and *Bohemia*, 1 July 1883 (M), published the results. See the comments in Klier, *Deutschtum Prags*, pp. 63-65, and Stölzl, *Kafkas böses Böhem*, pp. 48-49.

[80] The Jewish members were identified positively by comparing the membership list from SÚA Praha PP 1900-07 V/15/10: kt. 1966, 5832/pp 3542, to the register

Czech associations apparently remained small, but in 1879 Jews accounted for nearly forty percent of the German Casino's members and for similar portions of the other larger German groups.[81] While the middle-class and lower-middle-class Jews who joined in German public life still acknowledged that they were Jews, they also identified fully with Prague's German community:[82]

> We would have thought crazy anyone who would have said to us that we were not Germans. . . . In my family there were lawyers, physicians, and businessmen. All considered themselves good Germans, good Austrians, and in politics they supported the middle-class liberal party.

Jewish peddlers and the poorest shopkeepers, however, found access to German collective life no easier than did their Gentile counterparts.

The Czech-German division in Prague's public life was so striking by the 1880s that outside observers like the German liberal parliamentary leader Ernst von Plener were convinced that the two ethnic groups were moving toward complete isolation from one another:[83]

> Prague was once a city in which Germans and Czechs lived together in a certain mix, in sociable interaction, and with frequent joint dealings. Today—and it is always only the first symp-

---

of all Jewish heads of household in the city of Prague for 1870, who were obliged by law to contribute to the upkeep of the Jewish religious institutions. One could escape the taxes only by changing religion officially. In a few cases I have identified as Jews those who, although not in the register, seemed to be closely related to those who were. Still, the count is probably a conservative one because of the omission of those who resided in the suburbs and could not be identified as Christians or Jews on the basis of names alone. The register derives from Archiv židovského muzea, Praha, fond Židovské náboženské obce Prahy (Archive of the State Jewish Museum, Prague, fond of the Prague Jewish Religious Community; hereafter, AŽM-ŽNOP): Kniha poplatníků kultovní daně, 120718 (1870).

[81] AHMP fond spolků, Deutsches Haus: "Mitglieder-Verzeichnis des Vereines des Deutschen Casino, 1879-80," and AŽM-ŽNOP: Knihy poplatníků kultovní daně, 120718 (1870), 120730 (1891). See Chapter 4 for a more detailed socio-economic analysis of Jewish participation in the German associations from the late 1870s to 1897.

[82] Höllriegel, "Fahrt auf dem Katarakt," pp. 4-5. Cf. Max Brod, *Der Prager Kreis* (Stuttgart and Berlin, 1966), p. 40, and Mauthner, *Erinnerungen*, p. 126. For further discussion of the Jews' dual identification, see Cohen in *Central European History*, X, pp. 39-40, 45-54.

[83] Ernst von Plener, *Reden 1873-1911* (Stuttgart and Leipzig, 1911), p. 310, from a speech in the Austrian Reichsrat, 21 October 1885.

tom when such things begin among the educated—there is a complete separation and hostile division between the two nationalities. It will soon come about that the German colony in Prague will live as in a foreign country . . . and break off all intercourse with the Czechs.

By the late seventies Czechs and Germans in the Bohemian capital conducted in separate, ethnically exclusive bodies nearly all the social, cultural, and political activities which nineteenth-century liberals considered matters of legitimate collective or public concern. Catholic and Jewish worship and, to a lesser degree, education were the only significant areas of collective life where Czech-German interaction continued.

The division of public life into separate Czech and German spheres after 1861 established a clear social boundary between the two groups where there had been little separation before and where individual identities had often been ambiguous. Even if many were slow to take sides at first, the agitation of others and the division of public affairs on Czech-German lines ultimately forced the great majority of Prague's middle-class, lower-middle-class, and laboring elements to choose one allegiance or the other and articulate ethnic identities. Of course, not all those who defined ethnic loyalties in Prague in the sixties and seventies had the same choice between Czech and German allegiances. Insofar as middle-class liberals dominated German group life and the German associations upheld their values and interests, the great majority of the city's Catholic master artisans, small shopkeepers, clerks, and workers adhered to the Czech side with hardly a second thought.

The division of Czechs and Germans in public life did not necessarily mean that they separated at the same time and to the same degree in those affairs that were matters of individual or private concern. The private sphere of domestic life, personal consumption habits, and earning a living must be examined on its own. This is vital to the history of the Prague Germans and their relations with the Czechs, for if social boundaries developed between them in private as well as public affairs, there might be individuals in the Bohemian capital who identified as Germans and were perceived as such without participating in German public life. By the 1880s the Czech-German distinction was so deeply ingrained in the popular consciousness throughout the Bohemian Lands that individuals could acquire a German identity simply through being brought up in a German family or in a German district. Some of these, too, might number among the Germans of Prague.

The questions of how many Germans there actually were in the Bohemian capital, who they were, and how many of them the organized German community reached acquired crucial significance after 1879. The German liberals lost political dominance in Austria as a whole, and nearly everywhere they faced rising opposition, even within the German population. In Prague Czech political and numerical strength grew sharply, and the Czech middle class increasingly challenged the economic preeminence of the German burghers. The sheer numbers of Germans in Prague drew increasing concern among German leaders as well as among Czech nationalists. If there were German residents not involved in the liberal associations, their numbers might be used to strengthen an otherwise declining German community, or alternatively they might join in attacking it.

CHAPTER THREE

The Demographic Realities

The crucial importance of numbers has become a commonplace in the ethnic conflicts of the twentieth century, but statistics on ethnicity first attracted public attention in the Habsburg Monarchy in the 1880s and 1890s. Successive installments of suffrage reform in Cisleithania in 1883 and 1897 and the steady increase of state intervention in society and economy made officials ever more sensitive to the numerical strength of competing social interests. As the nationality conflicts intensified after 1880, the census statistics on ethnicity for the various mixed localities in Austria became the subject of intense public interest.

The census data on ethnicity were important for a minority group like the Prague Germans in several ways. The census returns provided minorities with statistical ammunition for demanding representation and educational or judicial services from the state, and they also indicated how well groups were actually surviving in environments which they might find increasingly inhospitable. The censuses from 1880 to 1910 brought the Prague Germans the unwelcome news that while the Czech population in the city and inner suburbs was growing from 213,000 to 405,000, the number of Germans—Catholics, Jews, and Protestants—declined relatively and absolutely from nearly 39,000 to 33,000 (see Table 3/1). Czech nationalists crowed that the Germans were melting away into the "Slavic sea" of Prague, and in the 1880s the Czech municipal officials proudly erected, outside the city hall in the Old Town, a graphic display of the relative sizes of the Czech and German populations.[1]

---

[1] Quoted in *Národní listy*, 19 June 1883 (evening), in a letter from a group of Young Czech deputies in the Bohemian Diet which compared the Prague Germans to a block of ice melting away in a lake. The first reference I have to the ethnic "thermometer" at the city hall is in the 1889 speech of Otto Forchheimer, *Die öffentliche Lage der Deutschen in der Landeshauptstadt Prag* (Prague, 1889), p. 4.

The census returns showed the difficulties the organized German community had in maintaining a German presence in Prague, as well as the extent to which German group life failed to embrace portions of the local German population. One could see in the censuses that the patterns of population growth in the Bohemian capital resembled those of many other cities in the German-Slavic frontier areas. Like České Budějovice, Plzeň, Olomouc, and Ljubljana, Prague acquired a large Slavic majority as it grew, and the once dominant German element declined to a small and relatively weak minority. German leaders in each of these cities studied the census returns carefully to determine the extent of the decline and the identity of the remaining Germans. For all of these cities, the censuses provided the best evidence of who actually identified as Germans after ethnic differences became clear; of their origins, occupations, and settlement patterns; and of the causes for their decline.

By themselves, however, mere numbers cannot assure the survival of an ethnic group. For Germans to persist as members of a distinct ethnic group in Austria's mixed cities, they had to share a conscious group identity and some relationships which distinguished or separated them from their non-German neighbors. As we have seen for Prague, linguistic or broader cultural heritages did not irrevocably attach individuals to one group or another; many grew up speaking several languages or easily learned new ones. In the rural portions of the Bohemian Lands, Czech and German peasants lived largely isolated from each other and had distinct folk traditions, but cultural differences were much narrower and ties to group tradition more fragile in the mixed cities. Czechs and Germans who were of the same religion and roughly the same class and were long settled in the cities lived on close terms with each other and shared much in values and habits.[2] Of course, the Czech-German conflict magnified what cultural differences there were and helped to create new ones, from new national music and verse to fashions in clothing, but this resulted from contemporary political processes through which supporters of the national causes linked cultural differences with all the political, social, and economic distinctions between the two groups.

[2] See the works of Fredrik Barth and Milton Gordon as cited in the Introduction above. There is a great need for historical studies of popular culture in the Bohemian Lands to establish clearly and without nationalist prejudgments the real Czech-German differences. Even a cursory examination of newspapers, popular fiction, and associational life shows how much Germans and Czechs in late nineteenth-century Prague actually shared in general way of life and values.

The growing power of the Czech majority in Prague, particularly after the early 1880s, placed strong pressures on many who might otherwise have identified with the Germans to adopt the language and culture of the Czechs and to identify with them. If a certain amount of bilingualism was common and basic cultural differences narrow, individuals needed in the long run some distinction in occupations or separation in social connections to encourage them to define or retain a German identity, to give them a real sense of belonging to a distinct group in society. Contemporary observations, memoirs, and popular prose fiction, along with the census data, reveal just what social separations there were between Germans and Czechs in everyday life.

The Census and the Problem of Nationality

The Austrian government collected the first reliable statistics on ethnicity for the western half of the Monarchy in the 1880 census. The census of December 1869 was the first to count all residents, regardless of citizenship, and it introduced careful survey techniques, including, most importantly, separate questionnaires for every household.[3] There was no measure of language or nationality in 1869, but the 1880 census asked for the "language of everyday use" (*Umgangssprache, obcovací řeč*) for each resident who was a citizen of the western half of the Monarchy. The census officials steadfastly refused to concern themselves with either "the historical-ethnographic factors of the mother tongue or the political ones of nationality," but the government did need to know how many citizens spoke each of the major languages in all the lands and territories.[4] The constitutional laws of 1867 recognized no special political rights for the nationalities per se but obliged the state to provide educational and judicial services in all the languages generally spoken in each province.[5]

[3] The 1857 census tried to count only the native population and other legal residents. See Wilhelm Hecke, "Die Methode und Technik der öster. Volkszählungen," *Statistische Monatsschrift der öster. Statistischen Central-Kommission*, N. F., XVII (1912), pp. 466-74; and Heinrich Rauchberg, *Die Bevölkerung Österreichs* (Vienna, 1895), pp. 10-12.

[4] See Karl Theodor von Inama-Sternegg, "Die nächste Volkszählung," *Statistische Monatschrift*, N. F., V (1900), p. 455.

[5] See Erwin Melichar, "Die Rechtslage der Nationalitäten in Zisleithanien nach der Dezember-Verfassung 1867 im Lichte der Judikatur des Reichsgerichtes (1869-1918)," in L'udovít Holotík, ed., *Der österreichisch-ungarische Ausgleich 1867* (Bratislava, 1971), pp. 451-74; Gerald Stourzh, "Die Gleichberechtigung der Nationalitäten und die österreichische Dezemberverfassung," in Peter Berger, ed., *Der*

Language by itself does not denote ethnic identity, but, in the context of Austria's ethnic conflicts, politicians, demographers, and the general public quickly accepted the declaration of everyday language as an affirmation of ethnic or national allegiance. The intensity of the Czech-German disputes in the Bohemian Lands and the resulting political interest in the census returns made the question of everyday language a generally valid test of Czech and German group loyalties from its inception.[6] Politicians and journalists in both camps urged the populace to treat the census as a test of national strength. In 1880 Franz Schmeykal exhorted all Bohemian Germans "freely and openly to declare themselves Germans so that the rights and interests of the German race be properly safeguarded in the census." *Národní listy* preached in similar terms to Czechs.[7] Nationalist critics of the census complained that everyday language was an ambiguous concept compared to nationality and that multilingual persons could easily change their statements from one census to the next.[8] Yet individuals could have changed a statement of nationality or mother tongue just as easily if the census had asked for either of those. The census asked for only a single language; thus in mixed localities like Prague it gave those who still had not established a clear ethnic loyalty one more inducement to decide since now they had to report one language to the government. A sampling of the surviving manuscript returns for one Prague parish in 1880 shows that only around five percent of the respondents tried to report both Czech and German, and this number diminished sharply thereafter.[9]

österreichisch-ungarische Ausgleich von 1867: Vorgeschichte und Wirkungen (Vienna, 1967), pp. 186-218; and Josef Redlich, *Das österreichische Staats- und Reichsproblem*, II (Leipzig, 1921), pp. 591-671.

[6] Jan Havránek, like many other historians, simply identifies everyday language with nationality in "Social Classes, Nationality Ratios, and Demographic Trends in Prague 1880-1900," *Historica*, XIII (1966), p. 191n. See the general comments on the meaning of everyday language in Heinrich Rauchberg, *Der nationale Besitzstand in Böhmen*, 3 vols. (Leipzig, 1905), I, p. 13, and idem, "Die Bedeutung der Deutschen in Österreich," *Jahrbuch der Gehe-Stiftung zu Dresden*, XIV (1908), p. 134.

[7] *Bohemia*, 29 Dec 1880 (M); *Národní listy*, 19 Dec 1880 (M) and 29 Dec 1880 (M).

[8] See Rauchberg, *Nationale Besitzstand*, I, pp. 151-56, 304-05; Jan Srb, ed., *Sčítání lidu v král. hl. městě Praze a obcech sousedních provedené 31. prosince 1900*, 3 vols. (Prague, 1902-08), III, pp. 270-80; and the January 1909 interpellation in the Chamber of Deputies of the Reichsrat by Vladimír Srb, Karel Kramář, Karel Baxa, and Václav Klofáč, *Anhang zu den stenographischen Protokollen des Hauses der Abgeordneten*, XVIII. Session, 125. Sitzung (20 Jan 1909), pp. 13931-14001. See the Central Statistical Commission's defense of everyday language in Dr. Robert Meyer, "Die nächste Volkszählung," *Statistische Monatsschrift*, N. F., XV (1910), pp. 662-64.

[9] AHMP manuscript census returns (hereafter, MCR): sampled returns for parish

Even where individuals reported only a single everyday language, however, doubts might remain about ethnic identity. In Prague the old "Bohemian" ambivalence died out in the last decades of the nineteenth century, but some equivocation persisted even into the 1890s, particularly among some of the Jews. In the 1880 and 1890 censuses, for instance, the wealthy Jewish hardware merchant Bo-humil Bondy, a stalwart of the Old Czech Party in Prague, reported Czech as everyday language for himself, his children, and servants. His Vienna-born wife, on the other hand, declared the German language.[10] His response signified his social and political identification with the Czechs even if he may have spoken a considerable amount of German each day. In all likelihood, Mrs. Bondy's statement indicated simply that she did not speak Czech, not that she wanted to affirm a German identity at a time when her husband sat in the Old Czechs' highest councils. Fortunately for historical and sociological analysis, cases in which the declaration of everyday language clearly did not mean an ethnic or national allegiance were rare after 1880. In most of the few cases in which spouses or other near relatives living in the same household differed in everyday language, they were simply indicating diverging ethnic loyalties, not that they had to communicate with each other through trans-lators or through sign language.[11]

Overall, the census statistics on everyday language accurately measured the German minority in Prague after 1880. Czech politicians claimed that in Brno and the predominantly German in-dustrial regions of northern Bohemia, German employers and local authorities often pressured immigrant Czech workers into report-ing German as their language.[12] In Prague, however, both the Czech and German populations were too politicized and their leaders too vigilant for any significant coercion or tampering with the returns to pass unnoted. Both sides complained occasionally that workers and servants in the Bohemian capital were pressured one way or the other, but neither the newspapers, local political organizations,

of St. Henry, 1880. See Appendix I for a description of the sampling procedures. The 1880 returns also include some instances of families which were otherwise German-speaking reporting Czech language for their small children, presumably because of the Czech language of nearly all their maids and nurses.

[10] AHMP MCR 853-II 1880 and 1890.

[11] See the droll description by Vladimír Vondráček, *Lékař vzpomíná 1895-1920* (Prague, 1973), pp. 32-33, of the varied movements from one national camp to the other of members of one family at the turn of the century depending on marital alliances and employment.

[12] See n. 8 above.

nor their special committees for the census ever produced convincing evidence or pressed any serious complaints with the higher authorities.[13] The manuscript returns for Prague include numerous cases of servants or other employees who lived with their masters but reported a different language. Whatever the reality of their linguistic usage and the influence of their employers, these individuals followed their own ethnic loyalties in responding to the census.

The Dimensions of Decline

The continuing development of heavy industry along with the expansion of bureaucracy and the service sector caused the total population of Prague and the inner suburbs to double from 204,488 in 1869 to 442,017 in 1910 (see Table 3/1). As in other nineteenth-century cities, in-migration accounted for the greatest portion of Prague's growth: 60 percent of the residents of Prague and the inner suburbs in 1900 had been born elsewhere.[14] The great bulk of that migration, however, was Czech, and while the Czech population grew in the Bohemian capital, the Germans declined. In 1880, 15.3 percent of all the citizen residents indicated German as their everyday language, but only 7.0 percent did so in 1910.

Natural increase contributed little to Prague's expansion in the late nineteenth century compared to immigration. The birthrate in the city and inner suburbs began to exceed the overall mortality rate only in the early 1870s.[15] For the whole decade 1881-1890, the city had a net natural increase of only 3.1 percent.[16] After 1890 the rate of natural growth in the municipality actually decreased be-

[13] The manuscript returns included in the samples for this study showed alterations in the responses for everyday language by the census officials only when individuals reported both Czech and German or when servants who by birthplace and name were obviously Czech were reported with German language by German heads of household.

[14] Srb, ed., *Sčítání lidu v Praze 1900*, III, p. 476. The "city" here will follow Srb's usage unless otherwise indicated and refer to the eight districts included in the municipality in 1901: Old Town, New Town, Malá strana, Hradčany, Josefov, Vyšehrad, Holešovice, and Libeň. The "inner city" includes only the historic first five districts. The "inner suburbs" refers to Smíchov, Karlín, Žižkov, and Vinohrady.

[15] See Jan Havránek, "Demografický vývoj Prahy v druhé polovině 19. století," *Pražský sborník historický 1969-70* (Prague, 1970), pp. 82-86; Ludmila Kárníková, *Vývoj obyvatelstva v českých zemích 1754-1914* (Prague, 1965), pp. 145, 209-10; 219-23; and Rauchberg, *Besitzstand*, I, pp. 209-22.

[16] Rauchberg, *Besitzstand*, II, pp. 68-71. Rauchberg offers no statistics on net natural growth rates for the city and suburbs taken together.

Total Civilian Population and German Citizens of Prague I-VIII and the 4 Inner Suburbs, 1869-1910

		1869	1880	1890	1900	1910
I.	Old Town	46,060	44,027	42,332	37,888	35,504
	German-speakers		9,696[a] 22.4%[b]	7,818 18.7%	3,894 10.4%	3,885 11.1%
II.	New Town	73,277	74,335	75,734	84,462	81,760
			11,903 16.3%	12,058 16.2%	10,412 12.5%	8,650 10.7%
III.	Malá strana	22,140	20,963	20,447	21,161	20,374
			4,222 20.4%	3,512 17.4%	1,790 8.6%	2,204 11.0%
IV.	Hradčany	5,940	5,825	5,805	5,786	5,412
			530 9.2%	476 8.2%	397 6.9%	448 8.4%
V.	Josefov	10,296	10,668	11,535	9,047	3,376
			4,058 38.7%	2,666 23.5%	682 7.7%	678 20.5%
INNER CITY (I-V)		157,713	155,818	155,853	158,344	146,426
			30,409 19.7%	26,530 17.3%	17,175 11.0%	15,865 11.0%
VI.	Vyšehrad	3,460	3,831	4,546	5,328	5,251
			57 1.5%	19 0.4%	36 0.68%	26 0.49%
VII.	Holešovice	3,094	10,852	15,352	30,799	39,704
			446 4.2%	576 3.8%	717 2.4%	1,291 3.3%
VIII.	Libeň	5,845	9,601	12,536	21,242	27,192
			159 1.68%	159 1.27%	330 1.57%	420 1.55%

	1869	1880			1890			1900			1910		
PRAGUE I-VIII	*170,112*	*180,122*	*31,071*	*17.5%*	*188,287*	*27,284*	*14.7%*	*215,713*	*18,258*	*8.6%*	*218,573*	*17,602*	*8.2%*
1. Karlín	13,384	14,779	1,793	12.3%	17,461	2,075	12.1%	19,411	2,001	10.4%	22,457	2,428	10.9%
2. Smíchov	15,382	24,984	3,044	12.4%	32,644	3,214	10.0%	47,109	3,575	7.7%	51,744	3,861	7.5%
3. Vinohrady	5,610	14,831	1,672	11.5%	34,530	4,250	12.5%	52,501	4,769	9.2%	77,073	3,861	9.0%
4. Žižkov	[c]	21,212	1,011	4.8%	41,236	923	2.3%	59,296	802	1.36%	72,170	1,555	2.2%
PRAGUE I-VIII and 4 SUBURBS	*204,488*	*255,928*	*38,591*	*15.3%*	*314,158*	*37,746*	*12.2%*	*394,030*	*29,405*	*7.6%*	*442,017*	*32,332*	*7.0%*
(Active military German-speakers)		9,044	3,265	35.9%	8,861	3,215	37.4%	9,323	3,764	40.4%	6,038	2,024	37.4%)

[a] German-speakers include only citizens of the Austrian half of the Monarchy.
[b] German-speaking citizens as % of all citizen residents.
[c] Žižkov was included with Vinohrady in 1869.

Sources: Jan Srb, ed., *Sčítání lidu v Praze 1900*, I, pp. 110-16, 126; *Statistická knížka král. hl. města Prahy za rok 1890* (Prague, 1892), p. 60; and *Statistická zpráva král. hl. města Prahy za rok 1910* (Prague, 1912), pp. 54, 60-61.

cause of falling fertility. The generally younger and poorer population of the heavily industrial inner suburbs had a higher birthrate than the residents of the city proper, but here also in-migration, from both inside and outside the metropolitan area, comprised almost nine-tenths of the growth after 1880.[17] More than nine-tenths of the migrants to the Prague area from outside came from within the Bohemian Lands, and the great majority of these from Czech areas.

New jobs created by economic growth attracted the migrants, and the specific character of Prague's economic development determined their numbers and composition. After the vigorous expansion of the 1860s and early 1870s, industrial development slowed in the more advanced areas of Cisleithania between 1873 and the late nineties.[18] Development accelerated again in the boom years of the last decade before World War I. While industry in Prague diversified somewhat after 1873, machine manufacture remained the largest single branch. Mechanized textile and clothing production became relatively unimportant in the Bohemian capital. In 1902 these two branches and food processing each employed a work force around one-quarter the size of machine building. On the other hand, the more dispersed and traditional non-mechanized production remained strong: in 1902 non-mechanized clothing and jewelry manufacture employed 19,000 in Prague and construction 17,000, compared to the 13,000 in machine building.[19] In the meantime, the commercial and transportation functions that Prague performed as the focus for central Bohemian trade and as entrepôt for traffic between Austria's Alpine lands and the Elbe Valley expanded more rapidly than manufacture in the city. The numbers in commerce and transportation grew from 19.4 percent of all those gainfully employed in Prague and the suburbs in 1869 to 24 percent in 1900, while wage workers in all areas of manu-

[17] Havránek, in *Pražský sborník historický 1969-70*, p. 84, reports a net natural increase of 0.2% for the municipality in the year 1890, 0.7% for the four inner suburbs in the same year. Over the whole decade of the 1880s, the total population of the suburbs increased by 66.3%.

[18] Both David F. Good, "Stagnation and Take-off in Austria, 1873-1913," *Economic History Review*, XXVII (1974), pp. 72-87, and Richard Rudolph, *Banking and industrialization in Austria-Hungary* (Cambridge, 1976), pp. 11-13, minimize the interruptions in Austria's capital formation and industrial development caused by the "Great Depression." See also Herbert Matis, *Österreichs Wirtschaft 1848-1913*, (Berlin, 1972), pp. 260-341.

[19] Pavla Horská-Vrbová, "Pražský průmysl v druhé polovině 19. století," *Pražský sborník historický 1969-70*, pp. 66-67.

facture declined from 43.8 percent to 38.9 percent of all employed. The state bureaucracy and free professions kept pace with the general growth of the employed population, accounting for a steady 25-26 percent.[20] Compared to Vienna or Budapest, for example, Prague generally offered fewer opportunities to migrants who lacked manufacturing skills or experience in commerce and office work.

Prague experienced significant industrial growth after 1873, but it lacked the scope and scale of manufacture in metropolitan Vienna and Budapest. As a result, the Bohemian capital had declining rates of population growth after the 1870s, and it drew migrants from a more limited territory than the other great cities of the Monarchy. The total civilian population of Prague and the inner suburbs increased by 53 percent between 1869 and 1890, close to the 59 percent increase for Vienna and its suburbs; but in the next twenty years Vienna grew by another 51 percent to 2,031,498 while Prague and its suburbs increased by only 34 percent.[21] Budapest grew by 80 percent between 1869 and 1890 and then by another 74 percent in the next two decades, reaching 880,371 in 1910.[22] Vienna drew immigrants from throughout the Habsburg Monarchy; Budapest from all of Hungary, Galicia, the Bukovina, and Rumania as well. In contrast, only 8 percent of the non-native residents of Prague and the suburbs in 1900 had come from outside Bohemia itself. Only 3,411, 0.9 percent of all the civilian residents of Prague and the inner suburbs were native to Galicia, the Bukovina, and Hungary, and 4,556 (1.15 percent of the total), native to the Austrian Alpine provinces.[23]

Within Bohemia, Prague drew the overwhelming majority of its immigrants from predominantly Czech regions. In 1900 fully 93 percent of those who had immigrated from other parts of Bohemia or 85 percent of all the non-native residents of the city and the inner suburbs had come from regions of Bohemia with Czech majorities.[24] In Bohemia as a whole, Germans comprised a nearly constant 37 percent of the population after 1880, but the German

[20] Havránek, in *Pražský sborník historický 1969-70*, pp. 74, 79.

[21] Statistics for Vienna quoted in Arthur J. May, *The Hapsburg Monarchy 1867-1914* (Cambridge, Mass., 1951), p. 306.

[22] *Statisztikai és Közigazgatáse Évkönyve* (Budapest, 1914), XI: 1909-1912, p. 32.

[23] Srb, ed., *Sčítání lidu v Praze 1900*, III, p. 476. No comparable detailed analyses of the Prague population by place of birth are available for the other censuses 1880-1910.

[24] *Ibid.*

districts sent disproportionately few migrants to Prague until after 1918. In a special study of Prague I-VII in 1900, the Austrian Central Statistical Commission found that only 9,313 residents, 8 percent of all residents native to other parts of Bohemia, had come from districts with German majorities, compared to 105,922 from Czech districts (see Table 3/2).[25]

TABLE 3/2
Birthplaces of the Non-Native Bohemian
Residents of Prague I-VII, 1900

Native to administrative districts in Bohemia with	
87-100% German everyday language	6,524
51-87% German " "	2,789
51-100% German " "	9,313
87-100% Czech everyday language	97,146
51-87% Czech " "	8,776
51-100% Czech " "	105,922

The individuals' ethnicity before migration is unknown, but once in Prague only 5,100 of the 106,000 from predominantly Czech districts declared German as their everyday language.[26] Many of the latter were Jews who migrated from Czech towns to Prague, where they aligned themselves with the German minority.[27] On the other hand, nearly half of the 6,524 persons from districts which were 87-100 percent German affirmed Czech rather than German allegiance once in the Bohemian capital.[28] The limited migration to Prague from German Bohemia and other German areas of Austria and the tendency of some Germans in Prague to cross over to the Czechs caused the local German population to fall even farther behind the Czech majority.

Contemporaries adduced a number of reasons as to why so few

[25] Franz von Meinzingen, "Die binnenländische Wanderung und ihre Rückwirkung auf die Umgangssprache nach der letzten Volkszählung," *Statistische Monatsschrift*, N. F., VII (1902), p. 724.

[26] *Ibid.*

[27] Fritz Mauthner and the parents of Franz Kafka and Hans Kohn, for instance, were all born in small Czech towns. See Kestenberg-Gladstein in *The Jews of Czechoslovakia*, I, pp. 27-37, on the patterns of settlement and migration of the Bohemian Jews in the nineteenth century.

[28] Meinzingen, in *Statistische Monatsschrift*, N. F., VII, p. 724. Altogether only 4,649 of the 9,313 from districts with German majorities reported German as their everyday language once in Prague.

Germans migrated to Prague in the late nineteenth century. The demographer Heinrich Rauchberg, a long-time professor at the German University of Prague, argued that industrial development made the German areas of northern Bohemia regions of in-migration rather than the reverse; simple proximity caused Germans leaving Bohemia's southern fringes to choose Vienna over Prague.[29] Northern Bohemia did have a large net migration gain before 1900, but the aggregate figures obscure a significant movement from the German districts to other parts of Austria. Other observers came closer to the mark when they argued that the strength of the Czechs in Prague caused migrants from German Bohemia to prefer other destinations to the Bohemian capital.

The movement of Bohemian Germans to Vienna illustrates the situation well. In contrast to the Czech areas of central and eastern Bohemia, many more migrated from German villages and towns in northern Bohemia to the imperial capital than to Prague, despite much greater distance. In 1910 Vienna had 2,066 residents native to the administrative district of Cheb (Eger), a solidly German area in northwestern Bohemia, compared to only 640 natives of Cheb in Prague I-VIII and the six suburbs. 682 persons born in Jablonec (Gablonz), another German district in northern Bohemia, lived in the imperial capital, in contrast to 340 in Prague. Migrants from the Czech regions of central and eastern Bohemia, on the other hand, showed only a marginal preference for Vienna. The solidly Czech district of Pardublice, about as far from Prague to the east as Jablonec is to the north, counted 4,841 of its natives in Vienna in 1910 but only slightly fewer, 4,531, in Prague and the suburbs.[30]

Of course, a variety of social, economic, political, and psychological factors shape migration, but considerations of ethnicity best explain the tendency of German Bohemian districts to send disproportionately large numbers to Vienna rather than to Prague.[31] One would expect the larger size of the imperial capital—more than four times the population of Prague and its suburbs after

[29] Rauchberg, *Besitzstand*, I, pp. 304-06. Meinzingen, in *Statistische Monatsschrift*, N. F., VII, pp. 706-07, also makes this argument.

[30] From census data in *Österreichische Statistik*, N. F., I, 2. Heft, pp. 28-31. See the complete tables for the generality of this phenomenon in Bohemia.

[31] For general discussions of migration in Europe and America in the late nineteenth century, see the pioneering work of Adna F. Weber, *The Growth of Cities in the Nineteenth Century*, repr. (Ithaca, 1965), pp. 230-84; Dorothy S. Thomas, *Research Memorandum on Migration Differentials* (New York, 1938); and Dorothy Thomas and Simon Kuznets, ed., *Population Redistribution and Economic Growth*, 3 vols. (Philadelphia, 1957-64).

1880—and the greater economic opportunities there to have had a stronger attraction than Prague for migrants from nearly all parts of Bohemia, not just the German portions. Irrespective of ethnicity, one might expect a different pattern of migration from a predominantly agricultural region like that around Pardubice than from a strongly craft and industrially oriented area such as Jablonec. The economy of the Cheb district resembled more the area around Pardubice.[32] Nonetheless, German Cheb sent 3.2 times as many migrants to Vienna as to Prague. The ratio was close to even for migration out of Czech Pardubice, although Cheb is more than 400 km. from Vienna, twice the distance between Pardubice and Vienna.

The minority status of the Germans in Prague and the overwhelming predominance of the Czechs in the lower strata of the city's population in the latter part of the century apparently discouraged Bohemian Germans from migrating to the provincial capital. The leaders of the German Casino indicated their awareness of the problem in the 1880s and 1890s by making special appeals to German Bohemia to send migrants to Prague and by sponsoring groups to assist German workers and white-collar employees.[33] Few Germans from solidly German districts like that around Cheb knew any Czech, but unless migrants could join Prague's middle-class German community, the Bohemian capital provided them an almost exclusively Czech environment. Because of the German minority's origins in Prague's old German-speaking middle and upper strata, from the outset Prague offered little collective life oriented to workers. Moreover, there were too few lower-strata Germans in the Bohemian capital at any time to create for themselves any analogue to the rich community life that immigrant Czech workers, for instance, established in Vienna in this era.[34]

In a speech to the German Casino's political arm in March 1883, one of its leaders, Professor Philipp Knoll, lamented the decline of the Prague Germans. Among the causes he singled out the small

[32] The areas around Pardubice and Cheb had population densities of 100-125 per km^2; the density around Jablonec was over 300 per km^2. The article on Bohemia, "Čechy," in the *Ottův slovník naučný*, 28 vols. (Prague, 1888-1909), VI, pp. 1-208, provides a convenient geographical survey for the late nineteenth century.

[33] See Chapters 4 and 5.

[34] On the Viennese Czechs, see the works of Monika Glettler, *Sokol und Arbeiterturnvereine der Wiener Tschechen bis 1914* (Munich and Vienna, 1970), and *Die Wiener Tschechen um 1900* (Munich and Vienna, 1972).

migration from the German districts of Bohemia and the insufficient number of lower-strata Germans in the city. Only extraordinary measures could change the situation for working-class Germans in Prague:[35]

> How is the German worker or craftsman supposed to feel comfortable here, when totally isolated, without any solid footing, and lacking any source of refreshment and support from friendly meetings with others of his race, he wanders lost among men who do not even understand his language, when even in his leisure hours he must do without the feelings of being at home which intercourse with those of shared beliefs and origins imparts?

Although natural increase contributed little to the growth of Prague in the late nineteenth century compared to immigration, here too the German population was at a disadvantage. The relatively high concentration of the German population in the middle and upper economic strata throughout this era resulted in the Germans' having a lower rate of reproduction than the Czechs. Like middle-class elements elsewhere in Europe, many Germans in Prague limited the size of their families to assure comfortable standards of living for themselves and what children they had.[36] In 1900 the German families in the city with children had an average 2.23 children living with them, the socially more diverse Czechs, 2.43.[37] The net rate of reproduction cannot be calculated directly from census data, but the Czech historian Jan Havránek has approximated the rates in 1900 for Czechs and Germans in the city and inner suburbs. For each married woman in the twenty-to-forty-five-year age bracket among the Germans, there were only 0.53 German girls of ten years or less, one-third lower than the figure of 0.75 for the Czechs.[38] No data are available to compare the mortality rates of the Czechs and Germans, but the Germans' greater average prosperity probably gave them a slightly lower

[35] Philipp Knoll, *Beiträge zur heimischen Zeitgeschichte* p. 191.

[36] Cf. the classic work on late nineteenth-century English middle-class behavior by J. A. Banks, *Prosperity and Parenthood* (London, 1954).

[37] Havránek, in *Pražský sborník historický 1969-70*, pp. 100-01.

[38] *Ibid.*, pp. 101-02. The ability of a population to reproduce itself is best described by the female net reproduction rate (NRR), the number of daughters that will be born to a group of female infants divided by the number in the original group of prospective mothers, whether they all survive to the end of the child-bearing period or not. Calculation of the NRR requires a complete record of the actual births.

mortality rate, which would partially counterbalance their lower fertility.

Attrition by Assimilation

The decline of Prague's German population between 1880 and 1910 resulted from the combined effects of immigration, natural increase, assimilation, and migration out of the city. Emigration was apparently an insignificant part of the equation, compared to immigration and assimilation. In the absence of published statistics, only intensive study of geographical mobility for a large sample population could determine the real extent of emigration. The general omission of emigration from the many contemporary discussions of the Germans' decline, however, suggests that migration out of the city did not lie at the root of the problem.

German and Czech observers alike agreed that adoption of Czech loyalties in place of German was the principal cause for the absolute decrease of the German population (see Table 3/1).[39] The low rate of German in-migration made it impossible for the Germans to keep pace relatively with the increase of the Czechs, but German-Czech assimilation, in fact, caused the German minority to decline in absolute terms by 15 percent between 1880 and 1910. The realities of life in Prague to which Philipp Knoll pointed encouraged Germans native to the city, as well as many of the few Germans who did immigrate, to adopt Czech identities.

The processes of German-Czech assimilation worked selectively and affected German lower middle-class and laboring elements more than the well-to-do. The leaders of the German Casino realized as early as 1883 that lower-strata Germans faced the greatest pressures to conform to their Czech surroundings and were least attached to the social and political life of the German community.[40] To chart the dimensions of the assimilative process one can use the aggregate statistics comparing everyday language with religious affiliation which were published for the 1890 and 1900 censuses. German-Czech assimilation was not peculiar to any one religious group, but for the Jews and Lutherans who changed their allegiances from German to Czech, their religion continued to distin-

[39] See Rauchberg, *Besitzstand*, I, pp. 151-60, and Srb, ed., *Sčítání lidu v Praze 1900*, III, pp. 262-71, 309-18. The lacunae in the surviving census materials, tax records, and police records make any thorough studies of geographical mobility extremely difficult if not impossible.

[40] See Chapter 4.

guish them from the Catholic majority among the Czech population.

At the end of the century more than 4,000 of the 18,000 Jews in Prague proper switched from German loyalties to Czech in the census. This shift equaled about half of the Germans' net decline in the city and inner suburbs. In 1890 the Jewish population still had strongly German allegiances: 12,588 (74 percent) of the 17,806 civilian Jewish citizens in the municipality (districts I-VII) declared German as their everyday language. In the 1900 census the majority of the Prague Jews adhered to the Czechs: in that year only 8,230 (45 percent) of the Jewish citizen residents of Prague I-VII affirmed German as their language.[41]

The exchange of German loyalties for Czech occurred primarily among the poorer elements of the Jewish population. One cannot easily determine the exact composition of the German Jewish and Czech Jewish groups, but in 1890 and 1900 the Jewish residents of the most affluent neighborhoods in the city, particularly those around Wenceslas Square, showed the strongest German allegiances. Those in the poorest areas, such as Josefov and Holešovice, had the greatest Czech loyalties (see Table 3/3 for a summary).[42]

Here it is best to concentrate on the thirty-five census wards of the inner city, where 97 percent of all Jews in the municipality resided. One can measure the relative prosperity of the citizens in each census ward at the end of the century by using an analysis of the population according to housing cost made by the Prague Statistical Commission in 1900.[43] In both the 1890 and 1900 censuses, the portion of the Jewish citizens in each ward who reported German as their language correlated highly with the share of the ward's population which occupied housing in the most expensive of three categories, over 600 crowns per annum. The correlation between

[41] Jan Srb, "Obcovací řeč jako prostředek sesilující národní državu německou v zemích koruny české zvlášť," pp. 72-75, 78 (Appendix to Srb, ed., *Sčítání lidu v Praze 1900*, III). No published statistics relating religion to everyday language in Prague are available for prior to 1890. The civilian Jewish residents of Prague I-VII comprised 78% of all those in the city, Libeň, and the four inner suburbs in 1890, 71% in 1900. Jews accounted for 6.7% of the civilian population of Prague I-VIII and the inner suburbs in 1900, Catholics 91%, and Protestants 1.9%.

[42] Complete data in Srb, "Obcovací řeč," pp. 72-75, 78.

[43] Srb, ed., *Sčítání lidu v Praze 1900*, III, pp. 27-29. Using the same index of prosperity for the census wards in both 1890 and 1900 is justified since the relative standing of the various neighborhoods in the inner city changed little in the 1890s. Only when new, more expensive apartments began to go up in the cleared portions of Josefov and the Old Town after 1900 did a significant alteration occur.

Table 3/3
Everyday Language of Jewish Citizens, Prague I-VII, 1890-1900

	1890			1900		
	Cz.-speak. Jews	Ger.-speak. Jews	Ger. J. as % all Jews	Cz.-speak. Jews	Ger.-speak. Jews	Ger. J. as % all Jews
I Old Town	1,622	4,902	74.8	3,781	2,146	36.2
Up N. Town	718	1,569	68.5	1,765	2,357	57.1
Lo N. Town	754	3,439	82.0	2,370	2,882	54.8
II New Town	1,472	5,008	77.4	4,135	5,239	55.9
III Malá strana	47	61	56.5	146	41	21.9
IV Hradčany	23	6	20.7	12	4	23.5
V Josefov	1,118	2,549	69.5	1,427	634	30.6
VI Vyšehrad	12	0	0	13	6	31.6
VII Holešovice	164	62	27.4	366	160	30.4
PRAGUE I-VII	4,498	12,588	73.8	9,880	8,230	45.3
		(46% of all Ger. citizens)			(46% of all Ger. citizens)	

the portion of Jewish citizens who reported Czech language and the percentage of all the residents in the lowest housing category, 200 crowns or less per year, was equal or nearly as high (see Table 3/4).[44] The greatest shifts in allegiance between the two censuses occurred in the wards whose residents fell primarily in the intermediate and lowest housing categories (see Plates VI-IX for street scenes from the poorest sections of Josefov and the Old Town). One cannot conclude definitely from these correlations that the richest Jews all remained German or that it was overwhelmingly the Jews in the intermediate and poorest strata who went over to the Czech side in the 1890s.[45] Yet such conclusions are suggested by the strength of the correlations and the fact that a number of the wards with the strongest German affinities among the Jews had extremely few poor residents while the strongest Czech affinities accompanied the virtual absence of the wealthy.

TABLE 3/4
Correlations of Jews' Ethnic Loyalties
with the Prosperity of Wards, Prague I-V, 1890-1900

1890	
Correl. Ger. Jews/Jew. cit. *with* % wealthy residents	0.58
Correl. Czech Jews/Jew. cit. *with* % poor residents	0.58
1900	
Correl. Ger. Jews/Jew. cit. *with* % wealthy residents	0.58
Correl. Czech Jews/Jew. cit. *with* % poor residents	0.52

A number of factors helped to persuade such a large number of Prague's Jews to try to win favor with the Czechs by adopting Czech loyalties in the 1900 census. The decline of the German Liberal Party in the 1890s, the increasing militancy of the Czech nationalist parties, and the trauma of Czech anti-Semitic violence in 1897 diminished the rewards and greatly increased the costs of

[44] Statistics on the everyday language of the Jewish citizens in each ward derive from Srb, "Obcovací řeč," pp. 72-75, 78. The fraction of all the Jewish citizen residents who declared German or Czech as their language was used in the correlations rather than the absolute number of German or Czech Jews in order to gauge the propensity of the Jews to have one ethnic allegiance over the other, not to correlate the prosperity of a ward with the mere presence or absence of German Jews or Czech Jews. The slight drop in the second correlation for 1900 probably reflects the fact that the Czech allegiance was becoming less specific to the poorest Jews.

[45] On the pitfalls of the "ecological fallacy," see David H. Fisher, *Historians' Fallacies* (New York, 1970), pp. 119-20.

VI.   Courtyard of building on Cikánská street, čp. 179,
      Josefov, in 1909

VII.   Group of buildings in Josefov, čp. 220 & 167, north of the Staronová
       synagogue, cleared in 1903

VIII.   Celetná street no. 2 with shops, Old Town
        (ca. 1900) [Leo Baeck Institute]

IX.   Second-hand store on Pinkasová street, čp. 27, Josefov, before clearance in
      1908

the Jews' old German allegiances. Jews who could not converse in Czech learned it.[46] Still, the Jews who thus adopted Czech political allegiances did not abandon all their previous German affinities. As will be discussed later, the great majority of Jews in Prague continued to send their children to German primary and secondary schools through World War I.[47]

German majorities persisted after 1890 among the Jewish citizens in Prague's wealthiest neighborhoods, but this resulted from the Jews' economic interests, cultural and political predilections, and social connections, not from any special "German" character of those districts. The parish of St. Henry, for instance, which abutted Wenceslas Square and Na příkopě in the Lower New Town, consistently had the highest concentration of German residents, and it included many of the Prague's banks, the finest shops and cafes, and some of the most fashionable apartments.[48] Even here, though, the German citizens declined to a small minority at the turn of the century: 50 percent German in 1880, 42.7 percent in 1890, 29.7 percent in 1900, and 21.0 percent in 1910.[49] The adjacent parishes had high numbers of Germans, compared to the rest of Prague, but only half to two-thirds the percentage in St. Henry (see Map II for the 1900 figures). The German Jews in these prosperous neighborhoods chose to adhere to a declining minority group, to whose numbers they made a large contribution. Indeed, in the 1890 and the 1910 censuses Jews accounted for around two-thirds of all those who reported German as their everyday language in the two parishes of the Lower New Town, St. Henry and St. Peter, and the contiguous Old Town parish of St. Gall (Cz., Havel).[50]

The census returns for St. Henry, St. Peter, and St. Gall show that Jewish manufacturers, merchants, bank officials, insurance agents, professionals, and their families were those who tended to retain German loyalties after 1890. These had business connections, professional expertise, and upbringings that either circumscribed

[46] See the vignettes in the popular contemporary novel by Auguste Hauschner, *Die Familie Lowositz* (Berlin, 1908), pp. 72, 329.

[47] See Chapter 5.

[48] See the description of this district by Peter Demetz, *René Rilkes Prager Jahre* (Düsseldorf, 1953), pp. 30-34.

[49] The 1900 statistics derive from Srb, ed., *Sčítání lidu v Praze 1900*, I, pp. 91, 129-30; the 1880, 1890, and 1910 data from samples of the manuscript census returns in the collections of AHMP. See Appendix I for a description of the sampling techniques. The total population of St. Henry varied little over the whole period: 9,580 in 1869; 11,105 in 1890; 10,178 in 1900.

[50] See the raw data for the sampled census returns in Appendix II, Tables 1, 6.

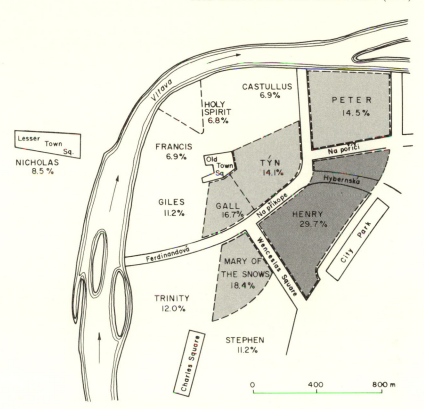

MAP II: Inner City Parishes with the Highest Percent German Citizen
Residents in 1900

their contact with Czechs or gave them personal horizons which
embraced Austria or Central Europe as a whole. As will be seen,
their standing in the middle class also gave them continued access
to the closed social life of the organized German community in
Prague.[51] The Jews in these neighborhoods who began to switch
to the Czech side were primarily small shopkeepers, salesmen, and
other commercial employees. These latter dealt constantly with
Czech colleagues, clients, and competitors; and after the mid-1890s
they faced at least threats of Czech reprisals and boycotts for pro-
German sentiments. As time passed, the willingness to abandon
German loyalties gradually spread to higher socioeconomic levels
among the Prague Jews.

[51] See Chapters 4 and 6, pp. 168-82, 258-63.

The heritage of the ghettoes and fear of Czech anti-Semitism affected Jews in special ways, and sheer numbers made the shift of Jews from German allegiances to Czech most conspicuous. Yet German-Czech assimilation was hardly unique to the Jews.[52] Lutheran and Catholic Germans also adopted Czech loyalties, but these too came from the lower strata of the German population. At the end of the nineteenth century, six out of every seven Lutherans in Bohemia were German. The Protestant minority among the Czechs was mostly Calvinist, and in 1890 Bohemia's Czech Lutheran superintendency, centered in Hradec Králové (Königgrätz), had only 12,430 communicants.[53] Nonetheless, 1,163 Lutheran citizens of Prague I-VIII and the four inner suburbs reported Czech as their everyday language in the 1900 census, compared to only 962 who indicated German.[54] Assimilation with the Czechs of the poorer German Lutherans best explains this anomaly.

The surviving census data permit no precise reckoning of how many of Prague's Czech Lutherans had once been German, but local officials concluded that German Lutherans, particularly the lower-middle-class and laboring elements scattered through the outlying districts, assimilated with the Czechs at a substantial rate.[55] As new industries developed on Prague's outskirts and as the city expanded territorially, the poorer segments of both the native and immigrant populations concentrated in the outlying areas, where they had lower housing costs and proximity to the factories.[56] Except in the prosperous sections of Vinohrady near Wenceslas Square and the city park, petty retailers, commercial and industrial employees, and workers comprised a larger portion of the German residents in the fringe areas than in the inner city. In the affluent inner city parish of St. Henry, for instance, German Lutheran citizens easily surpassed the Czech in 1900, ninety-two to thirty-

[52] Contrast Jan Havránek, "The Development of Czech Nationalism," *Austrian History Yearbook*, III (1967), pt. 2, pp. 225-26, who points to German-Czech assimilation in Prague only among Jewish residents and overlooks the less dramatic movement of German Catholics and Lutherans.

[53] *Ottův slovník naučný*, VI, p. 186.

[54] Srb, ed., *Sčítání lidu v Praze 1900*, I, pp. 88-96, III, p. 827. No comparable statistics are available from other censuses in the era.

[55] *Ibid.*, I, pp. 131-35, III, pp. 314-18.

[56] On the general movement of the poorer elements in Prague to the outlying areas see Kárníková, *Vývoj obyvatelstva*, pp. 222-23; Otto Lehovec, *Prag: Eine Stadtgeographie und Heimatkunde* (Prague, 1944), pp. 73-85; and Srb, ed., *Sčítání lidu v Praze 1900*, I, pp. 131-32, III, pp. 187-98.

two, but Czech Lutherans outnumbered the German in the largely proletarian districts of Žižkov and Libeň.[57]

The grim, crowded suburb of Žižkov had a particularly high rate of German-Czech assimilation among its Lutheran residents. Here Czech Lutherans outnumbered the German ten to one in 1900. Manuscript census returns do not survive for Žižkov and most of the other suburbs, but the aggregate statistics on the birthplaces of the Lutheran residents indicate at least the dimensions of the assimilative processes. In 1900 Žižkov had 294 Lutheran residents out of a total population of 59,296, and 123 of these were native to Prague and its suburbs. The ethnic background of those native to the Bohemian capital cannot be determined. Sixty-four of the non-native Lutheran residents of Žižkov, however, had been born in German areas: the German Empire (45), solidly German portions of Bohemia and Moravia (18), and the Austrian Alpine lands (1).[58] The census statistics on everyday language include only the 228 Lutheran residents who were citizens of Cisleithania, but remarkably only twenty-two of these gave German as their language. One cannot establish the birthplaces and occupations of the Lutherans with German loyalties without the manuscript returns, but by themselves those who were native to German parts of Cisleithania could have accounted for nearly all those in Žižkov who reported German as their language. That would leave in the Czech column all their spouses and children who might be native to Prague, together with all the other Lutheran residents born in the metropolitan area.

Occasionally the census caught the processes of assimilation in mid-course within individual families. Here the questionnaires themselves illustrate some of the social and economic conditions which favored the change. In the Old Town, for instance, Adalbert Wagner, a sixty-four-year-old Catholic porter born near the German Bohemian town of Stříbro (Mies), reported German as his everyday language in 1880.[59] Porters had little access to German public life in Prague, and in private affairs Wagner apparently had more contact with Czechs than with Germans. His wife Theresia, born in 1815 near Pardubice, and their son Bohumil, born in Prague, an official for the state lottery, both reported Czech language. In 1890 one found few Germans among Prague's artisans, but in Malá strana the retired glover Josef Reschka, a Catholic from

---

[57] Srb, ed., *Sčítání lidu v Praze 1900*, III, pp. 821-22.
[58] *Ibid.*, III, p. 476. [59] AHMP MCR 365-I 1880.

Vienna, his Prague-born wife, and their daughter all indicated German as their everyday language.[60] Their thirty-year-old son Wilhelm, on the other hand, was a typesetter who apparently had been absorbed into the Czech working class. He may have spoken German with his parents, but he reported Czech as his everyday language. Across the Vltava in the New Town in 1890, the Jewish bookkeeper Adolf Burg was apparently trying either to establish or to preserve a German identity despite his domestic circumstances. He indicated German as his everyday language although his wife, infant son, cousin, and servants all reported Czech.[61]

The German minority could have made up some of the losses to the Czechs had it been able to assimilate a comparable number from the Czech population, but assimilation of Czechs with the Germans declined to a low level in the late nineteenth century. Movement from Czech identification to German is even more difficult to measure than the reverse process; since Catholics accounted for 94 percent of Prague's Czech citizens in 1900, distinctive religion would not mark most of the Czechs who might assimilate with the Germans.[62] The diminishing numbers of Czech pupils in Prague's German public schools, however, suggest the low rate of Czech assimilation with Germans around 1900. Many Czechs attended the German schools merely to master the German language, but throughout the nineteenth century attending German schools was often the first significant step in the Germanization of Czech youth. In 1890 only 1,545 children whose mother tongue was Czech attended the municipal *Volksschulen* and *Bürgerschulen* which had German-language instruction, compared to 13,235 Czech pupils who attended the public schools with Czech as the principal language of instruction. By 1900 the number of Czech pupils in the German schools had declined to 952, by 1910, a mere 375.[63]

The low rate of German migration to Prague and the adoption of Czech loyalties by many former Germans, Christian and Jewish, caused the German population to decline after 1880 in both relative and absolute terms. German observers as well as Czechs realized at the time that the meager German immigration and the low re-

[60] AHMP MCR 306-III 1890.

[61] AHMP MCR 1116-II 1890.

[62] Srb, ed., *Sčítání lidu v Praze 1900*, III, p. 827.

[63] Statistics on school attendance derive from *Statistická knížka král. hlav. města Prahy za rok 1890*, p. 362; *Statist. knížka Prahy 1900*, pp. 384-87; and *Statist. zpráva Prahy 1910*, pp. 489-91.

tention of lower-strata Germans resulted in part from the special social and economic calculus of the German minority. Origins in Prague's old German-speaking middle and upper strata and the determination to preserve their claims to social superiority gave a peculiar cast to most of the German population and its social life. The patterns of migration and German-Czech assimilation together helped to guarantee the continuing predominance of businessmen, professionals, industrialists, and some white-collar elements in the German minority and minimal German representation among Prague's laboring elements.

The Occupational Profile of the German Minority

The Austrian census officials steadfastly resisted providing statistical ammunition for the nationality conflicts in the late nineteenth century. Consequently, it is as difficult to compare the occupational profiles of the Czech and German populations in Prague as it is to measure the effects of migration and assimilation on the two groups. The Central Statistical Commission first published comparisons of occupation with everyday language for the 1910 census; even then it offered only a summary, using general economic categories, for Prague and the inner suburbs. For earlier data and greater detail on 1910, one must sample the surviving manuscript census returns for various parts of the city.

The sheer volume of the manuscript materials and the lacunae in what survives make selective use necessary. Almost nothing remains for the suburbs from any of the censuses from 1880 to 1910, and the disarray and incomplete preservation of the returns for the city proper in 1880 and 1900 make the 1890 and 1910 censuses the only ones suitable for systematic analysis.[64] Moreover, the concentration of Germans was so low in many areas that unmanageably large samples would be needed to obtain statistically significant numbers of German residents if one drew randomly from throughout the city. Accordingly, occupational data will be presented for samples of the 1890 and 1910 census returns from three inner city parishes with relatively high German concentrations, St. Henry and St. Peter in the Lower New Town and St. Gall in the adjoining

[64] AHMP sčítací operaty. For the suburbs the collection in the Prague City Archive only includes summary sheets for some of the parcels in Smíchov. The holdings of the 1880 returns for the municipality range from nearly complete for some districts to more than half missing. The 1900 returns are out of the numerical sequence of the parcel numbers and appear to be only about two-thirds complete.

portion of the Old Town.[65] The Germans in these parishes were always at the heart of the social and political life of the German minority; in the last analysis they were the survivors among the Prague Germans. A sample of one parish with a low German concentration, St. Nicholas in Malá strana, together with the 1910 statistics for the whole city and the inner suburbs, will provide some counterbalance to the high proportion of Jews among the inner-city Germans and indicate how the Germans who were dispersed through the rest of Prague compared to the relatively affluent ones in the center.

At the end of the century, the most prosperous neighborhoods in the Bohemian capital generally showed the strongest German loyalties among the Jewish residents and the highest concentrations of German citizens, Christian and Jewish. Conversely, the poorest districts tended to have the lowest percentages of German citizens. Table 3/5 gives the figures for the eight richest and eight poorest of the census wards in 1900.[66] The parishes of St. Gall, St. Henry, and St. Peter were representative in most respects of the districts with relatively large numbers of Germans. While St. Henry, which was 30 percent German in 1900, was the most prosperous district of all, St. Peter, which stretched from Hybernská street north to the Vltava, also had a substantial number of German manufacturers, businessmen, and professionals and was 15 percent German in 1900. Nonetheless, the population here was generally less prosperous than in St. Henry and included proportionately twice as many workers. St. Gall, adjacent to St. Henry in the Old Town, had a more affluent population than St. Peter and was 17 percent German in 1900. Here more academics, state bureaucrats, and lawyers resided, due to the proximity of the main building of the Charles-Ferdinand University, the German Technical College, and the city hall. Yet the centuries-old open markets on Havelská and Rytířská streets and continuing craft production in the neighborhood also gathered a considerable number of small grocers, hawkers, and craftsmen here (see Plates X and XI).[67]

[65] See Appendix I for a description of the sampling procedures.

[66] The median rent levels per household for each ward derive from Jan Havránek, "Social Classes, Nationality Ratios, and Demographic Trends in Prague 1880-1900," *Historica*, XIII (1966), p. 189, based on data in Srb, ed., *Sčítání lidu v Praze 1900*, III, pp. 25-26, 39-40. The population totals for the German citizens also derive from Srb, ed., III, pp. 820-29. The Austrian census defined a household as a single living unit including live-in servants, boarders, and lodgers.

[67] See Appendix II, Tables 2-4, for the complete occupational data from the samples.

X. Vegetable market on Rytířská street in the parish of St. Gall, Old Town (ca. 1900)

XI. Egg market on Rytířská street in the parish of St. Gall, Old Town, late 1880s

TABLE 3/5
Median Rent per Household and Percent German Citizens
for 16 Census Wards in 1900

District	Ward	Annual Rent in Crowns	% Ger. Citizens	(Absolute no.)
Lo. New Town	XXIV	790	24.0	(1,021)
Lo. New Town	XXVI	705	29.8	(1,342)
Lo. New Town	XXV	695	30.7	(1,270)
Up. New Town	XXIII	661	21.5	(1,038)
Vinohrady	X	656	27.8	(1,122)
Up. New Town	XXI	646	19.3	(747)
Up. New Town	XIV	575	13.2	(548)
Old Town	V	566	19.8	(782)
Hradčany	XXXIV	140	6.9	(397)
Holešovice	XXXVI	127	1.3	(65)
Holešovice	XXXVII	124	1.8	(84)
Žižkov	XII	122	0.76	(38)
Žižkov	XI	118	0.79	(39)
Žižkov	IX	116	0.17	(8)
Smíchov	VII	110	1.8	(94)
Smíchov	IX	110	1.1	(45)

Jews accounted for a majority of the German citizens in the districts which had the highest German concentrations at the turn of the century. Prague's Jews were even more highly concentrated in the inner city than was the German population as a whole. Since German loyalties persisted so strongly among the Jews in the most affluent inner-city areas, the sampled inner-city parishes had disproportionately large Jewish contingents among their German residents: 66 percent in 1890, compared to their share of 46 percent among all German citizens in Prague I-VII. Jews accounted for 68 percent of the German citizen residents in the sampled parishes in 1910.[68]

While Czechs and Germans lived cheek by jowl in these densely populated areas, the occupational profiles of the two groups differed markedly (See Table 3/6).[69] In the heart of the city, of course, Czechs and Germans were both weakly represented in the manu-

[68] See Appendix II, Tables 1 and 6, for the absolute numbers in the samples. See Table 3/3 for the total numbers of German Jews in each district of the city in 1890; comparable statistics for all of Prague are not available for 1910.

[69] *Confidence Interval*: With 95% certainty, the confidence interval for the whole 1890 sample of 1,655 persons is ± 2.4%, for the 484 Germans, ± 4.46%; for the 1,171 Czechs, ± 2.86%. Thus any category of analysis for Germans that has less than 4.46% has doubtful significance.

Significance Test: Using the test for differences of proportions from direct random

facturing categories, compared to the whole metropolitan area. There was still a sizable body of handcraftsmen and industrial workers here, but Germans were nearly absent from their ranks. Only the presence of independent German manufacturers and qualified industrial employees raised the percentage of Germans in the industrial sector nearly to the level of the Czechs. Significantly, almost three-quarters of the German residents drew their livelihoods from commerce, the free professions, and rents; the Czechs were relatively weaker in all three of these categories. The presence of the German Jews, at least half of whom were in commerce, caused 47 percent of the German citizen residents to be dependent on commerce, compared to only 30 percent of the Czechs. The Czechs had relatively greater strength in domestic industries and state service.

TABLE 3/6

Gall-Henry-Peter, 1890: Distribution of Residents by Economic Sector

	Germans	Czechs
Ind.	9.5%	10.9%
Hand.	2.3	20.1
Com.	46.6	30.5
Bank	2.1	3.1
Trans.	1.03	4.1
State	4.5	11.2
Free	8.9	3.5
Army	—	1.0
Dom. Ind.	1.65	6.1
Rent.	18.0	5.5
Other	5.6	3.9
TOTAL	100% (484)	100% (1,171)

The statistics on status of employment for 1890 show that a majority of the employed Germans in the three parishes fell into the two highest categories. Yet even here one also finds traces of lower-strata Germans, who were all too easily ignored in Prague (see Table 3/7).[70] Seven out of every ten self-supporting German

samples, Z must be greater than 1.65 at a 95% level of certainty for a difference in percentages to be significant. The Z values for the differences between the Czech and German percentages in the handicrafts, commerce, state employment, free professions, domestic industry, and rents were, respectively, 9.3, 6.4, 4.27, 4.6, 3.8, and 8.0, all significant with 95% certainty.

[70] *Significance Test*: The Z values for the differences between the Czech and German percentages in the independent, employee, and worker ranks were, respectively, 4.27, 4.04, and 7.2, all significant with 95% certainty.

residents were independent/self-employed or qualified employees, compared to only one in three among the Czechs. The Czech population included a significantly larger percentage of domestic servants because Czech and German middle-class households alike employed almost solely Czech women, whom they recruited from the surrounding countryside. The Czech servants, many of whom spoke little German, were so ubiquitous in German households that they became a stock figure in Prague German fiction; they even drew the criticism of German politicians, who feared for the ethnic purity of German households.[71] But for an occasional nurse or governess, one found few German servants anywhere in Prague in the late nineteenth and early twentieth centuries. Throughout the Bohemian capital, the Czech population had a preponderance at the lower end of the economic scale, but there were German workers as well, and in the sampled inner-city parishes, wage workers accounted for one in every seven self-supporting Germans. Moreover, as a conservative estimate, at least a third of the German employees were petty clerks, bookkeepers, technicians, and lesser supervisors who lacked the income, education, and life-style requisite to the society of the German middle class. To complete the count of lower-strata Germans, one should add the number of small producers, peddlers, and the smallest shopkeepers who reported themselves as independent manufacturers and businessmen in the census, but there is no practical way of identifying them in the manuscript returns. It appears, though, that in Prague their numbers were generally small relative to the large body of independent manufacturers and traders who could be counted legitimately among the German middle class or more respectable lower middle class.

The 1890 statistics show the substantial advances which the Czech middle class had made over the preceding four decades. In absolute terms Czech independents and qualified employees in St. Gall, St. Henry, and St. Peter outnumbered their German counterparts three to two. Already dominant in the crafts, the Czechs achieved numerical superiority among Prague's smaller commercial and industrial proprietors in the eighties and nineties. In 1883 Philipp

---

[71] See such a critique in Philipp Knoll's speech to Prague's German Club on March 20, 1883 in Knoll, *Beiträge*, pp. 186-90. For fictional portraits of Czech servant women in German households, see Hauschner, *Die Familie Lowositz*; Max Brod, *Ein tschechisches Dienstmädchen* (Berlin, 1909); Franz Carl Weiskopf, *Das Slawenlied* (Berlin, 1931); and Franz Werfel, *Barbara oder die Frömmigkeit* (Berlin, Vienna, and Leipzig, 1929).

TABLE 3/7
Gall-Henry-Peter, 1890: Distribution of
Residents by Status of Employment

	Germans		Czechs	
Independent	21.9%	(106)	13.4%	(157)
Employee	12.2	(59)	6.3	(74)
Worker/day-laborer	6.6	(32)	21.0	(241)
Participating family	2.1		1.8	
Servant	5.5	(27)	17.1	(200)
All employed	48.3%		59.6%	
dependents	51.7		40.4	
TOTAL	100% = 484		100% = 1,171	

Knoll complained of the "gradual exclusion of the German language from petty commerce" as one of the most important signs of the Prague Germans' retreat, and after 1884 the German forces in the Prague Chambers of Trade and Manufacture retained majorities only in the sections for large commercial firms and large industries not based on agriculture.[72] There is insufficient data available for a comparison of income levels among the Czech and German middle classes in Prague, but many signs indicate that by the end of the century Czech merchants and industrialists had reached at least parity in numbers and wealth with their German counterparts.[73]

The declining representation of Germans in state service in the three sampled parishes reflects the increasing Czech dominance of all government employment in Prague at the end of the century.[74] Aspiring Czechs continued to look to state service as an avenue for upward mobility despite the declining status of much government employment, and Czech power in the Bohemian Diet and the Provincial Executive Council (Landesausschuss, Zemský výbor) after the early 1880s abetted the Czech influx into public service.[75] The Ger-

[72] Knoll, Beiträge, p. 186; Gruber, Handels- und Gewerbekammer, p. 33.

[73] Cf. Havránek, in Austrian History Yearbook, III/2, pp. 244-45. The general trend was noted in 1884 by the Prague German ethnologist, Josef Bendel, Die Deutschen in Böhmen, Mähren, und Schlesien, 2 vols. (Vienna and Těšín, 1884), II, p. 241.

[74] A comparison of the 1890 census data for St. Henry with a sample of the returns for 1880 shows the decline in German government employees. See Appendix II, Table 8 for the 1880 data. The comparison of the 1890 and 1910 data below also shows the decline.

[75] On the contrast between Czechs and Germans in Bohemia on occupational preferences, see Münch, Böhmische Tragödie, p. 466, and Wiskemann, Czechs and Germans, 1st ed., pp. 37-40, 53-63. Eugene N. Anderson and Pauline R. Anderson,

mans of Prague increasingly shared the preference of many Bohemian Germans already noted for careers in commerce and industry. The strident Czech nationalism of Prague's municipal
government in the last decades of the century only heightened
German disdain for the local officialdom.

The 1890 census returns for the parish of St. Nicholas near much
of the provincial administration in Malá strana illustrate the consequences (see Table 3/8).[76] The sample includes too few Germans
to permit detailed discussion of them, but it is significant that here
Czech governmental employees outnumbered the Germans five to
one. Moreover, the Czech public servants in the sample were
broadly distributed among local, provincial, and imperial agencies,
while the few Germans were primarily imperial bureaucrats. Understandably, the few German state employees who remained in
Prague after the early 1880s had little choice but to insist that the
city continue as provincial capital for both Czechs and Germans.[77]

The occupational statistics for the parishes of St. Gall, St. Henry,
and St. Peter in 1910 reflect the continued growth of the Czech
middle class, the movement of Jews into the Czech ranks, and an
increasing representation of Germans in the free professions. The
German share of the sampled population dropped from 29 percent

TABLE 3/8
St. Nicholas, 1890: Distribution of Residents by Economic Sector

	Germans	Czechs
Ind.	2.9%	14.4%
Hand.	—	19.1
Com.	7.1	18.1
Bank	5.7	—
Trans.	—	3.3
State	30.0(21)	12.6(81)
Free	2.9	4.2
Army	21.0	—
Dom. Ind.	—	10.9
Rent.	5.7	4.7
Other	24.0	11.2
TOTAL	100% = 70	100% = 640

(Absolute numbers, including dependents, in parentheses)

Political Institutions and Social Change in Continental Europe in the Nineteenth Century
(Berkeley, 1967), pp. 231-37, discuss the general decline in prestige of bureaucratic
service in Europe in the late nineteenth century.

[76] See Appendix II, Table 5 for the raw data. *Confidence Interval*: With 95% certainty, the interval for the 640 Czechs is ±3.88%; for the 70 Germans, ±11.7%.

[77] See Chapters 4 and 6.

to 21 in the two decades after 1890; in 1910 only 52 percent of the Jews affirmed German as their language compared to 87 percent in 1890. The statistics on status of employment demonstrate most clearly the flowering of the Czech middle class (see Table 3/9).[78] Even in these old centers of German strength, the absolute numbers of independent or self-employed Czechs now surpassed the Germans in all occupational sectors except the free professions; in toto the Czech independents outnumbered the Germans by more than two to one. Yet among the remaining Germans, independents accounted for an even larger share than in 1890, amounting to half of all self-supporting Germans in 1910.

Between 1890 and 1910 Germans in the inner city showed the greatest persistence in industry, the free professions, and the rentier category (see Table 3/10).[79] The significant drop in the percentage of Germans in commerce and the corresponding rise for the Czechs resulted primarily from the shift in ethnic loyalties of

TABLE 3/9
Gall-Henry-Peter: Distribution of
Residents of Status of Employment, 1890-1910

	Germans		Czechs	
	1890	1910	1890	1910
Independent	21.9%(106)	27.5%(92)	13.4%(157)	16.2%(204)
Employee	12.2 (59)	13.1 (44)	6.3 (74)	6.2 (78)
Worker/day-labor	6.6 (32)	5.1 (17)	21.0 (241)	19.5 (245)
Participating family	2.1	2.7	1.8	2.2
Servant	5.5 (27)	6.9 (23)	17.1 (200)	18.1 (227)
All employed	48.3%	55.3%	59.6%	62.2%
dependents	51.7	44.7	40.4	37.8
TOTAL	100% = 484	100% = 335	100% = 1,171	100% = 1,256

[78] See Appendix II, Table 6, for the raw data. Since the attrition of Catholic and Protestant Germans from the three parishes was nearly as great as the loss of German Jews, the religious breakdown of the German population in the three parishes hardly changed over the twenty years. In the 1910 sample, the Germans were 27.5% Catholic, 68.4% Jewish, and 4.1% Protestant.

Confidence Interval: With 95% certainty, the interval for the whole 1910 sample of 1,591 persons is ±2.45%; for the 335 Germans, ±5.36%; for the 1,256 Czechs, ±2.76%.

Significance Test for the 1910 sample: The Z values for the differences between the Czech and German percentages in the independent, employee, and worker ranks were, respectively, 4.75, 4.23, and 6.32, all significant with 95% certainty.

[79] *Significance Test for the 1910 sample*: The Z values for the differences between the Czech and German percentages in the handicrafts, state employment, free professions, domestic industry, and rentier categories are, respectively, 5.73, 3.69, 5.21, 3.64, and 6.23, all significant with 95% certainty.

Jewish businessmen and commercial employees. By 1910 very few Germans in the sampled parishes were in state service, but as long as Prague remained the administrative and financial center for all of Bohemia and a major focus for regional commerce and industry, Germans with the requisite capital or education continued to find livelihoods here as industrialists, qualified employees, physicians, lawyers, artists, and rentiers.

TABLE 3/10
Gall-Henry-Peter: Distribution of
Residents by Economic Sector, 1890-1910

| | Germans | | Czechs | |
	1890	1910	1890	1910
Ind.	9.5%	14.0%	10.9	12.6
Hand.	2.3	3.6	20.1	15.4
Com.	47.0	39.4	30.5	38.4
Bank	2.1	4.2	3.1	2.9
Trans.	1.03	0	4.1	1.67
State	4.5	2.7	11.2	8.6
Free	8.9	14.6	3.5	6.0
Army	0	0.3	1.02	1.35
Dom. Ind.	1.65	0.90	6.1	5.6
Rent.	18.0	14.3	5.5	4.7
Other	5.6	6.0	3.9	3.0
TOTAL	100% = 484	100% = 335	100% = 1,171	100% = 1,256

Germans survived in the greatest numbers in occupations that were insulated from the economic and political forces which affected lesser commerce and much of state employment in Prague at the end of the century. Property or specialized training assured at least some Germans a satisfactory livelihood in the Bohemian capital, regardless of the strength of the Czech majority. Such special advantages and the accompanying business or professional connections certainly kept some Germans in Prague. The relatively high numbers of German merchants, industrialists, professionals, rentiers, and qualified employees represented, of course, the combined effects of higher rates of economic survival in these occupations, and the deliberate choice of them by individual Germans after Czech strength began to grow elsewhere. The census totals include both the survivors and the products of occupational and geographical mobility.

The occupational statistics published with the 1910 census returns show that the German citizen residents of Prague and the inner suburbs as a whole had a significantly higher portion in the middle and upper economic strata than did the Czechs. To a great extent, the Prague Germans were "a prosperous upper stratum suspended in air" over the city's Czech majority, as some put it, or as the famed journalist Egon Erwin Kisch later described them:[80]

> They were almost exclusively grande bourgeoisie: owners of lignite mines; executives of the mining companies and the Škoda munitions works; hops merchants who traveled back and forth between Žatec and North America; sugar, textile, and paper manufacturers as well as bank directors; in their own circle professors, higher army officers, and state officials. There was no German proletariat.

In reality, independents, the self-employed, and all qualified employees comprised nearly three-quarters, 73 percent, of all self-supporting Germans compared to only 41 percent of the self-supporting Czechs (see Table 3/11).[81] In terms of economic sector, fully 51 percent—48 percent if the military are excluded—of the German citizens derived their livelihood from the free professions, rents, and state employment, compared to only one-quarter of all the Czechs. Equal portions of the Czech and German populations depended on commerce, but the paucity of German workers in industry and the handicrafts limited the Germans' overall involvement in manufacture.

There were so few German workers in the inner-city districts with the highest German concentrations that contemporaries easily ignored them, but the 1910 census data show that, in fact, more than one in five self-supporting Germans (22.1%) were wage workers or day laborers. As already suggested, at least one-third of the qualified employees at any time were poorly paid, minimally trained clerks and petty supervisors who also stood outside the middle class of property and education and the more respectable lower-middle-class elements. Contemporary politicians and journalists tended to

---

[80] E. E. Kisch, *Marktplatz der Sensationen* (Mexico City, 1942), p. 85. For similar views see Heinrich Rauchberg, "Nationale Haushaltungs- und Familienstatistik von Prag," *Deutsche Arbeit*, IV (1904-05), pp. 262-64; August Sauer, *Kulturpolitische Reden und Schriften*, ed. Josef Pfitzner (Liberec, 1928), pp. 2-3; and Friedrich Freiherr von Wieser, *Die deutsche Steuerleistung und der öffentliche Haushalt in Böhmen* (Leipzig, 1904), pp. 57-59.

[81] Statistics derive from *Öster. Statistik*, N. F., III, 8. Heft, p. 330. See Appendix II, Table 7 for the absolute numbers. The suburbs included here are Karlín, Vinohrady, Nusle, Vršovice, Smíchov, and Žižkov. No corrections could be made for the reporting of some state employees as independents by the census officials.

TABLE 3/11
Occupational Distribution of the Czech and German Citizen
Residents in Percentages, Prague and Suburbs, 1910

	Agr.-Forest	Mfg.	Commerce	Govt.-Free-Rent-Other	Total	
Czechs in %						
Independent	—	6.84	7.98	14.03	29.00	(74,237)
Employee	—	2.38	4.82	5.24	12.49	(31,966)
Worker/day-1	0.39	31.41	11.20	4.95	47.95	(122,753)
Part. family	—	—	0.60	—	0.89	(2,272)
Servant	—	2.12	3.18	4.27	9.68	(24,770)
All employed	0.70	43.02	27.78	28.50	100%	(255,998)
TOTAL (with	3,431	209,540	134,361	115,616	462,948	
dependents)	(0.7%)	(45.3)	(29.0)	(24.9)	(100%)	
Germans in %						
Independent	—	3.24	5.87	28.70	37.98	(7,945)
Employee	—	7.18	13.94	13.39	34.90	(7,229)
Worker/day-1	—	4.03	5.02	12.87	21.99	(4,600)
Part. family	—	—	0.21	—	0.33	(70)
Servant	—	0.83	1.08	3.15	5.13	(1,073)
All employed	0.37	15.40	26.11	58.12	100%	(20,917)
TOTAL (with	169	6,481	10,894	18,405	35,949	
dependents)	(0.5)	(18.0)	(30.3)	(51.3)	(100%)	

consider the Prague Germans as almost exclusively middle class, but the census data indicate that, conservatively estimated, one-third of all the self-supporting Germans in the city and inner suburbs fell into the laboring or lowest lower-middle-class strata. Confirmation for this comes from the fact that in 1910, 38 percent of the households headed by Germans lacked servants. Of course, this was still a remarkably small fraction of the German population; fully 84 percent of the households headed by Czechs had no servants.[82] Since few of Prague's German workers and petty employees resided in the inner city in the post-1880 era, the great majority of them were thinly dispersed in the more proletarian outlying districts of Holešovice, Libeň, Smíchov, Karlín, and Žižkov.[83]

The growth of the Czech majority in Prague, the patterns of

[82] *Öster. Statistik*, N. F., IV, 3. Heft, pp. 109-10. Havránek in *Pražský sborník historický 1969-70*, pp. 94-97, shows similar contrasts between Czech and German households in the employment of servants in 1900.

[83] The social composition of the German residents of the suburbs in 1900 is described in Srb, ed., *Sčítání lidu v Praze 1900*, III, pp. 315-18, although no supporting statistics are offered. Aside from middle-class pockets in Vinohrady and the

migration, and German-Czech assimilation resulted in what is best understood as the selective survival of Germans in certain social strata. The impress of the Germans' origins in Prague's old German-speaking middle and upper strata remained strong to the end of the Monarchy. The German population included relatively few workers and petty employees at any time, whether they were native to Prague or immigrants. As the city expanded and as the Czech majority grew, such lower-strata Germans as there were found themselves scattered in minute numbers in a largely Czech environment. The more prosperous German professionals, industrialists, and merchants persisted, many of them clustered in the more comfortable sections of the Old Town, New Town, and Vinohrady. The census data from after 1880 show that German workers, petty employees, and small retailers, both Christian and Jewish, tended to disappear, many through assimilation with the Czechs and an undetermined number through emigration.

Still, the origins of the German minority and the character of Prague's economic and demographic development do not fully explain the attrition from the German population. Contemporary observers like Philipp Knoll, Heinrich Rauchberg, and Friedrich von Wieser noted the loss of lower-strata Germans, and they clearly recognized that such elements failed to participate in the special pursuits and group life that separated middle-class Germans from Czechs in the Bohemian capital. This raises the question, however, of just where Germans and Czechs erected social barriers to separate the groups in everyday life.

Czech-German Relations in Daily Life

According to the standard lore of Austria's nationality conflicts, the warring groups in mixed localities established rigid barriers to minimize social and economic contacts across national lines. In Prague, a favorite example, Czechs and Germans are supposed to have had virtually no dealings in social or cultural affairs in the late nineteenth century; in Hans Kohn's phrase, a "voluntary segregation" existed between Czechs and Germans.[84] Czechs might

---

older parts of Smíchov and Karlín, the majority of the Germans in the suburbs were small retailers, petty employees, and workers in commerce and industry.

[84] Kohn, born in Prague in 1892, remembered the city thus in *Living in a World Revolution*, pp. 9-10. See also Ernst von Plener, *Reden 1873-1911* (Stuttgart and Leipzig, 1911), p. 310, and Joseph Wechsberg's hyperbolic description in *Prague: The Mystical City* (New York, 1971), pp. 16-19.

work as servants in German homes or employees in their businesses, but as Egon Kisch remembered it:[85]

> Other than for business affairs, the Prague German did not traffic with the half million Czechs of the city. He never lit a cigar with a match from the Czech School Society (*Matice školská*) nor did the Czech light his with matches from the German School Society (*Deutscher Schulverein*). No German appeared in the Czechs' Burghers' Club and no Czech entered the German Casino. Even the concerts were ethnically exclusive as were the public swimming facilities, parks, playgrounds, most restaurants, cafes, and businesses (sic!). The Czechs' corso was Ferdinandová (now Národní), that of the Germans, Na příkopě.

Kohn and Kisch recalled accurately the general tendency of politics and organized social life in Prague. Czech and German political leaders openly pursued the aim of separating the two groups as much as possible in group affairs, but no matter how great the separation in the public affairs that were the province of organized groups, Czechs and Germans continued to mingle extensively in the private matters of bread-winning, consumption of goods and services, and domestic life.

It is hard to describe precisely the development of Czech-German relations in private affairs between 1861 and 1914, but at least we can delineate the overall character of contacts in daily life around the turn of the century. The simple realities of numbers and residence patterns make clear the actual extent of Czech-German contacts. In physical terms the members of the German minority neither resided in nor did business within a ghetto. Germans lived surrounded by Czechs, not only in the outlying districts, where they were outnumbered more than ten to one after 1880, but also in the inner city areas of high German concentration. The civilian population of the Old Town was only 22 percent German in 1880, 10 percent in 1900; the New Town was 16 percent German in 1880, 13 percent in 1900 (see Table 3/1). As already noted, those sections of the Lower New Town and neighboring Vinohrady which had the very highest German concentrations were no more than 30 percent German in 1900 (see Table 3/4). Within those neighborhoods the German residents did not gather on some streets or even in certain apartment buildings to the exclusion of Czechs. Similarly, but for the fashionable Czech and German promenades of Ferdi-

[85] Kisch, *Marktplatz*, pp. 85-86.

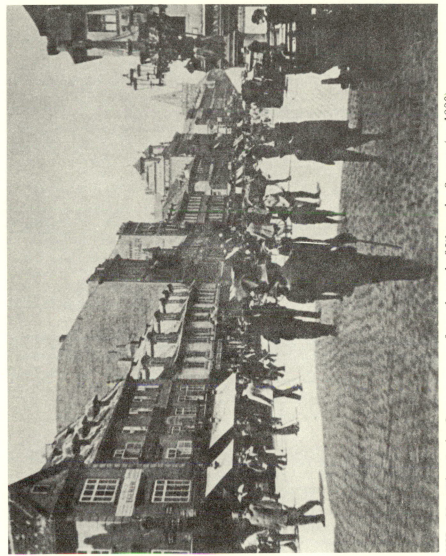

XII. Na příkopě, the German corso, from the end of Wenceslas Square (ca. 1880)

nandová and Na příkopě, Czech- and German-owned businesses stood side by side throughout much of the city.[86]

Convenience and practical economic considerations generally weighed more heavily than ethnic loyalties in determining business relations in Prague at the end of the century. After the early eighties politicians and voluntary associations on both sides repeatedly called for ethnic preference or outright boycotts in business dealings, but individual Czechs and Germans apparently followed considerations of economic advantage and continued to deal with each other as suppliers and customers, colleagues and employees.[87] The attempted boycotts generally had only limited success, and even nationalistic newspapers had to admit that neither Czech nor German businesses cared to do without customers of the other ethnic group.[88] Whatever their national loyalties, many Czech artisans, shopkeepers, and restaurateurs continued to provide bilingual signs or menus even into the era of nationalist violence in the late 1890s (see Plates XIV and XV). Even if some German proprietors could not speak enough Czech to deal with Czech customers themselves, many had Czech employees who did.[89] Indeed, it appears that at the turn of the century most businesses of any size in the Bohemian capital, whether in manufacture, finance, or commerce, employed both Czechs and Germans.

The group sociability that went on in pubs and cafes gave them a certain public character, and ethnic differences had a greater impact here than on other businesses. Individual establishments might be identified with one or another Czech or German voluntary association. No German would enter the beer halls identified with the units of the *Sokol*, any more than Czechs would go to the favorite pub of the German Gymnastics Society's members. Certainly, no Czech came into the restaurant and *Bierstube* on the ground floor

[86] See *Adressář král. hlav. města Prahy*, ed. Václav Lešer (Prague, 1891), passim; and *Adresář král. hlav. města Prahy*, ed. Vojtěch Kraus (Prague, 1910), passim.

[87] On the campaigns for boycotts or preferential business dealings, see Chapters 5 and 6, pp. 189-90, 240.

[88] See *Der Deutsche Volksbote*, 21 Nov 1897; the Old Czechs' *Politik*, 7 Jan 1903 (M); and Ernst Lustig's remarks in "Verhandlungsschrift über die am 4. Jänner 1909 in Deutschen Kasino in Prag stattgefundene Vorberatung des Zweiteilungsausschusses," SÚA Praha pozůstalost č. 73, Karl Urban, ct. 43, VII-tisky. On this point see also the reminiscence of Egon Kisch, *Marktplatz*, p. 36.

[89] *Bohemia*, 18 Sept 1897(M) commented on the continued bilingualism of many businesses. For vignettes on the mixing of Czechs and Germans as employees or customers, see Pavel Eisner, *Franz Kafka and Prague* (New York, 1950), pp. 20-22; and Vondráček, *Lékař vzpomíná*, pp. 30-33.

XIII.   Artist's rendering of the New German Theatre, Prague, opened 1888

XIV.   Melantrich House, Sirková street, čp. 471, Old Town, in 1895

XV. Houses on Ovocná street, čp. 374 & 375, Old Town, in 1894

of the German Casino unless he wanted to start a disturbance.[90] On the other hand, a small establishment not identified with any organization might have a mixed clientele. Naturally, the most honored figures of German artistic and literary life in the seventies and eighties had their own favorite cafes in the Lower New Town, just as their Czech counterparts had theirs clustered near the National Theatre. Nonetheless, at the turn of the century the younger intellectuals on both sides who rejected too thorough a separation of Czech and German communities sought each other out in other cafes. A Czech group including the Čapek brothers, František Langer, and V. V. Štech, which normally gathered in the Cafe Union, met frequently with Max Brod, Franz Kafka, Egon Kisch, Paul Leppin, and Franz Werfel at the Cafe Arco or in various "bilingual" establishments.[91]

Medicine and law had closer links to political affairs in Prague than did much of commerce, but here too practical considerations drove individual Czechs and Germans closer together than nationalist leaders cared to admit. Czech and German groups disputed the distribution of laboratory and clinical facilities between the Czech and German medical schools when the medical, legal, and philosophical faculties of the Charles-Ferdinand University were divided in 1882, and thereafter Czech leaders periodically raised complaints against various German-run medical facilities.[92] Nonetheless, Czech and German physicians and dentists continued to share most hospital facilities and referred patients back and forth. To a great extent they formed a single body of practitioners in which individual expertise apparently counted for more than ethnic loyalties.[93]

---

[90] Such a disturbance occurred in August 1897, as reported in *Národní listy*, 31 Aug 1897(M); and Allgemeines Verwaltungsarchiv, Vienna (hereafter AVA): Ministerium des Innern—Praesidium (MI—Praes.), 22 Böhmen 1897, ct. 853, 9195/MI, 8 Sept 1897.

[91] See Willy Haas, "Die Prager deutsche Gesellschaft vor dem ersten Weltkrieg," *Prager Montagsblatt*, 27 Dec 1937 (5. Beilage); Kisch, *Marktplatz*, p. 71; František Langer, *Byli a bylo* (Prague, 1971), pp. 167-68; and Utitz, *Kisch*, p. 36.

[92] On the division of the university, see further discussion in Chapter 4, p. 143, and the studies by Jaroslav Goll, *Rozdělení Pražské University Karlo-Ferdinandovy roku 1882 a počátek samostatné university České* (Prague, 1908), and H. Gordon Skilling, "The Partition of the University in Prague," *Slavonic and East European Review*, XXVII (1949), pp. 430-49. *Bohemia*, 23 April 1903(M), reported a meeting of Czech physicians and dentists to protest the treatment of Czechs in the hospital of the Merciful Brethren in Prague, and complaints against this hospital continued thereafter.

[93] Vondráček, *Lékař vzpomíná*, pp. 75-106, reminisces about Czech and German physicians almost indiscriminately.

Ethnic differences played a greater role in legal practice in Prague than in medicine. The nationality conflict made the language in which one litigated—and the loyalties of the lawyer who handled the case—a matter of considerable national pride among the politically aware. Further, many lawyers on both sides were too deeply engaged in politics to attract clients from the other ethnic group. Nonetheless, the separation was far from total. Czech law students outnumbered the German in Prague at the end of the century, and German lawyers regularly hired some of the Czechs as clerks in the eighties and nineties.[94]

The appearance of ethnic separation exceeded the reality in entertainment and education as well. Czech and German leaders alike insisted on the national character of the arts and their importance for a national movement, and after the opening of the provisional structure of the Czech National Theatre in 1862, Czech and German groups each developed their own theatrical establishments in Prague.[95] The Czech National Theatre and the German Provincial Theatre Company became objects of fierce national pride, and they served important political and social functions for the Czech and German middle classes in the Bohemian capital. Yet many concerts continued to attract mixed audiences, and individuals on both sides regularly crossed national lines to attend operatic performances by the two companies.[96] To minimize direct competition, Angelo Neumann, director of the German Provincial Theatre from 1885 to 1910, actually made an arrangement with his Czech counterpart, František Šubert, to give the Czech National Theatre rights to first local performances of new French and Italian works while the German company would have first rights to new German operas.[97]

---

[94] Karen Johnson Freeze, "The Young Progressives: The Czech Student Movement" (Ph.D. dissertation, Columbia University, 1975), pp. 153-54.

[95] On the Czech National Theatre, see Stanley B. Kimball, *Czech Nationalism: A Study of the National Theatre Movement, 1845-83* (Urbana, 1964). On the German Provincial Theatre Company, see Richard Rosenheim, *Die Geschichte der Deutschen Bühnen in Prag, 1883-1918* (Prague, 1938), and Heinrich Teweles, *Theater und Publikum: Erinnerungen und Erfahrungen* (Prague, 1927).

[96] With mixed audiences, visiting artists easily committed faux pas, as Hans von Bülow discovered when he brought the Meiningen orchestra to Prague in 1884 (*Bohemia*, 6 Dec 1884[M]). For instances of Germans attending the Czech National Theatre and vice versa, see Egon Basch, "Wirken und Wandern: Lebenserinnerungen" (mimeograph, n.d., LBI), pp. 16-20; Kurt Blaukopf, *Gustav Mahler* (New York and Washington, 1973), p. 71; Richard Kukula, *Erinnerungen eines Bibliothekars* (Weimar, 1925), pp. 37-38; and Langer, *Byli a bylo*, pp. 172-73.

[97] Teweles, *Theater und Publikum*, p. 136. Despite the arrangement, a dispute over performance fees allowed the Czech National Theatre to stage the first local pro-

German groups in Prague went to great trouble in building and maintaining a separate system of German public and private schools, but those schools did not isolate German children from Czechs or from the Czech-speaking environment of Prague. The German schools provided a German-language education, and they offered many German children their first sustained exposure outside the home to a situation in which German was dominant.[98] Nonetheless, many Czech parents in the city and throughout the Bohemian Lands also valued schooling in the lingua franca of Central Europe and continued to send their children to German-language schools after the 1860s. The numbers of Czechs who attended the German schools in Prague declined with the development of Czech society and the strengthening of Czech political forces, but a minority persisted until World War I. Pupils whose mother tongue was Czech comprised 40 percent of all those in the German municipal *Volksschulen* and *Bürgerschulen* in 1890, 17 percent in 1910.[99] The Czech enrollments were always lower in the German secondary schools; in 1910, for instance, Czechs accounted for 8 percent of the students in the German *Gymnasien*, 16 percent of those in the German *Realschulen*.[100] In contrast to the willingness of a minority of Czechs to send their children to German schools, virtually all Germans in Prague shunned the Czech schools once the dual systems were fully in place: never more than twenty or thirty German students attended all the Czech primary and secondary schools combined at any one time between 1880 and World War I.[101]

While the German parents, Christian and Jewish, overwhelmingly preferred German schools for their children, they did not reject all instruction in Czech. From the late 1860s on, Czech was offered as a non-required subject in the last three years of the German *Volksschulen*, all three years of the *Bürgerschulen*, and in six to eight years of the secondary schools. Parents could exempt their

---

duction of *Der Rosenkavalier* before World War I, and Richard Strauss himself conducted the work in the National Theatre. See Teweles, p. 184, and Kukula, *Erinnerungen*, p. 37.

[98] See the comments by Willy Haas, *Die literarische Welt* (Munich, 1958), pp. 10-11.

[99] *Statistická knížka Prahy 1890* (Prague, 1892), p. 362; *Statistická zpráva Prahy 1910* (Prague, 1912), pp. 489-91.

[100] *Statistická zpráva Prahy 1910*, pp. 477-79.

[101] Based on a review of the data in the statistical handbooks published annually by the city of Prague, taken at five to eight-year intervals, 1880-1910. For further discussion of Czech-German relations in Prague's schools, see G. B. Cohen, "The Prague Germans," pp. 551-73.

children from the instruction in Czech by simple request, but in contrast to the noisy rejection of Czech courses by German nationalists in northern Bohemia, typically 80 to 90 percent of the German pupils in Prague studied Czech in the primary schools.[102] It is hard to know how much Czech they actually learned in these classes, and the numbers enrolled fell off considerably at the advanced levels of the secondary schools. Nonetheless, German parents and their children were clearly willing to make some concessions to Prague's Czech environment in matters of schooling.

German and Czech children in Prague mingled in the schools, in the parks, and on the streets. While the memoirs, novels, and short stories of the Prague Germans describe the brawls that frequently erupted between groups of Czech and German schoolboys, they also portray the links of acquaintance and friendship that could develop.[103] At home, on the streets, and in the schools, those who grew up as Germans in Prague doubtless quickly learned the difference between German and Czech, who was friend and who foe; but they also learned that there was no escaping contact with Czechs as long as they lived in the Bohemian capital. Even within the German primary and secondary schools, Germans learned to deal with Czechs, came to know some of them, and studied their language.

Contacts between Czechs and Germans were generally fewer and more strained in the institutions of higher learning, where students and professors alike were highly politicized in the late nineteenth century. Still, the Czech and German academic communities were always aware of each other's presence and activities. They shared some facilities, and a few students occasionally crossed national lines.

Technical education went on in separate Czech and German colleges after 1869, but one needed only to understand the language of instruction to enroll in either college. Not surprisingly, never more than a handful of Germans were enrolled in the Czech Technical College at any one time. Although their numbers declined over the long term, a significant minority of Czechs attended the German College through most of the era before World War I. In 1900, for instance, no Germans attended the Czech College, but

[102] See G. B. Cohen, "The Prague Germans," pp. 567-70.

[103] See Demetz, *Rilkes Prager Jahre*, pp. 32-33; Hauschner, *Die Familie Lowositz*, pp. 36, 71, 121; Fritz Mauthner, *Der letzte Deutsche von Blatna* (Berlin and Vienna, 1913), pp. 31-50, passim; Gustav Janouch, *Conversations with Kafka*, 2d ed. rev. (New York, 1971), p. 114; and Franz Carl Weiskopf, *Das Slawenlied*, passim.

58 of the 461 in the German institution were Czechs.[104] By 1910 the German College had only 22 Czechs enrolled.[105]

The division of the Charles-Ferdinand University begun in 1882 was completed in 1891 with the inauguration of a separate Czech theological faculty, but the two universities continued to share the historic aula, library, and other facilities in the Karolinum and Klementinum. Here, too, individual students could matriculate at either institution, although by the end of the century few Czechs and even fewer Germans crossed national lines. In 1900, the German University had seventy-seven Czech students compared to 1,065 German, while the 2,868 students in the Czech University included no Germans.[106] As in the German Technical College, the trend of Czech enrollments in the German University was downward: only 45 Czechs matriculated in the summer term of 1910.[107] It is difficult to tell how many on either side crossed over on an occasional basis to hear lectures or seek advice on research. Albert Einstein, for instance, had a number of Czech students attend his lectures and do research with him during his brief tenure at the German University in 1911-1912.[108]

Mingling of Prague's Czechs and Germans in everyday affairs reached even into the confines of home life. It is difficult to determine the true character of Czech-German domestic relations and to differentiate the experience of various segments of the German population, but it is clear that most Germans found themselves surrounded by Czechs even in their home life. Not only were there no German neighborhoods as such, but even in the areas of highest German concentration, German families shared the same apartment buildings with Czechs. For example, German residents were found in only 28 of the 46 buildings in the 1890 samples for the parishes of St. Gall, St. Henry, and St. Peter. Yet even if one ignores the Germans' Czech servants, Germans lived alongside Czechs in all but 3 of these structures. In the 1910 samples, Germans resided in 31 of the 46 buildings, and Czechs were found in all the buildings where there were Germans.[109] The Czechs typically belonged to

[104] *Statistická knížka Prahy 1900*, pp. 372-73. 1,070 Czechs were enrolled in the Czech Technical College in 1900.

[105] Wilhelm Winkler, *Die soziale Lage der Deutschen Hochschulstudentenschaft Prags* (Vienna and Leipzig, 1912), p. 19.

[106] *Statistická knížka Prahy 1900*, pp. 372-73.

[107] Winkler, *Die soziale Lage*, p. 19.

[108] Philipp Frank, *Einstein: His Life and Times* (New York, 1947), pp. 81-82.

[109] For the statistics on each building in the samples broken down by ethnicity and religion, see G. B. Cohen, "The Prague Germans," pp. 603-05.

other households in the buildings, but they might also be lodgers or co-resident relatives of the German householders.[110] With so much mixing of Czechs and Germans in apartment buildings in the inner-city areas, where Germans were relatively numerous, it is likely that there was even more contact in the outlying districts, where the German population was more thinly dispersed.

Of course, German residents may not have had intimate relations with Czech neighbors in apartment buildings, but they had closer contacts with Czech lodgers, Czech servants, and, if they had any, Czech relatives. The rate of intermarriage is perhaps the most obvious and important gauge of Czech-German intimacy in daily life and of whether behavior in private affairs served to preserve or to widen Czech-German differences. Unfortunately, intermarriage between Czechs and Germans is virtually impossible to measure since marriage registries included no indication of ethnicity, and one cannot determine from the census returns how many individuals adjusted their responses to the question of language to conform with their spouses. There was little discussion of intermarriage by Czechs and Germans in Prague at any point in the late nineteenth century. As time passed, the depth and pervasiveness of ethnic differences in politics and formal social life can only have made Czech-German marriages increasingly difficult, particularly among middle- and upper-strata families on both sides, where ethnic loyalties and social prejudices were strong. Nonetheless, occasional instances noted in memoirs and differing responses by spouses to the question of language in the census suggest that intermarriage occurred throughout the pre-World War I era, even if at a low rate.[111] Although the numbers are too small to be statistically significant, the 1890 samples from the parishes of St. Gall, St. Henry, St. Peter, and St. Nicholas included 7 couples in which one spouse reported the German language, the other Czech, compared to 83 in which both reported German. The 1910 samples included 2 couples with differing responses, compared to 64 where they were both German.[112]

The patterns of employment, commerce, education, and resi-

[110] My sampling methods did not permit counting the number of Czech lodgers or relatives found in households headed by Germans, but they were present in an appreciable minority of the households.

[111] See, for example, the amusing vignette in Vondráček, *Lékař vzpomíná*, pp. 32-33.

[112] See Appendix II, Tables 1, 5 and 6, and G. B. Cohen, "The Prague Germans," pp. 608-12.

dence in Prague indicate that Germans had extensive and close dealings with Czechs in the essentially individual or private affairs of daily life. Indeed, personal convenience and simple economic considerations seem to have influenced these matters more strongly than did ethnic loyalties. However important organized German social life and group solidarity became for many of the German residents, jobs in commerce and the service sector, comfortable incomes, and urban middle-class tastes played major roles in gathering them in the largest numbers in the Old Town, New Town, and neighboring Vinohrady, keeping them there, and determining their basic consumption patterns. At the turn of the century, the Germans shared those realities of everyday life with many of their Czech neighbors to a much greater extent than many politicians cared to admit. For many in both groups, occupation, wealth, and class life-style probably had a greater impact on private life than did ethnic differences.

Religion clearly affected residence patterns and family life among the Prague Germans at the end of the century more strongly than did the simple Czech-German cleavage. At least in the Old Town and New Town, households that were largely or wholly German were generally found in the same apartment buildings with Czech households, but German Catholics tended to reside with Czech Catholic neighbors and seldom lived in the same buildings with Jews, whether German or Czech. For their part, the Jews in the sampled parishes resided primarily along with other Jewish families, whether German or Czech. While German Jews found great acceptance in German public life in Prague, they and the German Catholics seem to have avoided each other generally in the most intimate areas of private life; besides the residence patterns, few Jews converted or married non-Jews in Prague before World War I. The separation of the German Jews' family life from German Gentiles helped them to preserve a distinct Jewish group identity even while they participated extensively in Gentile public affairs.[113]

By comparison to the sharp separation of Czechs and Germans in politics and organized group life, members of the two groups in Prague had close, varied relations in everyday business affairs and domestic life throughout the era between 1861 and World War I. Social boundaries first developed between the groups in public

[113] See further discussion of this point by G. B. Cohen in *Central European History*, X, pp. 47-52. The numbers of German Protestants in the samples of the three parishes, twenty-four in 1890 and fourteen in 1910, were too small to be statistically significant.

affairs in the early sixties, and thereafter they apparently remained strongest in the affairs of public or group interest which voluntary associations and political action could control. The separation between Czechs and Germans never became as great in the private or individual affairs outside collective scrutiny. Yet if individual Czechs and Germans continued to have considerable contact in the private sphere, it was more despite the ethnic differences than regardless of them.

Ethnic conflict became so intense in public affairs and the consciousness of ethnic differences so general and so deep that few Czechs and Germans could easily ignore ethnic identity in any aspect of interpersonal relations. Even if they continued to deal with each other in business and domestic life, ethnicity at least colored many of those relationships. Given the distinctive occupational profile of the German minority, individual Germans often dealt with Czechs from a position of economic or educational advantage; even if contacts were frequent, this could only strengthen the sense of differences between the groups. The social separation between Czechs and Germans was not as clear and palpable in the private affairs of everyday life as in the public sphere, but a distinction still showed up in the terms of Czech-German relationships and the attitudes which accompanied them. Perhaps the German Jewish novelist Franz Carl Weiskopf, born in Prague in 1900, did not describe too strongly the feelings of many Prague Germans about their relations with Czechs:[114]

> So it was. One lived in the same city, saw the others daily. One heard them, spoke their language, even if only when compelled to. One dealt with them repeatedly, but one did not love them, know them, or want to know anything of them.

Czechs, in turn, complained of the arrogance, snobbery, and unbending behavior of many of the middle-class Germans.[115]

The question of just what set Germans apart from Czechs and gave them a sense of solidarity had growing importance after 1880 for those who worried about the survival of the German minority in the Bohemian capital. The self-image of the middle-class Germans as members of a cultured elite with a special unifying mission in Austria certainly distinguished them from their Czech neighbors. The Germans' special occupational profile also contributed to the

---

[114] Weiskopf, *Das Slawenlied*, pp. 84-85.

[115] For examples, see Ignát Herrmann, *Ze staré Prahy* (Prague, 1970), p. 74; and Štech, *Vzpomínky*, I, pp. 51, 95.

differences, but overall the Germans' advantages diminished as the Czech middle class matured and offered increasing competition in all sectors of the local economy. Simply identifying as a German in Prague did not automatically give individuals a social experience as part of a distinct German community. In the long run, the network of German associations provided the principal vehicle, really the firmest basis, for functioning German group solidarity in the city. If a separate German group existence depended much more on organized political, social, and cultural affairs than on any separation from Czechs in business or domestic life, then the task of maximizing the Germans' numbers and minimizing their decline became largely a matter of involving more people in German public life.

After the early eighties the leaders of the German Casino worried especially about bringing more lower-strata elements into German group life, for the Prague Germans could not survive merely as a middle-class elite "suspended in air." Franz Schmeykal, Philipp Knoll, and their colleagues recognized that they were attracting few lower-strata Germans as migrants to the city and that significant numbers in Prague were assimilating with the Czechs. Those who joined the Czech majority did so not simply because they lived in poor, strongly Czech neighborhoods and failed to share the interests and life-style of the middle-class Germans. Lower-strata Germans also abandoned their German loyalties because, by all appearances, they failed to participate significantly in any ongoing German group life. Certainly, they were largely excluded from the associational network directed by the liberal notables of the Casino.[116]

The strongly liberal, middle-class character of German group life in Prague from its inception virtually condemned the German population to decline. In the early 1880s, when German liberals found themselves squarely on the defensive at all political levels, the leaders of the German Casino realized that they could insure the survival of the German minority only by lowering the class barriers to participation in German community life. At the same time, however, they were still determined to maintain the liberal political order in the community and to combat the growth of ideological divisions and of religious or racial limits to German

---

[116] For further discussion of the social experience of the lower-strata Germans, see Chapter 5.

solidarity. The liberal leaders soon discovered that they were pursuing conflicting aims. In the next two chapters we turn to their efforts to meet the new political challenges of the eighties and nineties and to create a closer relationship with lower-strata Germans.

CHAPTER FOUR

Defense of the Liberal Community

The German community in Prague assumed a new defensive stance in the early 1880s. The middle-class Germans, of course, had already faced challenges from Czech nationalists and clerical-conservatives in the two preceding decades, but German liberal control of the Austrian government and the economic strength of the Austrian Germans had given the Prague community confidence in its ability to maintain itself. After 1879, however, demographic decline, a series of electoral defeats, and adverse administrative actions confronted the German minority in the Bohemian capital with a whole new situation. The old conservative and Czech nationalist adversaries won superior strength by joining a new coalition which took control of the Cisleithanian government and by exploiting a growing mass revolt against the rule of the German liberals. Among the German population throughout Austria, radical German nationalists and socialists soon began to mobilize large numbers of the lower middle classes and workers to join in the attack on the liberal notables. Faced by new, more powerful challenges on all sides, the liberal Germans of Prague now found their whole social and political situation seriously endangered.

The Prague Germans' demographic and economic decline vis-à-vis the Czechs was too gradual and piecemeal at first to elicit direct group responses, but the political setbacks after 1879 shocked the German burghers and forced them to undertake new defensive measures. Between 1879 and 1883 the German Liberal Party lost control of the Cisleithanian ministry, the higher officialdom, the Reichsrat, and the Bohemian Diet to a conservative-Slavic coalition. The Prague Germans now found it much harder to obtain reversals of adverse decisions by the Czech local authorities. In addition, the growth of divisions between moderates and radical nationalists in German middle-class politics throughout Austria after 1885 forced the moderates in Prague into a bitter struggle with the radicals for the loyalty of lower-middle-class Germans in the city and in German Bohemia as well. The Cisleithanian government's repression of the Social Democrats in the 1880s and the small number of German workers in Prague at first limited the direct threat of socialism to the German Casino, but the rise of a militantly democratic Marxist movement in Austria in the nineties undercut further the bases of liberal politics. As will be seen, Prague's liberal German community had to take up new defensive activities, create new organizations, and mobilize popular support both to insure the survival of the German minority in the city and to try to preserve the liberal political and social order. As the defensive efforts proceeded, the contradictions in the liberals' aims quickly became apparent. To understand the new conditions which the liberal community confronted and its response to them, we must turn first to the political events between 1879 and early 1884 which led to the German liberals' loss of power in Austria and Bohemia. These developments first brought home to the liberal community in Prague how threatened it was.

The End of German Liberal Dominance in Austria and Bohemia

The fall of Austria's German liberal ministry in 1879 and its replacement by a coalition of conservatives and Slavic parties under the emperor's old friend Count Eduard Taaffe initiated a gradual change in the Prague Germans' perceptions of their political position. Their new outlook did not solidify until 1884. By then middle-class Germans in Prague clearly saw themselves as a beleaguered minority excluded from the governmental bodies which controlled their own future. Spokesmen for the German community talked as if its very existence were threatened by the Czech and clerical-conservative adversaries. The leaders of the Casino could not speak so freely, however, about the menace from radical German nationalists, but by the mid-1880s they faced serious attacks from that source as well.

The initial setbacks for the German liberals in Austrian politics came at the hands of a new alliance of conservatives, Czech nationalists, and Poles. Angered by German liberal opposition to Austrian control of Bosnia and Herzegovina, Emperor Francis Joseph asked Count Taaffe to form a new government in 1879 when Prince Adolf Auersperg's liberal ministry broke up. After the resignation of the last German ministers in 1880, Count Taaffe tried to unite behind a neo-conservative program all the German and Slavic forces in Austria which were opposed to the Liberal Party except the Social Democrats. The Taaffe government worked assiduously to deprive the German liberals of power in Austria's bureaucracy and representative bodies and of support among the electorate. With Count Taaffe's aid, Czech nationalists in Prague took the last of the city's seats in the Reichsrat and the Bohemian Diet from the German minority and won a Czech majority in the Prague Chambers of Trade and Manufacture.

In a more piecemeal and less consistent manner than that of Bismarck in Germany, Count Taaffe tried to advance a basically authoritarian political project by exploiting the social and economic grievances of farmers, urban lower-middle classes, and workers during the difficult years of the 1880s. Both statemen tried to suppress socialism while offering workers protectionist legislation and welfare programs, but Taaffe was much more of an aristocratic reactionary than Bismarck.[1] Whereas the latter played on the divisions among Germany's liberals and attempted to ally big business and industry with conservative agrarian interests, Taaffe waged a multi-front war on the whole German liberal movement in Austria. As Count Taaffe's policies developed, he tried to use revived corporate ideals to unite aristocrats, farmers, small producers, and shopkeepers of all nationalities in a new mass-based Right against the largely German great industrial, commercial, and financial interests, which were so closely identified with the Liberal Party. Taaffe's alliance with the conservative Poles and Old Czechs prevented his government from winning much support among the German lower middle classes. Yet by the mid-1880s, the lower-middle-class revolt he helped to encourage bore fruit in an anti-liberal German nationalist movement.

The full import of Count Taaffe's pro-Czech and anti-German liberal leanings became apparent only gradually in the Bohemian Lands. In April 1880 Minister of Justice Stremayr ordered that henceforth all officials in Bohemia and Moravia must deal with the citizenry in whichever language, Czech or German, was used by the petitioners. Most Liberal Party spokesmen in solidly German areas sharply attacked the ordinance, but in mixed Prague Franz

---

[1] On the Taaffe government see William A. Jenks, *Austria under the Iron Ring* (Charlottesville, 1965), pp. 158-220; Kolmer, *Parlament und Verfassung*, III, pp. 357-89; and Hans Rosenberg, *Grosse Depression und Bismarckzeit* (Berlin, 1967), pp. 227-52. On the contradictory character of some of Count Taaffe's economic policies, see Heumos, *Agrarische Interessen und Nationale Politik*, pp. 128-38.

Schmeykal was willing to consider some concessions to the Czechs. The leader of the German liberals in the Bohemian capital was more concerned with Count Taaffe's ultimate intentions than with linguistic rights in themselves.[2]

The parliamentary debates over the future of the Charles-Ferdinand University in 1881 increased national hostilities in Prague and offered more indications of the Czechs' new strength. Tension rose in the Bohemian capital in the spring of 1881 as the Taaffe government tried to find a way to meet Czech demands for full Czech-language university education while preserving complete courses of German instruction as well. Political animosities erupted in violence between German students and Czech residents outside Prague on June 28, 1881. Although the initial division of the university's property, facilities, and privileges satisfied neither Czechs nor Germans, the creation of separate Czech and German faculties in the long run gave both sides what they had wanted. German liberal leaders in Bohemia had particular cause for satisfaction, for in the early 1870s Eduard Herbst and Philipp Knoll had themselves proposed the establishment of separate Czech and German universities.[3] Nonetheless, the anti-German responses to the nationalist violence by the Czech aldermen of Prague and the Taaffe government, as well as the ministry's announced aim to extend the suffrage, convinced the leaders of the German Casino that the government and Czech nationalists wanted to deprive the Prague Germans of equal protection under the laws. Some German liberal spokesmen even asserted that the Czechs wished to extinguish the German minority in the Bohemian capital.[4]

The suffrage reform that the Taaffe government enacted in 1882 greatly aided the Czech cause in Bohemia. The law signed by the emperor in October 1882 refashioned the great landowners' curia in the Bohemian Diet to give control to the conservative nobility and to the Czechs and reduced the suffrage requirements for the urban and rural curias in the Reichsrat to five florins in direct tax payments. German liberal politicians were certain that as a result

[2] Heinrich Pollak, *Dreissig Jahre aus dem Leben eines Journalisten*, 3 vols. (Vienna, 1894-98), III, p. 274, quotes Schmeykal as saying that the Germans would happily grant Czech linguistic rights if their demands would stop there.

[3] On the division of the university, see Jenks, *Iron Ring*, pp. 71-89; Skilling, in *Slavonic Review*, XXVII (1949), pp. 430-49; and Goll, *Rozdělení pražské university*.

[4] German responses are quoted in *Bohemia*, 1 July 1881(M), and SÚA Praha PP 1900-1907 V/15/10 Deutscher Verein: 5214/pp, 3 July 1881 police report on the meeting of the Constitutional Society on 2 July.

they would suffer heavy losses in new elections to the Diet and the Reichsrat and that Count Taaffe's "Iron Ring" coalition would then have full control of both bodies.

Czech nationalists and German liberals hotly contested the elections for the Bohemian Diet in June 1883. At the beginning of 1883, the Prague Germans retained only the seats for Malá strana, still heavily Jewish Josefov, and the Prague Chambers of Trade and Manufacture. The growth of the Czech population made the loss of the mandates for Malá strana inevitable. As in previous elections, the Czech parties made special appeals to Prague's Jewish voters in 1883 and argued against their continued identification with the Germans. The Czechs urged conciliation between Czechs and Jews and imputed anti-Semitic sentiments to some of the local German liberal leaders. The Czech overtures did not persuade the more prosperous and better assimilated German Jews, however, and a saying circulated among them that it was "better to be a German arrogant Jew than a Polish dirty Jew or a Czech kept Jew."[5] On the other hand, the less prosperous Jews, some newly enfranchised, were beginning to see the merits of a Czech political alignment. In the end Jewish sentiment was so sharply divided that Prague's chief rabbi had to withhold his customary endorsement of the German liberal candidates. The two pro-Czech candidates in Josefov narrowly defeated the two Jewish candidates of the Liberal Party. In Malá strana the Czechs won nearly two-thirds of the votes cast, thanks to the abstention of a number of German liberal bureaucrats.[6]

By late 1883 the Liberal Party had lost control of both the executive and representative branches of the Bohemian provincial government, and the Prague Germans saw their remaining political power rapidly fading. A conservative Czech coalition won control of the Diet after the 1883 elections, and among all the bodies which represented the Bohemian capital, Germans now retained a majority only in the Prague Chambers of Trade and Manufacture. The Chambers, in turn, provided the German Casino with its last directly controlled seats in the Diet and two of its three remaining seats in the Reichsrat. In January 1882, however, Count Taaffe's Minister of Commerce had requested the Chambers to reform their

[5] *Bohemia*, 29 June 1883(M), reviewed the whole effort to win the Jewish vote. See Stölzl, *Kafkas böses Böhmen*, pp. 48-49, on political trends among Bohemian Jews in the early eighties. Auguste Hauschner, *Familie Lowositz*, pp. 329-30, recounts the contrasting Czech and German appeals to Jewish voters.

[6] The election results were reported in *Bohemia*, 1 July 1883(M).

suffrage to give a greater voice to small business and the handi-crafts—and hence to Czech interests. In January 1884 the Vienna government ordered such a change over German objections.[7] The German members of the Chambers vigorously protested the min-istry's actions, but Czechs won a majority in the next elections for the Prague Chambers and retained control thereafter.[8]

New Czech Offensives in Local Government

Czech-German hostilities in Prague's municipal affairs also entered a new phase in the 1880s. Czech nationalists increasingly used the city government as a forum for the assertion of Czech rights to superiority over Germans in the Bohemian Lands, and almost no Germans remained in the local administration to rebut them. Czechs defeated the last German liberals who held seats on the board of aldermen in the early eighties without resort to suffrage reform. Despite the retention of the restrictive three-class franchise for the municipality, only five German liberals remained among the ninety aldermen in 1882, four of them German Jews from Josefov and the Old Town. In the face of steady defeats, the Ger-man Casino had stopped even running candidates for alderman in most races in the 1870s. Only one German was elected in 1883, and none ran in the November 1884 and January 1885 elections.[9] In 1888 the term expired for the last prewar German alderman in Prague, Dr. Ludwig Bendiener, a director of the Casino's Ger-man Club and a leader in the Prague Jewish community.

Radical Czech nationalists among the aldermen and city coun-cilmen used every opportunity to attack what they considered the Prague Germans' inflated claims to social prestige and to public services. By the early 1880s middle-class politicians in Bohemia generally denied the ability of members of one national group to represent the other fairly, and Prague's Czech city officials made little show of evenhandedness. The considerable autonomy with which the German liberals had earlier endowed municipal govern-

[7] On the evolution of the suffrage for the Chambers, see Gruber, *Handels- und Gewerbekammer*, pp. 189-333.

[8] For typical German responses see Philipp Knoll's articles for the *Münchner All-gemeine Zeitung*, September 1884, repr. in his *Beiträge*, pp. 385-96; and the speech of Otto Forchheimer in SÚA Praha ČM 1889-1900 30/41/3 Deutscher Verein in Prag: 29 June 1884 police report, and PP 1900-1907 V/15/10: NE 5734 pp/965, 29 June 1884.

[9] Election results reported in *Bohemia*, 25 Nov 1884 (M) and 3 Jan 1885(M).

ment in Austria now served Czech nationalists in asserting proprietorship over local administration in Prague, and they used the municipality to conduct a great propaganda effort on behalf of Czech state rights.[10]

As party loyalties changed among the Czech aldermen and city councilmen in the 1880s and 1890s, ethnic conflict increased. In the eighties the number of Young Czechs rose steadily at the Old Czechs' expense, and after the virtual disappearance of the Old Czechs in the mid-nineties the Young Czechs' own radical wing gave birth to more extreme nationalist groups. The latter competed with the mainstream Young Czechs in appeals to the lower-middle-class and laboring elements whom the Old Czechs had neglected, and at times Young Czechs as well as their more radical successors whipped up anti-German feeling to advance their own political fortunes.[11]

In matters of substance, Czech-German contention after 1879 focused mainly on the continuation in Prague of German-language public education and administrative services. The Czech municipal authorities consistently tried to limit expenditures on the German public schools and to gain greater control over the German district school board. The Czech aldermen wanted primarily to prevent Czech children from attending the German schools, but German community leaders viewed the Czech efforts as ultimately intended to close the schools or make them Czech.[12] A speech by Otto Forchheimer, Schmeykal's second in command in the Casino, typified the response of the German liberal elite. In December 1888, Forch-

[10] Cf. Janáček, ed., *Dějiny Prahy*, p. 524. The propaganda effort reached a peak in 1891 with the Bohemian provincial exhibition in Prague as evidenced by the dispatches of the Bohemian Governor Count Franz Thun to Count Taaffe in Arthur Skedl, ed., *Der politische Nachlass des Grafen Eduard Taaffe* (Vienna, Berlin, and Leipzig, 1922), pp. 579-80, 595-97, 626-31.

[11] On Czech politics in the eighties see H. Gordon Skilling, "The Politics of the Czech Eighties," in *The Czech Renascence of the Nineteenth Century*, ed. Brock and Skilling, pp. 254-81; and Říha, ed., *Přehled československých dějin*, II, pp. 621-23, 649-51. On the evolution of the Young Czech movement, see Garver, *The Young Czech Party*, passim, and Winters, in *Slavic Review*, XXVIII, pp. 426-44.

[12] The German position is expressed in Carl Broda, "Die deutschen Volks- und Bürgerschulen in Prag, Vortrag gehalten im Deutschen Verein in Prag, 11 Nov 1885" (Prague, 1886) in SÚA Praha PP 1900-1907 V/15/10 Deutscher Verein; and "Die unverfälschte Wahrheit über die Verhältnisse an den öffentlichen Prager deutschen Volks- und Bürgerschulen" (Appendix to the memorandum, "Den deutschen Schulen ein deutscher Bezirksschulrat!," pamphlet, no date) in SÚA Praha PP 1900-1907 V/7/33: 4044/pp. For a representative Czech view see "Pravda o poměrech německého obecného školství v Praze" (Prague, 1896).

XVI. Czech nationalist assemblage on Wenceslas
      Square for the funeral of Miroslav Tyrš,
      co-founder of *Sokol*, 1884

XVII. The Habsburg authorities—Governor Franz Thun and Provincial
       Military Commander Gen. Grünne inspecting flood damage in Josefov,
       1890

heimer told the Casino's political arm that the Czech authorities' generally shabby treatment of the German schools deprived German citizens of their basic rights and swindled the prosperous German community out of the large sums which it paid in school taxes.[13] Appeals to higher authorities generally blocked the municipal government's attempts to halt German administrative services or meddle with the German educational system. Indeed, the near certainty of action at higher levels to block gross violations of minority rights made many of the aldermen's actions regarding German public services no more than symbolic gestures.

Symbols of group strength, however, assumed ever-greater importance for Austria's competing nationalities in the last decades of the nineteenth century. With the rise of mass politics among both Czechs and Germans in Bohemia, nationalist politicians increasingly resorted to demonstrations of national group strength to rally support. The mayors and many aldermen in the Bohemian capital made every effort to have Prague appear to be a Czech city. They repeatedly pointed to the Germans' numerical decline and constantly referred to "Golden Slavic Prague."

The decision of the aldermen in 1892 to replace Prague's formerly bilingual street signs with exclusively Czech ones particularly incensed the German community. While Czech signs would actually inconvenience few of the German residents, they would reinforce the general impression of Prague as a Czech city with a small, subordinate German minority. Seeing it as a question of group survival as well as pride, leaders of the German community insisted that two equal peoples resided in the city and that it remained the capital for both Czech and German Bohemia. Each step in the symbolic transformation of Prague into a Czech city further encouraged German Bohemia to abandon support of the Prague Germans and the Casino's leadership. Moreover, some German spokesmen in Prague asserted that the actions of the city government helped to further the decline of the German minority by discouraging German immigration and speeding German-Czech assimilation.[14] When the Cisleithanian highest administrative court finally upheld the change in the street signs in 1896, all that the

---

[13] *Bohemia*, 20 Dec 1888(M), and SÚA Praha ČM 1889-1900 30/41/3: 114746pp, 19 Dec 1888 police report on the 18 Dec meeting of the Deutscher Verein.

[14] SÚA Praha Praesidium českého místodržitelství (Presidium of the Bohemian Governor's Office, hereafter PM) 1881-1890, 8/5/15/57: ad Praes 11609/889, police report, 17 Nov 1889, on the speech of Prof. Ferdinand Höhm for the fifth anniversary of the founding of the German Handworkers' Society.

German Casino could do was provide German landlords with German signs to affix to their buildings.

The German Liberal Response: Retreat and Regrouping

In general the responses of the German liberals in Prague to their deteriorating political situation in the eighties and nineties followed in step with the development of German liberal politics throughout Austria, and that evolution passed through four major phases between 1879 and the great crisis of 1897.[15] The first phase, from 1879 to 1885, saw the initial reactions of the Liberal Party to Count Taaffe's conservative, pro-Slavic policies and a general strengthening of German nationalist elements in the party program. The party leaders were fortunate in that they did not have to contend with any significant left-liberal force at this time. On the one hand, Austria's ethnic rivalries enforced a certain amount of unity in German middle-class politics; on the other hand, a nationalistic German liberalism here attracted the radical elements who, were it Germany, might have moved in the direction of more egalitarian politics.[16] In the second half of 1881, the need for a united German front against the Taaffe government brought moderate German liberals together with the existing nationalistic splinter group, the Progressives, in a new United Left Party. The United Left was committed to defending a centralized government and the privileged position of Germans in Austria against the incursions of the federalist conservatives and their Slavic allies. As a response to the Stremayr language ordinances for Bohemia and Moravia, the United Left agitated for legislation to make German the official state language for Cisleithania.[17] Franz Schmeykal and the other

---

[15] On the general evolution of German liberal politics in this era see Charmatz, *Deutsch-österreichische Politik*, pp. 240-43, 299-335; H. Gordon Skilling, *The Czech-German Conflict in Bohemia, 1867-1914* (unpubl. revision of a University of London Ph.D. dissertation, 1940; typescript, Toronto, 1967), Chapters Four to Eleven; and Jenks, *Iron Ring*, passim. On offshoots of the German Liberal movement, see Diethild Harrington-Müller, *Der Fortschrittsklub im Abgeordnetenhaus des österreichischen Reichsrats 1873-1910* (Vienna, Cologne, and Graz, 1972); Paul Molisch, *Geschichte der deutschnationalen Bewegung in Österreich* (Jena, 1926); and Andrew G. Whiteside, *The Socialism of Fools: Georg Ritter von Schönerer and Austrian Pan-Germanism* (Berkeley and Los Angeles, 1975).

[16] John W. Boyer makes this point in "Freud, Marriage, and Late Viennese Liberalism: A Commentary from 1905," *Journal of Modern History*, L (1978), pp. 76-77.

[17] On the question of German as state language, see Jenks, *Iron Ring*, pp. 90-103; and Skilling, *Czech-German Conflict*, Chapter Five, pp. 20-32.

liberal leaders in Prague strongly supported the union of German political forces and a concerted defense of German ethnic interests as they tried to steer a middle course between moderates and radical nationalists. When Schmeykal and his colleagues reorganized the Constitutional Society of Germans in Bohemia in February 1882 and renamed it the German Club in Prague (*Deutscher Verein in Prag*), they signaled a measured shift in the nationalist direction designed to strengthen their position with Bohemian Germans.[18]

In 1882 and 1883 the deputies of the United Left in the Reichsrat as well as the German liberal leaders in Prague had increasing difficulty in maintaining German unity. The suffrage reform of 1882, the Czech victory in the 1883 elections for the Bohemian Diet, and new conservative public school legislation in 1883 all contributed to rising tensions in German liberal ranks. With their sights set on the "little man," radical nationalists increased their demands for a more democratic politics and a commitment to German national solidarity at the expense of the liberals' cherished individualism. The United Left tried to make a show of German unity in the Reichsrat elections of June 1885, but even though they added a number of radicals to their ticket, they still lost fifteen of their former 151 seats in the Chamber of Deputies. In Prague, though, liberal leaders could still mobilize impressive support among German voters when they chose to run candidates: Franz Schmeykal's token candidacy drew 1,803 votes, 24 percent of all ballots cast.[19]

The dissension among liberals over German nationalism grew deeper in the next phase of political development, from the 1885 elections to late 1888. Within months of the Reichsrat elections, the question of "Austrianism" versus German nationalism split the United Left into rival German-Austrian and German parliamentary clubs.[20] In addition to these two groups, three deputies declared themselves followers of Georg von Schönerer's radical Pan-Germanism. The German Casino in Prague remained basically sympathetic to the German-Austrian club and its leader, Ernst von

[18] SÚA Praha PP 1900-07 V/15/10: 1822/pp1452, 15 Feb 1882, Schmeykal to the Prague police, and NE 1822/FS 337, 28 Feb 1882, police report on the 27 Feb meeting of the Deutscher Verein.

[19] On the overall results of the election, see Jenks, *Iron Ring*, pp. 116-19; Kolmer, *Parlament und Verfassung*, IV, pp. 1-5; and Macartney, *The Habsburg Empire*, pp. 614-15. *Bohemia*, 4 and 5 June 1885(M) published the results for Prague.

[20] See Ernst von Plener, *Erinnerungen*, 3 vols. (Stuttgart and Leipzig, 1911-21), II, pp. 190-99; and Skilling, *Czech-German Conflict*, Chapter Ten, pp. 30-35.

Plener, but the liberal leaders in Prague were determined to maintain some unity in Bohemia between their moderate friends and the German nationalists who were gaining strength in the towns of the northern districts. In fact, a mediator's role suited well the widely respected Schmeykal, who was at his best in behind-the-scenes negotiations and quietly inspirational talks.[21] The German Casino even tolerated the formation in Prague in February 1886 of a new German political association, the German-National Club, which included both young lower-middle-class radicals and older respectable liberals who were open to a shift to the nationalist left.[22] Although the German-National Club initially supported the German club in the Reichsrat and drew greater lower-middle-class support than did the Casino, the new group remained within the limits of the broad German liberal consensus which Schmeykal desired. In the meantime, supporters of Count Taaffe were urging a new Economic Party (*Wirtschaftspartei*) on Bohemian Germans to divert loyalties from national issues to protection of economic interests, and the leaders of the German Casino sensed a greater danger in late 1886 and 1887 in the Economic Party than in the German-National Club.[23]

Between late 1886 and autumn 1888, continued pressure from Count Taaffe's coalition gradually persuaded all but the most nationalistic Germans in the Reichsrat to reunite with the moderate German liberals. The collapse of the German club in the lower house paved the way for a new consolidation of German forces. The club split over the question of anti-Semitism in February 1887, and the anti-capitalist, mostly anti-Semitic radicals led by Otto Steinwender and Ernst Bareuther established their own *Deutschnationale Vereinigung* in May 1887.[24] The more moderate members of the German club drifted back to the German-Austrian ranks, and together they formed a new United German Left in autumn 1888. In the meantime in Prague, the most prominent radicals in

[21] For a portrait of Schmeykal's dignified but modest character, see Pollak, *Dreissig Jahre*, II, pp. 78-81. See [Klaar], *Schmeykal*, pp. 44-46, on the efforts to maintain unity among the Bohemian German political forces.

[22] Bylaws and membership lists are included in SÚA Praha ČM 1889-1900 30/41/15: 18283/1199, 8 Feb 1886 "Statuten," 10 May 1886 membership list.

[23] In February 1887 Schmeykal wrote to Ernst von Plener of a German-Austrian Casino founded in Prague in support of the Economic Party by a group of German Jews; Haus-, Hof-, und Stattsarchiv, Vienna (HHStA hereafter), Nachlass Plener, ct. 19, no. 49, Schmeykal to Ernst von Plener, 18 Feb 1887.

[24] See Molisch, *Deutschnationale Bewegung*, pp. 126-28; Skilling, *The Czech-German Conflict*, Chapter Ten, pp. 38-47; and Whiteside, *Socialism of Fools*, pp. 118-21.

the local German-National Club left the board of directors in February 1887, and over the following year the Casino's own political association gradually absorbed most of the other members.[25]

All the German deputies in the Reichsrat except the radical nationalists, democrats, and socialists remained in the United German Left through the next phase of development, from 1888 to 1895. In late 1889 and 1890, Ernst von Plener, Franz Schmeykal, and Josef M. Baernreither represented German liberal interests in negotiations with Count Taaffe and the Old Czechs on national rights in Bohemia.[26] The German liberals in Prague supported the abortive efforts to reach a compromise in hopes of getting the ethnic division of Bohemia's administrative, judicial, and legislative affairs so much desired by Germans in the border areas while still protecting the rights of Germans in the provincial capital. After the fall of the Taaffe government in 1893, the German Left joined Prince Alfred Windischgrätz's coalition of conservatives, liberals, and Poles, but in mid-1895 the controversy over a proposed Slovene *Gymnasium* in the Styrian town of Cilli brought down the ministry and sundered the United German Left.

Dissension erupted again among the German middle-class forces in Austrian politics in 1895. The moderate liberals under Plener had shown some willingness to compromise on national questions in return for a share in the government. Now in revolt against Plener, German liberals from the Bohemian Lands and Styria who demanded a firmer line on national questions formed a new Progressive Party. Still committed to individualist social and economic doctrines, the Progressives drew the support of the German Casino in Prague, but they were only one among several parties which competed for German middle-class and lower-middle-class support in Cisleithania after 1895. Divided among Plener's Free German Union, the Progressive Party, Steinwender's German People's Party, and Schönerer's Pan-Germans, the German middle-class forces confronted the new ministry of the conservative Pole Count Casimir Badeni in 1896-1897 in considerable disarray. In Vienna there was no longer any strong, united German liberal parliamentary force, and in Prague the leaders of the German Casino could

[25] SÚA Praha PP 1888-1892 V/14/7: 1416/pp 1108, 7 Feb 1887, report from the German-National Club on the election of a new board of directors; NE 1213 pp VS 281, 5 Feb 1887, police report on the 4 February meeting; 11317/pp 3825, 2 Nov 1889, deposition by Prof. Josef Bendel for the Smíchov district police.

[26] See Jenks, *Iron Ring*, pp. 239-71; and Skilling, *Czech-German Conflict*, Chapter Four, pp. 25-28; Chapter Six, pp. 14-30.

depend no more on the united support of German political groups in Bohemia or even in their own city.

The Völkisch Movement in the Bohemian Borderlands

German liberals in Prague in the 1880s confronted mostly accustomed antagonists in the clerical-conservative and Czech nationalist forces, but the German liberal groups had to deal with a new and in some ways more problematic challenge in the anti-liberal, radical nationalism which won growing support among Germans in the Bohemian borderlands. The radicals appealed to the grievances of small farmers, urban lower middle classes, and some skilled workers against free-trade economics and deferential politics. The German nationalists blamed the troubles of the German little men on Czech interlopers, international socialists, Jewish swindlers, and their protectors in the corrupt Liberal Party. Schmeykal and the other liberal notables in Prague were accustomed to broad German acceptance of the Liberal Party's policies and leadership in Bohemia. The radicals, on the other hand, wanted to supplant the German liberal political order with a new popular—völkisch—politics which would involve the lower social strata more directly, intervene in the economy to protect small producers, and establish separate governance for Germans and Slavs in Austria. The völkisch movement would substitute a new, more exclusive sense of Germanness based on blood for the old one founded simply on language and conscious identification.[27]

In the mid-1880s small farmers, craft producers, and small businessmen in Bohemia's German border areas eagerly lashed out against the liberal notables. They were suffering the combined effects of agricultural depression and the ongoing mechanization of manufacture, and the liberals offered little relief. Völkisch spokesmen could blame the liberals for rapid industrialization and the emancipation of the Jews. Broad German national solidarity, restrictive laws against the Jews, and political separation of the Czech and German sections of Bohemia had great attraction for the lower middle classes and many workers in the German borderlands. Yet although deeply opposed to the radical nationalists' views, many

---

[27] On the rise of German nationalism in Bohemia and Cisleithania as a whole, see Molisch, *Deutschnationale Bewegung*, pp. 111-34; Skilling, *Czech-German Conflict*, Chapter Three, pp. 19-23, Chapter Ten, pp. 14-47; Andrew G. Whiteside, *Austrian National Socialism before 1918* (The Hague, 1962), pp. 13-20, 51-60; and idem, *Socialism of Fools*, pp. 9-42, 107-40.

liberal leaders like Franz Schmeykal hesitated to break openly with them. Heightened nationalism had too wide an appeal, and the liberals were too interested in maintaining a united German front to face the conservative-Slavic coalition to take such a step until pushed to the limit.

After the 1883 Diet elections, complaints rose in German Bohemia that the German liberal leaders in Prague were not defending German national interests adequately and that the Prague Germans were unworthy of further support. In October 1883 the newspaper in Franz Schmeykal's own home town, Česká lípa, put the question baldly:[28]

> Why should German Bohemia follow Prague? Its own house is not in order. Over the past twenty years they have been driven out of the municipal board of aldermen. . . . Last summer they lost the last Diet mandate for their own city. . . . Residents of German Bohemia will not forget that overnight Prague's Jewish quarter was half "Wenzelized" but for some large industrialists and lost to the Germans.

Hostility to the liberals in Prague made it difficult to raise funds in the border areas in 1883 and 1884 for the new German theatre which the leaders of the Casino proposed for the provincial capital. This weak support contrasted sharply with the great outpouring for the Czech National Theatre throughout the Bohemian Lands in the sixties and seventies, and in the end the lavish New German Theatre was built mostly with the contributions of a few aristocrats and industrialists as well as the German population of Prague itself (see Plate XIII).[29]

The Casino tried to maintain ties with moderate elements in the border areas and sent speakers to the German Bohemian towns. As before, prominent members of the Casino continued to stand

---

[28] Reprinted from the *Böhmisch-Leipaer Zeitung* in *Politik*, 30 Oct 1883. Attacks on the German Casino by radical nationalists in German Bohemia were also reported in *Národní listy*, 31 Oct 1883(M), and dispatches from the Bohemian Governor's Office to the Ministry of Interior, 25 and 29 Oct 1883, in SÚA Praha PMT 1883 178/83 and 180/83.

[29] Comments on the difficulties in raising funds were included in a dispatch from the Bohemian Governor to the Ministry of Interior, 8666pp, 25 Oct 1883, in SÚA Praha PMT 1883 178/83. On the building of the Czech National Theatre, see Stanley B. Kimball, *Czech Nationalism: A Study of the National Theater Movement 1845-1883* (Urbana, 1964). On the New German Theatre, see Rosenheim, *Geschichte der deutschen Bühnen*, pp. 71-79.

for election to the Diet and the Reichsrat in German Bohemia.[30] After the collapse of the United Left in 1885, however, moderate liberals faced increasingly powerful nationalist opposition in German Bohemia. Schmeykal still tried to conciliate the more tractable nationalists in the late eighties, but the liberals' commitment to the existing constitutional structure in Austria and to a civic life that rejected any religious or racial discrimination obliged them to repudiate all Pan-German and anti-Semitic tendencies.[31]

Radical German nationalists and the leaders of the Casino alike recognized that the revolt against the liberal notables went beyond matters of political power and influence and impinged on the very survival of the German minority in the Bohemian capital. As the newspaper in Česká lípa pointed out in 1883, the Prague Germans depended on German Bohemia for more than just political support if they were to escape continuing decline:[32]

> The haughtiness with which some of the Prague Germans view the artisan class has pushed the latter into the Czech ranks, so that today, as the well-informed point out, there is not even a single German tailor. . . . The Prague Germans are lacking the broad and firm basis of a small-craft *Mittelstand*. Therefore, they must rely upon the German towns and rural districts or they will be lost.

Although most leaders of the organized German community in Prague clung to their liberal ideology after 1879, some of them, at least, were ready by 1883 to make the same diagnosis of their political and demographic problems.

The Liberal Perspective on the New Era in Prague

The elite of the German community in Prague retained its libertarian, essentially anti-democratic beliefs through the eighties and nineties despite the growing strength of the conservative, Czech,

[30] In 1878 six liberal lawyers from Prague won seats in the Bohemian Diet in German districts according to *Bohemia*, 21 Sept 1878(M). In 1895 after Schmeykal's death, three Pragers still won seats in German Bohemia, *Zprávy zemského statistického uřádu království českého*, I, 1. sešit, pp. 20-21.

[31] Statements by liberal leaders on this issue are included in Knoll, *Beiträge*, p. 189, and in speeches of Schmeykal quoted in SÚA Praha PMT 1886 22/86, 3469, Police Director Stejskal to Governor Kraus, 26 March 1886, and *Bohemia*, 25 April 1887 (M).

[32] Quoted in *Politik*, 30 Oct 1883.

and German nationalist adversaries. Most members of the German Casino still saw the incomplete work of establishing constitutional government in Austria, destroying all corporate privilege, and creating all the conditions needed for free economic development as their only proper political agenda. All persons, whatever their nationality, must enjoy equality in the marketplace and in the eyes of the state, but these moderate liberals still believed at heart that the formation of public policy should be entrusted to an elite, not of birth but of individual achievement.[33] The liberals only hardened their middle-class social conservatism in the face of lower-strata demands for a more egalitarian social and political order.

Under attack, the German liberal notables in Prague strengthened their belief that the Germans, particularly the middle-class elements, had played a special civilizing role in the history of Prague, the Bohemian Lands, and Austria as a whole. Further progress, they thought, depended on maintaining a centralized Austrian state led by the Germans; and Franz Schmeykal joined in the demands for recognition of German as the state language.[34] Whatever the accomplishments of the Czechs and their national movement, many of the German middle class in Prague as well as the other mixed cities of the Bohemian Lands continued to view Czechs as socially and economically inferior and politically immature. Writing more in sympathy for the Czechs than in derogation, Rainer Maria Rilke, who was born in Prague in 1875, caught the essence of the German burghers' outlook. For him the development of the Czech nation was "the story of the child who grows up among adults."[35]

While the leaders of the German community in Prague held on to their liberal ideals, Count Taaffe's policies, the electoral defeats, and the first anti-liberal stirrings in German Bohemia convinced some by late winter 1883 of the need for new defensive measures. In Vienna in January 1883 the prominent left-liberal Professor Victor von Kraus warned of the dangers to the Prague Germans

---

[33] See Charmatz, *Deutsch-österreichische Politik*, pp. 43-53; and Boyer, in *Journal of Modern History*, L, pp. 73-76. For expressions of these views by Prague spokesmen see Knoll, *Beiträge*, passim, and [Klaar], *Schmeykal*, pp. 100-19, passim.

[34] See Jenks, *Iron Ring*, pp. 95-96.

[35] Rilke has a Czech character utter this sentiment in "Die Geschwister," in *Erzählungen und Skizzen aus der frühzeit* (Leipzig, 1930), pp. 224-25. See also Rilke's other Prague story, "König Bohusch," *ibid.*, pp. 142-43. Julius Lippert, "Prag, die deutsche Stadt," *Deutsche Arbeit*, VIII (1908-09), pp. 332-48, makes the conventional assertions of the superiority of German contributions to Prague's economy and cultural life.

posed by the recent Czech political advances.[36] In March Professor Philipp Knoll, at a meeting of the German Club in Prague, gave a seminal address on the Germans' situation.[37] Knoll argued that the rising Czech-German conflicts were causing a new, stronger German group identity to supplant supranational Austrian loyalties among Germans in Prague and throughout Bohemia. Still, all German organizations in the provincial capital must work vigorously to develop national consciousness among all German residents in the city and unite them into a single social and political entity. The Germans' daily activities were too deeply enmeshed with the Czechs to permit them to seal off their lives and ignore their Czech neighbors, but they must cultivate their own group identity and insist on their linguistic rights in all areas of public life. A defeatist attitude would be suicidal; the Germans should enter every election, try to win some sort of proportional representation, and use their own organizations to defend their interests wherever they lacked direct access to governmental bodies.

Knoll led the way among German liberals in the Bohemian capital in insisting that the survival of the German minority depended on the cultivation of a broader, more diverse popular base. The German leaders in Prague would do well to follow the examples of the Czech movement, Count Taaffe, and the German radicals and seek greater support among lower-strata Germans in Prague and the Bohemian borderlands. If the middle-class elements in the organized German community believed in their own liberal doctrines of social mobility based on individual achievement, they must seek a steady flow of recruits from below, ". . . for even the prosperous bourgeoisie will decline if they lack the broader popular strata from which they can rejuvenate themselves by adding those who had to struggle up and therefore have started out on their life tasks with greater energy and devotion."[38] If the Prague community was without a significant artisanal and laboring segment, one must be created. Knoll urged the Prague Germans to maintain close, cordial relations with German Bohemia, recruit more lower-strata Germans into the city, and engage artisans and workers in German

[36] Professor Dr. Victor von Kraus, "Über die politische Lage der Deutschen in Böhmen," lecture to the Deutscher Verein, Vienna, 26 Jan 1883 (pamphlet, Vienna, 1883) in HHStA Nachlass Plener, ct. 29. On Kraus and the Deutscher Verein in Vienna, see William J. McGrath, *Dionysian Art and Populist Politics in Austria* (New Haven, 1974), pp. 36, 170-72, 199-202.

[37] Knoll, *Beiträge*, pp. 162-96.　　　　[38] *Ibid.*, p. 191.

collective life in the city. In the remaining years of the 1880s and 1890s, the German liberal community in Prague worked to find ways of carrying out Knoll's program.

Ethnic Defense and the Liberal Associational Network

Inevitably, the burden of the German liberals' new efforts at ethnic defense fell to the network of German voluntary associations. If the German minority could no longer elect representatives to the municipal board of aldermen or the Bohemian Diet and if the local authorities refused to provide sufficient German-language public education, the German associations would lobby with the higher authorities or provide services on their own. Friedrich Freiherr von Wieser, the brilliant economist at the German University of Prague, aptly described the new activities and substitutive political functions which the associations took on in the era of ethnic defense:[39]

> We are poor people who must cook with the water of associational resolutions. . . . With our suffrage right as good as lost and excluded from the great political dealings, we have grabbed on to the next best thing and in an era of rhetoric have worked quietly and assiduously at home. The German associations in Prague are thus the creations of national self-government, one complementing the functions of the next, so numerous and united that we can say that we have founded *a smaller German city within the larger city by means of our associations.* [Emphasis added]

Like other minority groups in Austria, the Prague Germans had to adapt their community life to new defensive functions in the era of increased ethnic conflict after 1879. As a strongly middle-class group with liberal traditions, however, the organized German community here faced the critical question of whether ethnic defense would serve the preservation of liberal politics and the existing social hierarchy or bring with it the little man's democracy preached by radical nationalists.

German associational activity in Prague expanded greatly after 1879 in response to the new political situation. As in other centers of ethnic conflict, existing organizations undertook new defensive functions, and numerous new associations arose devoted to ethnic

[39] *Bohemia*, 16 Nov 1902(M), from a speech given on the fortieth anniversary of the German Casino. For a brief appreciation of Wieser and his contribution to Austrian economic theory, see William M. Johnston, *The Austrian Mind* (Berkeley, 1972), pp. 81-82, 85-86.

defense. In 1890 German groups accounted for 130 of the some 700 independent voluntary associations registered in the Prague police district, a substantial number for a German population of less than 40,000.[40]

Schmeykal, Knoll, Forchheimer, and the other leaders of the Casino were proud indeed of the strength of German associational life in Prague.[41] In 1886 Franz Schmeykal urged critics in German Bohemia to accept the vigor of the associations as tangible proof of the Prague Germans' determination to defend their national interests, for, he asserted, "there is no German district, no German town in Bohemia which has such a multi-faceted, well-developed associational life as among the Prague Germans."[42] The new threats to the community, however, made the dominant middle-class elements more conscious than ever of their social identity as a declining middle- and upper-strata elite. Ostensibly, the associational network undertook new activities to assist Germans of all social strata, but the middle-class notables who remained in charge did their utmost to make ethnic defense serve the continuation of the liberal political and social order in the community.

Specialized organizations for ethnic defense, *Schutzvereine*, such as the local chapters of the German School Society (*Deutscher Schulverein*) and the German League for the Bohemian Woods (*Deutscher Böhmerwaldbund*), were the most obvious expressions of the Prague Germans' new defensive posture. In 1880 the Viennese group of young, nationalistic left liberals, which included Engelbert Pernerstorfer, Heinrich Friedjung, Viktor Adler, Max Menger, Otto Steinwender, and Georg von Schönerer, originated the idea of a voluntary organization to finance and operate German schools in districts which lacked sufficient numbers of German pupils for state-supported German instruction. The German School Society quickly won the endorsement of moderate liberals and radicals,

[40] Statistische Central-Commission, *Handbuch der Vereine in den im Reichsrate vertretenen Königreichen und Ländern, 1890* (Vienna, 1829), pp. 200-16. The numbers reported here are approximate because the handbook omits the multiple local chapters of the great Czech and German associations for ethnic defense. Otherwise all voluntary associations are included except cooperatives and corporations directly engaged in production, consumption, and finance.

[41] See, for example, Forchheimer, "Die öffentliche Lage der Deutschen in Prag," pp. 4-5.

[42] Quoted in [Klaar], *Schmeykal*, p. 89. Robert Weltsch commented on the Prague liberals' special need to prove their fidelity to the German national cause to German Bohemia in "Max Brod and His Age," *Leo Baeck Memorial Lecture 13* (New York, 1970), p. 7.

and with the sponsorship of Liberal Party leaders drew broad support among middle-class and lower-middle-class Germans. At the high point in 1887, the myriad local chapters in Cisleithania had 120,000 members.[43]

Liberals and radical nationalists competed for control of the German School Society throughout Austria in the eighties and nineties. Moderate liberals dominated the Society in the Habsburg Hereditary Lands and the Bohemian Lands in the early years, and in 1885 and 1886 they defeated the attempts of Schönerer and his followers to win acceptance of extreme nationalist and anti-Semitic principles. *Völkisch* elements persisted in many local chapters, however, and won approval at the Society's general conference in 1899 for the formation of their own anti-Semitic units.[44]

The liberal notables in Prague succeeded in harnessing the local chapters of the School Society and, indeed, most of the new defense groups for the preservation of their own social and political position. The Casino had been operating German kindergartens, elementary school classes, and an adult school through the German School-Penny Association (*Deutscher Schulpfennig-Verein*) since 1872, and in September 1881 Franz Schmeykal founded a general Prague chapter of the German School Society. Leading members of the Casino directed the group throughout the pre-1914 era and established a women's chapter in the inner city and additional units in Karlín, Malá strana, Smíchov, Vinohrady, Libeň, and Vršovice.[45] While from the late eighties on, contention between liberals and nationalists wracked many local chapters in Lower Austria, Styria, Moravia, and northern Bohemia, the Prague units remained staunchly liberal and continued to accept Jewish membership and Jewish pupils in their schools.[46]

[43] Franz Perko, "Die Tätigkeit des deutschen Schulvereines in Böhmen," *Deutsche Arbeit*, III (1904), p. 388. On the history of the German School Society in Austria, see also August von Wotawa, *Der Deutsche Schulverein 1880-1905* (Vienna, 1905); McGrath, *Dionysian Art*, pp. 167-70; Molisch, *Deutschnationale Bewegung*, pp. 135-39; and for the Bohemian Lands, Jiří Kořalka, *Všeněmecký svaz a česká otázka koncem 19. století*, Rozpravy Československé akademie věd Řada společenských věd, LXXIII, sešit 12 (Prague, 1963), pp. 16-20.

[44] See Wotawa, *Schulverein*, pp. 23-28; Eduard Pichl, *Georg Schönerer*, 6 vols. in 3 (Berlin, 1938), II, p. 271ff.; and Whiteside, *Socialism of Fools*, pp. 124-25, 291.

[45] SÚA Praha PP 1908-1915 V/40/13 Deutscher Schulpfennig-Verein: bylaws, lists of officers, members, and contributors, 1872-1915; PP 1908-1915 V/40/1-2, ct. II/2790 Deutscher Schulverein: bylaws, lists of officers and contributors, 1882-1915.

[46] Jewish participation in the local chapters of the School Society drew sharp attacks from the *völkisch* groups in Prague in the 1890s as, for example, in *Der Deutsche Volksbote* (Prague), 16 Jan 1891.

The German School Society functioned as an extension of the liberal associational network in Prague. Nominally, the Prague chapters were engaged in raising funds to support the general Austrian organization and the operation of their own German primary schools in Holešovice, Libeň, and Vršovice. The names of the directors and contributors suggest that the central Prague chapters drew their most active supporters from the same strata as the Casino, which provided meeting space.[47] The units in the outlying industrial districts functioned more to link German white-collar employees, managers, and skilled workers with liberal industrialists, merchants, and professionals; and the chapters here served general German social life in addition to supporting the schools. In Karlín and Libeň respected members of the German *Bürgertum* generally presided over the local chapters while the other directors were mostly lower middle class. Here the School Society received funds from wealthy individuals and pro-German banks, as might be expected, and also from some of the great industrial firms, which, whatever their politics, were willing to support German elementary schools for children of their German employees.[48]

The German liberal leadership in Bohemia had tight control over the German League for the Bohemian Woods from its inception in 1884. Schmeykal, Eduard Herbst, and Philipp Knoll hoped that an organization for the assistance of threatened German settlements on the ethnic frontier would win broad popular support, particularly among the lower middle classes.[49] The three chapters in Prague did bring together various middle-class and lower-middle-class elements in the eighties and nineties, and the Casino gave them generous support as well as direction.[50]

From the perspective of the evolution of urban public life, the rise of German as well as Czech organizations for ethnic defense

[47] SÚA Praha PP 1908-1915 V/40/1-2 includes extensive reports of meetings and lists of officers but hardly any membership lists.

[48] SÚA Praha PP 1908-1915 V/40/1-2: Fasc. II, Ortsgruppe Libeň, "Verzeichnis der subskrierenden Firmen 1908, 1909," and a request for police approval for the collection of funds, 20576/pr, 3 Oct 1913.

[49] AHMP fond spolků: Deutscher Schulpfennig-Verein, broadsheet from the Deutscher Böhmerwaldbund, Ortsgruppe Prag, February 1885. See Kořalka, *Všeněmecký svaz*, pp. 14-17, on the general significance of the League and other similar groups.

[50] AHMP fond spolků: spolkový katastr, protokoly XXII-17, XXII-23, XXII-88; and Deutsches Haus, annual reports of the directors.

[51] AHMP fond spolků: Deutsches Haus, "Bericht der Direktion des Kasino, 18 Jan 1905."

in the Bohemian Lands represented only one aspect of the increasing specialization of voluntary associations throughout Central Europe in the late nineteenth century. If middle-class notables wished to retain political power locally, they had to extend their webs of deference and control to all new organizations. In Prague the German Casino expanded the services it provided for more specialized German groups as a response to the growth of associational activity. Even more than before, the Casino functioned as the physical center of German community life. In 1903-1904, for instance, other organizations used the Casino's facilities for more than 500 gatherings.[51] To attend meetings and soirées at the Casino, eat in its restaurant, or merely sit in the well-appointed reading and game rooms gave German residents in Prague a concrete sense of belonging to the still proud German minority; and many naturally continued to look to the doyens of the Casino for leadership.

Increased ethnic conflict and the additions to the associational network after 1879 resulted, in fact, in a strengthening of the Casino's hold on German public life in Prague. The tendency of nearly all German associations to have leaders who were prominent members of the Casino intensified after 1879 until the split between local liberal and *völkisch* elements in 1888, and it continued thereafter in the liberal groups.[52] The Casino's control over the leadership of the other groups was itself both a contributing cause and consequence of the survival of the liberals' deferential order.[53] Some individuals, of course, could use service in the smaller special-purpose groups to advance their status in the German community at large, but more typically leaders of the specialized associations held those positions because of their prior status in the Casino, the German Club, or one of the larger German professional associations. As a result, the leadership of the liberal associations displayed a remarkable continuity and homogeneity in the 1880s and 1890s.

A few examples can illustrate the durability of the liberal notables who led German community life in Prague. Most of the directors of the Casino and German Club in the eighties and nineties meas-

[52] See Chapter Five for discussion of the split between liberal and *völkisch* groups.
[53] Cf. the comments on the survival of liberal deferential politics in municipal government in Germany in Helmut Croon, "Das Vordringen der politischen Parteien im Bereich der kommunalen Selbstverwaltung," in Croon et al., *Kommunale Selbstverwaltung im Zeitalter der Industrialisierung* (Stuttgart, Berlin, Cologne, and Mainz, 1971), pp. 17-29, 36; and James J. Sheehan, "Liberalism and the City in Nineteenth-century Germany," *Past and Present*, n. 51 (1971), pp. 116-37.

ured their service in decades rather than in years.[54] Franz Schmeykal remained as president of the Casino and the German Club until
his death in 1894. The commodities trader Otto Forchheimer succeeded him in both positions, serving the political group until 1903
and the Casino until his death in 1914. Karl Ritter von Wolf-Zdekauer, head of the Zdekauer banking house and president of the
Böhmische Escomptebank for a time, served on the board of the Casino
from 1870 to 1914, the German Theatre Society from its inception
in 1883, and the German Municipal Affairs Association in the
1890s. Dr. Karl Klemens Claudi, a lawyer and long-time director
of the *Böhmische Sparkasse/Česká spořitelna*, was on the board of the
Casino for almost as long as Zdekauer. Most of the leaders of the
School-Penny Association and the general Prague chapter of the
German School Society showed similar longevity.

The old liberal elite retained such a strong grip on German
community life in Prague during the eighties and nineties that new
men found it difficult to enter the leadership. Individuals such as
Karl Broda, a *Realschule* professor, and Ferdinand Höhm, a professor at the German Girls' Lyceum, had to serve long apprentice-
ships as officers of special-purpose groups before winning distinction in the Casino itself or the German Club. This resulted in part
from simple generational patterns, but it also stemmed from a
conservatism that was probably typical in the leadership of a declining and defensive middle-class minority.

Mobility into the liberal elite increased in the middle and late
1890s as German public life in Austria entered a new period of
crisis and the leaders who first came to the fore in Prague in the
sixties and seventies began to die or retire. The change was apparent in the rapid election of the aggressive thirty-two-year-old
Jewish lawyer Josef Eckstein to the board of the German Club after
he roundly criticized the group for general lethargy in the spring
of 1898.[55]

The German liberal elite had great success in maintaining control
of German associational life in Prague after 1879 as the number

[54] See Appendix II, Tables 9-10, for lists of the directors of the Casino and German
Club taken at intervals between 1870 and 1914, based on the complete lists of
officers and directors in SÚA Praha PP and AHMP fond spolků: spolkový katastr
and Deutsches Haus, papers of the association.

[55] SÚA Praha PP 1908-1915 V/15/61 Deutscher Verein: Ad Z 5278/pp, 19 March
1898 police report on the 17 March meeting of the German Club; 7513/pp, police
report on the meeting of 19 April 1898.

of groups increased and as they took up activities for ethnic defense. The leadership worked to incorporate the new organizations and functions into the fabric of German public life without altering the existing modes of social and political control. In fact, they had a relatively easy task with most ethnic defense groups and other special-purpose organizations, but it proved much more difficult to renovate local political action itself without altering the deferential order.

Liberal Community Politics in the Era of Ethnic Defense

The German liberal leaders in Prague tried to win increased local support for political activity in the eighties and nineties, but they would not open up the formation of policy and selection of candidates to the electorate or even to members of their political associations. In imperial affairs they, like moderate liberal leaders elsewhere, generally resisted expansion of the suffrage and basic changes in the constitutional structure; at the grass-roots level they tried to deal with new conservative, radical nationalist, and socialist opposition without changing their basic modes of decision-making.[56] For German liberals in Prague, defense of the German community before 1900 meant defense of deferential politics in principles and practice.

The political arm of the Casino, the Geman Club, did increase its membership and met more regularly after the reorganization in late 1881 and early 1882. The membership rose from 115 in 1881 to 426 in early 1888, but the latter figure still represented less than one-quarter of the 1,800 five-florin voters who cast ballots for Franz Schmeykal in the 1885 Reichsrat election.[57] Moreover, despite

---

[56] The literature on grass-roots organization of Austria's German liberals is generally thin, but useful perspectives can be found in John W. Boyer, "Church, Economy and Society in *fin de siècle* Austria: The origins of the Christian Social Movement, 1875-1897" (unpubl. Ph.D. thesis, University of Chicago, 1975); Felix Czeike, *Liberale, christlichsoziale und sozialdemokratische Kommunalpolitik (1861-1934)* (Vienna, 1962), pp. 14-26, 30-60; and William H. Hubbard, "Politics and Society in the Central European City: Graz, Austria, 1861-1918," *Canadian Journal of History*, V (1970), pp. 25-47.

[57] Membership totals derive from SÚA Praha PP 1900-1907 V/15/10 Deutscher Verein: NE 1822pp/LS 337, 18 Feb 1882 police report on the meeting of 27 February, and ČM 1889-1900 30/41/3 Deutscher Verein in Prag: "Namens-Verzeichnis der Mitglieder des Deutschen Vereines in Prag nach dem Stande mit Ende Feber 1888." Election results were published in *Bohemia*, 4 and 5 June 1885(M). In the three Prague constituencies the Old Czechs won 5,456 votes, Schmeykal 1,803, and the Young Czechs and Czech independents 248.

the increase, the membership of the German Club remained more exclusive in socioeconomic terms than that of the Casino itself. In 1888 individuals in the middle- and upper-middle-class strata comprised 83 percent of the German Club's members, compared to 77 percent of the Casino's members at the beginning of the decade.[58]

The German Club met monthly after 1882, but its gatherings did not offer the members an opportunity for open debate on all major issues or for real participation in the formulation of policy. Perpetuation of the closed politics of deference drew criticism from within the German liberal community as well as from outside, and the critiques occasionally captured both the essence of the liberal political system and the features that were most problematic in the new era. At a meeting of the German Club in February 1884, for instance, from which Franz Schmeykal was absent, the journalist Heinrich Teweles listed the organization's faults:[59]

> The topics for the programs are never timely. Only after a question has been discussed at length elsewhere and all the national associations in German Bohemia have gone ahead with resolutions does the German Club in Prague get permission to express itself on the issue as well. But beyond these questions, there are a great number of issues which have not been raised at all. . . . The German population which is supposed to be assembled in this hall but which is not here is told nothing of what goes on and knows nothing of the leaders' motives.

Teweles blamed some of the disaffection in German Bohemia on these shortcomings and asked that in the future the leaders avoid long speeches and allow more free discussion. Pointedly, he proposed that the directors distribute speaking duties more widely so that speakers "not all be drawn from one tiny circle."

Complaints like those of Teweles had little effect on the conduct of politics in the liberal community until after the fall of the Taaffe government in late 1893 and the death of Schmeykal in 1894. Thereafter meetings of the German Club saw timelier and more open discussions than before on a wide range of issues. The change,

---

[58] Membership list for the German Club in 1888 as in n. 56. Data on the Casino derive from AHMP fond spolků, Deutsches Haus: "Mitglieder-Verzeichnis des Vereines des Deutschen Casino, 1879-80." The membership of the Casino will be examined further below.

[59] SÚA Praha PP 1906-1907 V/15/10: leaflet, "Aus dem Deutschen Vereine in Prag, 15 Februar 1884," including minutes of the meeting on 29 Jan 1884. Dr. Franz Wien made similar criticisms of the German Club at the first meeting after Schmeykal's death in 1894, as reported in *Prager Tagblatt*, 15 Nov 1894(M).

however, reflected a weakening of discipline as much as any desire of the leaders for broader participation in the formation of policy. In April 1896, for instance, when the German Club took up the proposal of Minister-President Badeni for a new curia in the Reichsrat to be based on universal manhood suffrage, the principal speaker began with sharp criticism of the hostility to universal suffrage of many "musty bookworms" among the German liberals.[60] While insisting that German liberals must have a truly national, popularly based party, he went on to condemn the ministry's proposal for mixing equal suffrage with interest-group representation by retaining the curial system. The other members present roundly attacked the whole treatment of the issues by the German liberal deputies, but at the end of the discussion they accepted the resolution prepared by the local leadership which rejected the Badeni initiative.

Although the German liberals in Prague did not change their modes of decision-making, they did augment their local political organization in the early nineties. The Casino sponsored the founding of the German Political Association in Vinohrady in 1890 and the German Municipal Affairs Association in 1893 to meet the growth of Prague's suburbs and the increased need for defense of German interests in local government. By the early eighties the German community in the inner city had absorbed much of the formerly autonomous German group life of Smíchov and Karlín, but the rapid, large-scale development of new middle-class and lower-middle-class neighborhoods in Vinohrady thereafter created a significant new concentration of German residents there.[61] The lawyer Adalbert Werunsky, a veteran liberal deputy in the Bohemian Diet, presided over the creation of a new German liberal political association in October 1890 to rally the Germans of Vinohrady and deal with the local authorities in their name.[62]

In general character the German Association in Vinohrady strongly resembled the German Club. The directors and members of the Vinohrady group, in fact, included many who were also

[60] SÚA Praha PP 1908-1915 V/15/61: 5785pp, 16 April 1896, police report on the meeting of 15 April.

[61] See Table 3/1. In 1890 Vinohrady with 4,250 German citizen residents had the highest number of any of the inner suburbs and the highest relative concentration, 12.5%.

[62] SÚA Praha PP 1900-1907 V/15/25 Deutscher politischer Verein in kgl. Weinberge: 10609/pp 7280, 13 Oct 1890, police report on the organizational meeting on 12 Oct 1890.

active in the Casino or German Club. The new group reflected its local constituency in counting more engineers, commercial employees, and railroad personnel among its members than were in the German Club: in 1891 only 65 percent of the 391 members in the Vinohrady association fell in the middle and upper-middle-class strata which comprised over 80 percent of the German Club.[63] The presence of more lower-middle-class elements in the Vinohrady group and the relatively modest locale of its meetings in a large restaurant occasionally even attracted German workers as visitors.[64]

A new, younger group of German liberal leaders which began to emerge in Prague in the mid-1890s organized the German Municipal Affairs Association in October 1893 in a belated move toward a more activist approach to problems of local government. Hitherto the German Club and the German Association in Vinohrady had relied primarily on parliamentary interpellations by German liberal deputies and on appeals to the higher executive authorities in dealing with local questions. Yet increasing dissatisfaction among Prague Germans with the blatant Czech nationalism of the local officials and specific grievances over the delivery of public services in German led to calls for better organized, locally based lobbying on municipal questions and new efforts to provide services denied by the local authorities.

Although the founders of the Municipal Affairs Association all had good standing in the German Casino, men such as Professor Adolf Bachmann, Dr. Emil Lingg, and Professor Emil Pfersche belonged mostly to a younger and more popularly oriented generation of leaders than that of Schmeykal, Forchheimer, and Knoll. The new group quickly established special sections for schools, public sanitation, technical affairs, poor relief, and urban problems, although many of its proposed activities overlapped with those of the Casino and the German liberal delegations in the Diet and

[63] SÚA Praha PP 1900-1907 V/15/25: 4756/pp 3393, "Verzeichnis der Mitglieder am Ende 1891 des Deutschen politischen Vereins in der Stadt kgl. Weinberge." The largest occupational groups among the 391 members were lawyers with 11.7%, businessmen (16.5%), managers and employees (12.7%) bank officers (9.3%), and railroad employees (7.9%). The Jewish membership was probably as high as in the German Club, but an exact count is not possible without the tax registries of the Jewish Religious Community in Vinohrady.

[64] Such instances are reported in *Bohemia*, 8 May 1890 (M), and SÚA Praha 1900-1907 V/15/25 Deutscher politischer Verein in kgl. Weinberge: 9647, 22 April 1894 police report on the meeting of 21 April, and ad N 1837pp VL 223, 31 Jan 1897 police report on the meeting of 30 January.

Reichsrat.[65] The group's activism and popular orientation collided with the old liberals' habits of quiet, private negotiation in early 1894 when the Municipal Affairs Association proposed an ambitious program to combat the imposition of the Czech street signs. Franz Schmeykal informed the directors in February 1894 that he was already engaged in private discussions in the Diet and Provincial Committee whose success would obviate most of the proposed program, and he forced the tabling of everything but a proposal to sponsor voluntary posting of German or German-Czech signs on German buildings.[66] With the death of Schmeykal later in the year, however, and the gradual retirement of other leaders of his generation, the Municipal Affairs Association was able to gain control over various charitable and educational activities. Community interest in such affairs was apparent in the Association's large membership: at the end of 1896 the group had 1,100 members, apparently drawn from much the same social strata as the Casino's members.[67]

Through the mid-1890s German liberal notables in Prague succeeded in preserving their individualist ideology and deferential politics with little change. They adapted their local political organizations to defend their own power as well as German ethnic interests against the new dangers, and as a consequence the liberal ordering of German community life actually reached its peak only after 1879. The local leadership accomplished this, however, largely because they dealt with a community which retained a predominantly middle-class and lower-middle-class composition and a relatively stable social hierarchy based on property and education.

The Survival of German Middle-Class Society, 1879-1897

The patterns of participation in the liberal associational network between 1879 and 1897 show clearly the survival of the social structure first established in the sixties and seventies. Individuals might participate in German collective life in various ways, and each mode

[65] SÚA Praha PP 1900-1907 V/7/33 Deutscher Verein für städtische Angelegenheiten in Prag: 16237/pp 11932, 3 Nov 1893, police report on the organizational meeting on 30 October; 15517/pp 11367, first list of officers. On Adolf Bachmann see the biography by his grandson, Harald Bachmann, *Adolf Bachmann: Ein österreichischer Historiker und Politiker* (Munich, 1962).

[66] SÚA Praha PP 1900-1907 V/7/33: NZ 5141pp, police report on the meeting of the directors of the German Municipal Affairs Association on 28 Feb 1894.

[67] SÚA Praha PP 1900-1907 V/7/33: 5099pp, 17 March 1898 police report on the meeting of the Municipal Affairs Association on 14 March.

of involvement was subject to its own social criteria. Doubtlessly, many German residents hardly ever joined in any manner in associational activities but still considered themselves part of the German minority. Others may have attended meetings and cultural activities and occasionally contributed funds or joined organizations but still left few traces of their presence. Still others belonged to one or several of the associations on a continuing basis. All participation in group life was contingent on at least some social scrutiny, but the last and highest degree of involvement was generally subject to the most rigorous screening. Membership and honors in the associations depended variously on an individual's socioeconomic position, family connections, friendships, and the exclusivity of the groups in question. Naturally, formal memberships and contributions are the best documented modes of participation, but they demonstrate well the persistence into the nineties of the status distinctions first defined three decades earlier.

In the mature associational network of the eighties and nineties, organizations which had the broadest social and political functions tended also to have the most clearly articulated social criteria for membership. These groups included general-purpose organizations such as the German Casino, the German Merchants' Club, and the German Handworkers' Society, and political groups such as the German Club and the German Political Association in Vinohrady. The liberals' special-purpose organizations generally had less clearly defined criteria and often recruited broader, more varied, memberships. The German Theatre Society may have had standards as high as the Casino, but other specialized groups like the Gymnastics Society and the suburban chapters of the School Society offered those who could not qualify for the Casino or the Political Association in Vinohrady what amounted to a second-class membership in the liberal community. Since most special-purpose groups left only scanty documentation of their membership, one must try to generalize about the whole social structure from the general-purpose groups and the few specialized organizations which left any data.

Although liberal spokesmen in the eighties and nineties often spoke of opening up local German public life to Germans in all social strata, the memberships of the leading organizations remained as exclusively middle class as before. The Casino and the German Club maintained that exclusivity, however, by indirect, gentlemanly means. An applicant for membership had to be sponsored by a member and win approval from a majority of the association's directors. While the leading groups almost never made an explicit determination of an applicant's social standing, they almost never had occasion to reject anyone. The requirement that new members be sponsored by old apparently guaranteed that applicants already moved in the proper social circles.[68]

The German Casino had a formidable membership throughout the period. The total rose slightly from 1,200 in 1879 to 1,282 in 1898-1899.[69] Effective formal participation in the Casino was much larger, for each member normally represented a whole family. The only women who belonged formally were widows of former members. If one counts a wife and a rough average of two children along with each male member, the effective membership in 1879 can be estimated at nearly 4,800, roughly 13 percent of Prague's German population in 1879; the comparable figure for 1898-1899 was 17 percent. Although comments in police documents and annual reports of the Casino indicate that significant numbers of people attended the various gatherings of the Casino as guests or spectators, there is no way to measure the level of informal participation.

The remarkable strength of the Casino's membership resulted from both the general need for such an organization to help to preserve German group identity and the ability of Prague's middle-class Germans to maintain a unitary public life. The contrasts in the associational life of the Czech middle class in the city underscore this. The closest Czech equivalent to the Casino, the Burghers' Club (*Měšťanská beseda*), consistently had a smaller membership despite the great disproportion between Czechs and Germans in the city. At the end of 1879, the Burghers' Club had only 1,012 members; in 1913 it had 1,019, compared to 1,235 in the German Casino.[70]

---

[68] AHMP fond spolků, Deutsches Haus: bylaws and minutes of the directors, 1867-1914. The minutes of the directors of the Casino record only a single rejection of an application for membership, a case decided on 13 March 1913 in which the directors feared the applicant only wished to further his business interests.

[69] AHMP fond spolků, Deutsches Haus: "Mitglieder-Verzeichnis des Vereines des Deutschen Casino, 1879-1880" and "Mitglieder-Verzeichnis des Vereines des Deutschen Casino, 1898-1899."

[70] AHMP fond spolků, no. 53, Měšťanská beseda: "Výkaz počtu členů k valné hromadě Měšťanské besedy v Praze dne 29. unora 1880," and "Výkaz o stavu členstva za rok 1913"; Deutsches Haus: "Bericht der Direktion an die 52. Vollversammlung des Vereines des Deutschen Casino, 17 Februar 1914." Otto Forchheimer's self-congratulatory remarks on the size of the Casino's membership in 1889 indicate that German liberal leaders were aware and proud of the numerical difference, SÚA Praha PP 1900-1907 V/50/10: 6800/pp 4902, 3 July 1889 police report on the meeting of the German Club on July 2.

In the eighties and nineties, the Czech middle class had clerical-conservative and Young Czech alternatives to the Old Czech Burghers' Club, but the German burghers could not afford such political diversity and never developed any respectable alternative to the Casino in the inner city.

Despite the large numbers, the Casino's membership was even more strongly middle class in 1898 than at the end of the seventies. In 1898-1899, 81 percent of the members had occupations which were middle class or upper middle class by contemporary standards, compared to 77 percent in 1879-1880 (see Table 4/1).[71] Except for the less prosperous segment of the merchant/businessman category, all of the occupations listed above the subtotal line belonged to the middle class of property and education. In the eighties and nineties these elements still had the freest access to the collective life of the liberal community, and virtually all the officers and directors of the Casino and most other liberal groups came from these strata.

To a great extent the membership of the Casino simply reflected the special character of the German minority and the heavy concentration of the inner city's Germans in the middle and upper strata. Few state officials, for instance, belonged to the Casino after 1879 because of the declining number of German bureaucrats in Prague; many of those who remained in the Bohemian capital may also have wanted to avoid public involvement in German organizations.[72] The profile of the Casino's members, however, also resulted from the continuing exclusion of lower-middle-class and laboring elements from equal participation in German community life. Those in the lower occupational strata who lacked comfortable incomes, advanced education, and good personal connections had little entrée to any of the more prestigious German associations in the inner city. As already noted, the German Club had a smaller and even narrower membership than the Casino. While the German Merchants' Club included many small retailers and some commercial employees among its 700-800 members, it lacked prestige comparable to the Casino or to the German Club.[73] Lower-middle-

[71] Sources as in n. 69.

[72] German officers in the Austrian military forces stationed in Prague generally abstained from local German associational life except for the annual opera balls sponsored by the German Theatre Society and a few of the great social events sponsored by the Casino. Public educators, on the other hand, participated in the German associations in relatively large numbers.

[73] SÚA Praha PP 1888-1892 V/24/23 Deutscher Kaufmännischer Verein: annual reports, lists of officers and directors, and police reports on meetings. Unfortunately, no membership lists are included.

TABLE 4/1
Casino Members by Occupation in Percentages

	1879-1880		1898-1899	
Banker/bank director	1.3%		1.5%	
Manufacturer	8.7	(104)[a]	10.0	(130)
Lawyer	8.6	(103)	13.0	(167)
Physician	2.3		3.1	
Merchant/self-employed bus.[b]	36.0	(434)	32.6	(418)
Government official	3.1	(37)	1.8	(23)
University professor/docent	4.2	(51)	5.8	(74)
Gymnas. prof./school director	2.4		1.4	
Bank/insurance co. officer	3.6	(43)	5.1	(65)
Architect/engineer/chemist	2.8		2.3	
Landowner	1.5		0.8	
Rentier/independent	2.8	(34)	3.7	(48)
	77.3%	(927)	81.1%	(1,040)
Supervisor/official/agent	7.1	(85)	8.3	(107)
Bookkeeper	3.7	(45)	0.7	(10)
Retail clerk	0		0	
Government clerk/worker	0.3		0.2	
Military	0.8		0.1	
Shop-foreman	0.1		0.1	
Skilled trade	0.8		1.3	
Worker	0		0	
Construction	0.6		0.5	
Railroad/transportation	2.3		1.6	
Teacher	0.3		0	
Theatre/arts/journalism	4.3	(52)	4.7	(61)
Student	0.4		0.1	
Widow	0.3		0.3	
Retired	1.0		1.5	
Miscellaneous	0.7		0.1	
TOTAL	100%	(1,200)	100%	(1,282)

[a] Absolute numbers given for categories comprising 3% of the members or more.
[b] Includes small retailers.

class elements apparently comprised a larger portion of the informal participants in the Casino's activities than of the members, but a wide gulf separated occasional guests from the members.

Changes in the Casino's membership between 1879 and 1898 actually suggest a decline in the status of white-collar elements and an upward movement of status-group boundaries in Prague's German middle-class society. In 1879 bookkeepers probably had the least respectability among the occupations with substantial representation in the Casino. By the end of the century they had virtually disappeared from the Casino's membership and from meaningful participation in German middle-class life in general, although a significant body of German bookkeepers remained in the city.[74] In 1898 small independent businessmen, supervisors in commerce and industry, artists, and journalists were the largest groups in the lowest quartile of the Casino's membership. Bookkeepers and petty employees were losing status in middle-class society elsewhere in Central Europe at this time, but the ethos of a declining middle-class minority contributed to the development among the Prague Germans.[75] Complaints about the stultifying atmosphere in the community indicated that the German *Bürgertum* here only heightened its sense of class and status differences when put on the defensive.[76]

A larger portion of Prague's German population joined the liberal special-purpose organizations than the more prestigious general groups. Nonetheless, even the specialized groups apparently failed to engage any substantial part of the German petty employees and workers who resided in Prague. Since the Austrian laws of association required only political associations to report all members to the police, one cannot determine from the surviving police records the numbers or identity of the members in most non-political groups.[77] Among the special-purpose groups, the five suburban chapters of the German School Society were among the most consistently successful in attracting lower-strata members, but each unit typically had no more than a total membership of around 100. The German Gymnastics Society, which generally had 400 to 500 members, seldom included more than 170 white-collar employees,

[74] Bookkeepers continued to play a prominent role in the German Merchants' Club and helped found the Association of German Commercial Employees in 1899; SÚA Praha PP 1888-1892 V/24/23 Deutscher Kaufmännischer Verein: annual reports, lists of officers, police reports on meetings, 1867-1892; and AHMP fond spolků, spolkový katastr: protokoly, XX-188 Verein deutscher Handelsangestellten.

[75] On the general trend in Central Europe, see Jürgen Kocka, *Unternehmensverwaltung und Angestelltenschaft am Beispiel Siemens 1847-1914* (Stuttgart, 1967), pp. 148-98, 254-314, 463-546.

[76] Max Brod remarked on the rigidity of class and status distinctions among the Prague Germans in *Streitbares Leben 1884-1968*, rev. ed. (Munich, Berlin, and Vienna, 1969), p. 154. Richard A. Bermann, who wrote under the pseudonym Arnold Höllriegel, complained of the Prague Germans' stiffness and conservatism in social life, politics, and cultural tastes in his autobiography, "Die Fahrt auf dem Katarakt" (unpubl. typescript in Leo Baeck Institute, New York, no date), pp. 21-27.

[77] On the distinctions Austrian law made among various types of voluntary associations, see Friedrich Tezner, *Österreichisches Vereins- und Versammlungsrecht*, 5th ed. (Vienna, 1913), pp. 469-600, passim.

retail clerks, and skilled workers.[78] Such figures fell far short of the at least 7,000 self-supporting German workers and lesser employees who resided in the city and inner suburbs at any time in the eighties and nineties. A much larger share of the German lower strata may have participated informally in the German special-purpose groups, but occasional attendance at their meetings or entertainments or even sending one's children to the schools of the German School Society would not suffice to incorporate individuals into German collective life.

While the German middle class of property and education widened, if anything, the social distance between itself and the German lower strata after 1879, the distribution of honors within the *Bürgertum* showed strong continuity through the nineties. The basic composition and even individual identities of community leaders hardly changed, as the lists of directors for the Casino and the German Club clearly demonstrate.[79] Those who directed associational affairs did so by virtue of the high social status accorded them, their desire for such honors, and perhaps a special interest in a group, but generally not because of any personal expertise or special constituency.

Those who held the highest honors in the community had a fairly consistent profile throughout this period. Whether they were successful lawyers, university professors, or proprietors of large businesses or medium-sized industries, nearly all either were self-employed or were public educators with considerable independence. No public employees except the educators figured in the leadership. Since few great industrialists took part, other than the textile manufacturer Alexander Richter, few of the leaders had any experience in managing large organizations and most were accustomed to acting as relatively independent agents. As members of the middle or upper middle class, all enjoyed high standards of living and had attended at least a *Gymnasium* or *Realschule*, if not a university. None of the leaders possessed aristocratic titles, and most resided in the districts of highest German concentration in the Old Town and New Town. The liberal leadership stratum naturally excluded the commercial and industrial supervisors and lesser employees who were the most visible among the German lower strata in Prague.

[78] See Chapter 5, pp. 193-96, for further discussion of the German Gymnastics Society.

[79] See Appendix II, Tables 9 and 10.

German associational life in Prague saw much the same increase in female participation at the end of the century as elsewhere in Western and Central Europe as middle- and lower-middle-class women sought a wider social life outside the home. Not surprisingly, though, the liberal women's groups maintained a status hierarchy fully consistent with that of the male-dominated organizations. In fact, most of the women who held positions of leadership did so because they were the wives or daughters of respected men in the community. Otto Forchheimer's wife Johanna and Gabriele Krasnopolski, the wife of a distinguished Prague law professor, for instance, led the Women's and Girls' Chapter of the German School Society over many years. Similarly, wives and daughters of directors of the Casino, the German Club, or the Municipal Affairs Association ran the ladies' section of the latter group.[80]

Despite the stresses of the new era after 1879, the German *Bürgertum* in Prague succeeded well in preserving the social hierarchy they had first instituted in the sixties. The survival of that social structure made possible in turn the preservation of much of the community's liberal ideology and deferential politics. The retention of the liberal social and political order in the German community was perhaps most striking—and most problematic in light of *völkisch* opposition—in regard to the continuing role of Jews in German group life. In the middle and late 1880s the continued participation of Jews became one of the crucial tests for maintaining the liberal order in the community. If the liberal notables were determined to make ethnic defense serve the preservation of their existing social and political system, then they had to defend the involvement of liberal, middle-class Jews in German public life.

Community Defense and the Status of the German Jews

The rise of political anti-Semitism and the exclusion of Jews from Gentile society in Bohemia, Moravia, and the Habsburg Hereditary Lands are commonly seen as inevitable consequences of the deepening nationality conflicts after 1879. Moved by violent outbursts of both German and Czech anti-Semitism in 1897, Theodor Herzl first popularized the view that heightened nationalism led each of

[80] According to *Bohemia*, 16 March 1898(M), those in charge of the women's section of the Municipal Affairs Association in 1898 were the wives of Dr. Theodor Altschul, Viktor von Ottenburg, Friedrich Elbogen, and Zdenko Ritter von Wessely, all prominent members of the Casino or the German Theatre Society.

Austria's peoples to attack Jewish supporters of rival groups and to reject its own Jewish adherents.[81] Later political analysts have gone on to argue that as each national group revolted against the liberal Austrian state, it turned against the Jews, the most obvious and vulnerable beneficiaries of liberal constitutionalism.[82] Regarding Prague, the hotbed of Czech-German rivalry, it is commonly asserted that Jews there gradually became alienated from both Czech and German middle-class society.[83]

The Christian Social movement and nearly all the radical nationalist parties, in fact, developed anti-Semitic strains, but Austria experienced in the eighties and nineties what was essentially a mass revolt against the deferential politics of liberal, middle-class notables. Except for small extremist groups like Georg von Schönerer's, there was no proto-fascist revolt against the state itself. Austrian Jews became victims of their previous identification with German liberals, and militant anti-Semitism typically accompanied assaults on the German liberals.[84] One should not try to generalize about social relations between Jews and non-Jews without extensive local studies, but there is no reason to assume that all Jewish-Gentile interaction ceased with the decline of liberal politics. Moreover, Jews could still join with non-Jews in group life where German liberals or liberal elements among the other ethnic groups defended their old social and political values and continued to affirm Jewish equality.[85]

[81] Theodor Herzl, "Die Jagd in Böhmen" and "Die entschwundenen Zeiten," from *Die Welt*, November 1897, reprinted in Herzl, *Gesammelte Zionistische Werke*, 5 vols. (Berlin, 1934-35), I, pp. 216-22, 249-54.

[82] See, for example, Hannah Arendt, *The Origins of Totalitarianism*, 2d ed. (New York, 1958), pp. 42-45.

[83] For examples see Brod, *Streitbares Leben*, pp. 153-54; Pavel Eisner, *Franz Kafka and Prague* (New York, 1950), passim; Eduard Goldstücker, "Über die Prager deutsche Literatur am Anfang des 20. Jahrhunderts," *Dortmunder Vorträge*, no. 70 (1965); and Hans Tramer, "Prague—City of Three Peoples," *Leo Baeck Year Book*, IX (1964), pp. 305-39. Brod himself presented a less extreme view in *Prager Kreis* (Berlin, 1966), pp. 37, 40, 58, 67, where he rejected interpretations of the work of the Prague Circle as having resulted from the isolation of the German Jews within the German community and the latter's thorough isolation from Czech Prague.

[84] On Austrian anti-Semitism the judicious works of Dirk van Arkel, *Antisemitism in Austria* (publ. Ph.D. dissertation, University of Leiden, 1966), Peter G. J. Pulzer, *The Rise of Political Anti-Semitism in Germany and Austria* (New York, 1964), and Stölzl, *Kafkas böses Böhmen*, pp. 44-90, provide useful correctives to Hannah Arendt's sweeping generalizations.

[85] A series of local studies is needed to explore this question properly, but the memoirs of Ernst von Plener, *Erinnerungen*, 3 vols. (Stuttgart and Leipzig, 1911-21),

After the early 1880s, the Prague Jews did confront anti-Semitism among some radical Czech nationalists, German radicals in the Bohemian borderlands and Prague's German University, and some of the lower-strata Germans in the city. Still, the German liberal community continued to welcome Jewish participation and rejected anti-Semitism. While German Christians and German Jews in Prague remained largely separated in their private lives, the involvement of middle-class and lower-middle-class Jews in German public affairs generally increased after 1879. As small minorities in Prague, the liberal, middle-class German Christians and German Jews needed each other too much to permit any religious or racial rift. Some Christian members of the liberal community doubtlessly harbored traditional prejudices against Jews, and the German Jews remained highly sensitive to any action or gesture they considered anti-Semitic. Yet throughout this period, the German liberal leaders in the Bohemian capital refused to tolerate any public expression within the community of either the traditional or new, political anti-Semitism; and they ostracized all those who refused to conform. As a consequence, the alliance between German Jews and Gentiles remained so close that, in the words of Felix Weltsch, a friend of Franz Kafka and Max Brod, "the Jews did not feel themselves to be allies at all but simply identified themselves with the Germans."[86]

The role of Jews both as members and officers in the leading German liberal groups steadily increased between 1879 and 1897. Jewish membership in the German Club grew from 30 percent of the total in 1882 to 35 percent in 1888, the last date in this period for which complete lists are readily available.[87] The Jewish share of the Casino's membership increased from 38 percent of the total in 1879-1880 to 45 percent in 1898-1899, almost equal to the Ger-

---

II, pp. 233-34, and the Social Democratic journalist Friedrich Stampfer, *Erfahrungen und Erkenntnisse: Aufzeichnungen aus meinem Leben* (Cologne, 1957), pp. 10-12, and the many complaints from pro-Nazi elements between the world wars in Austria and the Sudetenland indicate that German liberals did defend Jewish participation in German civic life where they could.

[86] Felix Weltsch, "The Rise and Fall of the Jewish-German Symbiosis—The Case of Franz Kafka," *Leo Baeck Institute Year Book*, I (1956), p. 255.

[87] Membership lists for the German Club derive from SÚA Praha PP 1900-1907 V/15/10: "Namens-Verzeichnis der Mitglieder des Deutschen Vereines nach dem Stande mit Ende Dezember 1882," and ČM 1889-1900 30/41/3: "Namens-Verzeichnis der Mitglieder des Deutschen Vereines in Prag nach dem Stande mit Ende Feber 1888." The Jewish members were identified positively by use of the tax register for the Jewish Religious Community, AŽM-ŽNOP: Kniha poplatníků kultovní daně, 120730 (1891).

man Jews' share of the total German-speaking population in Prague I-VII.[88] The ten directors of the German Club regularly included two or three Jews, among them Otto Forchheimer and the lawyers Friedrich Ritter von Wiener and Ludwig Bendiener. Typically, four or five Jews sat among the twenty-four directors of the German Casino. Jews served with comparable frequency on the boards of the more important special-purpose organizations such as the German Theatre Society, the Gymnastics Society, and the chapters of the German School Society.[89] Membership lists do not survive for most of the special-purpose groups, but Jews comprised one-third of the Gymnastics Society, for instance, in 1887.[90]

The "Germans of Israelite religion," as they were sometimes described, achieved prominence in German public life in Prague without having to cut all ties to the Jewish religious community. This contrasted with the experience of Jews in Vienna, who found that ultimately upward mobility in the less tolerant lower Austrian Catholic society usually required abandonment of all Jewish identity. In Budapest's caste-ridden Magyar society, aspiring Jews had to give up most of their Jewish traditions and identify fully with the Magyars even if they avoided formal conversion.[91] In the German community of Prague, on the other hand, Jewish dignitaries generally held honors in Jewish religious and charitable bodies equal to those they enjoyed in the German associations, and they clearly identified as both Germans and Jews. Ludwig Bendiener, for instance, who was the last German liberal alderman and a long-time

[88] Membership lists for the Casino derive from AHMP as in n. 69 above. Jewish members were identified with reference to AŽM-ŽNOP: Knihy poplatníků kultovní daně, 120718 (1870), 120730 (1891), and 120840 (1901). The few in Prague during this era who formally renounced Judaism or were descended from converts are excluded from this reckoning.

[89] See Chapter 6 for discussion of the role of Jews in the leadership of the liberal associations after 1897.

[90] SÚA Praha 1888-1892 V/39/1 Deutscher Verein in Prag: "Verwaltungsbericht des Vorstandes des Deutscher Turnvereins in Prag für das Jahr 1887" (Prague, 1888). Jewish members were identified by comparison with the tax registries for the Jewish Religious Community of Prague as in n. 88 above.

[91] On the assimilation of Viennese Jews see the essays in Josef Fraenkel, ed., *The Jews of Austria* (London, 1967), and Hans Tietze, *Die Juden Wiens: Geschichte—Wirtschaft—Kultur* (Leipzig, 1933). On Budapest and Hungary see George Barany, " 'Magyar Jew or: Jewish Magyar'? (To the Question of Jewish Assimilation in Hungary)," *Canadian-American Slavic Studies*, VIII (1974), pp. 1-44; Victor Karady and Istvan Kemeny, "Les Juifs dans la Structure des classes en Hongrie," *Actes de la recherche en sciences sociales*, no. 22 (1978), pp. 25-60; and William O. McCagg, Jr., *Jewish Nobles and Geniuses in Modern Hungary* (New York, 1972), passim.

director of the German Club, presided over the orthodox High
Synagogue in the nineties and served on the council of the Jewish
Religious Community of Prague for four decades.[92] In the eighties
and early nineties, the textile manufacturer Sigmund Mauthner
simultaneously presided over the German Merchants' Club and the
chief local Jewish charity, the Central Society for the Care of Jewish
Affairs. The insurance broker Philip Falkowicz succeeded Mauthner in both positions. German-Jewish notables retained control of
the Jewish religious and charitable institutions at the end of the
century despite the abandonment of German political loyalties by
many Jews, and, in fact, they used their power to combat the Czech-
Jewish and Zionist movements within local Jewish circles.[93]

So thorough was the acceptance of Jews in German public life
in Prague that they won admission and honors according to much
the same social and economic criteria as Catholics and Protestants.
The occupational distribution of the Jewish participants differed
from the Christians' insofar as the Jewish population as a whole
had a distinct economic profile, but a comparison of Jewish to non-
Jewish members in the Casino in 1898-1899, for example, shows
that Jews were not subject to appreciably higher standards for entry
(see Table 4/2).[94] The large number of Jewish merchants and businessmen among the members, of course, reflects the high proportion of all Prague Jews in commerce. The large number of businessmen, in fact, artificially inflates the portion of the Jewish
membership which can be properly considered middle class. Nearly
nine-tenths of the Jewish members of the Casino came from the
wealthier half of the Jewish population, but a significant portion
of the businessmen had relatively modest means and were really
lower middle class.[95] The numbers of Jewish members in the various
professions reflect the comparatively strong representation of Cen-

[92] See the biographical sketch published in *Selbstwehr*, 2 Sept 1910, on the occasion
of Bendiener's seventieth birthday.

[93] See the discussion in G. B. Cohen, "The Prague Germans," pp. 532-51, and
below in Chapter 5, pp. 226-28.

[94] 1898-99 membership list for the Casino derives from AHMP as in n. 69 above.
Jewish members were identified by comparison with AŽM-ŽNOP: Knihy poplatníků
kultovní daně, 120730 (1891) and 120840 (1901).

[95] A comparison of the 1898-99 membership of the Casino to the 1901 tax register
for the Jewish Religious Community of Prague indicates that 86 percent of the
Jewish Casino members ranked in the wealthier half of the Jewish population and
55 percent in the highest quartile, assuming a rough correlation between the grad-
uated tax payments and wealth. I have not been able to establish the formula by
which tax payments to the religious community were calculated.

TABLE 4/2
Occupational Profile of the Members of the German Casino, 1898-1899

	Non-Jewish Members in Percentages		Jewish Members in Percentages	
Banker/bank director	1.6		1.2	
Manufacturer	10.6	(75)	9.6	(55)
Lawyer	9.2	(65)	17.8	(102)
Physician	2.5	(18)	3.8	(22)
Merchant/indep. business[a]	23.8	(168)	43.0	(250)
Government official	3.0	(21)	0.4	
Univ. prof./docent	7.8	(55)	3.3	(19)
Gymn. prof./school dir.	2.0		0.7	
Bank/insurance officer	5.9	(42)	4.0	(23)
Architect/engineer/chem.	3.8	(27)	0.5	
Landowner	1.1		0.2	
Rentier/independent	2.7		5.1	(29)
SUBTOTAL	74.0%	(523)	89.6%	(516)
Superv./employee/agent	9.5	(67)	5.2	(30)
Bookkeeper	0.4		1.2	
Government clerk/worker	0.3		0	
Shop foreman	0.1		0	
Skilled trade	1.6		0.9	
Construction	0.7		0.2	
Railroad/transport	2.7		0.3	
Teacher	2.0		0	
Arts/journalism	7.4	(52)	1.6	
Student	0.1		0.2	
Widow	0.3		0.3	
TOTAL	100% = 707		100% = 575	

[a] Includes small retailers.

tral European Jews in the late nineteenth century in medicine and law and their limited involvement in government service, the academy, and technical pursuits. At the low end of the social hierarchy, poor Jewish bookkeepers, clerks, peddlers, and workers found entry into such associations as the German Casino as difficult as did their Catholic and Protestant counterparts.

It is hard to know what Catholics and Protestants in the German liberal community really thought of the Jews' prominent role. *Völkisch* spokesmen in Prague vociferously attacked Jewish participation in German public life, but, as outsiders noted, the liberal community maintained a taboo on the expression of anti-Jewish sentiments as strong as that against publicly fraternizing with Czechs.[96] Christian liberals left few memoirs or letters which might

[96] See, for instance, Margarete Jodl, *Friedrich Jodl*, pp. 117-18.

offer private viewpoints. In any case, they accepted the Jews' participation and contributions, and they clearly did not treat them as unwelcome but necessary clients, who were to be given the social honors they desired at the highest price and in the least amount.

The German Jews, for their part, did not behave as craven suppliants for status in Gentile society. In late 1883, for instance, when the first wave of the new political anti-Semitism crested in Austria and Hungary, a number of Jews briefly boycotted the German Casino to protest the actions of a small anti-Semitic clique.[97] In 1887 another Jewish group, angered by the liberal leaders' efforts to conciliate the more tractable German nationalists in northern Bohemia, temporarily withdrew from the Casino to support the pro-Taaffe Economic Party.[98] These were not "kept Jews" in the sense of the 1883 election slogan. If the leaders of the Casino valued Jewish adherents, they dared not compromise their liberal principles regarding religion and race.

Through most of the eighties and nineties, the stance of the local German liberal leaders against anti-Semitism gave Jews little cause for complaint. Beginning in 1883, Schmeykal and his colleagues maintained a policy of strongly condemning racial anti-Semitism and of resisting its intrusion into German public life in Prague and elsewhere. The leaders of the Casino still hoped for unity among all German forces in Bohemia, but Schmeykal, Knoll, and others in Prague consistently made it clear that they welcomed Jewish support for the German cause and considered racial anti-Semitism and pan-Germanism as pernicious, demagogic attacks on the essence of the German liberal tradition in Austria.[99]

Schmeykal and his colleagues rejected anti-Semitism in principle, but in practice until 1888 they tried primarily to mute anti-Semitic dissidence and avoid open splits. Like German liberal leaders elsewhere in Austria, they wanted to win over the more flexible nationalist critics. Even while condemning anti-Semitism, liberal leaders admitted that centuries of ghetto life had engendered unpleasant traits among European Jews; but the cure for this, they argued,

[97] *Politik*, 30 Oct 1883, and SÚA Praha PMT 1883 177/83, 8682pp, Prague police to Bohemian Governor Kraus, 25 Oct 1883.

[98] HHStA Nachlass Plener, ct. 19, no. 49, Schmeykal to Ernst von Plener, 28 Feb 1887. Neither Schmeykal's letter nor the papers of the German Casino in AHMP identify the Jewish secessionists.

[99] For examples see Knoll, *Beiträge*, pp. 184-85, from a speech of 20 March 1883; Julius Lippert, "Der Antisemitismus," *Sammlung gemeinnütziger Vorträge*, no. 88 (Prague, 1883); and another speech of Knoll's reported in *Bohemia*, 28 June 1888 (M).

lay in complete equality of status and fuller integration of Jews into Gentile society, not renewed exclusion.[100] The disarray of German liberal forces in Austria between 1885 and 1888 gave the leaders of the Casino little choice but to seek a modus vivendi with German nationalist groups even within the Casino itself and the German Gymnastics Society.[101]

German liberal leaders walked a tortuous path in trying to keep the confidence of both Jews and German nationalists, and by May 1888 the leaders of the German Casino concluded that they must expel the uncompromising *völkisch* elements from their own community life. Schmeykal and his colleagues apparently realized that they would have to sacrifice much more in basic principles and support from their old middle-class constituency, Christian and Jewish, by attempting to placate the *völkisch* movement than they might gain from joining in *völkisch* appeals to the German lower strata. Any new overtures to German petty employees and workers in Prague must be pitched in a liberal key. The decision was difficult for the cautious Schmeykal, but the trial of Schönerer in April 1888 for his attack on a Viennese newspaper and the movements in the Reichsrat toward a new union of German deputies convinced the Prague leadership that the time was ripe to isolate the radical nationalists.[102] The Casino satisfied Prague's German Jews with this action, and there were no further outbreaks of anti-Semitism within the liberal associational network before World War I. What implications the expulsion of the *völkisch* elements had for relations between the liberal community and the German lower strata in Prague will be examined in the next chapter.

The overlapping memberships, interlocking directorates, and common social and political outlook of the German liberal associations guaranteed a strong sense of community among all the participants as they adapted to the requirements of ethnic defense after 1879. The German burghers of Prague expressed that com-

[100] Lippert, in *Sammlung gemeinnütziger Vorträge*, no. 88, is representative of this line of argument. See further discussion of the liberals' position in Stölzl, *Kafkas böses Böhmen*, pp. 55-57.

[101] See the discussion of the events in the Gymnastics Society in Chapter 5, pp. 196-202. Of the anti-Semites in the Casino, the papers of the directors in AHMP fond spolků and the police reports in SÚA Praha identify only the leader Dr. Heinrich Osborne.

[102] SÚA Praha PMT 1888 48/88 secret Prague police report on Schmeykal's activities to Governor Kraus, forwarded to Count Taaffe, 11 April 1888.

munity feeling most clearly at the celebrations held in the Casino to mark important milestones in their civic life. All major German associations sent delegations to celebrations such as that for Franz Schmeykal's sixtieth birthday in 1886. On December 3, 1886, six hundred persons heard praises heaped on Schmeykal by Ernst von Plener and representatives of the German School Societies of Austria and Germany, Prague's German Casino, the German Jurists' Society, the Reading Hall of German university students in Prague, the German Handworkers' Society, and the local German journalists. Speaking for all the local groups, Eduard Ritter von Zahn singled out Schmeykal's untiring efforts on behalf of all German organizations in the city, which together "form(ed) a great family."[103]

Yet the sense of German community solidarity expressed so strongly at such gatherings had important components of class and ideology. In 1897 the associational network which carried on community life still served best the interests of the liberal middle class. The new political threats had forced those who shared in German collective life in Prague to become more conscious of their group identity in social and ideological as well as cultural terms. Whether they admitted it or not, the German burghers used ethnic defense to uphold the interests of a German middle class of property and education, its rigid social hierarchy, and individualist ideology. The German Jews remained in the community not simply because of their numbers but also because they met its social criteria and supported its ideology.

The liberal middle-class Germans still needed recruits and support from the lower social strata if they were to survive. Even if the liberal notables failed to open up groups at the center of community life to workers or petty employees, they still wanted to attract more lower-strata Germans to the city and attach them somehow to German collective life. The creation of the German Handworkers' Society and the suburban chapters of the German School Society together with other steps were part of a larger effort to coopt lower-strata elements. The development of that program and the fate of those who refused co-optation on the liberals' terms must now be examined.

[103] Reported in *Bohemia*, 4 Dec 1886(M), *Prager Tagblatt*, 4 Dec 1886(M), and [Klaar], *Schmeykal*, pp. 88-89.

CHAPTER FIVE

The German Lower Strata, 1883-1897:
The Co-opted, the Outcasts,
and the Passive

The liberal community found it difficult to increase the numbers of lower-strata Germans in Prague and engage them in liberal group life. Poorly qualified employees, workers, and their dependents comprised around one-third of the German citizens of Prague and the inner suburbs after 1880. Their total numbers ranged from around 13,000 in 1880 to about 10,000 in 1900. Yet they were too mobile and too thinly dispersed in the poorer districts to be easily reached by the liberal community, and it was hard for them to sustain any public life of their own.[1]

The dispersion and high transiency of the German lower strata make it hard to identify them even now. Without manuscript census returns for the outlying districts, one cannot define their origins precisely. Descendants of the few lower-strata German-speakers in the city in the 1840s and 1850s comprised some of the German craftsmen, employees, and workers at the end of the century. Downward mobility out of the German middle class also contributed to the German lower strata. The largest portion, however, probably derived from migration after 1860 from German districts of Bohemia and Moravia or from south Germany.[2] In the long run,

[1] The high transiency of the urban poor is characteristic of modern industrializing societies and has received particular attention from American urban historians. See, for examples, Stephan Thernstrom, *Poverty and Progress: Social Mobility in a Nineteenth Century City* (Cambridge, Mass., 1964), and idem, *The Other Bostonians* (Cambridge, Mass., 1973).

[2] The extensive analysis of the 1900 census returns, *Sčítání lidu v Praze 1900*, ed. Jan Srb, published by the Prague Statistical Commission, compares the birthplaces of the residents with religion but not with everyday language. Using the example of the Lutherans in Žižkov cited in Chapter 3 above, the 19 residents of the district

(184)

of course, only a larger immigration and an end to the assimilation of poorer Germans with the Czechs could reverse the numerical decline of the Prague Germans.

Low incomes and jobs in the industrial districts obliged many lower-strata Germans to live in overwhelmingly Czech neighborhoods removed from the affluent centers of German group life in the Old Town and New Town. Many of them ultimately disappeared, either through assimilation or through migration out of Prague. As already noted, the more than 4,000 Jews who shifted from German loyalties to Czech between the 1890 and 1900 censuses came primarily from the intermediate and poorest strata.[3]

The poorer Germans in Prague gave other signs of their presence, in addition to the cold census statistics. Lower-strata Germans in Holešovice, Libeň, Vršovice, and Žižkov sent their children to local kindergartens and primary schools operated by the German School Society. The German lower strata claimed certain pubs and cafes as their own in the inner city as well as in some of the industrial districts. Even Žižkov had at least one German beer hall.[4] The German liberal groups remained the only significant German political forums despite the rise of opposition in Prague in the late eighties, and German craftsmen and workers occasionally sought them out when stirred by political events. The meetings of the German Club in the Casino were too staid and exclusive for workers, but the gatherings of the German Political Association in Vinohrady were less intimidating.[5] Yet the atomized existence of many of the poorest Germans meant that involving them in German group life on a continuing basis would require powerful efforts.

The scantiness of the surviving records for the German lower strata reflects their marginality to the collective life of the German middle class. Newspaper and police reports on the activities of lower-class German groups are fragmentary at best. But what made most of the German petty employees and workers insignificant to contemporary journalists and bureaucrats makes them crucial to understanding the social structure of a declining ethnic group. The

---

born in German areas of Bohemia, Moravia, and the Habsburg Hereditary Lands probably comprised most of the 22 Lutheran citizen residents who declared German as their everyday language in 1900. See Chapter 3, n. 54 and n. 58.

[3] See Chapter 3, pp. 100-108.

[4] *Bohemia*, 13 Nov 1905 (noon), reported the sacking of the pub "Zur Eintracht" in Žižkov by a Czech crowd during the Social Democrats' campaign for universal equal suffrage.

[5] See Chapter 4, pp. 166-67.

various efforts by liberals and their opponents to create a group life for lower-strata Germans in Prague reveal much about social and political relations in the German minority.

The Handworkers' Society and the Tactics of Co-optation

The leaders of the German Casino responded slowly to Philipp Knoll's urgings to enlarge the popular base of the German community. After Knoll's speech of March 1883, they took no action to carry out his proposals until late 1884. The liberal notables had more urgent concerns in the meantime: the elections for the Bohemian Diet in spring 1883, an anti-Semitic incident in the Casino and a brief Jewish boycott in October 1883, suffrage reform and new elections for the Prague Chambers of Trade and Manufacture in early 1884. The German School Society's expanding net of local chapters began to engage more lower-strata Germans in liberal associational life in 1883 and 1884, but Knoll had envisioned something different. He was convinced that only programs directed specifically at the social and economic needs of lower-strata Germans in Prague could rally them.

In November 1884 the leaders of the German Casino founded the German Handworkers' Society (*Deutscher Handwerkerverein*) as the principal instrument for attracting more German artisans and workers to Prague and rallying them to the liberal community. Professor Ferdinand Höhm of the German Girls' Lyceum described the practical aims of the new group at the organizational meeting in the Casino. The Society was "first to defend the German handworkers of Prague from losing their national identity and becoming renegades and then to establish a loan fund and a hostel for German apprentices and assistants, who now cannot find lodgings in Prague."[6] The liberals' emphasis on craftsmen and handworkers echoed the familiar appeals of lower-middle-class radicals in Central Europe to small masters and skilled workers. Like many of the radicals, the moderate liberals of the German Casino in the 1880s made no sharp distinctions among self-employed artisans, workers in small shop production, and skilled operatives in factories.

The liberal leaders in Prague intended the Handworkers' Society to serve as a general social organization for lower-strata Germans, but they themselves played a major role in the association from the

---

[6] SÚA Praha PP 1888-1892 V/20/20 Deutscher Handwerkerverein: 9931pp, 17 Nov 1884, report from the Handworkers' Society to the Prague police.

outset. Liberal notables like Höhm generally served as directors alongside small businessmen and artisans, and they guaranteed close links with the Casino. The first board of the Handworkers' Society included Höhm and Dr. Josef Holzamer, a professor at the German Commercial Academy, as well as a barber, printer, shoemaker, bookbinder's assistant, and retailer of straw hats. Friedrich W. Sauer, a small hardware producer, presided.[7] The Casino showed its support at the start by corporately joining the Handworkers' Society, contributing 100 fl., and donating periodicals.[8]

The Handworkers' Society was something of an organizational hybrid. It combined the functions of the general-purpose social groups developed by the Central European middle classes in the sixties and seventies with the activities of the organizations for ethnic defense of the eighties and even something of the economic interest-group associations which became popular in the nineties. Nonetheless, the Handworkers' Society remained anchored in the liberal associational network headed by the German Casino. The Society established its own quarters to provide lower-class Germans with a place to gather and to socialize just as the Casino served as a focus for the group life of the higher German strata. Also like the Casino, the Handworkers' Society maintained a library and sponsored lectures, classes, and reading groups for its members.[9]

The Handworkers' Society directed its economic services primarily to the needs of self-employed artisans and skilled workers. The founders wanted the Society to help to recruit more German skilled workers to Prague and to sustain them there.[10] The Society also wanted to assist German domestic servants and proposed a free labor exchange and employment service to find positions with German employers for German servants and skilled workers. Unskilled laborers received no special attention from the German

[7] SÚA Praha PP 1888-1892 V/20/20: 10099pp, 18 Nov 1884, report from the Handworkers' Society to the Prague police.

[8] AHMP fond spolků, Deutsches Haus: "Protokoll der Direction, 20 Nov 1884," "Bericht über das Vereinsjahr 1883-84," 19 Jan 1885, and SUA Praha PP 1888-1892 V/13/5 Verein deutsches Casino: 63/pp 41, police report on the general meeting of 19 Jan 1885.

[9] The activities of the Society were outlined formally in the bylaws, SÚA Praha PP 1888-1892 V/20/20: 9465/pp 6296, "Statuten," 29 Oct 1884, and in the announcement by the directors in *Prager Tagblatt*, 9 Dec 1884(M).

[10] The Prague economy gave the Society little need to distinguish workers in small shops from those in factories. On the general evolution of the Prague work force see Pavla Horská-Vrbová in *Pražský sborník historický 1969-70*, pp. 52-69, and idem, in *ČSČH*, V (1957), pp. 108-36.

Handworkers' Society. In fact, the unskilled never achieved visibility in any German group in Prague before World War I; they were apparently too few for any specific appeal to have results.

The Handworkers' Society quickly launched a variety of programs. The placement bureau for German domestic servants began to operate in February 1885, and a general employment service followed soon after. In October 1885 the Society established a credit union and a sickness and disability fund for its members. The most ambitious undertaking, a privately funded industrial continuation school, began in the autumn of 1886. Within a year's time the school had 114 pupils.[11] The Society rented quarters from a large pub until after 1900 and provided space for its own gatherings, the meetings of other German groups, and a reading room. In a real sense the Handworkers' Society became a second, less distinguished, German Casino.

In the first years the Handworkers' Society won a large following, apparently drawn from all strata of the local German population as well as from several other Bohemian German communities. In January 1886, it had 2,557 members; by the end of 1887 there were 3,631, three times the strength of the Casino.[12] The effective membership of the Handworkers' Society cannot be reckoned as simply as the Casino's: one cannot determine without membership lists how many of those who paid the one florin in annual dues were not residents of Prague or were women or young men who did head their own households in the Bohemian capital. Although intended primarily for artisans and skilled workers, the Society also drew small businessmen and many adherents from the higher social strata.[13] The membership remained close to 4,000 through the late eighties, but the scanty police reports from the 1890s suggest a gradual loss of membership.[14] The infrequency of press notices for the Handworkers' Society after the mid-nineties implies a general decline in activity as well.

[11] SÚA Praha PP 1888-1892 V/20/20: 9886/pp 7084, 13 Oct 1886, Bohemian Governor's Office to the Prague police directorate, and "Dritter Jahresbericht des Deutschen Handwerkervereines Prag, Vereinsjahr 1887" (Prague, 1888).

[12] SÚA Praha PP 1888-1892 V/20/20: 660/pp 517, police report on the meeting of the Handworkers' Society on 24 Jan 1886, and "Dritter Jahresbericht des Deutschen Handwerkervereines in Prag."

[13] SÚA Praha PM 1881-1890 8/5/15/57 Deutscher Handwerkerverein: 4939 ai 1886, 3 July 1886, Governor Alfred von Kraus to the Ministry of Interior on the character and activities of the Handworkers' Society.

[14] There were 3,966 members in 1889, SÚA Praha PP 1888-1892 V/20/20: "Fünfter Jahresbericht des Deutschen Handwerkervereines in Prag, Vereinsjahr

The participation of middle-class and upper-middle-class elements in the Handworkers' Society went well beyond token representation of liberal notables. The president and the chairmen of
the various sections were almost always self-employed craftsmen.
On the other hand, the vice-president or secretary and around one-
third of the other directors were usually professors, respected merchants, lawyers, or industrialists. In 1889, for instance, Ferdinand
Höhm, Philipp Knoll, Schmeykal's law partner Dr. Eduard Langer,
the merchant Simon Klauber, and the factory owner Philipp Bu-
miller, Jr., served as directors, along with a shoemaker, tailor, typesetter, shop foreman, and several other skilled workers.[15] Middle-
class and upper-middle-class elements probably comprised an
equally large portion of the general membership. Jews played a
smaller role here than in the other liberal associations, but the
directors of the Society generally included several Jewish businessmen, lawyers, or managers.[16]

The leaders of the Handworkers' Society emphasized the group's
educational and economic services in trying to attract lower-strata
support. They made blatant appeals to all Germans in Prague to
hire German workers and to patronize German small businessmen
and artisans. In a speech to the German Club in April 1885, for
instance, Eduard Langer praised the efforts of the Handworkers'
Society to strengthen German loyalties among craftsmen and skilled
workers in Prague, and he argued the necessity of directing all
German consumption to members of the Society.[17] In the same
month Professor Friedrich Kick, the head of the German Gymnastics Society in Prague, spoke to the Handworkers' Society on
how German artisans could increase their clientele.[18] Kick had pre-

1889" (Prague, 1890). The police dossier for the following seven years, PP 1893-
1899 V/22/13, includes no membership lists or any statement on the number of
members. There are indications of a decline in membership in the speeches of
Ferdinand Höhm on 10 Feb 1894 and 27 Sept 1897, and of Philipp Knoll and Josef
Bendel on 24 Nov 1894. The police dossiers for the periods 1900-1907 and 1908-
1915 could not be located in SÚA Praha.

[15] SÚA Praha PP 1888-1892 V/20/20: 1436, 1 Feb 1889, report from the Handworkers' Society to the Prague police on new officers.

[16] Ferdinand Höhm took pains to deny rumors of anti-Semitism in the Society at
the general meeting held on 10 February 1894, SÚA Praha PP 1893-1899 V/22/13:
3334pp ai 1894, 11 Feb 1894, police report.

[17] SÚA Praha PP 1900-1907 V/15/10 Deutscher Verein in Prag: 3604/pp 2510, 18
April 1885, police report of the meeting on 17 April.

[18] SÚA Praha PP 1888-1892 V/20/20: 3924/pp 2735, 27 April 1885, police report
on the meeting of 26 April.

sided over the German workers' society Concord in 1868, and he retained a strong interest in the lower strata. Taking a leaf from the Czech nationalist doctrines of "from one's own to one's own" (*Svůj k svému*), he recommended that a list of all German craftsmen in Bohemia be distributed to all German inhabitants so that they might patronize Germans only. Such proposals were common in Austria's mixed cities and towns in the late nineteenth century, but the expense of producing lists and government regulations against economic boycotts generally prevented carrying out of the proposals. Little came of Kick's suggestion, but the Handworkers' Society and the liberal leadership at least demonstrated their moral support for preferential hiring and purchasing.

The leaders of the liberal community apparently believed that creating a service organization for the German lower strata and urging the whole German population to patronize only German retailers and craftsmen were the best means of building lower-strata support. Such measures could do little to increase the German population or to stop German-Czech assimilation, but most of the liberal notables avoided any deep analysis of the Prague Germans' predicament. Few shared Philipp Knoll's candor in assessing the social dynamics of the liberal community. Most found it easier to blame the loss of lower-strata Germans on the Czechs in local government, the economic boycotts urged by Czech politicians, and the myriad other pressures exerted on Germans by the Czech environment.[19] Yet the creation of the Handworkers' Society in itself signified an admission that the group life of the liberal community had previously had no place for German workers and many of the petty employees.

The Handworkers' Society maintained close ties with the local German liberal leaders throughout the eighties and nineties. Both the middle-class supporters of the Society and its lower-strata members had an interest in cooperation. The liberal notables of the Casino, of course, expected the Handworkers' Society to co-opt lower-strata elements into the liberal community, but the political ferment among the Central European lower middle classes and workers in the 1880s also made it wise for the Casino to keep the Society on a tight rein lest it spawn opposition. Seeing the potential for anti-liberal politics among lower-strata Germans, those who

[19] Ferdinand Höhm made such arguments at meetings of the Handworkers' Society in December 1884 and November 1889, SÚA Praha PP 1888-1892 V/20/20: 10656 pp/7164, 8 Dec 1884, police report, and 11845/8768, 17 Nov 1889, police report.

vainly tried to win support for Count Taaffe and the Economic Party among Prague Germans in spring 1886 proposed their own association for German handworkers in addition to a new "German-Austrian" casino.[20]

In addition to assisting the Handworkers' Society in concrete ways, liberal leaders in Prague used every ceremonial opportunity to demonstrate their solidarity with the group and with the German lower strata in general. In September 1886, for instance, Schmeykal, Forchheimer, Knoll, Dotzauer, Kick, and Alexander Richter all attended the dedication of a monument to Emperor Joseph II in the garden of the Handworkers' Society.[21] At the celebration of his own sixtieth birthday in December 1886, Schmeykal singled out the Society for praise and assurances of community support.[22] The liberal notables had particular need for such avowals of unity as long as the community leaders resisted legislative protection of small producers and workers from larger business and financial interests.

The various services of the Handworkers' Society and the liberal leaders' affirmations of support did win over some lower-strata Germans in Prague. Yet the artisans, small retailers, and skilled workers who joined the Handworkers' Society were those who could accept co-optation on the liberal notables' terms. These individuals apparently wanted the limited access to liberal community life, educational and social programs, and support for some of their economic interests that the liberal establishment offered. In fact, the liberal community offered no more economic assistance than the training programs, employment services, and promises of patronage. German barbers, grocers, and typesetters could participate in German community life through the Handworkers' Society, but they still won no significant social honors in the liberal community.

Within the limits set by the liberal notables, the Handworkers' Society could achieve only modest results in recruiting lower-strata Germans. It could not become an association truly of and for German artisans and workers, nor could it prevent the rise of anti-liberal politics among some of Prague's lower-class Germans. The Handworkers' Society gradually declined in the nineties as, first,

---

[20] Eduard Langer described the whole project at a meeting of the German Club in May 1886, SÚA Praha PP 1900-1907 V/15/10: ad VS 958/NE 5629pp, 29 May 1886, police report. See the discussion of the Economic Party in Chapter 4 above, p. 151.

[21] *Bohemia*, 27 Sept 1886(M).

[22] *Bohemia*, 4 Dec 1886(M), and *Prager Tagblatt*, 4 Dec 1886(M).

radical German nationalist and, later, Social Democratic organizations began to articulate lower-strata interests more forcefully. In the end the Society served the purposes of the liberal community. The founder of the first German Social Democratic group in the city put it succinctly:[23]

> We have another German workers' society here in Prague, that is the Handworkers' Society. It is an offshoot of the German Casino, and one puts there the people who, because of their inelegant attire, are not welcome in the Casino.

The Seedbed of Völkisch Opposition

An aggressive and persistent anti-liberal movement first arose among Prague's German lower strata in 1888. By then German lower-middle-class and laboring elements had abundant reasons for opposition to the notables of the Casino: the old social tensions exacerbated by depression conditions, the liberals' deferential politics, their resistance to protectionist economics, and their inability to counter the growing strength of the Czech nationalists. Throughout Austria, leftist voices now attacked middle-class liberalism without hesitation, and radical German nationalists were gaining popularity in northern Bohemia and in the Alpine lands. In light of such great incentives, the belatedness of the first full-fledged revolt against the liberal order among the Prague Germans is perhaps more interesting than its basic causes.

Anti-liberal groups, of course, faced the same problems as the liberals in reaching lower-strata Germans in the Bohemian capital. Even if völkisch and Social Democratic ideologies appealed more directly to the poorest Germans, their small numbers, atomized existence, and often weak German identification impeded radical nationalists and German socialists as much as the liberals. In addition, the numerical strength of the middle-class liberals within the German minority and their hold on existing German group life made it difficult for any opposition to develop. The intensity of the Czech-German conflict actually worked to the liberals' advantage by encouraging diverse German interests to maintain solidarity in the face of national danger. As a consequence, liberals and radical

---

[23] SÚA Praha PP 1893-1899 V/7/48 Verein deutscher Arbeiter in Prag: 4487pp, 24 March 1896, police report on the meeting of 22 March. For discussion of the German Social Democratic group, see Chapter 6, pp. 249-52.

nationalists split apart significantly later in Prague than in most solidly German towns in the Bohemian Lands.

Although radical German nationalism had roots in Prague dating back several decades, it flowered rapidly in the second half of the 1880s. As will be seen, the *völkisch* movement developed gradually in some of the local German student societies throughout the seventies and eighties. Nationalist radicalism first appeared among adult German residents in the German-National Club in 1886 and 1887. The Club offered no direct threat to liberal hegemony, however, because neither it nor the Casino wanted an open break. During its brief existence the German-National Club did provide a forum in Prague for such radical voices as Engelbert Pernerstorfer.[24] It also served to identify radical activists among the German lower strata and brought them together with the more volatile student elements. Within a year the German Gymnastics Society gave birth to a radical nationalist movement of lower-class adults and university students which the liberal notables could neither co-opt nor silence.

The special character of the Gymnastics Society suited it well to give birth to the first enduring *völkisch* group within Prague's German minority. Unlike most of the associations in the liberal network, middle-class adults comprised only a small minority in the Gymnastics Society. Moreover, while liberal notables dominated the general administration of the Gymnastics Society, commercial employees, skilled workers, and university students controlled various sections.

The Gymnastics Society had a dual organizational structure. Older men with high standing in the liberal community held largely honorific positions on the general board of directors alongside young men drawn from the senior active gymnasts. The president, vice-president, and two or three other members of the twenty-four-man general board always came from the elite of the Casino, but the rest of the directors and a board of senior gymnasts were almost all young bookkeepers, commercial clerks, university students, and occasionally workers.[25] The senior gymnasts managed gymnastic practice, competitions, and the accompanying singing and drinking parties.

[24] Pernerstorfer addressed 200 persons on 1 July 1886, SÚA Praha PP 1888-1892, NE 6750pp, 1 July 1886, police report; *Bohemia*, 3 July 1886(M). On the German-National Club see Chapter 4, pp. 151-52.

[25] See Rychnovsky, *Turnverein*, passim. Lists of officers and directors are included

The membership of the Gymnastics Society showed a more complex stratification than did its officers and directors. In most years nearly one hundred firms and individuals from the upper middle class subscribed as contributing members, but few of these took any active part. The regular membership was split betweeen young adults in middle-class occupations and a larger group of commercial employees, students, and some skilled workers (see Table 5/1 for the membership in December 1887).[26] Hardly any workers from Prague's outlying districts joined the Gymnastics Society, but the lower strata of the German population in the inner city comprised a larger portion of the regular members than in any other major German group. Any male over eighteen of good repute and of German ethnicity could join the Gymnastics Society simply by filing with the directors and paying a nominal entry fee of one florin and monthly dues of 80 kreuzer.[27] Individuals in middle-class occupations comprised over 40 percent of the regular members in 1887, but these tended to be young men with little distinction in liberal society. The university students, who comprised 16 percent of the regular membership, derived mostly from middle-class families in Prague and elsewhere in Austria. On the other hand, commerical and industrial employees, the largest German lower-strata groups in the inner city, provided fully 37 percent of the members. One-third of all the regular members were Jews, slightly less than the Jewish share in the Casino in the eighties, and Jews participated in the direction and all the activities of the Gymnastics Society.[28] Still, the large student and lower-strata contingents gave the Gymnastics Society a different constituency from most liberal groups. Moreover, the dual organizational structure facilitated the development of lower-strata leadership outside the Casino's direct control.

---

in SÚA Praha PP 1882-1887 V/43/5 and PP 1888-1892 V/39/1 Deutscher Turnverein in Prag, and ČM 1889-1900 30/41/5, 8, 15, 25. The dual structure resembled that of some English amateur football societies in the late nineteenth century and apparently served many of the same social functions. See Stephen Yeo, *Religion and Voluntary Organisations in Crisis* (London, 1976), pp. 186-96.

[26] Membership data derive from "Verwaltungsbericht des Vorstandes des Deutschen Turnvereins in Prag für das Jahr 1887" (Prague, 1888) in SÚA Praha PP 1888-1892 V/39/1.

[27] SÚA Praha PP 1882-1887 V/43/5: 12083, "Grundgesetz des Deutschen Turnvereins in Prag" (no date; found among papers for 1883).

[28] As with the Casino and the German Club, the Jewish members of the Gymnastics Society were identified by comparing the rosters with the tax registries of the Jewish religious community, with allowances for the fact that many members of the gym-

TABLE 5/1
Membership of the German Gymnastics Society,
December 1887, Compared to the German Casino, 1879-1880

	Gymn. Soc.	Casino
Banker/bank director	1.9%	1.3%
Manufacturer	5.7	8.7
Lawyer	9.9	8.6
Physician	3.8	2.3
Merchant/self-empl. bus.[a]	16.9	36.0
Government officer	0.9	3.1
University prof./docent	1.1	4.2
Gymnas. prof./school dir.	1.7	2.4
Bank/insur. co. officer	0	3.6
Engineer/architect	1.1	2.8
Landowner	0	1.5
Rentier/independent	0	2.8
SUBTOTAL	43.0%	77.3%
Supervisor/official/agent	13.5	7.1
Bookkeeper	19.3	3.7
Retail clerk	3.8	0
Government worker/clerk	0.4	0.3
Military	0	0.8
Shop-foreman	0	0.1
Skilled trade	1.9	0.8
Worker	0.6	0
Construction	0	0.6
Railroad/transportation	0	2.3
Teacher	1.1	0.3
Student	16.1	0.4
Theatre/arts/journalism	0.2	4.3
Widow/retired	0	1.3
Miscellaneous	0	0.7
TOTAL	100% (472)	100% (1,200)

[a] Includes small retailers.

The Gymnastics Society's functions and traditions also prepared the ground for opposition to the liberal notables. German gymnastics societies throughout Central Europe provided members with a variety of social and cultural services, including lectures, excursions, and drinking parties, in addition to the regular gymnastic practice and competitions. Although women and children

nastics group were too young to head their own households. The university students will be discussed further below, pp. 209-214. Anton Kiesslich, *Heitere Erinnerungen aus meinem Turnerleben* (Most, 1922), offers fictional vignettes about the lives of German commercial employees in Prague from an anti-Semitic perspective.

could not join most of the groups, they often reserved special hours in the gymnastics halls for children and admitted women as guests to some of the social events. By sponsoring such multifarious activities the German Gymnastics Society in Prague approximated a general-purpose social club for young men of the German lower strata in the inner city. The Austrian laws on associations prohibited such an organization from having formal political discussions, but the German gymnastics movement as a whole enshrined a strong Romantic German nationalism, which could be turned against the pro-Habsburg sentiments of Austria's German liberals.

The German Gymnastics Society in Prague participated in the larger German gymnastics movement through membership in the *Deutsche Turnerschaft*, the principal union of German gymnastics groups in Germany and Austria. Organized in 1868, the *Turnerschaft* saw the movement's purpose in building the individual's body and character so that he might help to unify and strengthen the whole German nation.[29] This general association of local groups sponsored regular meetings and gymnastic competitions at the regional, all-German or all-Austrian, and international levels. Such gatherings helped to reinforce the sentiments of German national solidarity within the movement and to propagate new ideological currents. Encouraged by contacts with German nationalists from elsewhere and frustrated by the growing weakness of the Prague Germans in local politics, members of the German Gymnastics Society became ever more determined in the mid-eighties to assert their nationalist feelings.[30]

Völkisch *Dissidents in the Gymnastics Society*

Anti-Semitic, *völkisch* tendencies arose in some of Austria's German gymnastics societies in 1885, but they only took hold in the Prague unit in late 1887 and early 1888. In the mid-eighties Georg von Schönerer won the first organized support for his militant anti-Semitism and Pan-Germanism in gymnastics groups and student fraternities in and around Vienna.[31] Schönerer attacked all the

[29] See Rychnovsky, *Turnverein*, pp. 1-21, and the general histories of the German gymnastics movement, Josef Recla, *Freiheit und Einheit: Eine Turngeschichte in gesamtdeutscher Beleuchtung* (Graz, 1931), and Eduard Neuendorff, *Geschichte der neueren deutschen Leibesübungen vom Beginn des 18. Jahrhunderts bis zur Gegenwart*, 4 vols. (Dresden, 1930-36).

[30] See Rychnovsky, *Turnverein*, pp. 25-30.

[31] See Paul Molisch, *Geschichte der deutschnationalen Bewegung in Oesterreich*, pp. 125-

barriers he perceived to the unity of the German nation: the Habsburg dynasty, Roman Catholicism, the Austro-Hungarian Compromise, great capitalist interests, and, above all, the Jews.

Schönerer's message struck responsive chords in gymnastic and student groups which already had traditions of radicalism, German nationalism, and hostility to the Habsburgs. After the Austro-Prussian War and the working out of the Austro-Hungarian Compromise, radical German youth in Austria had shown increasing hostility toward the remnants of bureaucratic absolutism in Austrian government and the elitism and cosmopolitanism of the moderate German liberals. These sentiments grew after the Franco-Prussian War and the financial crash of 1873, but most young radicals found a political outlet in the Progressive faction of the German liberal movement rather than in opposition to all liberals.[32] Now in the mid-eighties, students, who came primarily from middle-class and lower-middle-class families, confronted the economic uncertainties brought on by structural crisis in agriculture and a new commercial recession. Lower-strata elements in the gymnastics societies had even greater economic concerns. In politics all faced the new situation created by the collapse of German liberal power in Austria and the new strength of the conservative and Slavic forces. The conditions quickly ripened for a sharp break with the German liberal movement.

Vienna provided the impetus for the emergence of a *völkisch* movement in Prague. In October 1885 supporters of Schönerer founded the first avowedly anti-Semitic gymnastics club in Vienna, and members of this group gained control of the larger First Viennese Gymnastics Society (*I. Wiener Turnverein*) in March 1887. The split within the German club in the Reichsrat over anti-Semitism a month earlier indicated that the *völkisch* ideology was gaining strength elsewhere in German public life in Austria, and the *völkisch* members of the First Viennese Gymnastics Society soon began to seek converts in other gymnastics associations. In August 1887, at an all-Austrian gymnastics competition in Krems, Lower Austria,

---

48; idem, *Politische Geschichte der deutschen Hochschulen in Oesterreich von 1848 bis 1918* (Vienna and Leipzig, 1939), pp. 101-28; and Eduard Pichl, *Georg Schönerer*, 3rd ed., 6 vols. (Berlin and Oldenburg, 1938), II, passim.

[32] Although Austria's German student fraternities and gymnastics groups differed in social composition and activities, they shared much in general political development. On the young radicals up through the early 1880s, see Molisch, *Deutschnationale Bewegung*, pp. 69-115; idem, *Politische Geschichte*, pp. 68-103; and Whiteside, *Socialism of Fools*, pp. 43-63.

völkisch gymnasts from Vienna tried to win over sympathetic elements from elsewhere. Among others, the Viennese gained the support of Anton Kiesslich and Theodor Fischer, respectively chairman of the senior gymnasts and instructor for the German Gymnastics Society of Prague.[33] In the following nine months a vigorous *völkisch* group developed within the Prague association under the leadership of Kiesslich.

Anton Kiesslich's career in Prague's German liberal groups up to 1887 epitomized what ambitious lower-strata Germans might achieve in liberal social life. Kiesslich's background typified the lower-middle-class elements who stood at the fringes of Prague German society. Born in Prague in 1858, the son of a Catholic cafe owner, Kiesslich worked as a cashier and sometimes bookkeeper in a small commercial bank in the Lower New Town.[34] His energetic and dedicated service to the German Gymnastics Society won him election to the general board of directors in 1879 at age twenty-one, and in February 1883 he was elected gymnastics director.[35] Such distinctions in the Gymnastics Society gave Kiesslich opportunities for preferment in other liberal associations that a young bank cashier would have lacked otherwise. He served as one of three auditors for the German Merchants' Club from 1882 to 1888, and the German Club accepted him as a member in May 1883.[36] Still under thirty, Anton Kiesslich had risen rapidly through the lower ranks of local German liberal society by 1887. He had ambition and apparently charm and administrative talent as well, but Kiesslich could rise no higher in the liberals' status hierarchy without wealth, higher education, or a secure position among the self-employed. His experience in the liberal associations, however, gave him an intimate knowledge of the social and political order which he repudiated when he embraced the *völkisch* cause.

[33] Rychnovsky, *Turnverein*, pp. 63-65.

[34] The limited personal data on Kiesslich available derives primarily from police reports on the voluntary associations to which he belonged and his own thin police dossier, SÚA Praha PP 1908-1915 K/19/9 Anton Kiesslich. The *Israelitische Gemeindezeitung* (Prague), 15 Feb 1899, claimed that the cafe which Kiesslich's father owned and where his grandfather had been headwaiter had a largely Jewish clientele.

[35] SÚA Praha PP 1882-1887 V/43/5: NE 1696/pp VS 378, 28 Feb 1883, police report on the meeting of the Gymnastics Society of 27 February.

[36] SÚA Praha PP 1888-1892 V/24/23 Deutscher Kaufmännischer Verein: 10457/pp7469, 27 Dec 1882, report from the directors to the Prague police, and 1932/pp 1503, 26 Feb 1888, police report on the annual general meeting; and PP 1900-1907 V/15/10 Deutscher Verein in Prag: 4087/pp 2902, 9 May 1883, report of new members to the Prague police.

Kiesslich left no statement of his motives, but it is clear that he was increasingly attracted in the mid-1880s to a general ideological radicalism and to extreme nationalism in particular. Sometime before autumn 1883, he abandoned Roman Catholicism to join in the Old Catholic protest against papal authority and the actions of the first Vatican Council.[37] In early 1886 Kiesslich joined in founding the German-National Club in Prague. He did not openly espouse anti-Semitism, however, before August 1887, and he continued until then to have close connections with Jews in the Gymnastics Society and the German Merchants' Club.[38]

The *völkisch* movement in Prague's German Gymnastics Society had a short, stormy career. Neither Kiesslich and his followers nor the German liberal leadership proved willing to compromise their conflicting ideologies or to back away from confrontation. The interests of German solidarity could hardly unite groups which differed fundamentally in their notions of German ethnicity. Anti-Semitic literature began to circulate among the Prague gymnasts in the months after the competition at Krems in August 1887, and a *völkisch* group grew rapidly around Kiesslich. In late October the gymnasts' social club, *Tafelrunde* (Round Table), which Kiesslich headed, openly declared itself anti-Semitic.[39]

The response to the *völkisch* gymnasts by the leaders of the German Casino offers an object lesson in the liberal notables' determination to control all German public life in Prague during the difficult years of the eighties. Initially, the liberal majority among the directors of the Gymnastics Society reacted to the developments in Round Table by forcing all members who were leaders of the

[37] SÚA Praha PP 1882-1887 V/43/5 Deutscher Turnverein: ad NE 8087/pp a 883, 4 Oct 1883, deposition by Dr. August Rihl, president of the Gymnastics Society, in which Kiesslich is identified as an Old Catholic.

[38] In 1885, for instance, Kiesslich's vice-chairman for the board of senior gymnasts was a Jew, Albert Bondy; they reversed roles in directing the gymnasts' monthly drinking parties, SÚA Praha PP 1882-1887 V/27/10 Deutscher Turnverein: "Verwaltungsbericht des Vorstandes des Deutschen Turnvereins in Prag für das Jahr 1885."

[39] In the absence of any *völkisch* or Czech accounts of the events in the German Gymnastics Society between August 1887 and June 1888, one must rely on German liberal and police sources, including Rychnovsky, *Turnverein*, pp. 63-75; the report of Friedrich Kick, the president of the Society, to the regional council of the Turnerschaft, SÚA Praha PP 1888-1892 V/39/1: 30 June 1888, hectographed copy; "Verwaltungsbericht des Vorstandes des Deutschen Turnvereins in Prag für das Jahr 1887" (Prague, 1888); 30 Jan 1888 police report on the general meeting of 28 Jan 1888; and the 19 June 1888 police report on the general meeting of the Society, 18 June 1888, NE 5671x5693/pp 4326x4338.

Gymnastics Society to resign their offices. Thereafter, Professor Friedrich Kick, the president of the Society, and the liberal directors worked closely with Franz Schmeykal and other leaders of the Casino in trying to silence the dissidents' anti-Semitism, which the liberals set as the condition for continued membership in the Society. In December 1887, Kick and Schmeykal met with Kiesslich to ask him to disavow anti-Semitism, but the latter refused to make the sweeping denial that Kick wanted. The dispute nominally focused on anti-Semitism, but that was only the centerpiece in a general dispute over the understanding of the German national cause. The anti-Semitic faction grew to around sixty by spring 1888, and sparring between it and the liberal leadership continued until June.

The conflict in the Gymnastics Society ended with an open break between the liberal and *völkisch* elements. In May the *völkisch* members requested use of the gymnastics hall for separate exercise periods, and Kiesslich avowed himself unequivocally as an anti-Semite. Kick refused to make any concessions, and on June 18 he announced at a special general meeting of the Gymnastics Society that sixty-four members had resigned.[40] Kick asserted that the group's anti-Semitism was the sole cause of the secession. Philipp Knoll followed Kick to the rostrum to demonstrate the Casino's solidarity with the liberal directors of the Gymnastics Society. Knoll condemned both the earlier attempt of the *völkisch* group to gain autonomy within the Society and their latest request to use the gymnastics hall. Those in attendance then approved a resolution proposed by Knoll in support of Kick's actions.

Those who joined in the *völkisch* secession cannot be identified precisely. The police received no list of the sixty-four who initially left the Gymnastics Society, and the new German Men's Gymnastics Society (*Deutscher Männerturnverein*), which they founded, left no membership lists.[41] Altogether, the names of 107 non-Jews who were members of the German Gymnastics Society at the end of 1887 failed to appear on the new roster a year later, and in occupations the 107 had much the same character as the whole membership of the Gymnastics Society.[42]

[40] *Bohemia*, 20 June 1888(M), and SÚA Praha PP 1888-1892 V/39/1: NE 5671x5693/pp 4326x4338, 19 June 1888 police report on the 18 June meeting.

[41] SÚA Praha PP 1893-1899 V/43/3 Deutscher Männerturnverein in Prag, includes annual reports, lists of officers and directors, police reports on meetings, 1888-1899, but no membership lists.

[42] 1887 membership from "Verwaltungsbericht" as in n. 26 above, late 1888 mem-

The rupture between German liberal and *völkisch* elements came relatively late in Prague. The skilled workers, students, and young lower-middle-class elements who followed Anton Kiesslich in 1888 did not act in Prague in a vacuum. Rather, they were latecomers who took their cues from Vienna and from other German communities in Austria. Hitherto the liberal notables of the Casino had successfully stifled any hint of opposition within Prague's German organizations, and until 1888 the German Handworkers' Society had encountered no serious German rival for the support of lower-strata elements in the city. The Gymnastics Society, however, had its own distinctive nationalist traditions and a large, organized contingent of small retailers, craftsmen, clerks, and university students. By 1887-1888 the members were well primed for anti-liberal radicalism, and the radicals' organizational base in the board of senior gymnasts and Round Table made it difficult for the liberal leaders to break up the group. Refusing to tolerate any open *völkisch* activity in their associational network, the liberals had no choice but to force the dissidents to leave the Gymnastics Society. The German Gymnastics Society continued to operate under liberal control until after World War I, while the *völkisch* gymnasts survived all further efforts by the liberal notables to silence them.[43]

When a revolt against liberalism finally occurred among the Prague Germans, it involved individuals who had had a place in the liberal community structure. Anti-liberal mass politics did not arise here or elsewhere in Austria simply through a welling up of the lower strata whom a restricted suffrage and elitist liberals had formerly excluded from public life. The intellectuals who at first led most of the mass parties and the majority of the university students who served as the shock troops for radical German nationalism had themselves belonged to middle-class society. Yet the small retailers, white-collar employees, and skilled workers who joined the *völkisch* movement in Prague had also had some access to liberal middle-class public life through associations such as the Gymnastics Society and the German Merchants' Club. Like Anton Kiesslich himself, some had even been able to win limited social honors there. Many knew well what they now attacked in the liberal social and political order.

---

bership from SÚA Praha PP 1888-1892 V/39/1: "Verwaltungsbericht des Vorstandes des Deutschen Turnvereins in Prag für das Jahr 1888" (Prague, 1889). Bookkeepers with 22%, businessmen and shopkeepers (18%), supervisors, agents, and employees (17%), and students (14%) were most numerous among the 107 Gentiles who left.

[43] Rychnovsky, *Turnverein*, pp. 70-91.

It was the limits on the power and status which lower-middle-class elements could achieve in liberal society which incited much of their protest in Prague and throughout Austria in the late seventies and eighties.[44] Political and economic adversity led most German liberals to a heightened defense of individualist economics and of the privileges of the German *Bürgertum*. Liberal ideologues in all national camps had previously held out promises of economic advancement and upward social mobility to persuade the poor to accept deferential politics, but such assurances were belied by the recessions of the mid-seventies and mid-eighties and the liberals' increasing social conservatism. In cities and towns throughout Austria a variety of anti-liberal forces took the opportunity to lead revolts of the lower middle classes and workers against the moderate liberals' unremitting demands for deference. In Prague the efforts of liberal notables to defend a declining German middle-class minority against the Czech majority and opposition in German Bohemia only added to the rigidity of the liberals' social and political order.

Lower-strata Germans in the Bohemian capital who wanted an alternative public life to that of the liberals had few options available before the mid-nineties. Social Catholicism had little appeal to Bohemian Germans in the late nineteenth century: popular piety was often weak here and anti-clericalism strong compared to Moravia and the Habsburg Hereditary Lands, and in Prague both the lower clergy and the hierarchy were closely identified with the Czechs.[45] Social Democracy suffered from governmental repression in Austria until 1891, and thereafter German industrial workers in Prague proved too few and scattered to develop their own socialist organization until 1896.[46] In the interim the Czech Social Democrats welcomed German support. For most of the nineties, the *völkisch* groups which sprang up around the Men's Gymnastics Society offered the German lower strata the only alternative to the German liberal community, short of joining Czech groups.

[44] Cf. John W. Boyer in *The Journal of Modern History*, L, pp. 72-76, who argues that the Christian Socials enjoyed much of their success in Vienna to their affirmation of the unity of the *Bürgertum* and of lower-middle-class claims to *bürgerlich* status and respectability without deference to the liberal notables.

[45] On the politics of the Catholic Church and the Christian Social movement in the Bohemians Lands, see Garver, *Young Czech Party*, pp. 283-88, and Barbara Schmid-Egger, *Klerus und Politik in Böhmen um 1900* (Munich, 1974), passim.

[46] See Chapter 6 for discussion of the German Social Democratic group in Prague before 1914.

The Völkisch *Outcasts*

Continuing hostility from the German liberals forced the *völkisch* elements in Prague to create their own associational network in isolation from the liberal groups. While the *völkisch* bodies offered a clear alternative to Catholic and Protestant Germans who might be dissatisfied with the liberal order, the radical nationalists had difficulty in winning popular support here. They faced all the problems inherent in any appeal for German lower-strata support, as well as treatment as outcasts by all the organizations under liberal control. Moreover, the liberal notables benefited from a continuing tendency of Germans in all strata to equate German ethnic solidarity with acceptance of the Casino's leadership. The success of German liberal "census candidates" in Reichsrat elections even after the suffrage reforms of 1882, 1896, and 1907 demonstrated that continuing support even if liberal associations themselves did not attract large numbers of lower-strata members.

Kiesslich and the other *völkisch* gymnasts organized the German Men's Gymnastics Society on September 15, 1888. A revived German-National Club, several small singing societies, and a dozen local chapters of the League of Germans in Bohemia (*Bund der Deutschen in Böhmen*) followed in the next fifteen years. At first the *völkisch* organizations hoped to coexist peacefully with the German liberal associations in Prague and even requested aid. Yet the refusal of the Casino to temporize further with the radical nationalists and the widening split between the German liberal and nationalist forces in parliamentary politics encouraged the local *völkisch* groups to become increasingly belligerent. After 1890 they missed no opportunity to attack or ridicule the values and activities of the liberal community. Later in the nineties, the radical German nationalists even began to sponsor an annual "Peasants Ball," which the more humble Germans in Prague might attend in homespun in mock imitation of the elegant affairs sponsored by the Casino and the German Theatre Society.[47]

The *völkisch* movement throughout Austria adopted many of the organizational forms developed earlier by the German liberals.[48]

---

[47] Announced in *Der Deutsche Volksbote*, 9 Jan 1898; reported in *Bohemia*, 11 Feb 1912(M).

[48] See Jiří Kořalka, *Všeněmecký svaz a česká otázka koncem 19. století*, Rozpravy Československé akademie věd, Řada společ. věd, LXXIII, no. 12 (Prague, 1963), pp. 12-22. Whiteside, *Socialism of Fools*, pp. 107-40, 188-224, recounts the devel-

In Prague, however, the small number of followers and their dispersion in the city limited the diversity of *völkisch* associations and prevented the rise of any preeminent group analogous to the German Casino. Like their liberal counterparts, the *völkisch* groups indulged in formalities to satisfy the members' cravings for social honors, and they reserved the highest offices for individuals who were respectable by conventional middle-class standards. The physician Dr. Alexander Hnilitschka and Dr. Heinrich Osborne, the lawyer who had led the anti-Semitic clique in the Casino, each served a term as president of the Men's Gymnastics Society in the first years. Many of the initial directors had previously sat on the board of senior gymnasts in the German Gymnastics Society. Anton Kiesslich took over the presidency of the Men's Gymnastics Society after Osborne's sudden death in 1890, and he presided almost continuously until 1918.[49]

Like many other *völkisch* groups in Austria, those in Prague hoped to win a broad following by avoiding extreme Pan-Germanism. Although the Prague organizations were openly anti-Semitic, they hesitated to adopt racial principles as formal policy, and the bylaws of the Men's Gymnastics Society in its first nine years did not explicitly exclude Jews from membership.[50] This drew complaints in February 1896 from local members of the Pan-German cultural league, the *Germanenbund*. The critics asserted that the Men's Gymnastics Society was not yet sufficiently anti-Semitic and asked why it remained in the *Deutsche Turnerschaft*, which still permitted Jewish members. Such extremism had an alien ring in Prague even in the *völkisch* groups; the police officer in attendance reported that the critics were mostly students who had come from Vienna.[51] Kiesslich responded that the Society fully supported an Aryans-only policy. For the time being, though, it was tactically better to remain in the *Turnerschaft*, where anti-Semitic groups already had a majority, than to start a new union.[52] Kiesslich finally recommended withdrawal from the *Turnerschaft* and formal exclu-

opment of the Pan-German organizations without asking whether they resembled any liberal bodies.

[49] SÚA Praha PP 1893-1899 V/43/3 Deutscher Männerturnverein in Prag: lists of officers and directors, 1888-1898; and reports on the Men's Gymnastics Society in *Der Deutsche Volksbote*, 1891-1910.

[50] SÚA Praha PP 1893-1899 V/43/3: 7721, "Grundgesetz" (1888).

[51] SÚA Praha PP 1893-1899 V/43/3: 1955pp/1561, 9 Feb 1896, police report on the meeting of 8 February.

[52] SÚA Praha PP 1893-1899 V/43/3: 2980pp, 1 March 1896, police report on the meeting of 29 February.

sion of Jews in November 1897 at the height of the German nationalist outcry against the language ordinances proposed by the
Badeni government. As Anton Kiesslich pointed out, however, the
change in the bylaws would only "correspond with what had already been the actual practice."[53]

The Men's Gymnastics Society attracted a sizable membership in
the first years of its existence. In February 1889 it had 302 regular
members, compared to the 514 in the German Gymnastics Society
in Prague.[54] In March 1895, the Men's Gymnastics Society had 411
regular members.[55] In the face of official hostility to radical nationalist groups, neither the gymnastics association nor any of the
other *völkisch* organizations in the city volunteered membership lists
to the police. Apparently none published yearbooks with rosters
of members like those of the larger liberal groups. Police reports
on the activities of the Men's Gymnastics Society consistently noted
the presence of large numbers of university students, who comprised perhaps half of all the participants. The association of students from the districts of Česká lípa, Zelená hora, and the Ohře
valley (*Leipaer-, Grünberger-, und Egerländer Landtag*) and the student
fraternities Teutonia and Ghibellenia supplied particularly large
contingents.[56] White-collar employees, small retailers, and a few
skilled workers apparently provided most of the balance. The directors of the Men's Gymnastics Society divided almost evenly
among small businessmen, commercial employees, and university
students.[57]

The Men's Gymnastics Society served as the base for a network
of interconnected *völkisch* institutions in Prague. In September 1890
the trustees of the German-National Party in Cisleithania agreed
to support a *völkisch* newspaper in Prague under Kiesslich's edi-

[53] SÚA Praha PP 1893-1899 V/43/3: ad Z 18568/pp, 15 Nov 1897, police report
on the meeting of 6 November. See Chapter 6, p. 238, for discussion of the Badeni
ministry.

[54] SÚA Praha PP 1893-1899 V/43/3: NE 2216, 27 Feb 1889, police report on the
meeting of the Men's Gymnastics Society on 25 February; and PP 1888-1892 V/39/
1: "Verwaltungsbericht des Vorstandes des Deutschen Turnvereines in Prag für das
Jahr 1889" (Prague, 1890).

[55] SÚA Praha PP 1893-1899 V/43/3: 4 March 1895, police report on the annual
general meeting of 2 March.

[56] SÚA Praha PP 1893-1899 V/43/3: 2292/pp 1634, 7 March 1891, police report
on the meeting of 2 March; Z 11436, 20 Oct 1892, police report on the meeting of
19 October.

[57] SÚA Praha PP 1893-1899 V/43/3 Deutscher Männerturnverein: lists of officers
and directors, 1888-1899.

torship, and *Der Deutsche Volksbote* began publication as a bi-monthly on January 1, 1891.[58] After the founding of the *Volksbote*, Kiesslich made a full-time career of German nationalist politics and journalism. Schönerer's lieutenant Karl Hermann Wolf contributed the lead article in the first number, and in the second issue Kiesslich began the vituperation of the local German liberal establishment that became a regular feature of the *Volksbote* in the next two decades.[59]

At the end of January 1891, a group of thirteen reorganized the German-National Club in Prague to serve as the local unit of the German-National Party. Kiesslich presided, and the others present, mostly commercial employees and small businessmen, were all prominent in the Men's Gymnastics Society.[60] The German-National Club initially announced its dedication to the ideals of Georg von Schönerer, but the group proved more loyal in subsequent years to German nationalist leaders in northern Bohemia. The Prague organization joined most of the northern Bohemian leaders in 1893 in repudiating Schönerer's intransigent extremism and his repeated attacks on the Habsburg dynasty. In 1895 the Club formally joined the German People's Party led by Otto Steinwender and Ernst Bareuther.[61] Kiesslich openly condemned the futility of Schönerer's politics, but this contributed little to winning support for a *völkisch* political organization in Prague.

The German-National Club attracted even fewer members among Prague's lower-strata Germans than did the liberal political associations. The *völkisch* group seldom had more than fifty members from the metropolitan area at any time between 1891 and World War I.[62] Several hundred students might attend the Club's meetings on occasion, but Austrian law permitted only those who had reached their majority to join a political association.[63] Small

[58] Pichl, *Schönerer*, IV, pp. 178-80; VI, p. 187.

[59] *Der Deutsche Volksbote*, 1 Jan and 16 Jan 1891.

[60] SÚA Praha PP 1893-1899 V/32/10 Deutsch-nationaler Verein: 1017 pp702, 31 Jan 1891, police report on the organizational meeting of 30 January. Pichl, *Schönerer*, IV, pp. 270-76, discusses the group from a Schönerianer perspective.

[61] Pichl, *Schönerer*, IV, pp. 1-21, 409-12.

[62] Like the earlier German-National Club in 1886 and 1887, the *völkisch* organization included some members from outside Prague. In May 1892, 27 of the 53 members resided outside of Prague and its suburbs; in November 1903, 11 of the 58 came from outside, SÚA Praha PP 1893-1899 V/32/10: 4927/pp 3514, 1 May 1892, membership list; PP 1908-1915 V/15/131: 19378/pp, 30 Nov 1903, membership list.

[63] See Tezner, "Vereinsrecht," in Mischler and Ulbrich, ed., 2nd ed., IV, pp. 712-22.

shopkeepers, managers, and other qualified employees from throughout the city and suburbs comprised nineteen of the twenty-six members in May 1892 who were residents of Prague. Only four of the Prague members were in learned professions, while three were students at the German University or the German Technical College.[64] Since none of the members from Prague were workers in the handicrafts or industry, all might have found some place in the liberal associations. Indeed, three of them belonged to the German Casino at this time although they could not express their *völkisch* sentiments there.

Of all the *völkisch* organizations, only the chapters of the League of Germans in Bohemia had any real success in winning members among the German white-collar employees and skilled workers dispersed through the poorer districts of Prague. Modeled on the liberals' German League for the Bohemian Woods and the equivalent Czech National Union of the Bohemian Woods (*Národní jednota pošumavská*), the League of Germans provided financial aid for German farmers and businessmen in communities on the boundaries between German and Czech settlements and tried to recruit German settlers for those areas. The League also campaigned for the exclusive hiring of Germans by German employers and disseminated *völkisch* propaganda. Although officially non-political, the myriad chapters of the League provided a grass-roots network for the radical German nationalist movement in Bohemia, and they formed links with the Pan-German League in Germany.[65] Anton Kiesslich joined in founding the League of Germans in Bohemia in July 1894 and served as vice-president and director of its central administration in Prague until World War I.[66]

Together the various chapters of the League in Prague attracted the largest membership of any *völkisch* organization in the city before 1914. Kiesslich and a young lawyer, Dr. Josef Feiler, presided over the first meeting of the General Local Chapter for Prague on October 6, 1894.[67] A week later members of the German Men's

[64] Membership list, 1 May 1892, as in n. 62.

[65] On the League of Germans in Bohemia, see Jiří Kořalka, "La montée du pangermanisme et l'Autriche-Hongrie," *Historica*, X (1965), pp. 232-34; idem, *Všeněmecký svaz*, pp. 17, 27-32; Molisch, *Deutschnationale Bewegung*, p. 176; and the contemporary report by Franz Jesser, "Der Bund der Deutschen in Böhmen," *Deutsche Arbeit*, X (1911), pp. 463-67.

[66] SÚA Praha PP 1908-1915 V/10/36 Bund der Deutschen in Böhmen: leaflets, announcements, lists of officers, and police reports on meetings in the Prague area, 1894-1915.

[67] SÚA Praha PP 1908-1915 V/10/36: ad X 23.350/19.015pp, 7 October 1894,

Gymnastics Society organized their own chapter, and a women's group and five student chapters followed in the next seven months.[68] Additional chapters appeared later in the peripheral districts of Prague: Vinohrady (May 1896), Žižkov (February 1897), Smíchov (November 1897), and Malá strana-Hradčany (May 1901). By 1900 the League's potent combination of radical nationalism, protectionist economics, anti-Semitism, and general opposition to the liberals had drawn around 60,000 members throughout Bohemia.[69] It is hard to find totals for all the Prague chapters in any single year. Excluding the student chapters, most of whose members came from outside the city, the League's units in the provincial capital had more than a thousand members in the first years of the twentieth century (see Table 5/2 for the 1904 totals).[70] The actual number of individuals who belonged to the League in Prague was something less than this since some belonged to several chapters simultaneously.

In the absence of rosters one can only extrapolate the social composition of the League's membership from the identity of its

TABLE 5/2
Members of the League of Germans in Bohemia, Prague, December 1904

	Founding Members	Regular Members
General Chapter, Prague	83	193
Women's and Girls' Chapter	7	140
Gymnasts' Chapter, Prague	17	197
Malá strana-Hradčany	—	40
Karlín	—	161
Smíchov	1	78
Vinohrady	3	166
Žižkov	7	113
TOTAL	118	1,088

police report on the organizational meeting of 6 October for the Allgemeine Ortsgruppe Prag, Bund der Deutschen in Böhmen.

[68] SÚA Praha PP 1908-1915 V/10/36: 12988, 14 October 1894, police report on the founding of the Turnerortsgruppe, Prag; 27778/pp27822, 21 Nov 1894, announcement of the organizational meeting for the Frauen- und Mädchenortsgruppe, Prag.

[69] Franz Jesser, *Zehn Jahre völkische Schutzarbeit: Festschrift anlässlich der Feier des 10-jährigen Bestandes des Bundes der Deutschen in Böhmen* (Prague, 1904), p. 19 [In SÚA Praha PP 1908-1915 V/10/36: Bund der Deutschen in Böhmen, ct. II/2426].

[70] SÚA Praha PP 1908-1915 V/10/36: "Bericht über die Tätigkeit des Bundes der Deutschen in Böhmen im elften Vereinsjahr 1904" (Prague, 1905). The report offers no explanation for its omission of the student chapters.

officers and directors. Commercial and industrial employees, independent craftsmen, small businessmen, engineers, a few physicians, and many students served as directors of the General Chapter in Prague in the middle and late nineties.[71] Police reports on the activities of the chapters suggest that the same elements, along with a number of wives and unmarried daughters, comprised the great majority of members in the city proper. Students played a much smaller role in the suburban chapters, where engineers and commercial or industrial employees predominated among the directors.[72]

Support for the Völkisch *Movement: Students and Lower-Strata Residents*

University students apparently provided the largest share of participants in nearly all the *völkisch* groups of the inner city. Indeed, the police and German liberal leaders tended to view *völkisch* activity among adult German residents as largely incidental to that among students.[73] Such observations must be discounted somewhat since the police were especially sensitive to the students' extremist rhetoric and to their propensity for violent confrontations with Czech groups. Members of the liberal community, on the other hand, doubtlessly found it reassuring to be able to blame local *völkisch* manifestations on students from outside Prague rather than having to admit that any of the local German residents were involved. Still, all evidence indicates that university students played a decisive role in the *völkisch* groups of the inner city.

Little *völkisch* activity went on in the Old Town and New Town without substantial student participation. The General Chapter and Women's and Girls' Local Chapter of the League of Germans met

[71] SÚA Praha PP 1908-1915 V/10/36: 23.987/pp 19586, Bundesleitung des Bundes der Deutschen in Böhmen to the Prague police, 10 October 1894, reporting the names of officers and directors for the Allgemeine Ortsgruppe, Prag.

[72] SÚA Praha PP 1908-1915 V/10/36: police reports and lists of officers and directors for the various Prague chapters of the League of Germans in Bohemia, 1894-1915.

[73] Allgemeines Verwaltungsarchiv, Wien (General Administrative Archive, Vienna, hereafter AVA), Ministerium des Innern-Praesidialakten (MI-Praes.), in gen. 22 (1895-1897), Kt. 843, Pr 5/6 5774/MI 1897, Bohemian Governor Count Coudenhove to Minister-president Badeni, 31 May 1897; Else Bergmann, "Familiengeschichte" (unpubl. typescript in LBI New York; used by permission), p. 30; Arnold Höllriegel, "Die Fahrt auf dem Katarakt," pp. 24-25; and Emil Utitz, *Egon Erwin Kisch, der klassische Journalist* (Berlin, 1956), pp. 32-37, all present such views.

infrequently and apparently did little beside raising funds.[74] In contrast, the German Men's Gymnastics Society, the student chapters of the League of Germans, and the tiny German-National Club sponsored most *völkisch* lectures and social gatherings. The police officers who attended generally reported that students from the German University and German Technical College comprised the largest single group, often a majority, among the participants.[75] The sociology and politics of German students in Prague in the late nineteenth century merit independent study, but contemporary observers agreed that student support for the *völkisch* organizations came overwhelmingly from radically nationalistic student fraternities. These in turn drew the great majority of their members from outside the Bohemian capital.[76]

Many student groups in late-nineteenth-century Austria and Germany had traditions of political radicalism and German nationalism which dated back to 1848 or even to the Napoleonic wars.[77] Most of Austria's traditional duelling fraternities, the *Corps*, and the associations of students from various regions, the *Landsmannschaften*, were politically conservative throughout the nineteenth century. On the other hand, many of the younger *Burschenschaften* began to manifest radical German nationalism and some anti-Semitism in the fifties and sixties, well before the *völkisch* ideology had any important role in Austrian politics. Few Austrian university students came from the working class or identified with

---

[74] SÚA Praha PP 1908-1915 V/10/36: police reports on the Prague chapters of the League of Germans in Bohemia, 1894-1915.

[75] SÚA Praha PP 1893-1899 V/43/3 Deutscher Männerturnverein in Prag, V/32/10 Deutsch-nationaler Verein; and PP 1908-1915 V/10/36 Bund der Deutschen in Böhmen, V/15/131 Deutsch-nationaler Verein: police reports on meetings, 1888-1915.

[76] See Antonín Slavíček, "Dějiny a archiv spolku Lese- und Redehalle der deutschen Studenten in Prag" (unpubl. diploma essay, Philosophical Faculty, Charles University, 1973) for a brief history of German student politics in Prague in the late nineteenth century and a survey of archival holdings in the Charles University Archive. Slavíček, p. 63, upholds the contention of Brod, *Streitbares Leben*, 2nd ed., pp. 152-54, and others that the *völkisch* groups tended to recruit students from outside Prague while Prague students joined the liberal Reading Hall.

[77] On German nationalism among Austrian students see Molisch, *Politische Geschichte*, passim, and Whiteside, *Socialism of Fools*, pp. 43-63. For Central Europe as a whole, see Hermann Haupt, ed., *Quellen und Darstellungen zur Geschichte der Burschenschaft und der deutschen Einheitsbewegung*, 17 vols. (Heidelberg, 1910-1940), and Konrad Jarausch, "The Sources of German Student Unrest, 1815-1848," in Lawrence Stone, ed., *The University in Society* (Princeton, 1974), pp. 553-70.

it before 1900, and Marxian socialism began to find support among German students in Cisleithania only in the late 1890s.[78]

As in the Gymnastics Society, the *völkisch* ideology developed late in Prague's German student groups compared to elsewhere in Austria. Exclusion from the new Germany after 1866 turned the nationalism of some of Austria's German students against the Habsburg state, but through the middle seventies most of the student radicalism found a resting place in the Progressive wing of the German liberal movement in Austria.[79] The crash of 1873, the ensuing financial and political scandals, and the inflexibility of many German liberals stimulated opposition to all liberals and growing anti-Semitism in some of the *Burschenschaften* of Vienna and Graz. In 1878 student groups in each of those cities began to support the Pan-Germanism and extreme anti-Semitism of Georg von Schönerer. Over the following six years *Burschenschaften* in Vienna and Graz took formal action to exclude Jews.[80] *Völkisch* politics won adherents among students in Lower Austria and Styria before it had much strength among the adult public in those lands. In Prague, on the other hand, German student politics developed more in phase with the general evolution of Bohemian German public life.

Through the mid-eighties the Czech-German conflict in Prague exerted strong pressures on the local German student groups to maintain political unity. Liberal forces benefited from those pressures in the student fraternities just as they did among adult German residents in the city. Conservative *Corps* predominated among the student groups in Prague until around 1876, when more nationalistic *Burschenschaften* began to gain ascendancy. Nonetheless, the *Burschenschaften* remained within the pale of German liberal politics until 1885.[81] Two of the largest in Prague, the Carolina and the Ghibellenia, denounced anti-Semitism as late as 1882.[82] Only

[78] Molisch, *Politische Geschichte*, pp. 137-42.

[79] See Molisch, *Politische Geschichte*, pp. 58-97; Whiteside, *Socialism of Fools*, pp. 48-52, 68-74; Harrington-Müller, *Der Fortschrittsklub*, pp. 14-26; and William J. McGrath, *Dionysian Art and Populist Politics in Austria* (New Haven and London, 1971), pp. 33-52.

[80] Molisch, *Politische Geschichte*, pp. 80-97; and Whiteside, *Socialism of Fools*, pp. 61-63, 73-80.

[81] See Molisch, *Politische Geschichte*, pp. 80-97; and Wolfgang W. von Wolmar, *Prag und das Reich: 600 Jahre Kampf deutscher Studenten* (Dresden, 1943), p. 356.

[82] Oscar Hackel, "Geschichte der akad. Burschenschaft 'Carolina,'" in *70 Jahre akad. Burschenschaft Carolina zu Prag* (Karlový vary, 1930), pp. 48-49.

in 1884 and 1885, as tensions grew between moderates and radicals in the German liberal ranks and as the Schönerianer began to attack the liberals more vigorously, did a number of local *Burschenschaften* adopt *völkisch* views and informally begin to exclude Jews.[83]

For some students *völkisch* politics expressed a general revolt against the values of their parents' generation, but many of those who took up radical nationalism in Prague in the mid-eighties did so at the same time that their parents in German Bohemia were beginning to oppose the liberal notables. Although *völkisch* spokesmen indulged in revolutionary rhetoric, they also played on conventional concerns about future economic security which many students shared with their elders. The *völkisch* emphasis on the social, economic, and political solidarity of the German people proved reassuring to middle-class and lower-middle-class elements in the face of hard times in agriculture and commerce in the mid-eighties.[84]

Radical nationalism strengthened in many of the Prague *Burschenschaften* in the late eighties, but the *völkisch* students did not break formally with the liberals until 1890-1891. Only then, after the German nationalists had emerged as an independent, organized force in Austrian politics, did all the *völkisch* student associations in Prague adopt new constitutions with anti-Semitic clauses. All the German nationalist members withdrew from the liberal-dominated Reading Hall of German Students in July 1891, and founded their own reading and lecture society, the Germania, in May 1892. In the meantime, the Reading Hall lost half its membership, and other liberal student groups sustained similar losses.[85]

The growing hostility in German Bohemia toward the German community in Prague in the eighties and nineties added a special

---

[83] *Ibid.* According to *Geschichte der Prager Burschenschaft "Arminia," 1879-1929* (Prague, 1929), p. 22, Arminia only stopped accepting Jews as members in 1889. Wolmar's Nazi interpretation, *Prag und das Reich*, pp. 373-74, asserts that anti-Semitism developed earlier in the Prague Burschenschaften.

[84] Contrast this interpretation of German student politics in Prague with the discussions of Austrian student radicalism in McGrath, *Dionysian Art*, pp. 19-21; Whiteside, *Socialism of Fools*, pp. 57-58; and Adam Wandruszka, "Österreichs Politische Struktur," in Heinrich Benedikt, ed., *Geschichte der Republik Österreich* (Munich, 1954), pp. 376-77, which emphasize the elements of adolescent revolt and generational conflict. Systematic studies of a broad range of student groups using anthropological techniques are needed to clarify the bases of student radicalism.

[85] Hackel in *70 Jahre Carolina*, p. 50; Wolmar, *Prag und das Reich*, p. 374. Slavíček, "Dějiny a archiv," p. 57, reports that the Lesehalle had 635 members in 1891 and only 334 in 1892.

dimension to *völkisch* politics among the university students. Sociological surveys of the German students are not available from before 1900, but in 1910 only one quarter of the 2,200 students in the German University and German Technical College came from Prague itself. Despite a decline in the number of students from German Bohemia and from other parts of Austria after 1897, 60 percent of the student body in 1910 still derived from Bohemian locales outside Prague and 14 percent from the rest of Cisleithania.[86] Prague's liberal German burghers expected from the students the same deference they asked of the parents, and as dissatisfaction with the old liberal leadership spread in German Bohemia and the students developed more radical tendencies, liberals in Prague viewed the transient student population with increasing fear and resentment. One *völkisch* student later reminisced, "The German society that separated itself strictly from the Czech also cut itself off mistrustfully from those [students] of its own people who came into the city."[87] Contemporary accounts all agreed that youth from German Bohemia and the Habsburg Hereditary Lands provided the great bulk of support for the *völkisch* student groups in Prague.[88]

The conditions of life for German students in the Bohemian capital only added to the animosity that those from outside might feel toward Prague's proud German middle class. Hardly any of the students in the German University and German Technical College came from impoverished homes: in 1900 less than 1 percent of all the students' fathers were workers, while 38 percent were self-employed in all economic sectors, and 33 percent were salaried employees in public service or in the free professions.[89] Nevertheless, a shortage of dormitory facilities for German students and general competition for housing in the inner city forced many of

[86] Wilhelm Winkler, *Die soziale Lage der Deutschen Hochschulstudentenschaft Prags* (Vienna and Leipzig, 1912), pp. 23-24. 94.3% of the students in the two institutions in 1910 gave German as their mother tongue, 3.1% Czech.

[87] Karl Hans Strobl, *Heimat im frühen Licht* (České Budějovice and Leipzig, 1942), pp. 336-37. See Bergmann, "Familiengeschichte," p. 30, and Utitz, *Kisch*, pp. 31-32, for the perspective of German Jews in Prague on German students from outside the city.

[88] Slavíček, "Dějiny a archiv," p. 63. See also Brod, *Streitbares Leben*, rev. ed., p. 153; Höllriegel, "Fahrt auf dem Katarakt," pp. 24-25; and Utitz, *Kisch*, pp. 32-33. Membership lists for Germania could not be located in SÚA Praha or the Charles University Archive. The officers lists in SÚA Praha PP 1893-1899 V/20/8 show that nearly all the officers came from outside the Bohemian capital.

[89] Winkler, *Die soziale Lage*, p. 26.

the students from outside to make do with shabby, rented rooms scattered all over the city.[90] Many also had to scrape to find odd jobs or tutoring to augment meager living allowances. Moreover, students from German Bohemia or the Hereditary Lands often faced open hostility from the adult Czech population and from Czech students, in addition to the cool reception from the city's German burghers. All these conditions helped to embitter relations between the German students from outside and the liberal community and heightened the students' taste for radical nationalism.

Apart from the groups which had strong student support, the *völkisch* movement in Prague showed vitality only on the left bank of the Vltava and in the suburbs. Few students participated in the League of Germans in Bohemia in Malá strana-Hradčany, Smíchov, Karlín, Vinohrady, and Žižkov. Mainly adult residents from the lower middle class and working strata joined the League here. The local chapters met regularly for lectures, discussions, and social events and functioned much like general social organizations for lower-strata Germans.[91] In this they competed almost directly with the local units of the German School Society controlled by liberals.

In the 1890s, the League of Germans in Bohemia apparently won greater support from lower-strata Germans in the suburbs than did liberal groups. In Vinohrady, for instance, membership in the German School Society held steady at around ninety in the mid-nineties, and this included many from the middle class. Riding the crest of German nationalist feeling in late 1897, the more strongly lower-strata chapter of the League in Vinohrady had 160 members. At the same time, the local unit of the League in Žižkov had over 100 members, although there were only 800 German-speaking citizens in the whole district at the end of the century.[92]

The *völkisch* organizations offered Germans in the outlying districts a greater degree of egalitarianism in group life than did the liberal associations. The German residents of the suburbs were generally not only poorer but also more thinly dispersed and more predominantly Christian than those in the Old Town and New

[90] *Ibid.*, pp. 35-94, passim.
[91] SÚA Praha PP 1908-1915 V/10/36 Bund der Deutschen in Böhmen: lists of officers and directors and police reports on the local chapters in the Prague suburbs.
[92] SÚA Praha PP 1900-1907 V/10/25 Bund der Deutschen in Böhmen: 16986/pp 14757, 14 Oct 1897 police report on the Vinohrady chapter; ad 2083pp, 27 Feb 1898 police report on the annual general meeting of the Žižkov chapter, 2 February 1898.

Town. Even though the suburban chapters of the German School Society and the German Handworkers' Society tried to attract humbler elements, they still insisted on the primacy of the propertied and educated in public life. The League of Germans in Bohemia, in contrast, glorified the "little man." A narrower social distance separated leaders from the led in the suburban chapters of the League than in any of the liberal groups. Teachers, clerks, industrial employees, and skilled workers might direct the activities of the League's units. Among the chief attractions of the *völkisch* organizations in Prague was the fact that they offered the German lower strata both the means to protest their confinement to the bottom of the liberals' social and political hierarchy and the opportunity to engage in a more equal group life.

The Liberal Tactics of Containment and Isolation

The support that *völkisch* groups won among permanent German residents of Prague represented a considerable achievement since the liberal community did its best to stifle all radical German nationalism in the city. After the secession of the anti-Semitic group from the Gymnastics Society in 1888, the liberal leadership invoked a policy of excluding all openly *völkisch* elements from accepted German society and denying them all assistance from the liberal organizations. The liberal leaders banned all *völkisch* groups from the facilities of the Casino, the Handworkers' Society, and the German Gymnastics Society. *Bohemia* and the *Prager Tagblatt*, like other German liberal newspapers in Austria, by omitting notice of most of their group activities, made it difficult for the radical nationalists to attract support.[93] There was a certain irony in the fact that Angelo Neumann, the famous Wagnerian in charge of the German Provincial Theatre Company, aided the liberals' efforts. He gave discounts on tickets to members of the liberal Reading Hall of German Students but not to the *völkisch* student groups. Of course, Neumann's company depended on the support of the liberal notables, and he himself had Jewish origins.[94] The leaders of the Casino

[93] See the comments of Wolmar, *Prag und das Reich*, p. 375, on the liberal tactic of *Todschweigen*.

[94] *Der Deutsche Volksbote*, 19 Feb 1894. On Neumann, see Heinrich Teweles, *Theater und Publikum*, passim; Willy Haas, "Werfels erster Lehrmeister," *Witiko*, II (1929), pp. 137ff; and Richard Rosenheim, *Die Geschichte der Deutschen Bühnen in Prag 1883-1918*, pp. 30-34, 87-194, passim.

permitted a few *völkisch* sympathizers to remain in some of the larger liberal bodies after 1888, but they could neither express their political sentiments there nor win any distinctions.

Although the police had no interest in aiding the German Casino in the late eighties and nineties, their general opposition to radical nationalists helped the liberals' efforts to quell *völkisch* activity. The police and the Bohemian Governor's Office refused to authorize a number of *völkisch* projects which would have duplicated social services already provided by German liberal associations. In spring 1895, for instance, the League of Germans in Bohemia proposed an employment service for Germans in Prague. The director of the Prague police recommended rejection of the proposal, and he informed the Governor's Office that the German Merchants' Club and the Handworkers' Society already provided such services. At base, though, he objected to the League's political purposes:[95]

> One can assume with certainty that the League does not have a humane purpose of securing bread and work for the jobless. Rather, this employment service is only a means for gaining influence in the populace, for making dependent on the League those persons who would turn to it to find a job and thereby make them adaptable to the goals and purposes of the League.

The *völkisch* organizations could only vent their indignation at such treatment. With a characteristic lack of inhibitions, Anton Kiesslich and his colleagues simultaneously bemoaned the lack of support of *völkisch* projects from Prague's Catholic and Protestant German notables and denounced their liberal politics and philo-semitism.[96] The liberals' claims that all German associations in the city were represented in the great celebrations held at the Casino particularly galled the *völkisch* outcasts.

The hostility of the German liberals, the police, and the Czech population forced the *völkisch* groups in Prague to link tightly together. These organizations showed even greater mutual interdependence and sharing of leadership than did the liberal associations. Anton Kiesslich dominated the whole *völkisch* movement locally until World War I, and the *Volksbote*'s editorial offices served as headquarters from 1891 to the paper's demise in 1910. The

[95] SÚA Praha PP 1908-1915 V/10/36: 11.042pp, 10 May 1895, Prague police director to the Bohemian Governor. The Governor's Office rejected the League's proposal, 29 May 1895, 13889/pp 1249.

[96] *Der Deutsche Volksbote*, 9 Jan 1898, published a typical *völkisch* denunciation of the liberal notables.

antagonism of the liberal community and the limited means of most *völkisch* supporters made finances tenuous for the radical nationalist organizations. They had to rely on what little they could raise among their Prague members and aid from the League of Germans in Bohemia, the various German nationalist parties in Cisleithania, and the Pan-German League in the German Empire.[97]

The *völkisch* groups were the only German bodies which competed with the liberal associations for the support of lower-strata Germans in Prague until the founding of a German Social Democratic organization in 1896.[98] The liberals' response to the radical nationalists showed how closely linked were German group identity, liberal ideology, and deferential politics in their concept of ethnic defense. Even though the Casino's own efforts to engage lower-strata elements in German group life had only limited success, the liberal leaders would not tolerate any other attempt to rally the lower strata if it were not based on religious and racial equality, an individualist ideology, and acceptance of the multinational Habsburg state. Both the liberals and *völkisch* radicals claimed to defend the German presence in Prague, but ethnic interests failed to unite them. The liberal and *völkisch* elements had very different understandings of German group identity itself, and they conducted group activities in separate, antagonistic bodies.

Ethnic Defense in Religious Affairs

If the leaders of the German Casino could not win over a significant number of lower-strata Germans to regular participation in liberal public life in Prague, they at least wanted to stop their assimilation with the Czechs. Losses to the Czechs posed a much greater threat to the ultimate survival of the German liberal community than did the limited support which *völkisch* groups won in Prague at the end of the century. The number of German-speaking citizens counted in the city and inner suburbs declined by more than 9,000 between the 1880 and 1900 censuses; in contrast, the League of Germans in Bohemia, the strongest *völkisch* body, had only 1,100 members in Prague just after 1900, including students. Stopping or impeding assimilation with the Czechs was a vital concern for the German liberal leaders, and they directed toward this end much of the

[97] Police reports on the *völkisch* associations and the *Volksbote* suggest the sources of financial support although no financial records as such survive in the Prague collections. Pichl, *Schönerer*, VI, p. 187, comments on the operation of the *Volksbote*.

[98] See discussion of the German Social Democrats in Chapter 6.

defensive work of the Handworkers' Society, the German School Society, and the Municipal Affairs Association.

German liberal leaders also worked within Prague's Catholic and Jewish religious bodies to impede the assimilation of Germans with the Czechs. Little effort was needed to defend German interests in the Protestant churches because Czech and German Protestants had separate congregations in the city throughout the late nineteenth century. In any case, Protestants comprised less than 4 percent of all German citizens in the city and suburbs in 1900. Catholics, on the other hand, accounted for 57 percent of the Germans, and Jews still comprised 39 percent in 1900 despite the heavy attrition of the nineties.[99] Czechs and Germans confronted each other directly in the Catholic and Jewish religious institutions, which had unitary structures. There can be no general examination here of the political and social history of the churches and synagogues, but the efforts to protect German interests in the religious sphere shed additional light on the whole project of ethnic defense.[100]

Political realities limited the defensive measures that the German liberals could undertake within Prague's Catholic bodies. The German Liberal Party and Bohemia's conservative, pro-Czech Catholic hierarchy had fought each other since the early 1860s, and there were few Germans among the clergy at any level in Prague at the end of the century. The three Prince-Archbishops of Prague between 1849 and World War I—Prince Friedrich Schwarzenberg, Count Franz Schönborn, and Count Leo Skrbenský—each had close connections with the conservative aristocracy and opposed the development of Czech-German cleavages in the institutional structure of the Church. In general, the archdiocese was committed to preaching, hearing confession, and teaching in the vernacular of the parishioners, Czech or German. Nonetheless, each parish in Prague had a single body of clergy regardless of ethnic differences among the believers. Cardinal Schwarzenberg blocked the

[99] Census data derive from Srb, ed., Sčítání lidu v Praze 1900, III, p. 827. For discussion of the German Protestant bodies see G. B. Cohen, "The Prague Germans," pp. 527-31.

[100] The literature on the Catholic Church in Bohemia in the late nineteenth century is thin. For an introduction see Barbara Schmid-Egger, Klerus und Politik in Böhmen um 1900 (Munich, 1974), passim. On the Jewish religious communities see Ruth Kestenberg-Gladstein in The Jews of Czechoslovakia, I, pp. 21-71; Michael A. Riff, "The Assimilation of the Jews of Bohemia and the Rise of Political Anti-Semitism, 1848-1918," passim; Christoph Stölzl in Bohemia: Jahrbuch, XIV, pp. 179-221, XV, pp. 129-57; idem, Kafkas böses Böhmen, passim; and Hugo Stransky, "The Religious Life in the Historic Lands," Jews of Czechoslovakia, I, pp. 330-57.

division of the theological faculty of the Prague University into separate Czech and German bodies until 1890. The appointment of a single German suffragan bishop for the German portions of the archdiocese in 1901 marked the only other significant concession to ethnic diversity at the turn of the century.[101]

In the eighties and nineties German groups repeatedly complained of the lack of German priests in the Prague parishes. Indeed, Bohemia as a whole had a shortage of German Catholic clergy, which German politicians blamed on the pro-Czech bias of the hierarchy and seminary faculties.[102] Since Czechs comprised 70 percent or more of the communicants in every Prague parish after 1880, all parish clergy had to be able to preach and teach in Czech, something few German priests could do competently. Some of the parishes with the largest German populations may have had German vicars or chaplains from time to time, but Czech priests predominated in the Bohemian capital.[103] The only Catholic clergy who ever appeared in any of the larger secular German associations were the German professors of theology from the university, who also served occasionally as canons of the Cathedral of St. Vitus or of the Collegiate Church of All Souls, and the superiors of several monastic orders in Prague, particularly the Merciful Brethren in the Lower New Town and the Benedictines at the Emmaus monastery.[104] Simply maintaining German-language services alongside the Czech in an adequate number of Prague churches was difficult,

[101] H. Gordon Skilling, "The Partition of the University of Prague," *The Slavonic and East European Review*, XXVII (1949), p. 442; Schmid-Egger, *Klerus und Politik*, pp. 250-58. On Wenzel Frind, the first German suffragan bishop, see Robert A. Kann, "Ein deutsch-böhmischer Bischof zur Sprachenfrage," in Hugo Hantsch and A. Novotny, ed., *Festschrift für Heinrich Benedikt* (Vienna, 1957), pp. 162-78.

[102] See Schmid-Egger, pp. 26-28, 198-207, 250-68. For contemporary German comments, see Philipp Knoll, *Das Deutschtum in Böhmen* (Dresden, 1885), p. 20; and Victor von Kraus, "Über die politische Lage der Deutschen in Böhmen" (Vienna, 1883) [In HHStA Nachlass Plener, Kt. 29].

[103] No survey of the ethnicity of the Catholic clergy in Prague in the late nineteenth century could be located in the Archive of the Prague Archdiocese in SÚA Praha. Perhaps the only reliable way of surveying them now would be to check their responses to the question of language on the manuscript census returns. The rectory of St. Peter's in the Lower New Town, for instance, was included in my sample of the 1890 returns. The rector, two chaplains, music director, sexton, and parish clerk were all Czechs, AHMP MCR 1156/II 1890.

[104] Father Alban Schachleitner, later a supporter of Hitler, was at the Emmaus monastery between 1901 and 1920 and led campaigns against the *Los von Rom* movement in German Bohemia, Archive of the Prague Archdiocese, SÚA Praha, Ordinariat, kt. 31, Hnutí "Los von Rom," Director of the Emperor's Cabinet to Cardinal Schönborn, 6 Jan 1902.

and even in the cathedral German services lapsed briefly in the early nineties. As might be expected, churches in the poorest sections of the inner city and in the suburbs most often failed to provide German-language preaching, while the more prosperous parishes in the Old Town and New Town most frequently held services in both Czech and German.[105]

The German liberal leaders in Prague remained strongly anticlerical in general politics after 1879, but they tried to protect German rights to Catholic religious observance in the German language as part of ethnic defense. The Casino and other liberal bodies regularly lobbied for German services in additional parishes, and the German Municipal Affairs Association included such efforts in its activities from the first year onward. Dr. Josef Sprinzel, a professor of Catholic theology at the German University, served as a director of the Association for several years and helped to revive German services in the cathedral and the parish of St. Thomas in Malá strana.[106] As with most of the defensive projects, however, what success the German liberal groups had with these efforts was largely confined to the more prosperous parishes of the Old Town and New Town. There it was in the Church's own interest to meet the needs of significant numbers of German communicants. In 1902, the only year for which data are readily available, fifteen inner-city parishes and the church in Smíchov had both Czech and German preaching. None of the churches in the poorest areas of the Old Town, in Josefov, the Upper New Town, Vyšehrad, Karlín, Žižkov, or in Holešovice offered German-language services.[107]

The German liberal notables showed little interest in local Catholic group life after 1879, beyond the issue of German worship services. They complained about the lack of German clergy but did nothing to change the situation. The liberal associations expressed no collective interest in Catholic lay activities, and relatively few Prague Germans participated individually in local lay bodies. The great conservative Catholic lay groups, such as the Catholic Club (*Katolická beseda, Katholische Ressource*) and its political arm, the Catholic Political Union (*Katolicko-politická jednota, Katholisch-politischer Verein*), were almost exclusively Czech after 1880.[108] Czech Christian

---

[105] See the survey for 1900-1902 in Josef Schindler, *Das soziale Wirken der katholischen Kirche in der Prager Erzdiöcese* (Vienna, 1902), pp. 16-53.

[106] SÚA Praha PP 1900-1907 V/7/33: NZ 28105, 28 Nov 1894, police report on the meeting of the Municipal Affairs Association on the same day.

[107] Schindler, *Das soziale Wirken*, pp. 15-53.

[108] AHMP fond spolků: spolkový katastr, protokoly XI-12 Katolická beseda (1869) and XXI-2 Jednota Katolicko-politická v král. Českém (1871).

Social bodies first appeared in Prague in the mid-nineties, but Social Catholicism had no organized German following in the Bohemian capital until 1910. In that year a small group, composed mostly of Austrian governmental employees, founded a self-improvement society, the Catholic German People's Society (*Katholischer deutsche Volksverein*).[109] The only other German lay associations in Prague before 1914 were several small organizations which supported missionary activity, Catholic education, and publishing.[110] Close identification of the Catholic Church in the Bohemian capital with Czech political and social interests apparently prevented German Catholic lay activity from developing on any larger scale.

German liberals defended their interests more vigorously in the Jewish religious and charitable institutions than in the Catholic bodies. Since the total Jewish population at the end of the century surpassed the number of Gentile Germans by a ratio of nearly three to two, Jewish support had a singular importance for the survival of the German minority. The Jewish organizations proved more adaptable to German liberal purposes than the Catholic, and, encouraged by the Casino, German Jewish notables were able to work within them to impede the spread of Czech loyalties among their Jewish brethren. The Austrian Ministry of Religion and Instruction authorized a single corporate body to administer all Jewish religious affairs in each locality, but the elected Jewish community councils were free of the authoritative hierarchy and governmental meddling that characterized the Catholic establishment. Jewish bodies throughout the Bohemian Lands strongly supported the Liberal Party in the sixties and seventies, and, as already noted, leaders of Prague's Jewish community often enjoyed equally high honors in the German liberal associations in the last decades of the century.

As increasing numbers of Jews adopted Czech political allegiances in the late eighties and nineties, the German Jewish elite worked to maintain control over the principal synagogues and Jewish charities. Many Jews may have had little interest in the politics of the religious and fraternal bodies, but all had at least some dealings with the religious communities. Austrian law obliged all

[109] SÚA Praha PP 1908-1915 V/26/136: officers lists and 9336/pr, "Bericht über das 2. und 3. Vereinsjahr des katholischen deutschen Volksvereins in Prag, vom 28. März 1911 bis April 1913" (Prague, 1913).

[110] J. Ježek, *Čtyřicet let Katolického spolku tiskového v Praze* (Prague, 1911), pp. 39-42; SÚA Praha PP 1908-1915 V/40/2 Katholischer Schulverein für Österreich, Pfarrgruppe zu Maria Schnee in Prag: bylaws, officers lists; Archive of the Prague Archdiocese, Ordinariat, kt. 30: Katolické spolky 1899-1918, "Zpráva o činnosti katolických vzdělávacích spolků v Praze za rok 1905."

Jewish heads of household to pay taxes to maintain the synagogues and cemeteries unless they formally renounced their religious affiliation. Moreover, only rabbis and burial societies authorized by the religious communities could conduct Jewish weddings and funerals.[111]

Pro-German merchants, manufacturers, and lawyers succeeded in retaining power in all the major Jewish bodies after 1879. In the case of the council of Prague's Jewish Religious Community, this resulted largely from a suffrage system which weighted votes according to tax payments to the community. But the pro-German elite also benefited from the continuing respect among Prague Jews for liberal individualism and German learning.[112] Despite the erosion of the Jews' German loyalties in general political affairs at the end of the century, the members of all the larger synagogues and charitable groups continued to defer to the old pro-German notables. Indeed, the leaders of Prague's Jewish establishment showed even greater continuity than was the case in some of the German liberal associations.

The German Jewish notables had a particularly strong hold on the council of the Prague Religious Community. In 1894-1895, for instance, all eighteen members belonged to the German Casino, and at least eight had also belonged to the German Club in the preceding decade.[113] Many of the same individuals led the largest synagogues and Jewish charities in the city. Ludwig Bendiener and Sigmund Mauthner, to name only two, played important roles at the highest levels of the German liberal community.[114] The Prague Jewish council also showed particularly strong continuity. Leading figures in 1894 such as Arnold Rosenbacher, Ludwig Bendiener,

[111] See Rudolf Herrmann von Herrnritt, "Juden: Israelitische Kultusangelegenheiten," in Mischler and Ulbrich, ed., 2nd ed., II, pp. 971-81.

[112] See Felix Weltsch in *LBI Year Book*, I, pp. 255-78; and G.B. Cohen in *Central European History*, X, pp. 31-40.

[113] See Appendix II, Table 11, for the complete list. The membership of the council derives from *Jahrbuch für die israel. Cultusgemeinden Böhmens 1894-95* (Prague, 1894), p. 24. Membership in the German Casino and German Club was verified by comparison with "Mitglieder-Verzeichnis des Vereines des Deutschen Casino 1879-1880" and "Mitglieder-Verzeichnis . . . 1898-1899" in AHMP fond spolků, Deutsches Haus; and with "Namens-Verzeichnis der Mitglieder des Deutschen Vereines in Prag nach dem Stande mit Ende Feber 1888" (Prague, 1888) in SÚA Praha PP 1900-1907 V/15/10.

[114] In addition to serving on the council of the religious community, Bendiener, for instance, presided over the orthodox High Synagogue for many years, and Schneider, Elbogen, Austerlitz, Mauthner, and Schmelkes sat on the board of the "neolog" New Temple.

Moritz Hahn, and Sigmund Haurowitz were all still serving as late as 1910.[115] Until 1918 the German Jewish elite ensured that the religious community conducted all its administrative affairs in German and appointed only German-educated rabbis. Czech achieved parity with German in the Jewish communities of Prague and the various suburbs only at the founding of the Czechoslovak Republic.[116]

The service of Jewish notables in both the German liberal organizations and the Jewish bodies made it possible to coordinate action in the two spheres for the defense of German liberal interests. In 1891, for instance, the Central Society for the Care of Jewish Affairs consulted with the German liberal political leaders before sponsoring a lecture by Rabbi Josef Bloch, the controversial exponent of Jewish rights in the Chamber of Deputies of the Reichsrat.[117] In 1895 Dr. Ludwig Schlesinger, the leader of the German Progressives in Bohemia and Intendant of the German Provincial Theatre, asked the president of the Jewish council in Prague for his assent to a plan to stage Theodor Herzl's "The New Ghetto." To avoid controversy, Arnold Rosenbacher vetoed the production of Herzl's attack on the partial assimilation of Austrian Jewry.[118] The German Jewish elite openly used its power to combat the Czech-Jewish movement and Zionist activity.

The political and social history of the Czech Jewish groups awaits thorough exploration, but the outlines of the institutional development are clear.[119] In the early seventies Jewish residents of pro-

[115] *Selbstwehr* (Prague), 25 Feb 1910, 14 Oct 1910.

[116] The Jewish religious community of Libeň kept all of its records in German until March 1919, when it abruptly switched to Czech, AŽM-ŽNO Libeň, n. 42341. The records of the Jewish burial society in Karlín were all in German until January 1918, AŽM-ŽNO Karlín, n. 34928. The Jewish religious council in Vinohrady adopted bilingualism for all publications and announcements in May 1918; its own minutes remained in German through 27 Oct 1918. Beginning on 24 Nov 1918 and thereafter the minutes were in Czech, AŽM-ŽNO Vinohrady, n. 29682, "Protokollen des Vorstandes des Kultusgemeinde," n. 53 (5 May 1918), n. 60 (27 Oct 1918), and n. 61 (24 Nov 1918).

[117] HHStA Nachlass Plener, Kt. 19, n. 291-97, Franz Schmeykal to Ernst von Plener, 2 Nov 1891.

[118] Teweles, *Theater und Publikum*, pp. 119-25. The play is discussed in Desmond S. Stewart, *Theodor Herzl* (New York, 1974), pp. 146-57.

[119] On the Czech Jewish movement, see the brief chronicle, *Dějiny českožidovského hnutí* (Prague, 1932), published by the Svaz Čechů-Židů; Egon Hostovský, "The Czech Jewish Movement," in *The Jews of Czechoslovakia*, II, pp. 148-54; M. A. Riff, "The Assimilation of the Jews," passim; and Josef Vyskočil, "Die Tschechisch-Jüdische Bewegung," *Judaica Bohemiae*, III (1968).

vincial Czech towns, students in Prague from those towns, and a number of small retailers and clerks in the Bohemian capital began to support the Czech national cause. The students organized the Association of Czech Academic Jews (*Spolek českých akademiků-židů*) in 1876, and the students' association produced most of the leadership for the whole movement in the next two decades. In 1884 the student group gave birth to the *Or Tomid* Society (Hebr., "eternal light"), which worked throughout Bohemia to introduce Czech for the vernacular portions of Jewish worship services.

In politics, the Czech Jews struck an early alliance with liberal elements in the Young Czech Party in opposition to the conservatism of the Old Czechs. One of the earliest Czech Jewish leaders, the lawyer Jakub Scharf (1857-1922), began directing Young Czech agitation in Prague's old Jewish quarter in the early 1880s. In 1893 Scharf and several other young lawyers and academics founded an educational and cultural society, the Czech-Jewish National Union (*Národní jednota česko-židovská*), to agitate for the Czech cause among Bohemian Jews.[120] A political association followed in the next year. The Czech Jewish groups campaigned vigorously in Prague for members and the representation of Czech Jewish interests in the religious councils of the city and the suburbs, but they had little success in either pursuit.

The Czech Jewish movement simply could not overcome the old German affinities of Jews in the Bohemian capital. While increasing numbers of Jews dropped their support of German candidates in local elections after 1883 and a massive number shifted from German to Czech allegiance in the censuses between 1890 and 1900, the great majority of Jewish residents retained elements of their old German loyalties in social considerations and educational matters. Their continued acceptance of the leadership of the pro-German elite in Jewish organizations was only one sign of this. Even more telling was their persisting strong preference for German primary and secondary schooling over Czech. Ninety-seven percent of the 1,863 Jewish pupils enrolled in the municipal primary schools in 1890 attended the German institutions. Despite the changing political situation, the German primary schools still had 91 percent of the Jewish public enrollment in 1900 and 89 percent in 1910. Virtually all the Jewish pupils who attended private primary schools received German-language instruction. Jewish enrollment in Czech secondary schools reached levels only slightly higher than in the

---

[120] *Politik*, 5 Sept 1893.

primary schools: 17 percent of the Jewish students enrolled in Prague's public *Gymnasien* and *Realschulen* in 1910 attended the Czech schools, and this included a number of students who came into the city from the smaller Central Bohemian towns.[121] Thus, while many Prague Jews at the turn of the century found it politically expedient to vote for Czech candidates and indicate Czech language in the census, the great majority, rich and poor, was no more ready to abandon its old belief in the superior value of German learning than to drop its long-standing deference to a German-speaking, liberal middle-class elite.

Under such conditions, Czech Jewish organizations could win but few members in Prague before World War I. They attracted support in the 1880s primarily among university students, small shopkeepers, and commercial employees who had come recently from the Czech countryside. In the nineties the movement won followers somewhat more broadly among Jews of intermediate and low incomes, who saw little advantage in siding with the German minority and increasingly feared Czech retribution for any pro-German sentiments. Yet at their peak before the Czech nationalist violence of December 1897, membership in all Czech Jewish groups in Prague amounted to no more than 2 or 3 percent of the 26,000 Jewish residents. In January 1897 the local unit of the Czech-Jewish National Union, for instance, had only 282 members.[122] *Or Tomid* had somewhat over 300 members in Prague in the mid-nineties, and in 1897 it had not yet raised sufficient funds for a permanent house of worship.[123] The Czech-Jewish National Union remained tied to the Young Czech Party; the Union and most other Czech Jewish groups lost members after 1897 in the face of new outbursts of Czech anti-Semitism and the failure of the Young Czechs to denounce all Jew-baiting.[124] Data are not available on the everyday

[121] Statistics for all the public schools derive from *Statistická knížka král. hl. města Prahy r. 1890* (Prague, 1892), p. 362; *Statist. knížka města Prahy r. 1900* (Prague, 1903), p. 387; and *Statistická zpráva král. hl. města Prahy r. 1910* (Prague, 1912), pp. 477-91, 495. The statistical handbooks do not offer the same detail on pupils in private schools, but apparently at any given time throughout this era an additional 300-400 Jewish children attended private primary schools, nearly all of them with German-language instruction.

[122] Karel Fischer, ed., *Kalendář česko-židovský na rok 1897-1898* (Prague, 1897), p. 193. The National Union claimed a total membership in Bohemia of 1,200.

[123] *Ibid.*, p. 199, and *Jahrbuch für die israel. Cultusgemeinden Böhmens 1894-95*, p. 87.

[124] On the anti-Semitic violence of 1897, see Chapter 6. On Czech anti-Semitism at the turn of the century and the ritual-murder trial of Leopold Hilsner, see František Červinka, "The Hilsner Affair," *Leo Baeck Year Book*, XIII (1968), pp. 142-

language of the Prague Jews in 1910, but throughout Bohemia only 51.5 percent of the Jews declared Czech as their language in 1910, compared to 56 percent in 1900.[125]

Wherever possible, the German Jewish notables used their hold on the major Jewish religious and fraternal bodies in Prague to combat the Czech Jewish movement and prevent it from gaining a foothold in the synagogues and charities. The pro-German elements were abetted by the numerical weakness of the Czech Jewish groups and the desire of the Ministry of Religion and Instruction for centralized administration in each religious community. In 1887, for instance, the Bohemian Governor's Office gave *Or Tomid* only limited authority to conduct religious services in Prague. The group might hold normal worship services, but only rabbis appointed by the council of the Jewish Religious Community could officiate at weddings.[126]

The Czech Jews did somewhat better at the turn of the century in Vinohrady. There, in the favored district of the Czech middle class, the German Jewish elite had to make concessions to a Czech Jewish force which was stronger than in the city proper. The council of the Vinohrady Jewish Community gave Czech equal status with German in 1896 at the dedication of a new synagogue building, and in early 1897 the council decided to engage a second rabbi, competent in both Czech and German, to assist the incumbent, who officiated only in Hebrew and German.[127] Even after the appointment of a second rabbi, however, the council upheld the seniority of the first and prohibited his Czech colleague from undertaking any German-language functions.[128] Czech Jews continued to agitate for equal rights in Vinohrady and elsewhere after 1897, but pro-German rabbis and members of the community councils retained the upper hand throughout Prague and the suburbs.

Zionism presented less of a challenge to Prague's German Jews at the turn of the century than did the Czech Jewish movement.

57; and Ernst Rychnovsky, ed., *Thomas G. Masaryk and the Jews* (New York, 1941), pp. 148-234. Garver, *The Young Czech Party*, pp. 302-03, minimizes the tolerance of some Young Czech elements for anti-Semitism although he notes that Young Czechs and members of the various radical nationalist successor parties exploited anti-Jewish feeling.

[125] *Oester. Statistik*, LXIII, 3. Heft, p. 178, and N. F., I, 2. Heft, pp. 54-55.

[126] *Bohemia*, 9 April 1887(M).

[127] AŽM-ŽNO Vinohrady: "Protokollen des Vorstandes des Kultusgemeinde, 22 März 1896-15 März 1903," n. 1 (22 March 1896), n. 7 (16 July 1896), n. 8 (4 Aug 1896), n. 18 (18 March 1897).

[128] AŽM-ŽNO Vinohrady: "Protokollen des Vorstandes," n. 8 (24 Sept 1901).

The concept of a distinct Jewish nationality gained little support before World War I among Jews in Prague and Bohemia as a whole. Zionism won a larger mass following to the east in Galicia, Russia, and the Bukovina, where Jews had lived for centuries in separate towns and villages and found assimilation much more difficult. Before emancipation Bohemian Jews, like those in Germany, had resided in ghettoes within Christian communities. The great social and geographical mobility which Bohemian Jews experienced after 1860 and their thorough acculturation with non-Jews made most of them resistant to the notion of a separate Jewish nation. Even the growth of anti-Semitism among radical nationalists in both the German and Czech camps failed to reverse the assimilationist tendencies of Bohemian Jews.[129]

Jewish nationalist activity in Prague began in the mid-nineties in the German University and German Technical College. In 1899 Jewish nationalists founded the Society of Jewish University Students in Prague, *Bar Kochba*; and a chapter of the principal Zionist organization in Austria, the Jewish People's Society, *Zion*, appeared in the city in the same year. Additional Zionist associations followed in the succeeding decade, most of them German-speaking but also several Czech groups. A weekly newspaper, *Selbstwehr* ("self-defense"), began publication in 1907. *Bar Kochba* attracted a group of brilliant intellects in the first two decades, including Hugo Bergmann, Oskar Epstein, Sigmund Kaznelson, Hans Kohn, and Robert Weltsch. Yet, despite their intellectual élan, all the Zionist student groups combined never had more than 150 to 200 members at any time before World War I. This contrasted sharply with the average of more than 700 Jews enrolled each year in all the German and Czech faculties. The Jewish People's Society drew support primarily from small businessmen and white-collar workers in Prague and other nearby towns, and it had nearly 200 members within several months of the founding.[130]

The German Jewish elite reacted with open hostility to the first signs of Jewish nationalism in Prague. The council of the Prague

[129] See Kestenberg-Gladstein in *The Jews of Czechoslovakia*, I, pp. 50-61; and Oscar K. Rabinowicz, "Czechoslovak Zionism: Analecta to a History," in *The Jews of Czechoslovakia*, II, pp. 20-24.

[130] On the early Zionist groups in Prague, see Stuart A. Borman, "The Prague Student Zionist Movement, 1896-1914" (unpubl. Ph.D. dissertation, University of Chicago, 1972), pp. 25-52, 76-85; S. Goshen, "Zionist Students' Organizations," in *The Jews of Czechoslovakia*, II, pp. 177-78; and O. K. Rabinowicz in *The Jews*, II, pp. 20-22. The membership estimates derive from Borman, pp. 26-28, 77, 151.

Religious Community tried to make financial aid to Jewish university students contingent on adherence to German liberal ideals.[131] In response, some Zionists attacked the German loyalties of the Jewish community leaders and demanded reform of the suffrage for the community council.[132]

The young Zionist intellectuals understood the resistance of most Bohemian Jews to their belief that long-term coexistence between Jews and Gentiles was impossible. Accordingly, the Zionist students in Prague stressed the cultural and spiritual reawakening of Jews rather than political action and colonization schemes.[133] Perhaps due to this moderation, the students eventually managed to develop good relations with the principal local Jewish charity, the Central Society for the Care of Jewish Affairs, and they jointly sponsored a number of cultural events after 1908.[134] Some Prague Jews even found support of the Zionist movement compatible with membership in German liberal groups. The local president of *Zion* in 1908-1909, for instance, also belonged to the German Casino.[135]

Although the membership remained small in Prague's Czech Jewish and Zionist organizations, the pro-German elite in the Jewish religious and charitable bodies could not extinguish the two movements. Even so, the Czech Jews and Zionists failed to shake the political loyalties of most of the more prosperous Jews, who remained German liberals until 1918. The actions of the two Prague chapters of the Jewish fraternal society *B'nai B'rith* demonstrated this poignantly. In a conciliatory gesture toward the Zionists, the older of these respected bodies declared itself neutral in 1906 on the question of Jewish nationalism. In 1910 the two chapters collaborated in founding a new Jewish youth group. Rather than give it a Judaic name, however, they chose to commemorate Johann Gottfried Herder, the German philosopher who had championed the intrinsic worth of all ethnic and national cultures.[136]

Ethnic politics in the Catholic and Jewish religious bodies demonstrates yet again how closely the German liberal groups identified ethnic defense with defense of their ideology, social hierarchy, and

[131] Borman, pp. 99-100.

[132] *Ibid.*, pp. 87-89.

[133] On the so-called "Prague orientation" in Zionism, see Rabinowicz in *The Jews of Czechoslovakia*, II, pp. 20-22.

[134] Borman, pp. 96-97.

[135] AHMP fond spolkú: spolkový katastr, protokoly, XXII-199 Jüdischer Volksverein in Prag, Einzelverein des "Zion."

[136] E. Starkenstein, ed., *Festschrift anlässlich des 30-jährigen Bestandes der Loge "Bohemia" I.O.B.B.* (Prague, 1923), pp. 173-75.

class interests. The liberal leaders wanted to protect German access to Catholic worship and religious instruction, but the enduring political enmity between the German liberals and the Catholic establishment prevented the liberal groups from taking any greater interest in the Catholic Church. In contrast, the Jewish Religious Communities of Prague and the suburbs had traditions of strong support for German liberal politics. The elite of the Jewish bodies doubled as a segment of the Casino's elite, and they acted in Jewish group affairs to defend their own power as well as German linguistic rights. Under the banner of ethnic defense, middle-class notables acted in the Jewish organizations as well as the secular German groups to preserve liberal political values and a social hierarchy based on property and education. Despite the new challenges of the eighties and nineties, the German liberals, both Christians and Jews, clearly retained their strong middle-class, liberal identity.

The liberal community entrusted the efforts to win over lower-strata Germans to the familiar instrument of its associational network. As we have seen, the strengths and weaknesses of the liberals' associational life largely explain the successes and failures in the program of co-optation. The German Handworkers' Society and the suburban chapters of the School Society attracted those who would accept the liberals' deferential politics in return for educational and social services and low-level involvement in the liberal community. When a *völkisch* group tried to rally university students and lower-strata elements in the German Gymnastics Society, liberal leaders won the support of a majority of the gymnasts for rejection of *völkisch* doctrines and exclusion of their adherents. Although the German Jewish elite could not expel Czech Jews from the Jewish religious bodies, they tried to deal similarly with the Czech Jewish movement, which looked for support from Jews who were marginal to German liberal society. The liberals' program of co-optation and group defense apparently succeeded best with persons who were prepared to accept their political system and social hierarchy, those with whom the struggle for allegiance was already half won. The defensive efforts failed to win over those who would not accept the liberals' ground rules, and the liberal elite was quite willing to ostracize those already involved in German group life who strayed from ideological conformity.

The liberal leadership failed in the end to engage any large portion of Prague's lower-strata Germans in German community life. The presence of large middle-class contingents in most of the groups aimed at the lower strata, and the absence of membership lists makes it impossible to measure precisely lower-strata participation. The number of German petty employees, workers, and their dependents who were citizen residents of Prague and the suburbs in the eighties and nineties ranged between 10,000 and 13,000, but apparently no more than around 2,500 of them belonged to all the liberal associations at any one time during the period. Moreover, little came of the liberal leaders' desires to increase migration to Prague from German Bohemia and to reverse the processes of German-Czech assimilation. The German Casino could not reverse the demographic tides.

Similarly, the elite of the Casino could not stop *völkisch*, Czech Jewish, and Zionist groups from winning adherents among university students and German-speaking lower-class elements who were disaffected or excluded from the liberal community. The German liberal leaders succeeded only in isolating the *völkisch* groups from liberal public life. In the Jewish religious bodies, the liberal notables merely managed to keep the Czech Jews and Zionists subordinate. Still, none of these rival movements won any stronger organized support from the lower strata than did the German liberals.

The weakness of the opposition groups had deeper causes than merely the enmity of the liberals. Belonging to voluntary organizations anywhere in Europe in the late nineteenth century demanded resources of time, money, and personal commitment that many small retailers, employees, and workers simply lacked. While the heated political atmosphere in Prague may have produced a higher level of general engagement than was typical in Central Europe, the dispersed, fluid character of the German lower strata here and their submersion in a strongly Czech environment made it hard to involve them formally in any German public life.[137] Neither the liberals, the radical nationalists, nor later the German Social Democrats could overcome the passivity of the German lower strata before World War I. The Czech Jewish movement appealed to a somewhat more cohesive body among the poorer Jews of Prague, but the Czech Jewish activists had to surmount decades of identification with Germans and deep anxieties about Czech anti-Semi-

[137] None of the existing community studies on associational life in Central Europe offers reliable estimates of the percentages of the population in various social strata who participated in associations in the late nineteenth century. See Chapter 2, n. 2, and Sources for titles.

tism. Zionist leaders themselves recognized the continuing resistance to Jewish nationalism in all strata of Prague's Jewish population.

Liberal spokesmen tried to put as good a face as possible on the disappointing results of their appeals to lower-strata Germans. Typically, they blamed the insuperable passivity of the poorest Germans in the city. As usual, Philipp Knoll spoke with the greatest candor about the middle-class elements' own contribution to alienating the lower strata. In November 1894, on the tenth anniversary of the founding of the Handworkers' Society, Knoll reminisced about community politics in the early sixties and the founding of the German Casino:[138]

> . . . It became clear immediately that it was solely a question of creating a rallying point for the highest strata of Prague's German population, and my warning not to abandon the German handworkers and small craftsmen of this city, who were then still numerous, elicited only surpassing derision.

Knoll went on to explain the limited success of the Handworkers' Society in trying to gather together German workers and craftsmen:

> To be sure, the Society could not fulfill all expectations. It could not resurrect the German spirit which had died in the intervening years among the intermediate and lower strata of Prague's population. Its activity here could only be a preservative one to prepare for subsequent better times. . . . The other expectation, to see the German handicrafts strengthened by the universal patronage of the well-to-do Germans, was also fulfilled in only a limited way.

Like most of his colleagues, Knoll tended to exaggerate the degree of popular German identification which had existed in Prague at mid-century, but there was no denying the steady loss of German lower-middle-class and laboring elements after the seventies. The liberals' failure over so many years to provide for meaningful participation by the poor in German group life contributed significantly to the attrition.

The leaders of the liberal community remained committed to their deferential politics, individualist ideology, and rigid social structure until after 1897. Ethnic defense continued into the early

---

[138] SÚA Praha PP 1893-1899 V/22/13 Deutscher Handwerkerverein in Prag: "Zehnter Jahresbericht des Deutschen Handwerkervereines in Prag, Vereinsjahr 1894" (Prague, 1895).

years of the new century on a course largely set in 1883 and 1884. In the end the liberals turned their backs on lower-strata Germans who refused to be co-opted on their terms. When the Casino was forced to choose, it preferred the support of Jewish merchants and professionals to that of Catholic or Protestant clerks and mechanics. Christian and Jewish middle-class elements remained the largest and most powerful constituency of the liberal associational network, and the leadership had little choice but to uphold its moderate liberal commitments and reject all *völkisch* and socialist doctrines if it was to protect their interests. Preservation of the liberal order, of course, meant continued loss of lower-strata elements, and in this respect defense of the community on liberal terms only contributed to further decline.

CHAPTER SIX

The Decline of Liberal
Society, 1897-1914

The development of Austrian society and politics entered a new
phase in the 1890s as the masses began to find their own voice in
public affairs. Together, the politicization of the masses, advancing
industrialization, and a new political culture transformed public
life. Willingly or not, the lower middle classes and workers had
previously deferred to the power and influence of landowners,
clergy, businessmen, and bureaucrats. In the 1880s even radical
nationalists had brought the masses into the political arena only in
crisis situations. Now the masses became a potent political force.
The urban lower-middle-class and laboring strata continued to increase with economic development although the population in
many of the older industrial centers now grew at lower rates than
in previous decades.[1] Here, as in Western Europe, advancing tech-
nology and economic development resulted in an increasing differentiation of group social and economic interests at all levels of
society. At the same time, a new political culture arose which insisted
on the direct representation of those competing interests in the
political arena.[2]

[1] On Prague and the other industrial centers of the Bohemian Lands, see
Kárníková, *Vývoj obyvatelstva*, pp. 213-48, and Havránek in *Pražský sborník historický
1969-70*, pp. 70-79.

[2] On the Bohemian Lands see Butvin and Havránek, *Dějiny Československa*, III, pp.
363-70; Garver, *The Young Czech Party*, pp. 277-319; and Prinz in Bosl, ed., *Handbuch*,
III, pp. 184-89, 215-17. On Austria in general, see Kann, *Nationalitätenproblem*, I,
pp. 96-108, 193-213; Macartney, *Habsburg Empire*, pp. 669-85, 792-806; and Adam
Wandruszka, "Österreichs politische Struktur," in Heinrich Benedikt, ed., *Geschichte
der Republik Österreich* (Vienna, 1954), pp. 291-97, 302-17, 423-36. On the parallel
developments in Germany, see Karl Erich Born, "Der soziale und wirtschaftliche
Strukturwandel Deutschlands am Ende des 19. Jahrhunderts," *Vierteljahrschrift für
Sozial- und Wirtschaftsgeschichte*, L (1963), pp. 361-76; James J. Sheehan, *German
Liberalism in the Nineteenth Century* (Chicago, 1978), pp. 239-57; and Hans-Ulrich
Wehler, *Das Deutsche Kaiserreich 1871-1918* (Göttingen, 1973), pp. 48-59, 90-95.

(233)

Throughout Austria new political formations sprang up to mobilize the populace. A host of occupational pressure groups developed to lobby bureaucrats and legislators, while political parties which addressed the needs of mass constituencies, the Social Democrats, Christian Socials, agrarians, and radical nationalists, grew rapidly after the mid-nineties. The addition to the Reichsrat of a new curia based on universal manhood suffrage in 1897 and the adoption of direct and equal manhood suffrage for the whole Chamber of Deputies in 1907 drove home the changes in political life. Yet the articulation of the new mass interests in society and the popular demands for direct representation of those interests actually preceded the steps to reform the suffrage and underlay the whole transformation.

Social conflict increased in Austria with the advent of mass politics. As political discussion passed from aristocratic estates, elite urban clubs, and parliamentary chambers to the streets, the radicalism and contentiousness of street politics passed back into the legislative and administrative bodies. The transformation of political values and structures caused the liberal parties of middle-class notables to disintegrate. As already seen, the United German Left broke apart in 1895; thereafter its successors, the German Progressives and Free German Union, competed with various nationalist, Pan-German, agrarian, and socialist parties for German voter support. The Old Czechs virtually disappeared after the Reichsrat elections of 1891, and after 1897 the Young Czechs steadily lost ground to the Czech Agrarians, Social Democrats, National Socialists, clerical groups, and various radical nationalist factions. All this meant that the naked conflict of social and economic interests supplanted the old contest between clerical conservatism and liberal individualism as the principal counterpoint to the nationality questions in Austrian politics. Whether the parties and pressure groups now spoke for some occupational group, a social class, or a whole nationality, they pressed ever more strongly the specific demands of their own constituencies as against the rest of society.

For a strongly middle-class minority such as the Prague Germans, the new social and political relations presented critical challenges to group survival. New Czech nationalist groupings raised more radical demands for Czech political and economic primacy in the Bohemian Lands than had their national liberal predecessors, and now radical German nationalists in the Bohemian borderlands were eager to abandon German interests in Prague if they stood in the way of partitioning Bohemia on ethnic lines. The Prague Germans' declining numbers made it increasingly difficult to counter German as well as Czech radical nationalists, and the rise of mass politics generated increasing tensions within the German minority itself.

The transformation of Austrian public life after the mid-nineties forced German leaders in Prague to find new means to meet group needs and to defend German ethnic identity. As before, the evolution of German group life in the city and the efforts to defend German group interests were contingent on the general course of social and political development in Austria. The liberal associational network which had previously met German needs for ethnic defense was prepared to assume additional responsibilities, but it presumed a deferential community order which, in fact, was now in decline. As will be seen, even middle-class and lower-middle-class elements that were formerly loyal to the liberals were developing occupational interests at the expense of their identification with a broader German *Bürgertum*. Habits of deference weakened, and the liberal associations found it hard to contain the growing centrifugal forces among their own members. In the meantime, any attempt to continue a narrowly liberal political course could only impede winning the broad German support elsewhere in Austria which the Prague groups needed more than ever before.

The leaders of the German liberal bodies in Prague felt truly besieged after 1897. The new perils presented by Czech nationalists and German opposition groups must be examined first since they helped to shape as well as to provoke the liberals' responses to the new era. Then the various efforts to renovate German group life and to preserve a sense of ethnic community can be analyzed.

A New Era of Ethnic Conflict

Conflict between Czechs and Germans sharply intensified in Bohemia between the mid-1890s and World War I. National quarrels repeatedly brought the Bohemian Diet to a standstill, and Bohemian deputies in the Reichsrat engaged in noisy demonstrations and brawls. Beginning with a week of anti-German riots in December 1897, the antagonisms in Prague periodically burst out in mass violence. When aroused, Czech radicals were willing to incite crowds to attack and loot German businesses, homes, and schools. Czech nationalists who viewed Germans as the historic oppressors of the Czech people and as interlopers in their capital city raised new demands for complete Czech control of local government, limits on support for German public schools, and boycotts of German firms.

Heightened conflict between Czechs and Germans in Bohemia

after the mid-nineties derived in part from growing social and economic competition between them. The continued movement of Czech workers, craftsmen, and shopkeepers into the industrial centers of northern Bohemia and the maturation of the Czech middle classes in the central Bohemian cities led to increased competition between Czechs and Germans for jobs, other economic advantages, and political power.[3] Yet some of the new antagonism stemmed from the development of nationalist politics itself.

At critical junctures Czech nationalist leaders as well as Germans proved willing to fan the flames of ethnic hatred to strengthen their own hands against competing mass parties. In many areas agrarian, Social Democratic, and Social Catholic politicians increasingly outbid the nationalists for popular support by combining direct appeals to specific class interests with commitments to national equality or their own promotion of national demands. Some of the existing nationalist formations, such as the German People's Party or the left wing of the Young Czech Party, responded with strengthened social and economic programs. In addition, new parties arose, such as the Czech National Socialist Party and the German Workers Party, which combined radical nationalism with direct appeals to workers and lower-middle-class interests. Yet if the nationalist parties wanted to remain truly national and unite diverse social and economic interests, they could not go beyond narrow limits in appealing to special interests. To compete with the class or interest-based parties and retain a broad popular appeal, most of the nationalists had little choice but to radicalize their nationalist rhetoric and push their national programs even harder than before.[4]

National conflict in Prague peaked in three waves of mass violence between 1897 and 1914. The anti-German riots after the fall

[3] See Whiteside, *Austrian National Socialism*, pp. 37-50; Wiskemann, *Czechs and Germans*, 1st ed., pp. 53-69; and Erich Zöllner, "The Germans as an Integrating and Disintegrating Force," *Austrian History Yearbook*, III, pt. 1 (1967), pp. 204-05, 223-33.

[4] On the Czech parties, see Garver, *The Young Czech Party*, pp. 154-231; Stanley B. Winters, "The Young Czech Party (1874-1914): An Appraisal," *Slavic Review*, XXVIII (1969), pp. 429-30; idem, "Austroslavism, Panslavism, and Russophilism in Czech Political Thought, 1870-1900," in Winters and Joseph Held, ed., *Intellectual and Social Developments in the Habsburg Empire from Maria Theresa to World War I* (Boulder, 1975), pp. 186-88; and Zdeněk Šolle, *Dělnické hnutí v českých zemích koncem minulého století* (Prague, 1951), pp. 52-67, 182-225. For a conceptual overview, see G. B. Cohen in *The Journal of Modern History*, LI, pp. 767-72. On the German parties, see Wandruszka in Benedikt, ed., pp. 309-15, 380-82, and Andrew G. Whiteside, "The Germans as an Integrative Force in Imperial Austria: The Dilemma of Dominance," *Austrian History Yearbook*, III, pt. 1 (1967), pp. 184-200.

of Count Casimir Badeni's government in late November 1897 established a pattern for subsequent outbursts in 1904-1905 and 1908. The combination of specific triggering events varied from one instance to the next, but the same basic forces were at work each time. In each case rioting followed some major setback for the Czech nationalist parties or a period of special frustration for the Czech nationalists' programs. In these circumstances, some minor expression or demonstration of the German presence in the Bohemian capital—a noisy gathering of German university students or the normal Sunday processions of the student fraternity members in their caps and ribbons—would spark Czech protests, brawls, and mob attacks on German businesses and homes.

The deep crisis of the Young Czech Party in the late nineties underlay the massive riots of 1897. Defeat of the Old Czechs in elections for the Bohemian Diet in 1889 and for the Reichsrat in 1891 left the Young Czechs at the head of the Czech national movement. Lower-middle-class radicals in the party called for the unity of all Czechs who were opposed to the social and political status quo, and they demanded quick imperial recognition of autonomy for the Bohemian Lands under Czech leadership.[5] By late 1897, though, it was clear that the Young Czechs could not achieve either aim. In practical terms, advancing the cause of Czech state rights required a new grand anti-German coalition in Cisleithania like Count Taaffe's as well as Magyar approval for altering the arrangements of the Austro-Hungarian Compromise. Now, however, the imperial court, high officials, and conservative politicians were less interested in rebuilding the Iron Ring to combat German liberals and nationalists than in making alliances with German as well as Slavic moderates to settle the Czech-German wrangling and prepare for the next renewal of the economic agreements with Hungary. Magyar leaders, for their part, were more opposed than ever to any serious concessions to Slavic nationalism.

In the meantime the Young Czechs began to lose support among the Czech populace to the competing mass movements. In the 1890s the Czech Social Democrats rapidly won a large following among Czech industrial workers for a program of universal suffrage, industrial reform, national equality, and an eventual end to capitalist exploitation. Organizations of small and intermediate Czech farm-

[5] See Garver, *The Young Czech Party*, pp. 154-216; Říha, ed., *Přehled*, II, pp. 927-29, 933-34; and Stanley B. Winters, "Kramář, Kaizl, and the Hegemony of the Young Czech Party 1891-1901," in Brock and Skilling, ed., *The Czech Renascence*, pp. 288-314.

ers grew increasingly defiant of Young Czech leadership after 1895, and by the end of 1898 they were ready to form their own Czech Agrarian Party. The agrarian movement won strong farmer support by attacking the inroads of industrial society on village life and advocating extensive economic protection for the lesser farmers, together with realization of the Czech state-right program.[6]

To counter the Social Democratic and agrarian movements, spokesmen for the Young Czechs and various smaller nationalist groups could only reiterate the overriding importance of national goals and increase their nationalist agitation. Young Czech radicals heightened their attacks on the iniquities of the Bohemian Germans and demanded that Austria follow a pro-Slav foreign policy. In spring 1897 during the campaign for the first Reichsrat elections after the addition of the fifth curia, radical leaders in Prague such as Jan Vašatý, Václav Březnovský, and Václav Klofáč engaged in unrestrained anti-German and anti-Semitic demagoguery. The Czech Social Democrats won 30 percent of the popular vote in Bohemia's Czech districts in the 1897 elections, but the Young Czechs increased their strength in the Chamber of Deputies from 37 seats to 60.[7] When the Young Czechs tried to convert their national program into reality, however, they suffered humiliating defeat.

In Prague the Young Czechs' failure to advance their national goals led to the first major anti-German outburst of the new era. The Young Czechs had agreed in early 1897 to support Count Casimir Badeni's coalition ministry, in return for promises of a major role in the government and equality for Czech and German in the internal usage of the officialdom in Bohemia and Moravia. Badeni's strategy depended, however, on support from moderate German elements.[8] The Bohemian leaders of the German Progressive Party, including those from the Casino in Prague, rejected Badeni's proposals, and German nationalists obstructed the Reichsrat. Townspeople in German Bohemia and German nationalist stu-

---

[6] On the rise of the Czech Social Democracy, see Šolle, *Dělnické hnutí*, and Říha, ed., *Přehled*, II, pp. 682-700, 710-25. On the agrarian movement, see Říha, ed., II, pp. 930-32, 1290-92; and Andrew Paul Kubricht, "The Czech Agrarian Party, 1899-1914: A Study of National and Political Agitation in the Habsburg Monarchy" (unpubl. Ph.D. dissertation, Ohio State University, 1974).

[7] For complete election statistics, see *Österreichische Statistik*, XLIX, 1. Heft. Garver reviews the Young Czechs' showing in *The Young Czech Party*, pp. 234-37; and Šolle, the Social Democrats' performance in *Dělnické hnutí*, pp. 233-34.

[8] See Berthold Sutter, *Die Badenischen Sprachenverordnungen von 1897*, for a thorough review of the politics of the Badeni ministry.

dents in Vienna and Graz staged increasingly violent street demonstrations through the spring and summer of 1897. On November
28, Badeni's cabinet finally resigned, and the emperor charged a
new minister-president with the task of proposing language ordinances more acceptable to the Germans. German liberal and nationalist students gathered together in Prague on November 29 to
celebrate the fall of Badeni. Brawling erupted between bands of
Czech and German students, and by evening Czech mobs began
smashing windows and looting businesses and residences they identified as German or Jewish.

Czech nationalist rioting continued for a week until the Austrian
government declared a state of emergency. In a scenario repeated
in 1905 and 1908, crowds of Czech students, workers, unidentified
young men, and some middle-class adults assembled on Na příkopě
in front of the Casino, the better German shops, and the offices
of the Bohemian German and Viennese banks.[9] There the demonstrators began breaking windows, insulting German passersby,
and looting stores; and then they roamed the city in bands, attacking edifices which symbolized the German presence. German
schools, theatres, and nearly one hundred businesses, some of them
Czech, suffered assault in 1897.[10]

The mobs attacked Jewish property whether or not the owners
supported the German cause. Some Czech national extremists had
freely mixed anti-German and anti-Semitic rhetoric, and many in
Prague's Czech populace still habitually identified Jews with the
Germans. The journalist Willy Haas later recalled the screaming
of the rioters: "Germans! Jews! . . . Germans and Jews: they were
nearly identical at that time for Czech Prague and both, Germans
and Jews, were equally hated."[11]

---

[9] There are no published studies of the mass violence in Prague at the turn of the
century that have systematically examined all arrest records, police reports, and the
various journalistic accounts. My discussion of the 1897 disturbances is based on a
comparison of the reports published by the Czech conservative *Politik*, the radical
Young Czech *Národní listy*, the Social Democratic *Právo lidu*, the German liberal
Bohemia and *Prager Tagblatt*, and the German nationalist *Der Deutsche Volksbote*.
Národní listy, 3 Dec 1897(M), noted the respectable character of some of the rioters.

[10] *Politik*, 1 Dec 1897(M), and *Právo lidu*, 3 Dec 1897, described the work of the
roving bands.

[11] Willy Haas, *Die literarische Welt* (Munich, 1958), p. 10. *Politik*, 1 Dec 1897(M),
reported the following colloquy in one band of rioters: "The call went up, 'To the
synagogues!,' to which was answered, 'No, to the Schulverein school in Vršovice!' "
The novel by Viktor Dyk, *Prosinec* (Prague, 1906), treats the 1897 disorders from
the perspective of nationalistic Czech youth.

Czech nationalist leaders and the municipal authorities only added fuel to the flames by continuing to make anti-German statements during the riots. On the first day, for instance, the Young Czech mayor, Jan Podlipný, inveighed against the German students at a meeting of the city aldermen:[12]

> I have heard complaints that the German students are conducting themselves provocatively in the streets and squares (Calls: For shame! Březnovský: Jewish rabble!), that they themselves were purportedly incited by the professors (Calls: The knife to the professors!), that with their uniforms they provoked our peaceful people in a daring, indeed impudent manner, and in Czech Prague, on this Slavic soil, they dare to sing the *Wacht am Rhein*!

Czech nationalist newspapers gave full coverage to accusations of German provocation, and the Czech Social Democrats' *Právo lidu* was virtually alone among the Czech press in its condemnation of the riots.[13]

In the wake of the Badeni affair, some Czech nationalist groups renewed the previous efforts to invoke a general Czech boycott of German businesses in Prague and in the rest of Bohemia. As before, the advocacy of boycotts and runs on German banks frightened many German businessmen, but popular compliance with the boycott in Prague fell short of the radicals' goals. *Bohemia* dryly commented, "The intelligent know that an economic partitioning of Bohemia on national lines would be an impossibility and Czech businessmen and tradesmen cannot do without either German manufacturers or German customers."[14] Czechs and Germans in Prague apparently continued to traffic in each other's businesses after each new outbreak of nationalist violence even if some occasionally felt obliged to enter by the back door.[15]

The disturbances of December 1897 traumatized the German residents of Prague and sent shock waves through the rest of Austria. The repeated outbursts of nationalist violence after 1897 and new calls for anti-German boycotts convinced many German residents that their persons and property were no longer safe in Prague and that Czech nationalists were determined to drive out all Ger-

[12] Published in *Bohemia* and *Politik*, 30 Nov 1897(M).
[13] *Právo lidu*, 3 Dec 1897.
[14] *Bohemia*, 18 March 1898(M).
[15] See the reminiscences of Egon Erwin Kisch, *Marktplatz der Sensationen*, p. 36, and Vladimír Vondráček, *Lékař vzpomíná 1895-1920*, pp. 30-32.

man residents.[16] In 1912 the non-partisan Bohemian German journal *Deutsche Arbeit* bitterly described life in Prague: "In an unbelievably stubborn and agonizing daily battle, the Czechs led by the municipal authorities are trying to purge the city of everything that is German and to make the Germans loathe living in the city."[17]

During the disturbances German groups that were otherwise sworn political enemies had little choice but to look to each other for aid. Under normal circumstances *völkisch* students, for instance, would not gather in the German Casino under the gaze of the liberal notables and acclaim a figure such as Otto Forchheimer, the Jewish president of the Casino; but they did so during the 1897 riots.[18] The Casino and the liberal political organizations were still the most influential German bodies in Prague, and they assumed the principal responsibility during and after each crisis for petitioning the provincial and Cisleithanian authorities to uphold the rights of all German residents to a peaceable existence in the city.

The disorders in Prague in 1904-1905 and 1908 presented variations on the basic themes of 1897. The Young Czechs suffered significant losses to the Czech Agrarian Party after 1901 in both the Reichsrat and the Bohemian Diet. The recession of 1901-1903 briefly slowed the growth of Czech Social Democracy, but after 1903 a new wave of strike activity and a vigorous campaign for suffrage reform won the Czech Marxian socialists strong support in Prague and in other Bohemian industrial centers. Various Czech radical nationalist elements—left-wing Young Czechs, National Socialists, and Radical State-Rightists—tried to regain popular support in 1904 and 1905 by using Austria's tariff dispute with Serbia and the Russo-Japanese War as instances for increased anti-Ger-

[16] Dr. Franz Wien spoke of a system in the Czech actions in an address to the German Club in 1903, SÚA Praha PP 1908-15 V/15/61: ad Z1 7527 pp, 3 May 1930. A similar view is expressed in hysterical terms in the letters written to the politician Josef M. Baernreither during the 1897 riots by a female relative in Prague, HHStA Nachlass Baernreither, kt 50: "Briefe die such auf die Prager Excesse in Nov 1897 beziehen." The novel by the *völkisch* writer Karl Hans Strobl, *Die Vaclavbude* (Leipzig, 1902), presents much the same feelings.

[17] "Schutzarbeit: Das eiserne Prag," *Deutsche Arbeit*, XII (1912-13), pp. 192-93. See the accounts of individual reactions in Philipp Frank, *Einstein: His Life and Times*, pp. 80-85; Jozsef Illy, "Albert Einstein in Prague," *Isis*, CXX, no. 251 (1979), pp. 76-84; Willy Haas, *Literarische Welt*, pp. 10-12; Höllriegel, "Fahrt auf dem Katarakt," pp. 24-27; and Utitz, *Egon Erwin Kisch*, pp. 12-37. Franz Carl Weiskopf, *Das Slawenlied*, presents a novelistic portrait.

[18] *Bohemia*, 30 Nov 1897(M). The Casino hosted the *völkisch* students again during the 1908 disturbances according to Anton Kiemann, *Das fünfte Jahrzehnt des Vereines Deutschen Kasino in Prag 1902-1912* (Prague, 1912), pp. 35-36.

man, neo-Slav agitation.[19] At the first news of Russo-Japanese hostilities in February 1904, nationalist Czech students, lower-middle-class elements, and some workers went to the streets of Prague to show support for Russia and counter Social Democratic demonstrations against the Tsarist regime.[20] The Czech nationalist demonstrators viewed the German student fraternities' weekly processions (*Bummeln*) down Na příkopě as a provocation, and large Czech crowds gathered on successive Sundays in late February and March to assault the students and to attack German businesses.

Anti-German violence resumed in Prague in November 1905 at the peak of the Austrian Social Democrats' campaign for direct and equal suffrage. The Young Czechs had announced their own proposals for reform in September, and by early November Czech nationalist students were joining in the Social Democrats' suffrage demonstrations. In this case the antagonists of Czech nationalists and Social Democrats coincided, for up to this time the German liberal and nationalist parties had resisted reform out of fear of losing parliamentary seats. On November 4, participants in a Czech Social Democratic demonstration massed before the German Casino and began to attack German and Jewish establishments.[21]

The disturbances of 1904 and 1905 were minor, however, compared to the new outbreak in the fall of 1908. Earlier that year the ministry of Max Wladimir Freiherr von Beck had offered Czech nationalists major concessions on national rights, but opposition from conservative great landowners and German nationalists in Bohemia doomed Beck's proposals.[22] After German obstruction forced the dissolution of the Bohemian Diet on October 16, 1908, Václav Klofáč and the Czech National Socialists mounted mass protests against the actions of the German parties and Austria's annexation of Bosnia and Herzegovina. On six successive Sundays thereafter, thousands of Czechs gathered on Na příkopě to prevent

[19] On Czech politics in this period, see Garver, *The Young Czech Party*, pp. 277-319, and Říha, ed., *Přehled*, II, pp. 926-46.

[20] *Bohemia*, 29 Feb 1904(M), 7 and 8 March 1904(M); *Národní listy*, 7 March 1904 (M). The Bohemian Governor Count Coudenhove noted the politically diversionary character of the Czech nationalist agitation in a report to Minister-President Koerber, AVA MI-Praes., 22 Böhmen 1903-04, Kt. 2091, 2/3 1441/MI 1904, Governor's Office to the Minister-President/Minister of Interior, 1 March 1904.

[21] *Bohemia*, 4, 5, 6, and 7 Nov 1905(M); Germany, Auswärtiges Amt—Abt. A, Akten betreff. Böhmen, 1.XI.1905-31.V.1906, Band 21, A 21061, 25 Nov 1905, Imperial German Consul, Prague, to Chancellor Prince von Bülow (UC-I, reel 251).

[22] See Macartney, *Habsburg Empire*, pp. 793-95, and Johann Christoph Allmayer-Beck, *Ministerpräsident Baron Beck* (Munich, 1956), pp. 122-246.

the German student fraternities from marching. In the meantime, bands of Czechs sporadically stoned German schools and businesses, looted German and Jewish shops, and terrorized individual Germans in the streets. The Young Czech mayor of the city and various Czech deputies in the Reichsrat claimed that the German students' marches had provoked the disorders and demanded their prohibition.[23] The disturbances finally ended on December 2, when Beck's successor Count Richard Bienerth declared a state of emergency in Prague.

Prague experienced no further nationalist violence comparable to 1908, but a steady drumfire of Czech-German hostility continued in Bohemia until World War I. In 1905 moderates and conservatives from both sides had worked out a compromise on national rights in Moravia, but the repeated efforts of the Austrian government to work out a settlement in Bohemia failed. Frustrated by the rapid growth of the Social Democratic and agrarian parties after 1907 and the failure to achieve their national political goals, the more radical Czech and German nationalists increasingly committed themselves to maximalist positions on national questions. The more moderate Czech and German middle-class parties in Bohemia remained willing to try to negotiate solutions to the national disputes, but they were becoming increasingly dependent on simple appeals to national interests and the need for ethnic solidarity to counter the direct representation of class and economic interests by the new mass parties and special-interest groups. Under these circumstances, those who might otherwise want to take a conciliatory stand on some national issues feared being branded as traitors to their nationality by more radical elements, and no matter how close Czech and German negotiators came to agreement, all attempts at a compromise in Bohemia broke down. Czech-German wrangling paralyzed the Bohemian Diet for most of the period between 1908 and the outbreak of World War I, with German deputies leading the way in obstructing business. Czech nationalists in the Reichsrat responded by organizing a coalition with Ruthenian and Slovene deputies to defend Slavic interests, and they obstructed business in the Chamber of Deputies whenever national questions arose.[24]

[23] *Bohemia*, 19, 21, 26, 27, and 30 Oct 1908(M); AVA MI-Praes., 22 Böhmen 1908-18, Kt. 2095: Nov 1908-Jan 1909, PNr 11258/MI 1908, 12 Nov 1908, Count Coudenhove to the Minister of Interior, and 166 praes ai 1909 annex, Prague Police Director Křikava to the presidium of the Bohemian Governor's Office, 2 Jan 1909.

[24] On Austrian politics in this era, see the brief treatments by Macartney, *Habsburg*

As normal legislative mechanisms broke down after 1908, the central government resorted increasingly to rule by imperial decree, and career officials gained an even tighter hold on the Cisleithanian government than before. Despite their old commitments to constitutional rule and to representative institutions, German middle-class elements could take some comfort in this turn of affairs since they could expect the imperial bureaucrats to follow conservative social policies and to preserve a centralized polity favorable to German interests. Nonetheless, even the German middle classes feared the authoritarian tendencies of officials like Count Franz Thun, who served a second term as Bohemian Governor from 1911 to 1915, and Count Karl Stürgkh, Minister-President after November 1911, who looked ever more desperately for solutions to the national disputes if only to allow the other business of government to proceed.

Increased national conflict in Prague in the era after 1897 made efforts for ethnic defense even more necessary than before if the German minority was to survive as a distinct group in the city. As previously, the middle-class and lower-middle-class members of the German liberal groups organized to counter the threats posed by Czech nationalists. Now, however, the old liberal community also faced perils from German opponents whom it could neither isolate nor ignore.

German Nationalist and Social Democratic Opponents

German opposition added to the worries of German liberal groups in Prague after the mid-1890s. Radical nationalism and Social Democracy both won growing support among Prague Germans, and their followers refused to join forces with the liberals in a united response to the new Czech offensives. Solidarity between the *völkisch* students and the liberal groups during the outbursts of nationalist violence did not outlast the crises, and most German nationalist bodies in Prague and in the Bohemian borderlands continued their own attacks on the German liberal elite in the provincial capital. German nationalists were convinced that the riots and the anti-

Empire, pp. 792-806, and A. J. May, *Hapsburg Monarchy*, pp. 425-38. On the Moravian agreement, see Horst Glassl, *Der mährische Ausgleich* (Munich, 1967), and Josef Kolejka, " 'Moravský pakt' z roku 1905," *ČSČH*, IV (1956), pp. 590-615. On Bohemia, see Münch, *Böhmische Tragödie*, pp. 531-33, 721-26; and Zdeněk Tobolka, *Politické dějiny československého národa od r. 1848 až do dnešní doby*, 4 vols. in 5 (Prague, 1932-37), III, pt. 2, pp. 324-37, 512-22, 541-54, 573-79.

German actions of the local authorities in Prague only proved that the German liberals were now so weak that they could not even vouch for the physical safety of Germans in the city. *Völkisch* spokesmen argued that it was no longer prudent for Germans to go to Prague for education or for health care and that the city could not continue to serve as the capital of German Bohemia.

After each outburst of national violence, *völkisch* leaders in northern Bohemia vented their hatred for the German liberals in Prague by calling for the abandonment of German interests in the city. Radical German nationalists had sporadically urged moving the German University, Technical College, and hospitals out of Prague in the late eighties and early nineties; and in the midst of the 1897 disturbances *völkisch* students in Prague and political leaders in the north raised the cry of *Los von Prag* ("Out of Prague").[25] Students from German Bohemia assembled in Cheb at the end of December 1897 to discuss the removal of the university and technical college faculties from Prague. No action was taken at this time, but new calls of *Los von Prag* followed the subsequent anti-German riots in the Bohemian capital.

The *Los von Prag* campaigns demonstrated the vindictiveness of the radical nationalists toward Prague's liberal oligarchs. The German People's Party and the various Pan-German groups rejected any persisting claims by the German Casino to leadership in German Bohemia, and they denied that Germans in the border areas shared a common destiny with those in Prague. After 1897 German nationalists heightened their demands for the administrative partition of Bohemia on national lines. They tried to minimize the number of districts that they wanted designated as ethnically mixed, and most of their proposals treated Prague as a Czech district since it had such a small German minority. The German nationalists would not even request special provisions for official bilingualism in Prague if such a demand would impede a general agreement.[26] Supported only by the constitutional landowners and by the dwindling numbers of Progressive and Free German deputies, the German liberals in Prague had to make their own case for continued German rights in the city.

[25] See Wolmar, *Prag und das Reich*, pp. 393-96. Sutter, *Sprachenverordnungen*, II, p. 236, quotes a call for the removal of the German University to Liberec(Reichenberg) in the Liberec *Deutsche Volkszeitung*, 4 Dec 1897.

[26] On the German nationalist proposals for partition, see Harald Bachmann, "Der deutsche Volksrat für Böhmen und die deutschböhmische Parteipolitik," *Zeitschrift für Ostforschung*, XIV (1965), pp. 266-94.

The *Los von Prag* movement frightened the German liberal community nearly as much as the Czech violence. Possible loss of the German educational and medical facilities as well as the provincial administrative and judicial services for Germans threatened the survival of Prague's German minority even more than did the attempted commercial boycotts by the Czechs. After 1900, members of the free professions, public educators and employees, rentiers, and students living away from home accounted for 55 percent of all independent or self-supporting Germans in the city and inner suburbs.[27] Many of these could remain in Prague only if it continued to serve as the capital for German Bohemia.

The leaders of the Casino, editors of *Bohemia* and the *Prager Tagblatt*, and professors at the German University had to work hard to counter the appeal of *Los von Prag*. In early 1898, 1905-1906, 1908, and again at the end of World War I, they mounted propaganda efforts to persuade Germans in the border areas to support keeping the German provincial institutions in Prague.[28] Many radical nationalists scorned the German burghers of Prague as Jews and Jew-lovers, but spokesmen for the Prague community argued that the Germans of the borderlands had a national obligation to defend the German presence in the historic Bohemian capital, regardless of whether Jews were among the beneficiaries.

Völkisch organizations in Prague itself won increased popular support after each outbreak of nationalist violence, and they stepped up their anti-liberal agitation with each crisis through 1908. The strongest local body remained the League of Germans in Bohemia, which had particular success among university students in the inner city and among skilled workers in the outlying districts. In Vinohrady, for instance, members of the League increased from 160 in October 1897 to 253 in November 1898.[29] New chapters appeared in Karlín, Bubeneč, and Holešovice after 1900. The students, however, still provided the nucleus of support for the local *völkisch* movement, and the inner-city chapters in which they played the strongest role experienced the greatest growth. The League's

[27] See Appendix II, Table 6, for the census statistics from 1910 for the three sampled inner city parishes.

[28] See for examples, "Schutzarbeit: Das eiserne Prag," *Deutsche Arbeit*, XII (1912-13), pp. 192-93; and the speeches and articles of August Sauer, reprinted in his *Kulturpolitische Reden und Schriften*, ed. Josef Pfitzner (Liberec, 1928).

[29] SÚA Praha PP 1900-07 V/10/25: 16986/pp 14757, 14 Oct 1897, police report on the October 10 meeting of the Vinohrady chapter; 19657/pp 15285, 17 Nov 1898, police report on the November 16 meeting of the Vinohrady chapter.

following in Prague declined in the period of relative national quiet and economic recession between 1900 and 1904, but it again reached the levels of 1898 by the end of 1909 (see Table 6/1).[30]

The German liberals could take some comfort in the fact that radical nationalist politics as such attracted little formal support

TABLE 6/1
Prague Membership of the League of Germans
in Bohemia, 1904 and 1909 (Excl. of University Chapters)

Chapter	1904	1909
Bubeneč	—	102
Karlín	161	283
Prague, General	193	374
Prague, Women's and Girls'	140	146
Prague, Gymnasts	192	424
Prague, III and IV	40	54
Prague-Holešovice	—	72
Smíchov	78	207
Vinohrady	166	243
Žižkov	113	56

among Prague Germans after 1897. The local *völkisch* groups increased their efforts to create a comprehensive public life to rival that of the liberals, but the activities for ethnic defense and general sociability of the League of Germans attracted greater popular participation than did *völkisch* political action. The political association, the German-National Club, had less than seventy-five members throughout the decade after 1897.[31] The *völkisch* elements campaigned for the prominent German nationalist Rafael Pacher as their own token candidate in the Reichsrat elections of 1907, but he polled only 830 votes in Prague compared to more than 4,800 for the German liberals' Alexander Richter. Not surprisingly, Pacher drew a disproportionate number of votes from the outlying districts as compared to the distribution of liberal votes or the whole German population (see Table 6/2).[32]

[30] SÚA Praha PP 1908-15 V/10/36: "Bericht über die Tätigkeit des Bundes der Deutschen in Böhmen im elften Vereinsjahr 1904" (Prague, 1905), p. 13; "Bericht über die Tätigkeit des Bundes der Deutschen in Böhmen im 16. Vereinsjahr 1909" (Prague, 1910), p.19. As previously, the sum of all the chapters' memberships has little meaning since some individuals belonged to several chapters simultaneously.

[31] SÚA Praha PP 1908-15 V/15/31 Deutsch-nationaler Verein: police reports, lists of officers, and members, 1897-1917. In November 1903, the Club had 60 members, only 47 of them from Prague.

[32] Election results were reported in *Bohemia*, 15 May 1907(M) and 24 May 1907

TABLE 6/2
Geographical Distribution of German Liberal
and *Völkisch* Votes in the Reichsrat Election, May 1907

	Old Town & New Town	Prague III-VIII & 4 suburbs	Total
Liberal votes in %:	46.4%	53.6%	100% = 4,840
Völkisch votes in %:	27.8	72.2	100 = 833
Total German pop., 1910	36.3	63.7	100 = 32,332

Any support for the *völkisch* movement in Prague troubled the liberal groups, but the results of the 1907 election, in fact, showed the persisting strength of liberal loyalties among the Prague Germans. Richter won 7.3 percent of all the votes cast in the first balloting, virtually the same as the Germans' share of the total population in 1910. Germans comprised only 20 percent of the residents in the Lower New Town, but Richter drew one-third of all the votes cast in the run-off there.

The *völkisch* groups in Prague remained unremittingly hostile to the liberal community until after 1908. Only in the last five or six years before World War I did some begin to seek a modus vivendi with the liberals. The local chapters of the League of Germans in Bohemia, in particular, won some support for their charitable activities from liberal bankers and industrialists; and now even the Casino and the German Handworkers' Society occasionally granted use of their facilities.[33] German liberal dignitaries still abstained from joining the League, but respectable lawyers, *Gymnasium* professors, physicians, and state employees played a greater role in the local chapters after 1908.[34] The *völkisch* student groups, on the other hand, remained bitterly antagonistic toward the liberal as-

---

(M). Pacher had relatively greater strength than Richter in every district outside of the Old Town and New Town. See Appendix II, Table 12, for district-by-district totals.

[33] SÚA Praha PP 1908-15 V/10/36: 21544/pp 16819, report to the Prague police, 4 Nov 1908, from the Women's and Girls' Chapter, Prague, of the League of Germans in Bohemia.

[34] SÚA Praha PP 1908-15 V/10/36 Bund der Deutschen in Böhmen: lists of officers and directors for the general directorate of the League and the various Prague chapters.

sociations until World War I, although they were less vocally Pan-German after 1905 than at the end of the nineties.[35]

The transformation of the League of Germans in Bohemia, however, was not peculiar to the Prague chapters. The League softened its radicalism and gained in respectability in other communities as well after 1907-1908. This resulted in part from the organization's success in winning a broad following over the preceding decade, but it also reflected larger trends in German nationalist politics in Austria. The radicalism of the *völkisch* elements vis-à-vis other German middle-class parties generally diminished after 1901, although differences persisted on the issue of anti-Semitism.[36] The strong showing of the Social Democrats throughout Austria in the 1907 elections and Beck's attempt at a Bohemian settlement in 1908 provided powerful incentives for a rapprochement of German nationalists and liberals. Finally, in February 1910, all the "German" parties but the Pan-Germans and the Christian Socials formed a "German National Union" in the Reichsrat, although they still really agreed on little but the common opposition to the Slavic nationalists and Marxian socialists.[37]

The German liberals in Prague faced a new adversary in the Social Democratic group which began to find support among German residents of the city in the mid-1890s. The Educational Society of German Workers (*Bildungsverein der deutschen Arbeiter*) founded in 1896 asserted that the language and culture of German workers distinguished them from their Czech comrades and made separate organizations necessary. Still, the German socialists, like the early *völkisch* groups, rejected any alliance with the German liberal community and attacked its values and social hierarchy. In political matters the German Social Democratic group argued that German and Czech workers must join together on a basis of ethnic equality to fight for their common class interests.

The Marxist ideology of the Society of German Workers made it more resistant than some of the German nationalist groups to any accommodation with the German liberals in Prague. The small numbers and high transiency of German industrial workers here

[35] See Whiteside, *Socialism of Fools*, pp. 269-84, on the decline of Pan-German radicalism among German students in Austria.

[36] *Ibid.*

[37] On German politics in Austria between 1907 and 1914, see Molisch, *Geschichte der deutschnationalen Bewegung*, pp. 168-237; and Whiteside in *Austrian History Yearbook*, III, pt. 1, pp. 184-200.

limited the potential support for any German workers' group, but the Social Democratic organization experienced a respectable growth in the first two decades after its founding. The rapid rise of Social Democracy in all of Austria's industrial centers in the nineties encouraged the development of class consciousness among German workers in Prague. Yet those who were not ready to assimilate with the Czechs found it difficult to join the Czech-dominated Social Democratic organizations in Prague. Czech Social Democrats were committed to internationalism on basic social and economic questions and wanted to cooperate on an equal basis with workers of other ethnic groups. Nonetheless, after the mid-1890s most Czech socialists insisted on organizational autonomy for their own separate groups within an Austrian Social Democratic confederation.[38] Class interests might recommend that the small number of German workers in Prague join the Czech socialist groups and reject any alliance with the middle-class Germans, but even local Czech Social Democratic leaders recognized that the Czech character of their trade unions and clubs made distinct German bodies necessary. Accordingly, Czech leaders assisted a number of leftist German students and white-collar employees in founding the Society of German Workers, and thereafter they made Czech socialist facilities available to the German group.[39]

The Society of German Workers grew from 90 members in April 1897 to an estimated 300 in 1912-1913. In the latter year the German socialists also had a political club numbering 190 members.[40] No membership lists survive, but contemporary descriptions indicate that the Educational Society won support in the inner city

[38] See Ludwig Brügel, *Geschichte der österreichischen Sozialdemokratie* (Vienna, 1922), III, pp. 80-84; Hans Mommsen, *Die Sozialdemokratie und die Nationalitätenfrage im habsburgischen Vielvölkerstaat* (Vienna, 1963), I, pp. 155-234; O. Říha, ed., *Přehled*, II, pp. 626-45, 682-99; Zdeněk Šolle, "Die Sozialdemokratie und die tschechische Frage," *Archiv für Sozialgeschichte*, VI-VII (1966-67), pp. 315-90; Emil Strauss, *Die Entstehung der deutschböhmischen Arbeiterbewegung* (Prague, 1925), pp. 132-47; and idem, *Von Hainfeld bis zum Weltkriege: Geschichte der deutschen Sozialdemokratie Böhmens* (Prague, 1926), pp. 61-66.

[39] Karel Dědic and several other Czech Social Democratic leaders attended the organizational meeting according to the police report in SÚA Praha PP 1893-99 V/7/48 Verein der deutschen Arbeiter: 4487pp, 24 March 1896.

[40] SÚA Praha PP 1893-99 V/7/48: 6482/pp, 18 April 1897, police report of the meeting on April 11; AVA Sozial-Demokratische Parteistellen, Kt. 134, Böhmen-Organisation, Akten-Mappe BI, Prag: "Bericht der Bezirksorganisation Prag für die Zeit vom 1. Juli 1911 bis 30. Juni 1912," "Bericht der Bezirksorganisation Prag für die Zeit vom 1 Juli 1912 bis 30 Juni 1913." No police reports for the political organization could be located in SÚA Praha PP.

among printers, skilled workers in other specialized trades, commercial employees and wage earners, and university students. The growth of large factories on the northern and eastern fringes of Prague brought in additional skilled workers from southern Germany and German districts of Austria in the eighties and nineties, but apparently factory workers seldom accounted for more than a third of the German Workers' Society.[41] On the other hand, at least a third of those who attended the monthly meetings were university students.[42] They along with a group of mostly Jewish white-collar employees provided most of the early leadership.[43]

The German Workers' Society functioned primarily as a reading and lecture club, which met monthly in various Czech workers' pubs or Czech socialist quarters. The German socialists supported the Czech Social Democrats in political contests and attacked German liberal policies. Members of the Society often expressed their awareness of differences between Czech and German workers, but the group formally rejected any allegiance to German nationalism.[44] Occasionally, individual Social Democrats might heckle speakers at German liberal meetings, but the Workers' Society had no formal dealings with the liberal community. The only exception to this was an arrangement with the German Theatre Society and the director of the German Provincial Theatre Company after 1906 to give special performances for workers each year.[45]

In purely practical terms, the German Social Democrats in Prague represented little more than a nuisance for the German liberals compared to their other problems after 1897. Three hundred members of the Workers' Society was still a small number compared to the 4,600 German workers and day-laborers counted in Prague by the 1910 census. Even with the general rise of mass politics and the weakening of German liberalism, neither the Ger-

[41] See the discussion of migration data in Chapter 3, pp. 91-98.

[42] SÚA Praha PP 1893-99 V/7/48, PP 1900-07 V/7/7, and PP 1908-15 V/7/44 Verein der deutschen Arbeiter: lists of officers and police reports of meetings, 1896-1915.

[43] From Prague police reports as in n. 42. The founder Otto Pohl, the son of a German Jewish money-changer, had previously played a leading role in the joint Czech-German Social Democratic student organization in Prague and for a time edited its journal *Akademie*, HHStA Min. des Äussern: Informationsbüroakten 300, 1891, n. 42 and n. 141/4, 18 Jan 1892.

[44] Members criticized Czech workers for hostility toward their German comrades at the December 1896 meeting, SÚA Praha PP 1893-99 V/7/48: 20086/pp, 7 Dec 1896, police report on the meeting of December 5.

[45] Moritz Deutsch, "Erinnerungen aus der Anfangszeit," in *25 Jahre Arbeiter Vorstellungen des Bildungsvereins deutscher Arbeiter in Prag* (Prague, 1931), pp. 4-5.

man nationalists nor the Social Democrats could overcome the dispersion, transiency, and political apathy of many of the poorest Germans in Prague and engage them as regular participants. Most of the German workers were still lost to organized German group life in the city, liberal, *völkisch*, or Social Democratic, and were free to make their own informal social relationships or to assimilate with the Czechs. Yet German liberal circles could no more afford to ignore the German Social Democrats than the radical nationalists.
. For those committed to German group survival in Prague, political developments after 1897 gave increasing significance to maintaining solidarity among all German residents. The Germans' numerical decline, heightened ethnic conflict, and the *Los von Prag* movement all seemed to mandate unity among the Germans who remained. The old liberal bodies were determined to defend the German presence in the city and still hoped to use appeals for German solidarity to strengthen their control over local German public life. Despite all contrary developments, the leaders of the Casino still expected all Germans in Prague to accept the primacy of a middle-class elite and the old liberal values. Yet the growth of the local *völkisch* and German Social Democratic groups demonstrated that liberal values and community structures were weakening even in a minority population whose social and religious composition had uniquely favored liberalism before. While the liberal groups had failed to extinguish local German opposition before 1897, after, they even failed to contain its growth in their own midst.

The multiple perils of the era after 1897 required fundamentally new political responses by the liberal community if it were to defend the interests of even its own members. Some of the dangers, such as those posed by the Czech and German nationalists, had arisen before, but the advent of mass politics gave them new force and undermined the liberal community order itself from both within and without. The simplest response for the liberal groups would be merely to increase their old defensive activities on the same lines. The previous defensive efforts, however, had combined ethnic defense with protection of the power and status of a middle-class elite of property and education. After 1897 effective defense of the German residents' general interests required a more democratic political order that could deal with a myriad of social and economic needs. Simply forming more liberal voluntary associations and passing additional resolutions in support of civil equality, minority rights, and a centralized Austria would no longer meet the needs of even the old middle-class constituency. The mass parties and lobbyists for the most important economic interest groups virtually monopolized the attention of the administrators, technocrats, and noblemen who guided the Austrian government after the turn of the century. Spokesmen for an isolated minority group could win recognition only if they clearly represented significant economic interests or commanded a united and assertive popular following. In the new era liberal leaders in Prague had trouble mustering strength either way. German industrialists and bankers found other means of political representation besides the old liberal associations. Moreover, popular support for German nationalism and Social Democracy outside the liberal associational network and the advance of divisive interest-group politics within refuted any claims the Casino might still raise to united backing within the German minority.

Community Defense in the Post-Liberal Era

The liberal groups did their best to preserve control over German collective life in Prague after 1897. At first the liberal leaders tried to use the same means as before to meet the new challenges to local German interests; they founded new voluntary associations for ethnic defense, increased the responsibilities of existing groups, and invested additional money and effort in all the various special-purpose groups. The ability to carry on the local defensive work actually helped to prolong the survival of the liberal associational network here. In contrast to other German communities in Austria, liberal groups in Prague still showed considerable vitality in dealing with local political issues and in serving various social functions for middle-class and lower-middle-class German residents.

The programs for ethnic defense directed by the Casino sharply increased in the new era. In early 1897, for instance, when the Austrian German School Society had to cut support for its schools in Prague, the Casino responded by establishing a German School Maintenance Association (*Deutscher Schulerhaltungsverein*) to operate the schools.[46] Throughout the period after 1897, the various German educational groups and the Municipal Affairs Association lobbied assiduously in the Bohemian Governor's Office and the Cisleithanian ministries to combat the Czech local authorities. That

[46] See Perko, "Tätigkeit des deutschen Schulvereins in Böhmen," *Deutsche Arbeit*, III, p. 401. By 1912 the Austrian German School Society had recovered sufficiently that the schools in Prague could revert to its direct control.

the higher officials often treated the representatives of the German associations on a par with the municipal authorities indicates the effectiveness of the lobbying efforts.[47] The liberal groups continued to provide their own privately funded services when no redress was possible from the higher authorities. In January 1903, for example, the Prague board of aldermen voted to construct a new assembly hall to "symbolize the Czech character of the capital city." The leaders of the German Casino responded through the Handworkers' Society with a decision to erect an additional center for Prague's German associations.[48]

The liberal bodies continued to try to rally support in the Bohemian borderlands for German interests in Prague after 1897. Notables from the Casino went out to the German towns to combat the *Los von Prag* movement, and both *Bohemia* and the *Prager Tagblatt* assisted in propagandizing on behalf of the Prague Germans. In October 1901, the Prague-based Society for the Advancement of German Scholarship, Art, and Literature in Bohemia inaugurated a monthly, non-partisan cultural journal, *Deutsche Arbeit*, for all Bohemian Germans. August Sauer, a popular professor of modern German literature at the German University, edited the journal until 1918 and made it a sounding board for a variety of artistic expression and social commentary as well as news from German communities throughout Bohemia. On behalf of the Germans in Prague, Sauer published critiques of anti-Semitism and historical vignettes about the provincial capital along with poems and short stories of Rainer Maria Rilke and Max Brod.[49]

The liberal associational network expanded as a result of the new activities for ethnic defense. The *völkisch* and Social Democratic groups functioned independently, but the German Casino continued as before to provide direction, support, and facilities for nearly all other German associations in Prague. In 1890 all German voluntary associations in Greater Prague, including student organizations, numbered approximately 130; in 1912 there was a total of

[47] In 1907, for instance, the Ministry of Religion and Instruction treated the Prague municipal authorities and the German Association for the Care of Children's Recreation virtually on an equal basis in a dispute over use of a plot of public land, AVA Min. Kultus/Unterricht, 53225/08, 15 Vereine—Böhmen, Prag, fasc. 7588, 1907: 66532, 22 Feb 1907, and 17912, 17 April 1907.

[48] *Politik* and *Bohemia*, 6 Jan 1903(M), reported the aldermen's decision on the Reprezentační dům, now called Obecní dům. *Bohemia*, 26 Jan 1903(M), reported the action of the Handworkers' Society.

[49] For examples, see Hugo Herrmann, "Zur Judenfrage," *Deutsche Arbeit*, VII, 4. Heft (Jan 1908), pp. 277-81; and Julius Lippert, "Prag, die deutsche Stadt," *Deutsche Arbeit*, VIII, 5. Heft (Feb 1909), pp. 332-48, published after the riots of 1908.

232.[50] Use of the Casino's rooms by various groups increased from 404 separate occasions in 1901-1902 to 720 in 1912-1913.[51] The 1912 enumeration of German associations categorized them as follows:[52]

TABLE 6/3
German Voluntary Associations
in Greater Prague, 1912

Type	Number
Charitable	25
Ethnic defense	23
Gymnastic and athletic	20
Artistic	14
Scientific and scholarly	12
General sociability	7
Political	7
Self-improvement	3
Others	24
SUBTOTAL:	135
Occup./econ. interest	55
Mutual aid	6
Student Societies	36
TOTAL	232

Of the total, the liberal network accounted for some 100-110 associations in 1912. The 55 local organizations for the protection of specific occupational or economic interests were nearly all new since 1890; as will be seen, they increasingly competed with the general political and social functions of some of the older liberal bodies. The 1912 survey estimated that memberships in all the German associations amounted to some 60,000, compared to a self-supporting adult German population of around 20,000 and some 2,000 German students in the university and technical college.[53] The Casino's own membership reached 1,280 in 1898-1899 and remained nearly constant until World War I.[54]

[50] Wilhelm Winkler, "Schutzarbeit: Deutsch Prager Vereinsleben," *Deutsche Arbeit*, XIII (1913-14), pp. 527-28.

[51] *Bohemia*, 16 Nov 1902(M); AHMP fond spolků, no. 10: Deutsches Haus, "Bericht der Direktion an die 52. Vollversammlung, 17 Feb 1914."

[52] Winkler, in *Deutsche Arbeit*, XIII (1913-14), pp. 527-28. No comparable analysis is available for the German associations in 1890.

[53] *Ibid.* Census data derives from *Öster. Statistik*, N. F., III, 8. Heft, p. 330. See Appendix II, Table 7. University enrollment derives from Winkler, *Soziale Lage der Hochschulstudentenschaft*, pp. 9, 23.

[54] AHMP fond spolků, no. 20: Annual reports of the Board of Directors of the German Casino. The Casino had 1,313 members in October 1908, 1,263 in September 1911.

The liberal associations looked for some modus vivendi with the economic interest groups, but they could not integrate the new organizations fully into the old community structure, for they embodied a whole new principle of group formation. The speed of development varied from one region to the next, but throughout Central Europe after the late eighties, middle-class and lower-middle-class elements began to look to new local associations, each limited to a single occupational or economic interest, to represent them politically and to provide various educational and social services. Local associations for each interest banded together in regional, provincial, or national federations to press their demands for legislation and administrative action on legislators and bureaucrats. The larger local groups also provided their members with health and accident benefits, lectures, entertainment, and other social activities.[55]

The broad functions of the interest groups put them into direct competition with older liberal and conservative Catholic associations in many Central European towns. Liberal and Catholic group life had also combined political and social functions in the same bodies, but the older associations had brought together people with diverse economic interests in the name of broader ideological or class goals. The rise of the interest groups at the end of the century tended to fragment middle-class and lower-middle-class public life on occupational lines. The clerical-conservative and Social Catholic political movements in Austria could accommodate the new special-interest groups to some extent within their corporatist views of society.[56] German and Czech liberal national bodies, on the other hand, generally opposed the fragmentation of public life on economic lines and resisted demands for increased government intervention in the economy. Karl Eppinger, leader of the German Progressive Party in Bohemia in the early years of the new century, expressed well the liberals' hostility to interest-group politics. He argued that although the special interests had legitimate social and

[55] There has been next to no serious study of the rise of interest-group organizations in Austria. On the parallel development in Germany, see Karl Erich Born in *Vierteljahrschrift für Sozial- und Wirtschaftsgeschichte*, L (1963), pp. 361-76; Hans-Jürgen Puhle, "Parlament, Parteien, und Interessenverbände 1890-1914," in Michael Stürmer, ed., *Das kaiserliche Deutschland: Politik und Gesellschaft, 1870-1918* (Düsseldorf, 1970), pp. 340-77; and James J. Sheehan, *German Liberalism in the Nineteenth Century* (Chicago, 1978), pp. 249-51.

[56] On the relationship of the Christian Social movement in Lower Austria to various interest groups, see John W. Boyer, "Church, Economy, and Society in *fin de siècle* Austria," pp. 442-598, passim.

economic needs, ". . . the various occupational groups share so much in purely political, national, and libertarian questions, which can be represented without prejudice to their respective economic interests, that the establishment of separate class parties cannot be conceived as the basis for a healthy political development of the people."[57]

The older liberal associations could find ways to avoid open conflict with the special-interest groups at the local level, but there was no denying the basic incompatibility between them. Previously, middle-class liberals had had their own local occupational organizations, like the German Merchants' Society and the German lawyers' association in Prague, but such groups had looked to local liberal elites for leadership and undertook little or no political action of their own. The new interest organizations, in contrast, insisted on their political independence and cooperated with local liberal associations only when it suited their own needs.

Organizations for the protection of occupational interests won growing support among middle-class and lower-middle-class Germans in Prague after the mid-1890s. The need for unity in the face of conflict with the Czechs did not immunize Prague Germans against the rise of interest-group politics. Various attempts to establish German trade unions failed in the late nineties, but groups which served middle-strata occupations prospered.[58] An organization of German industrial supervisors and shop foremen, for instance, carried on a vigorous program of social, political, and educational activities after 1895. German commercial managers and employees organized their own group in 1899, and in 1904 public educators and state officials formed the "Association of State Officials of German Nationality in Prague" (*Verein der Staatsbeamten deutscher Nationalität in Prag*). Membership data for all the German special-interest organizations in Prague are lacking; within two years of its founding, the State Officials' Association, for example, had 1,250 members, some drawn from outside the city.[59]

With few exceptions, German interest groups organized separately from their Czech counterparts in Prague. Ethnic conflict was

---

[57] From the opening speech to the Bohemian congress of the German Progressive Party in 1907, published in the *Neue Freie Presse*, 18 Feb 1907 (evening).

[58] Between 1897 and 1906 unions for leather workers, glove-makers, tanners, chemical workers, hotel and restaurant workers, and stone masons were founded and quickly dissolved, AHMP fond spolků: spolkový katastr, protokoly, XX.

[59] SÚA Praha PP 1900-07 V/41/17 Verein der Staatsbeamten Deutscher Nationalität in Prag: 2186/pp, 1 Feb 1906, police report of the meeting on 30 Jan 1906.

so pervasive among the middle and lower-middle classes that the parallel Czech and German groups apparently had little to do with each other. Only through the all-Austrian confederations to which some belonged did the Czech and German bodies occasionally cooperate in lobbying efforts.[60]

The older liberal groups in Prague gained some advantage in local affairs from the ethnic loyalties of the German interest groups. The most active of the latter, the associations of public and commercial employees, acknowledged the Casino's direction of local ethnic defense programs and looked to the Casino for various forms of aid. In social affairs, the public and commercial employees at least still identified with the German middle-class community and accepted the liberal notables' continuing claims to prestige.

The industrialists, bankers, and great merchants in the Casino who still believed in the old liberal politics could hardly approve of the interest groups' special pleading at the higher levels of government, but they could not stop the advance of the new political alignments. The leaders of the Casino and the other liberal bodies had to be content with what support they could get from the new groups in local political questions and social life. Indeed, the liberal groups in Prague made no serious effort to combat the development of the special-interest organizations, and a number of younger liberal leaders even joined the new occupational groups.[61]

Increased ethnic conflict, mass politics, and the rise of the interest groups had little effect on status distinctions among Prague's middle-class and lower-middle-class Germans. Patterns of preferment in the Casino and the other liberal bodies changed little between 1897 and 1914. These groups continued to provide their members with valued signs of social status, and as before the same body of merchants, lawyers, industrialists, professors, and physicians led all of them.[62] The Casino's general membership showed no significant

[60] The question of ethnic divisions in the economic interest organizations of Prague and the rest of Bohemia merits separate, more intensive examination. Czech and German employees of the railways and postal service in Prague apparently had common associations, the Benevolent Society of Railway Officials, Sub-officials, and Employees in Prague (SÚA Praha PP 1908-15 V/17/7) and the Benevolent Society of Imperial-Royal Postal Employees for Bohemia (AHMP fond spolků: spolkový katastr, protokoly III-71).

[61] Professor Adolf Bachmann, for instance, who held high positions in the German Club and the Municipal Affairs Association, served on the first board of directors of the German State Employees' Association, SÚA Praha PP 1900-07 V/41/17: 18673/pp, 16 Nov 1904, report to the Prague police.

[62] See lists for the Casino and the German Club in Appendix II, Tables 9-10.

change between 1898 and 1907 (see Table 6/4).[63] Lower-middle-class elements and workers had no greater access to the principal liberal associations after 1897 than before.

The majority of Germans in the inner city apparently continued to accept the social hierarchy embodied in the liberal groups just

TABLE 6/4

Occupational Distribution of the Members of the
German Casino, 1898-1899 and 1907

		1898-1899	1907
Banker/bank dir.		1.5%	1.2%
Manufacturer		10.0	10.3
Lawyer		13.0	13.6
Physician		3.1	3.8
Merchant/self-empl. bus.ª		32.6	30.0
Government official		1.8	2.4
University prof./docent		5.8	5.6
Gymnas. prof./school dir.		1.0	1.1
Bank/insur. co. officer		5.1	5.6
Architect/engineer/chem.		2.3	2.4
Landowner		0.8	0.7
Rentier/independent		3.7	4.3
	SUBTOTAL	80.7	81.0
Supervisor/official/agent		8.3	7.5
Bookkeeper		0.7	0.4
Retail clerk		—	—
Government worker/clerk		0.2	0.1
Military		0.1	—
Shop-foreman		0.1	0.1
Skilled trade		1.3	0.8
Worker		—	—
Construction		0.5	0.5
Railroad/transport		1.6	1.4
Teacher		0.4	0.4
Theatre/arts/journalism		4.7	6.4
Student		0.1	0.2
Widow		0.3	0.3
Retired		1.5	1.0
Misc.		0.1	—
	TOTAL	100% = 1,282	100% = 1,329

ª Includes small retailers.

[63] Membership data derive from "Mitglieder-Verzeichnis des Vereines des Deutschen Casino, 1898-1899" and "Namens-Verzeichnis der Mitglieder des Deutschen Kasinos nach dem Stande vom 31. December 1907," AHMP fond spolků, no. 20: Deutsches Haus.

as they supported the direction of local ethnic defense by the liberal elite. The strong voter support for Alexander Richter in the 1907 Reichsrat elections was the most impressive sign of this.[64] Long-standing habits, of course, helped to uphold the old community order, and numerical decline and political adversity could be expected to strengthen the social conservatism natural to a strongly middle-class population. In inner-city parishes like St. Gall, St. Henry, and St. Peter, professionals, independent businessmen, manufacturers, rentiers, and their families comprised over 45 percent of the German citizens after 1900.[65] The liberal groups could still satisfy many of the collective needs of such a population despite the rising competition of the special-interest groups.

That 47 percent of the German residents in the inner city in 1900 were Jewish helped the liberal groups immensely. Those Jews who still identified as Germans would not readily abandon an ideology of civil liberty and equality or a social order based on individual achievement. The more prosperous Jews were equally unwilling to give up a community order which had accorded them positions of respect in Gentile society.

Jewish participation in German public life in Prague continued to grow after 1897 despite the *völkisch* pressures on the liberal community and the adoption of Czech political loyalties by many Jews. The leaders of the Casino wanted support for German interests in Prague from anti-Semitic German nationalists, but they refused to reduce the role of Jews in liberal group life. Jews, for their part, still mingled little with Christian Germans in domestic life: the previously low rates of conversion and intermarriage increased only slightly between 1900 and World War I.[66] Nonetheless, the Jews who retained German loyalties participated in liberal associational life in Prague even more intensively than before. The Jewish members of the German Casino increased from 575 (45 percent of the total) in 1898-1899 to 638 (48 percent) at the end of 1907.[67]

Jews gained in prestige as well as in numbers within the German liberal groups after 1897. Jews served as officers for the German School Society in the inner city and the suburbs despite the anti-

[64] See above pp. 247-48.   [65] See Appendix II, Table 6.
[66] See G. B. Cohen in *Central European History*, X, pp. 39-40, 47-48, and Riff, "The Assimilation of the Jews of Bohemia," pp. 207-33.
[67] Membership lists derive from AHMP as in n. 63. The Jewish members were identified by reference to the tax registries of the Jewish Religious Community of Prague as in Chapter 4.

Semitism of many local units elsewhere in Austria.[68] They predominated after 1910 among the leaders of the German Club: Josef Eckstein was president, the now aged Ludwig Bendiener served as vice-president, and Franz Kafka's cousin Bruno, a docent in the German law faculty, acted as secretary.[69] The *Los von Prag* movement and the agitation of the *völkisch* students in the German University and German Technical College put great pressure on the liberal Reading Hall to reduce the role of Jews, but even here Jews accounted for at least one-third of all officers and directors from 1897 to 1914.[70] If the Catholic and Protestant members of the liberal groups were merely tolerating the Jews' presence because they needed their support, individual Jews could not have achieved such honors and influence. Although declining, a body of liberal, middle-class German Catholics and Protestants remained in Prague which still accepted equal Jewish participation in German public life.

The German Jewish dignitaries took great pride in the status they enjoyed in local German society, but they could not ignore the strength of anti-Semitism in German politics elsewhere in Austria.[71] After 1897 the German Jewish elite in Prague became increasingly protective of its place in non-Jewish group life and wary of any tolerance that the local liberal bodies might show for *völkisch* views. In September 1899, during the furor over the Dreyfus affair in France and the concurrent ritual murder case in the Bohemian town of Polńa, four Jewish members of the German Casino demanded that the reading room stop taking the anti-Semitic *Deutsche Zeitung* of Vienna. In its place the petitioners asked for an additional copy of the liberal *Neue Freie Presse*. When the directors of the reading room replied that they had a responsibility to provide a

[68] Lists of officers in *Bohemia*, 12 May 1910(M), and SÚA Praha PP 1908-15 V/40/ 1-2 Deutscher Schulverein, ct. II/2790.

[69] AHMP fond spolků: spolkový katastr, protokoly, XXI-1.

[70] Lists of officers and directors in *Bohemia*, 13 March 1904(M), and AUK Lese- und Redehalle der deutschen Studenten, kt. 648, 649, 654: annual reports of the board of directors for 1896, 1899, 1903, 1909, and 1914. Contrast these findings with the recollections of Max Brod, *Streitbares Leben*, rev. ed., pp. 152-54, that the Gentile directors of the 'Halle made special efforts to limit Jews in leadership positions to a few baptized individuals or those from the most respected unconverted families. Felix Weltsch, in *Leo Baeck Year Book*, I, p. 257, recalled that Jews predominated in the literary section.

[71] The pride is expressed by Felix Weltsch, in *Leo Baeck Year Book*, I, pp. 255-58, and the unpublished memoirs in the Leo Baeck Institute Archive by Moritz Austerlitz, Egon Basch, and Else Bergmann.

broad spectrum of political views, several of the petitioners retorted with a request for the Jewish nationalist *Österreichische Wochenschrift*.[72] When German liberal leaders began negotiations for an alliance of all German parties after the 1907 Reichsrat elections, Jewish members of the Casino and the German Club objected angrily to offering the anti-Semites any concessions, real or symbolic.[73]

The most prominent Jews in the liberal bodies steadfastly insisted on equality of religion and race in German public life. Less assertiveness on their part would have made it easier for the German liberal groups in Prague to build bridges to the German nationalist parties, but in this the German Jewish elite showed that they still had a greater commitment to individualism and civil equality than to inclusion in Gentile society at any price.[74] The Jews who remained in the German liberal groups differed from their Zionist detractors in believing that a German civic life which treated Jews and Christians as equal—not necessarily identical—was still possible and desirable. Those Jews who spoke out in the Casino and the German Club against anti-Semitism obviously did not deny all Jewish identity or seek complete absorption into the German Gentile population. Many of the young writers and academics who initiated Zionist activity in Prague themselves had considerable experience in the social and cultural life of the German liberal community. It was a growing sense of insecurity and pessimism about the survival of liberalism throughout Central Europe, not exclusion and alienation from German society in Prague, that persuaded a Hugo Bergmann, a Max Brod, or, in his own way, a Franz Kafka, to abandon the Jewish-German symbiosis.[75]

---

[72] AHMP fond spolků, no. 20: Deutsches Haus, "Beschwerdebuch des Lesezimmers, 1899-1918," pp. 1-5, entries of 20 and 29 Sept 1899. On the Polná affair and the trial of Leopold Hilsner, see Rychnovsky, ed., *Masaryk and the Jews*, pp. 148-234; and Červinka in *Leo Baeck Year Book*, XIII, pp. 142-57.

[73] The confrontation between Dr. Karl Eppinger and Jewish members of the German Club on June 22, 1907 was reported in *Bohemia* and *Prager Tagblatt*, 23 June 1907(M), as well as the police report in SÚA Praha PP V/15/61: Ad Z 13.773 pp/F 1330, 23 June 1907.

[74] The anti-Semitic Imperial German Consul in Prague criticized the German Jews' assertiveness in a 1907 dispatch, Germany, Auswärtiges Amt-Abt. A, Akten betreff. Böhmen, 1 April 1907 to 18 July 1907, Bd. 23: A 10106 pr 28 June 1907, Imperial German Consulate, Prague, 24 June 1907 (UC-I, reel 251).

[75] Contrast my interpretation here and in *Central European History*, X, pp. 28-54, with Max Brod, *Streitbares Leben*, rev. ed., pp. 153-54; Eisner, *Franz Kafka and Prague*, passim; Eduard Goldstücker, in *Dortmunder Vorträge*, no. 70; and Tramer, in *Leo Baeck Year Book*, IX, pp. 305-39.

So much of the German liberal community order survived in Prague after 1897 because it still served functions useful to many middle-class and lower-middle-class German residents, both Christian and Jewish. The liberal associations performed well in providing for local ethnic defense, recreation, general sociability, and the articulation of status relations. The effectiveness in defending German ethnic interests, in particular, helped the old community structure retain so much vitality despite the advent of mass politics. Distinguished liberal social clubs survived elsewhere in Austria after 1897, but few in the intermediate and larger cities had the influence that the German Casino enjoyed among Germans in Prague.[76]

Even among the Prague Germans, however, the liberal groups' political competence was increasingly restricted to local concerns of ethnic defense. They gradually lost the ability to meet many of their own constituents' broader political needs. In public life the liberal elite had created a "preserve" to protect their local social and political order from their Czech nationalist, *völkisch*, and Social Democratic adversaries.[77] Nonetheless, while opposition rose from outside the community after 1897, narrow economic or occupational loyalties grew from within which undermined both the broad middle-class unity and the deference to an elite of property and education which were essential to the liberal order. Those in the liberal bodies who opposed complete fragmentation had to find new modes of political action if they were to preserve any meaningful sense of community for Germans in Prague.

In Search of a New Political Order

After 1897 German liberal politicians in Prague were forced to find new mechanisms to win broader, more active popular support and greater representation in the ruling bodies of Bohemia and Cisleithania. The process of change, however, was slow and halting. Many of the older notables still resisted opening up the processes of decision making or cooperating with non-liberal German politicians.

[76] For discussions of Brno, Graz, Ostrava, and Vienna, see Dřímal and Peša, ed., *Dějiny Brna*, II, pp. 36-38, 64-65; Hubbard, in *Canadian Journal of History*, V, pp. 25-47; Karel Jiřík and Blanka Pitronová, ed., *Dějiny Ostravy* (Ostrava, 1967), pp. 385-90; Czeike, *Kommunalpolitik*, pp. 30-60; and Boyer, "Church, Economy, and Society," pp. 442-728, passim. Among these only Hubbard addresses directly the evolution of German liberal local politics.

[77] Emil Utitz compared the liberal community to a *Naturschutzpark* in *Egon Erwin Kisch, der klassische Journalist*, p. 32.

The Casino's own political arm, the German Club, showed growing weakness at the turn of the century. The German Municipal Affairs Association took on most of the work connected with local ethnic defense after the death of Schmeykal in 1894. In theory this left the German Club free to address larger Bohemian and Austrian questions and plan initiatives on behalf of the community at the higher levels of government, but the Club's effectiveness in dealing with the larger issues, even the interest in discussing them, actually declined between 1897 and 1914.

Much of the activity of the German Club after 1897 merely supplemented the work of the Municipal Affairs Association and the local school societies. Despite the urgings of younger leaders, discussions in the Club focused mainly on local matters: anti-German actions by the municipal authorities, efforts to show German strength in elections and censuses, and the slum clearance in Josefov and the Old Town. Josef Eckstein and Bruno Kafka frequently warned the members that such a narrow approach to community politics could only lead to disaster; they argued that the German Club must address all the political concerns of the whole German minority and aggressively seek aid from Germans elsewhere. During the riots of November 1908, for example, Kafka bluntly told the Club that the German liberals needed no more voluntary associations and the German Progressive Party must end its self-defeating parliamentary tactics of obstruction and boycott.[78]

The membership of the German Club declined as its political perspective narrowed. The Club had over 400 members in the late 1880s, but by 1902-1903 it had only around 300. At the beginning of 1911, no more than 230 still paid dues.[79] As before, the Club's membership included many from the Casino and closely resembled the larger body in social exclusivity.

Lawyers and professors increasingly predominated among the leaders of the German Club after 1897. In part this merely reflected the strength of the middle class of education among the German residents of the inner city and the prominence of professionals and educators that was common to local liberal politics throughout Central Europe. In addition, in many towns of Germany and Austria,

[78] Kafka's critique was reported in *Bohemia*, 20 Nov 1908(M). *Bohemia*, 21 March 1901(M), reported an earlier warning by Eckstein.

[79] SÚA Praha PP 1908-15 V/15/61: ad Z 7700pp, 26 April 1902, police report of the meeting on April 25; ad Z 9253 pp/VI 890, 8 June 1904, police report of the general meeting on May 30; and 7700pp, 11 April 1911, police report of the meeting on April 10.

industrialists, bankers, and the wealthiest merchants themselves tended to withdraw from active roles in community politics around 1900.[80] The propertied elements of the upper middle class might retain their old honorific positions on the boards of social and cultural organizations such as the German Casino and the German Theatre Society in Prague, but increasingly they pursued political purposes through individual efforts or through specialized pressure groups. After 1900 many of the wealthiest Prague Germans could be found more readily in the loges of the German theatres or on country estates, hobnobbing with the nobility and military officers, than at meetings of the German Club or the Municipal Affairs Association.

Pleas for the German Club to broaden its perspective fell mostly on deaf ears. Many of the liberal rank and file in Prague openly resisted the changes in policies and tactics that the new era seemed to require; they were content to rely on their own associational network and programs of community self-help. When German Progressive leaders from elsewhere or the few Prague figures who still represented German Bohemian districts in the Diet or the Reichsrat advocated reconciliation of German liberals and nationalists or more aggressive policies on social and economic questions, they often faced hostile audiences in Prague. The German Club formally accepted parliamentary unions of German liberal and nationalist deputies in 1899 and again in 1910.[81] Even so, the Jewish members of the Club repeatedly complained against dealings with the anti-Semitic nationalist parties, and their Gentile colleagues did little to counter them.[82]

Programs for increased state intervention in economic and social affairs found little sympathy among German liberals in Prague before World War I. Despite the rise of interest-group politics all around them, many old liberal stalwarts clung stubbornly to the creed of possessive individualism: "We do not fool the farmer or the small craftsman with utopian promises and dreams of the guild

[80] See Sheehan in *Past and Present*, no. 51, pp. 130-31.

[81] Support was expressed for a coalition of German parties at the March 1898 meeting of the German Club, SÚA Praha PP 1908-15 V/15/61: ad Z 5278/pp ai 1898, 19 March 1898, police report on the March 17 meeting. On the United Front of 1899 and its Whitsun Program, see Macartney, *The Habsburg Empire*, pp. 681-82; Karl Hugelmann, *Das Nationalitätenrecht des alten Österreich* (Vienna, 1934), p. 204ff; and Molisch, *Geschichte der deutschnationalen Bewegung*, pp. 202-05. On the 1910 union, see n. 37 above.

[82] The most heated discussion of the issue occurred at the June 1907 meeting of the German Club cited in n. 73.

system but instead honorably show him the ways by which he can support and advance himself."[83] Those who might identify with the German liberal community otherwise but who wanted increased government intervention apparently found it more expedient to rely on the special-interest organizations than to agitate in the liberal political groups.

Few German liberals anywhere in Austria showed enthusiasm for the introduction of direct and equal manhood suffrage in the first years of the twentieth century, but on this issue many in Prague proved more resistant to change than liberals elsewhere. In 1905, when the inevitability of reform became apparent, a number of German Progressive leaders began to support change of the suffrage in one form or another.[84] In mid-November, two weeks after Emperor Francis Joseph had decided in favor of direct and equal suffrage for the lower house of the Reichsrat, *Bohemia* in Prague endorsed reform on the condition that it not reduce German representation substantially.[85] To persuade the German liberals in Prague to accept direct and equal suffrage, the Progressive Party leader Dr. Karl Eppinger came to the meeting of the German Club on December 20, 1905. He argued that although the German middle-class parties might lose mandates, a people with the cultural and economic significance of the Germans in Austria would inevitably benefit from the establishment of a new parliament which would address social and economic questions more vigorously and directly than before.[86] Dr. Karl Urban, the owner of real estate and a distillery in Prague, argued against Eppinger. Urban, who was prominent among the more conservative of the Progressive leaders in Bohemia, would accept some reform of the suffrage but opposed any diminution of German strength in the Reichsrat. If German industrial interests, in particular, would suffer from reform of the lower house, then the Progressive Party should demand compensation in the House of Lords.

Urban expressed the views of the older middle-class notables who had led the local liberal groups between the seventies and

---

[83] Quoted in *Bohemia*, 26 March 1901(M), from a speech by Professor August Fournier, a former Prague resident, to the 1901 congress of the German Progressive Party in Bohemia on the occasion of a visit to Prague by Fournier.

[84] On the German Progressives' attitudes toward direct and equal suffrage, see William A. Jenks, *The Austrian Electoral Reform of 1907* (New York, 1950), pp. 46-52, 120-25; and D. Harrington-Müller, *Der Fortschrittsklub*, pp. 135-45.

[85] *Bohemia*, 16 November 1905(M).

[86] SÚA Praha PP 1908-15 V/15/61: ad Z1 20788, 25 Dec 1905, police report of the December 20 meeting of the German Club.

early nineties and of the wealthier individuals who were still involved in community affairs. These elements still believed that political power and social status should belong to those who merited it by virtue of property, education, and contributions to society; the lower-middle-class and laboring strata had no special social and economic needs which required independent representation. Despite their concerns about the numerical decline of the German minority, the older and more conservative liberal notables were still unwilling to grant the lower strata a political voice on a par with their own. In 1900, Otto Forchheimer wrote in this vein to Josef M. Baernreither, one of the leaders of the constitutional landowners in Bohemia. Forchheimer, then sixty, insisted that any new Bohemian language ordinances must guarantee administrative bilingualism in Prague's suburbs as well as the municipality itself:[87]

> . . . in the suburbs, particularly Smíchov and Karlín, industry and commerce are to a great extent in German hands. One large factory makes a greater claim on the authorities than the thousand workers employed in it taken together.

The younger group of German liberal leaders in Prague who first emerged in the Municipal Affairs Association ultimately had to deal with the new forces of mass politics. The leading figures of the seventies and eighties gradually disappeared from the scene with the withdrawal of the wealthiest elements from local political action and the passage of time itself. Most of the generation of Franz Schmeykal and Alexander Richter retired or died in the decade or so after 1897.[88] The direction of the German Club and the German Political Association in Vinohrady passed after around 1907 to younger men who had not experienced the great constitutional struggles of the 1860s and 1870s. Dr. Josef Eckstein (b. 1866), Docent Bruno Kafka (b. 1881), and Professor Emil Pfersche (b. 1854) all proved more eager than their elders to address a broad public and to deal aggressively with popular social and economic concerns even if that meant compromising some property rights. Even this new generation, however, could do little to retard the disintegration of the bases of the old social and political order in the community. Eckstein, Kafka, and their colleagues responded as best they could to the ongoing structural changes and

[87] HHStA Nachlass Baernreither, Kt. 49: Otto Forchheimer to J. M. Baernreither, 22 May 1900.

[88] Schmeykal died unexpectedly in 1894, Schlesinger in 1899, Forchheimer in 1913, Richter in 1914, and Ludwig Bendiener not long thereafter.

to the day-to-day crises, but they never had the control over German collective life in Prague which Franz Schmeykal had enjoyed.

The younger liberal leaders in the Bohemian capital had no choice but to launch new efforts to make their political life more broadly inclusive and democratic than before. They, like their counterparts elsewhere in Austria, tried to find a basis for cooperation with other German parties which rejected parts of the old liberal creed and with interest-group organizations which put narrow economic concerns ahead of the broad middle-class interest which liberals had generally championed. The liberal leaders in Prague knew that unless the German middle-class and lower-middle-class parties could form a solid coalition, they could not hope in the long run to be an effective force in Austria's legislative bodies or to command the serious attention of the higher officials. The new generation of leaders came to accept the need for some representation of special economic interests and built alliances with the more cooperative German occupational groups in Prague. Still, they tried to appeal to an overriding community of ethnic interest in the whole German minority and to counter the centrifugal social and economic forces in the population. Once again local liberal leaders attempted to co-opt lower-middle-class and laboring elements into their public life through new organizations. Eckstein, Kafka, and Pfersche also experimented with efforts to move political discussions in the liberal community from the confines of select gatherings to public forums.

Like their predecessors in the eighties, the new generation of liberal leaders looked to lower-strata Germans in Prague to broaden their popular support and strengthen their hands against German opposition. In 1884 the Casino had established the Handworkers' Society as a liberal response to conservative and *völkisch* appeals to the lower middle class and workers; in 1909 the Casino and the Handworkers' Society created a liberal counterpart in Prague to the *völkisch* national socialist groups in the Bohemian borderlands.[89] On May Day, 1909, a disparate body of members of the Handworkers' Society, unaffiliated commercial and industrial workers, a few small businessmen, and members of the anti-Semitic German National Workers' League of Bohemia, as well as the Zionist workers' group, *Poale Zion*, gathered for the founding of a "German-

---

[89] On German national socialism in Austria, see Whiteside, *Austrian National Socialism.*

social local organization" (*Deutsch-soziale Lokalorganisation*).[90] The three skilled workers who presided condemned the nationalist prejudices of the Czech Social Democrats and the lack of national loyalty among the local German Social Democrats. The German-Social Organization would work for solidarity between nationally conscious German workers and German middle-class elements.

Although no prominent German liberals spoke at the founding, the liberal establishment in Prague apparently controlled the German-Social Organization from the inception. The Casino's allies in the Handworkers' Society and in the German Commercial Employees' Association organized the initial gathering and dominated the discussion. The national socialists in attendance proposed that the Prague group join the German National Workers' League, but a majority preferred an independent association open to Jews. This decision virtually guaranteed that the German-Social Organization would function merely as a lower-strata appendage to the liberal political groups. Prominent members of the Handworkers' Society assumed leadership of the new association, and by November 1909 it claimed about 300 members.[91] While the German-Social Local Organization had no great success in winning support among the German lower strata in Prague, it sponsored a busy schedule of political meetings and recreational activities through 1914, often in conjunction with other liberal bodies.

The younger liberal leaders in Prague turned to the German-Social Organization in their attempts to open local liberal politics to mass participation during the frustrating years between 1909 and 1914. On December 1, 1912, in the heat of the crisis over the First Balkan War, the German Club and the German-Social Organization sponsored an extraordinary "open people's assembly of the Germans in Prague" to discuss the implications of the Balkan situation for Austrian Germans and the failure of the most recent attempt at a Bohemian compromise.[92] Like their Czech nationalist opponents and the bureaucrats in charge of the Austrian government, German liberals in Prague were becoming increasingly sensitive to the connections between domestic politics and Austria's relations with the rest of Eastern Europe and particularly to the

[90] *Bohemia* and *Prager Tagblatt*, 3 May 1909(M).

[91] SÚA Praha PP 1908-15 V/54/363 Deutsch-soziale Lokalorganisation: 23.619/pp 3.XI.1909, police report of the meeting on 7 November 1909.

[92] *Bohemia*, 2 Dec 1912(M); SÚA Praha PP 1908-15 V/15/61 Deutscher Verein: ad Z 24114pr, 1 Dec 1912, police report on the meeting.

mutually reinforcing effects that instability in one sphere had on the other. Now, leaders of the liberal groups in Prague were willing to exploit the opportunities for whipping up popular enthusiasm by mixing appeals to their listeners' ethnic loyalties with advocacy of a particular course in foreign affairs.

The president of the German-Social Organization, Josef Eckstein for the German Club, and a representative of the liberal university students presided jointly over the December 1 meeting. This was the first open gathering sponsored by the German Club since it ceased running candidates for elective offices in the mid-1880s and the first large political meeting held jointly with an association for lower-strata Germans. The police estimated that 300 persons listened as Professor Emil Pfersche attacked the pro-Czech position taken in the compromise negotiations by the conservative nobility and by the Bohemian Governor, Count Thun. The audience cheered when Bruno Kafka urged limits to Serbian expansion, access to the Aegean for the Habsburg Monarchy, and the maintenance of a strong Austria led by its German citizens. That night liberal students held an outdoor rally around the statue of Marshal Radetzky in the Malá strana square.[93]

More mass meetings followed after 1912. At another critical juncture in February 1914, more than 1,000 people assembled in the Casino to protest the latest compromise on national rights in Bohemia proposed by Count Thun and by Minister-President Stürgkh and to demand full equality of Czech and German for all official usage in Prague.[94] The principal German liberal groups in Prague had previously looked askance at the politics of mass meetings; now they had no choice but to take to the streets and to public rostrums themselves.

The rise of new leadership in the local German liberal groups and the turn toward the methods of mass politics indicated only the waning of the old liberal order in the middle-class community, not its replacement by any settled new configuration of German public life. No integrated new structure had emerged by the coming of war in 1914. After the mid-nineties the middle-class Germans, Christian and Jewish, who rejected both radical nationalism and international socialism, searched for what the Viennese writer Ar-

[93] *Bohemia*, 3 Dec 1912(M), hyperbolically termed the gathering the "first German street demonstration" that Prague had seen.
[94] *Bohemia*, 16 Feb 1914(M); SÚA Praha PP 1908-15 V/54/723: Ad Z 4123, police report on the meeting of 15 Feb 1914.

thur Schnitzler termed a "way into the clear" out of the dying liberal culture.[95]

The German burghers of Prague had few ready alternatives to liberalism. Social democracy and national socialism had no attraction for those who still had a strong sense of belonging to a middle-class elite. That elitism also made unacceptable the populist ideology of radical German nationalism. Middle-class and lower-middle-class German residents in the inner city found it equally difficult to make any concessions to the anti-Semitism of the radical nationalists since Jews accounted for close to half their numbers. Still, the collapse of German liberalism as an effective force in Austrian public life and the decline of deferential politics among the Prague Germans themselves necessitated a quest for new political modes.

German public life in Prague showed a peculiar mixture of opposites in the last two decades before World War I. This resulted to a great extent from the Germans' situation as an ethnic minority and the requirements of ethnic defense. By 1900 liberals had little remaining power over local politics in Vienna and in most of their old strongholds in Lower Austria, Styria, and the German towns of Moravia and the Bohemian borderlands. In Prague, however, the needs of the German minority to protect its property, legal rights, and group life from Czech attacks gave the old liberal bodies continuing responsibilities in local political affairs. As elsewhere, the development of interest-group structures tended to fragment the public life of middle-class and lower-middle-class Germans who had formerly supported the liberal order. Yet the heightened national conflict of the new era sustained a broader, perhaps now shallower, sense of common interests as Germans which often worked to the advantage of the liberal groups.

The work of the Casino and the other liberal bodies in lobbying government officials on behalf of local German interests and in maintaining German educational and cultural services still drew the support of great numbers of Prague Germans after 1897. No other force in the German minority had the ability or the means. Some of the local *völkisch* groups tacitly recognized this when they began to use the Casino's facilities occasionally in the last several years before World War I. On the other hand, the occasional presence of even *völkisch* students in the Casino demonstrated the weak-

[95] See Carl E. Schorske's discussion of Schnitzler's novel *Der Weg ins Freie* (1908) in "Politics and the Psyche in *fin-de-siècle* Vienna: Schnitzler and Hofmannsthal," *American Historical Review*, LXVI (1961), pp. 930-46.

ening of the liberal elite and the waning of the old community order.[96] At heart the leaders of the Casino and the *völkisch* groups still had little sympathy for each other, but the *völkisch* organizations had nowhere else to turn and the liberal elite could no longer prudently deny them all hospitality.

World War I, the collapse of the Monarchy, and the creation of Czechoslovakia transformed the political and social situation of the German minority in Prague. Centripetal forces and German interests gained strength in Cisleithania during the early years of the war, but the formation of the Czechoslovak Republic completely transformed Czech-German relations. Germans had to give up any remaining pretensions to political and social primacy in Prague and in the Bohemian Lands as a whole. The new government proved generous to national minorities, but it was a republic of the Czechs and Slovaks. The Germans of Prague and German nationalists in the Bohemian borderlands drew even farther apart than before: the latter might engage in Pan-German irredentism, but the Prague population had to accept the status of a subordinate minority if they wished to remain in the capital of the new state.[97]

In the meantime, the erection of new national boundaries across old paths of migration caused the German minority in Prague to grow. In 1921, Greater Prague had 30,429 citizens of German nationality, 4.5 percent of the total, compared to 37,417 German-speaking citizens (6.1 percent) in 1910. By 1930, however, there were 41,453 German residents, 4.9 percent of the total.[98] After 1918 many came to Prague from German districts of Bohemia and Moravia who formerly would have migrated to Vienna or to other parts of Austria. The number of German university students in Prague also increased now that it was harder to go to study in

[96] AHMP fond spolků, no. 20: Deutsches Haus, annual reports of the directors, 1911-14.

[97] On German politics and Czech-German relations under the republic, see Johann Brügel, *Tschechen und Deutsche* (Munich, 1967), Victor S. Mamatey and Radomír Luža, ed., *A History of the Czechoslovak Republic 1918-1948* (Princeton, 1973), pp. 92-107, 167-87; and the polemical but richly detailed work of Jaroslav César and Bohumil Černý, *Politika německých buržoazních stran v Česloslovensku v letech 1918-1938*, 2 vols. (Prague, 1962).

[98] For a summary of the 1921 and 1930 census data on the Prague Germans, see Leo Epstein, "Das Wachsen des Prager Deutschtums," *Nation und Stadt*, IV (1930-31), pp. 408-09. See Havránek, in *Pražský sborník historický 1969-70*, p. 70, for a spatial definition of Greater Prague.

Vienna or in Graz.[99] All the social strata which were weakly represented among the Prague Germans previously grew after 1918: low-level white-collar employees, industrial workers, and even domestic servants.

The war and the establishment of the Czechoslovak Republic also transformed Prague's Jewish population and its relations to Czechs and Germans. Hundreds of Galician Jews came to the city during and just after the war. Their comparative piety, poverty, and lack of education made them unlikely candidates for integration into the German community. The Jewish immigrants constituted a new Jewish underclass in Prague and provided local Zionist groups an enlarged base of support. The founding of the republic naturally encouraged Jews who had previously been uncertain about national loyalties to side with the Czechs, but the new government also recognized a Jewish nationality in addition to the Czechoslovak, German, and Magyar. In 1900, 11,364 of the Jewish citizens in Prague I-VIII and the four inner suburbs had declared German their everyday language and 14,145 Czech. In 1921, only 7,070 Jewish citizens affirmed German nationality, compared to 14,953 Czechoslovak and 5,615 Jewish.[100]

German public life in Prague after 1918 reflected the increased size and diversity of the German population. The Casino, renamed the German House, survived as a community service center. Some German burghers still saw the German minority primarily as a propertied and educated elite, but divergent ideologies and varying notions of group identity now competed for the allegiance of Prague Germans on a more equal basis than ever before. Reform of the municipal suffrage and the introduction of proportional representation in all the legislative bodies of the republic gave Germans in Prague greatly expanded opportunities to elect their own representatives and encouraged vigorous competition for German voter support among left liberals, nationalists, and Social Democrats. After World War I, German leaders in Prague confronted a much different world from that which their forebears had envisioned with some confidence in the early 1860s. Society and politics had developed in the interim under the old Monarchy contrary to German middle-class hopes and heedless of the Germans' defensive efforts, and many Germans in Prague faced the new situation after 1918 with deep concern about what lay ahead.

[99] See the *völkisch* account in Wolmar, *Prag und das Reich*, pp. 505-55.
[100] A. Boháč, *Hlavní město Praha*, pp. 76-77.

Ethnic Identity, Group Solidarity, and Historical Change

If the history of Prague can serve as a guide, the German-speaking urban elites in Austria's Slavic territories developed ethnic identity and group solidarity only during the nineteenth century. Previously each of the cities and larger towns in the Czech and Slovene areas had a corporate social structure dominated by German-speakers drawn from the Habsburg Hereditary Lands, foreign countries, local pockets of German-speakers, and the assimilation of upwardly mobile Czech- and Slovene-speakers. High status and the Austro-German acculturation which automatically accompanied rank were what set the German-speaking elites apart from the rest of the local residents. The experience of the Prague Germans indicates that the German-speaking middle and upper strata only transformed themselves into self-conscious German groups, distinguished by a sense of German ethnicity and exclusive social relations, in response to demands for power and status by insurgent Slavic elements. Viewed broadly, both sides forged their group identities and aspirations in the course of the struggle for political and economic power.

Such a pattern of developing ethnicity in the mixed cities argues against a view of ethnic and national cleavages as simple constants in nineteenth-century Austria. The evolution of ethnic differences in Prague adds strength to arguments that ethnic cleavages in East-Central Europe underwent considerable change in the nineteenth and early twentieth centuries. Rather than affecting all other social and political conflicts as a sort of "first cause," ethnic solidarities and differences were themselves historically conditioned. In a mixed city like Prague, ethnic conflict grew directly out of the evolution of a modern class structure from a society of ranks and orders and the development, first, of deferential and, later, of mass politics.[1]

The Prague Germans essentially created an identity and group solidarity *de novo* after 1848 in reaction to the Czech nationalist challenge to their dominance. The Germans' ethnicity emerged as part of their efforts to deal with contemporary political and social developments that threatened their group interests. It did not spring from vague memories of a prior separate communal existence nor from some shared primordial attachment to distinctive popular customs, lineage, or home territory. The origins of the German-speakers at mid-century were too diverse and most had lived on close terms with Czech-speakers for too long for them to claim that any distinct lineage or group culture *qua* Germans already separated them from their Czech neighbors. In fact, even after ethnic differences widened in the late nineteenth century, Germans and Slavs in Austria's mixed cities still shared much more in modes of life, popular values, and day-to-day social relations than dedicated nationalists cared to admit. Some of the upper-middle-class Germans in Prague might build more luxurious villas and ostentatiously employ more servants than their Czech counterparts, but they had little else by way of customs and values other than language and political beliefs to set themselves off sharply as a group.[2]

In cities like Prague, struggles for power, status, and economic advantage lay at the root of the evolving differences between Germans and their Slavic neighbors. In the Bohemian capital, Czech nationalists wanted to supplant the old German-speaking upper strata and the social and political structures they dominated with a new Czech middle-class society; they fastened onto the Czech

[1] For interpretations on similar lines of Czech-German relations throughout Bohemia, see Friedrich Prinz, "Die Böhmischen Länder von 1848 bis 1914," in Bosl, ed., *Handbuch*, III, pp. 1-235, passim; idem, "Nation und Gesellschaft in den Böhmischen Ländern im 19. und 20. Jahrhundert," in Prinz, F. J. Schmale, und F. Seibt, ed., *Geschichte in der Gesellschaft: Festschrift für Karl Bosl zum 65. Geburtstag* (Stuttgart, 1974), pp. 333-49; Stölzl, *Die Ära Bach*, pp. 41-55, 120-46, 230-47; and Otto Urban, "K problematice rozkladu habsburské monarchie," in Jaroslav Pátek and Věra Šadová, ed., *Studie z obecných dějin: Sborník k sedmdesátým narozeninám prof. dr. Jaroslava Charváta* (Prague, 1975), p. 171.

[2] See the reminiscences of Ignát Herrmann, *Ze staré Prahy*, p. 74. On the numbers of servants employed by German and Czech families in Prague, see Havránek in *Pražský sborník historický 1969-70*, pp. 94-97, and *Öster. Statistik*, N. F., IV, 3. Heft, pp. 109-10.

language as the greatest common denominator in a diverse Czech population and made the civic rights of Czech-speakers the centerpiece of their political program. Local German-speakers responded in kind. By the end of the 1850s some began to define themselves as a distinct German group on the basis of what were virtually the only cultural traits which clearly distinguished them from Czechs: primary use of the German language and commitment to the primacy of German and German-speakers in the public affairs and economic life of Cisleithania. As Germans they could try to separate themselves from the assertive new Czech middle-class elements and defend some of their old advantages.

In more general terms, new patterns of ethnic identification arose here out of the political consciousness of groups which were trying either to modify or to maintain an unequal distribution of social advantages among popular elements which differed in major or minor cultural characteristics.[3] In Prague, as elsewhere in developing Western societies, heightened ethnicity was not an atavistic response to modernity: neither Czechs nor Germans cultivated ethnic solidarity to express a general resistance to social and economic development. Through the early 1880s both groups generally favored liberalization of the Austrian state and the abolition of corporate social and economic structures; they differed mainly on the terms of development and the relative advantages each side should reap.

Political processes have played a central role, of course, in the articulation of identity among all ethnic groups in modern Western societies, but upper-strata minorities generally seem to develop conscious ethnic identities only after being provoked by direct challenges from formerly subordinate groups or adverse changes in political structures. Elsewhere in Eastern Europe, for instance, the German- and Swedish-speaking elites of the Baltic and Finnish cities, like their German counterparts in Prague, had purely status-group identities through the mid-nineteenth century. They shared the same Lutheran faith and an allegiance to a society of ranks and orders with most of the subordinate Latvian, Estonian, and Finnish populations.[4] Wedded to the old social structure, the urban elites

---

[3] Michael Hechter offers such an analysis for the general evolution of ethnic consciousness in advanced societies in *American Journal of Sociology*, LXXIX, pp. 1151-54, 1177-78.

[4] See John A. Armstrong, "Mobilized Diaspora in Tsarist Russia: The Case of the Baltic Germans," in Jeremy R. Azrael, ed., *Soviet Nationality Policies and Practices* (New York and London, 1978), pp. 63-83; Gert Kroeger, "Zur Situation der bal-

were slow to respond to the rise of cultural and political movements among the subject peoples. Only at the very end of the century, when the Tsarist government began to attack the privileges of the local elites and the formerly submissive Baltic peoples began to assert themselves, did the urban elites establish new ethnic solidarities and demand rights as Germans and Swedes. Even then, most of the urban minorities here, like the Prague Germans, remained attached to their Baltic and Finnish native lands; and few embraced radical Pan-Germanism or Swedish irredentism.

From the beginnings of ethnic differentiation in Prague, most Germans cultivated a self-image as an elite of property and culture and a strong belief in German superiority over the Czechs. Accordingly, German group solidarity developed with sharp ideological and class limits. The organized German group life which evolved in the sixties and seventies served primarily the needs and interests of a middle class of wealth and education and those lower-middle-class elements which identified with the German *Bürgertum*. Acceptance in Prague's German group life required adherence to an ideology of liberal individualism and the primacy of the German middle class in Austria. The principal German organizations in Prague invoked no religious test. The common need for defense of liberalism and middle-class interests drew Christians and Jews together in the German community. What united the middle-class and lower-middle-class participants in German group life, however, effectively excluded workers, many petty employees, and, in fact, anyone who could not adopt the values of the liberal German burghers, even though they might identify with Germans otherwise.

The community structure created in the network of voluntary associations became a hothouse for German liberal values. The origins of most of the German population in the city's old middle and upper strata and the need for political unity felt by any embattled minority obviously contributed much to the social and ideological uniformity of German group life. But the character of the German community was not simply determined by inescapable, impersonal mechanisms: the members of the community themselves developed the criteria for group membership and defended

tischen Deutschen," *Zeitschrift für Ostforschung,* XVII (1968), pp. 601-32; Reinhard Wittram, *Baltische Geschichte: Die Ostseelande Livland, Estland, Kurland 1180-1918* (Munich, 1954), pp. 183-234; John H. Wuorinen, *Nationalism in Modern Finland* (New York, 1931), passim; and idem, *A History of Finland* (New York and London, 1965), pp. 7-11, 138-76.

them against mounting pressures to embrace a larger, more diverse population. The limits which the liberal groups imposed on participation in German community life had vital importance in deciding which individuals actually adopted or retained a German identity and were perceived as Germans in Prague.

Throughout the era before World War I, the social relations of Prague's German residents were separated most sharply from their Czech neighbors in the public sphere of collective action for political, cultural, and recreational purposes. Germans first articulated a distinct group identity and established a separate group existence by creating their own German public life, closed to Czech penetration. The separation of German and Czech public life became general by the 1870s, and thereafter only the schools and religious institutions operated or regulated by the state remained as major exceptions. The private sphere, on the other hand, did not see such a sharp division. In the affairs of individual work, consumption, home, and family, where collective controls could not reach so easily, it appears that individual Germans and Czechs continued to associate more freely down to 1914.

From what we can tell at this remove, ethnic differences came to color relations between Germans and Czechs in private affairs but did not cut off interaction. By the turn of the century, ethnic group loyalties and prejudices often affected the attitudes and demeanor of Prague's Czech and German residents in their daily contacts, but as individuals they continued to reside in the same neighborhoods and even the same apartment buildings, work in the same firms, patronize the same businesses, share friendships, and, at least to some extent, intermarry. Ethnic conflict may have strained some of these relations, but differences in ethnic identity and preferred language by themselves generally failed to stop individual interaction. Provided they maintained contact with other Germans in public, group affairs and perhaps in some of their individual relationships, many in Prague developed and maintained German identities despite frequent and close contacts with Czechs in their private lives. Where social barriers did arise between Germans and Czechs in private affairs, it was generally in situations where Czech-German distinctions coincided with sharp differences in class, religion, or geographic origin. Under the Monarchy, the social boundaries that were crucial to the formation and survival of a German group identity in Prague were to be found much more in the public sphere of daily life than in the private.

That the Prague Germans were more sharply separated from

Czechs in public life than in private affairs was probably typical of declining upper-strata minorities in the cities of East-Central Europe in this era. German and Swedish minorities in the cities of Austria, Finland, and the Baltic coast saw themselves as native citizens of lands in which their forebears had resided for centuries; and throughout their histories they had maintained close relations in everyday life with the majority peoples. To be sure, members of the old German and Swedish elites faced a changing world in their private affairs in the late nineteenth century, but developments in the public sphere threatened their group interests most directly once the formerly submissive majority groups began to challenge their dominance and the Habsburg and Tsarist empires reduced their privileges. For the once dominant elements to alter radically their private social relationships would be difficult and offered little as a response to their new predicaments. They could not easily isolate themselves in their daily individual relations like European colonists in Asia and Africa; nor would such action help much to shore up their declining political and economic positions.

Had a declining minority such as the Prague Germans confronted different historical circumstances, it would probably have established other social boundaries to insure group survival. At the opposite end of the spectrum of modern ethnic group experience, immigrant lower-strata minorities have often reacted to the general disruption in their lives caused by migration by limiting their closest personal relationships to others of the same group. In the United States this "ethnic enclosure" of close personal relations has played a vital role in sustaining ethnic identities even while members of the groups were being absorbed into the economic life and public affairs of the dominant majority.[5] The old dominant minorities of East-Central Europe, in contrast, did not suffer the multiple shocks of long-distance migration; the Prague Germans and the few other groups which have been studied made no concerted efforts to limit all their private relationships to others of the same group.[6] For

[5] Milton M. Gordon has developed the concept of ethnic enclosure in "Social Structure and Goals in Group Relations," in Morroe Berger, T. Abel, and C. H. Page, ed., *Freedom and Control in Modern Society* (New York, 1954), pp. 141-57; and *Assimilation in American Life*, pp. 19-95.

[6] On the response to decline of the Baltic Germans and the Swedish-speaking elements of the Finnish cities, see A. Henriksson, "The Riga German Community," passim; Kroeger in *Zeitschrift für Ostforschung*, XVII, pp. 623-32; Wittram, *Baltische Geschichte*, pp. 216-46; Wuorinen, *History of Finland*, pp. 8-11; and idem, *Nationalism in Modern Finland*, pp. 229-36.

them, the critical discontinuities occurred in public affairs, and ethnicity as such came to have a greater social meaning in the public sphere than in the private.

The group life of the Prague Germans retained its strong ideological and class limits to the end of the century despite the increasing need to broaden the popular appeal. By the early 1880s the leaders of the liberal community recognized that effective ethnic defense required a larger popular base, but white-collar employees, craftsmen, industrial supervisors, and workers found themselves no more at home in liberal society thereafter than before. The Prague Germans' past history and the various social and economic forces at work in Bohemia in the eighties and nineties sharply limited the numbers of lower-strata Germans in the provincial capital. Nonetheless, 30 to 35 percent of the citizens who declared themselves Germans at the turn of the century were petty employees, wage-earners, and their dependents. The liberal community's efforts to win lower-strata support on its own terms achieved meager results, and the lower-strata Germans by themselves were unable to develop any enduring group life of their own until the late eighties and nineties.

German public life as a whole in Prague began to show more ideological and social diversity only in the 1890s as the whole structure of Austrian society and politics entered a new phase. Once radical nationalists, Social Democrats, and Social Catholics began to build powerful mass movements in Austria in opposition to liberalism and deferential politics, the German lower strata in the Bohemian capital found sufficient stimulus and assistance to establish group life of their own. The majority of Prague's middle-class Germans, on the other hand, remained so strongly committed to a liberal political and social order in their community affairs that they refused any contact with *völkisch* and German Social Democratic elements in group life until well after 1900.

One might expect a common ethnic identity to unite the members of a beleaguered minority, but ironically in Prague conflicting notions of German identity worked to divide Germans from each other at the end of the nineteenth century. Various groups had their own concepts of German ethnicity which they used to combat others who had divergent ideological and class outlooks. The middle-class groups espoused their German identity as part of the defense of liberalism while the lower-strata *völkisch* bodies made theirs serve in the attack on liberal principles. Neither the growing dominance of the Czechs, nationalist violence, nor numerical decline could unite the Prague Germans or prevent new divisions from opening.

In this respect, however, there was nothing really unique about the experience of the Prague Germans. The evolving social and political conflicts which initially engender ethnic solidarity in developing or advanced societies may later produce new cleavages that divide people who otherwise share the same distinguishing cultural traits. In addition, migration and social mobility make it impossible for any modern urban minority to remain socially and economically homogeneous, whatever its origins. Compared to the German urban minorities in Austria, those of the Baltic, for example, developed conscious ethnic identities later and more rapidly, but there, too, political and social divisions widened among the Germans after 1900, just when declining power made unity more needed than before.[7]

In Prague the German liberals began to moderate their hostility toward radical German nationalists only in the last years before World War I, when the rise of economic interest groups had already begun to divide their own old middle-class base and when the mass parties had achieved dominance over popular political life in Austria. By then, however, the fragmentation of local German public life was irreversible, and the leaders of the German Casino had to face a pluralism of German political and economic interests as a permanent reality. In the meantime, the strongly liberal, middle-class tenor of German community life before 1900 had itself helped to diminish the German population.

At home and at the work place, most of Prague's few lower-strata Germans lived immersed in an overwhelmingly Czech environment. Many of them, in fact, were physically isolated from the areas of the city with the greatest German concentrations. German small retailers, clerks, and mechanics faced strong pressures to assimilate with the Czechs in the late nineteenth century. If the liberal community denied lower-strata elements any satisfying form of participation, and many were too dispersed to sustain a lasting group life of their own, they had little to assist them in maintaining a German identity in Prague. In the end many were simply absorbed into the Czech majority. Throughout the late nineteenth century the group relations of the liberal community did much more to aid the higher strata to survive as Germans in the city.

[7] See Kroeger in *Zeitschrift für Ostforschung*, XVII, pp. 627-31, and Wittram, *Baltische Geschichte*, pp. 232-46.

The very terms in which the German burghers of Prague first defined themselves as a group and the means they employed to insure group survival ultimately contributed to their own loss of strength. Most of the political and demographic forces which caused the Prague Germans to decline after 1861 were beyond their own control, and one could find similar conditions in Austria's other mixed German-Slavic cities. Yet the experience of Prague shows that by cultivating the self-image and collective life of a cultured and propertied elite, the German middle classes in these cities could make it nearly impossible to build a broader popular base. Otto Forchheimer spoke with more insight than he knew when he praised the accomplishments of the German Casino on its fortieth anniversary in 1902:[8]

> What we are, we are of ourselves; what we have achieved has come through our own efforts. Not only are we in our own house, but the number of members has risen more than threefold over the years despite the fact that the Germans in Prague have supposedly declined and many a brave German who finds himself in humble circumstances cannot dare to become a member.

Forchheimer assumed that the poorer German elements in the city were too intimidated by their Czech surroundings to try to join the Casino or to participate otherwise in German liberal group life. From his perspective as head of the Casino, he naturally failed to acknowledge that many Germans in "humble circumstances" did not "dare" join because of the social exclusivity of the Casino and the whole liberal community.

"What we are, we are of ourselves." The Prague Germans created their own identity and group solidarity in the second half of the nineteenth century. Their ethnicity was not simply the expression of a shared legacy of language or customs which drew them together instinctively regardless of divergent social and economic needs. Like other social formations in the modern world, ethnic groups fashion their own sense of self and their own group solidarity; and thereby they help to shape their own history. Perhaps if those involved in ethnic conflicts understood these processes better, they might more easily resolve their disputes and avoid lasting social hatred.

[8] Quoted in *Bohemia*, 16 November 1902(M).

Statistical Procedures

A. Sampling methods

The samples taken from the manuscript census returns were drawn indirectly. The Imperial-Royal Central Statistical Commission drew up census questionnaires for each household and distributed them in the cities to the owner of every developed parcel of land. The latter, in turn, gave one to the head of each resident household, who completed it. When the local officials in Prague collected and compiled the returns, they bound together all the questionnaires for each parcel, typically a single structure, and filed them under the number of the parcel.[1] Since the census takers prepared no general index of the population or of the heads of households, the only practical means of sampling is to draw the returns for a group of parcels in each district under study.

For simplicity and to facilitate time-series analysis, my samples included the same parcels in each census. The territorial definitions of the inner-city parishes established in 1870 were used throughout.[2] I drew systematic samples for the parish of St. Henry, beginning arbitrarily with the eleventh parcel and taking every twentieth parcel, and in the smaller parish of St. Gall every tenth parcel, beginning with the tenth. For the parishes of St. Peter and St. Nicholas, I renumbered the parcels consecutively and with a table of random numbers drew simple random samples of 10 percent of the parcels. I made no substitutions in any of the samples for parcels for which manuscript returns from one or more censuses were missing from the materials preserved in the Prague City Archive.

The systematic samples can be treated as random for purposes of this study. The parcel numbers in each of the five historic districts of the inner city generally run in ascending order in a radial pattern from the center of each district. Since the identity of each building's inhabitants had no apparent relationship to the parcel numbers, the systematic samples can be considered fully equivalent to the random samples.[3]

Once the manuscript census returns were drawn for the sampled parcels, all the civilian residents listed in the returns were counted. Statisticians

[1] See Wilhelm Hecke, "Die Methode und Technik der österreichischen Volkszählungen," *Statistische Monatsschrift*, N. F., XVII (1912), pp. 466-74.

[2] The parcels included in each parish as of 1870 are listed in Václav Hlavsa, ed., *Pražské matriky farní 1584-1870* (Prague, 1954), pp. 12-34.

[3] The numbers of the parcels included in the samples for the four parishes are listed in G. B. Cohen, "The Prague Germans," pp. 592-93.

term this a single-stage cluster sampling.[4] To simplify all calculations, however, I have treated all the samples as if they were direct and random.
Rigorous statistical procedure requires the use of special formulae for
calculating confidence intervals and testing for significant differences when
one draws clusters rather than sampling a population directly.[5] Using strict
procedures, one must draw a cluster sample that is larger in absolute terms
than an equivalent simple random sample in order to achieve the same
confidence interval. If the clusters are heterogeneous in composition, however, as was nearly always the case for the parcels in the samples used here,
the differences between the results of direct and cluster sampling are
minimal. Accordingly, I have used the simpler formulae pertaining to
direct random samples for all the significance tests and confidence intervals.

A number of simplifications were also made to facilitate work with the
manuscript census returns. All the civilian residents, citizen or alien, who
were reported in the census as present or only temporarily absent were
counted together. Moreover, all individuals in the samples were counted
as either Czech-speakers or German-speakers. The number of residents
who reported other languages was in any case nearly always less than 2
percent, and in most instances it seemed reasonable to count them with
the Czechs or Germans in whose households they lived. The French and
English governesses in some of the German households, for example,
usually reported their native tongues as their everyday language. Nearly
all these governesses also spoke German, and since there were not many
of them, it seems reasonable to count them along with the German population. Technical limitations and considerations of time required the tal-
lying of the totals for each parcel directly from the manuscript returns in
the Prague City Archive. The tally sheet used the same basic format as
Tables 1-6 in Appendix II.

B. Occupational categories

The Austrian Central Statistical Commission used the following general
categories in the censuses after 1880 for analyzing the sources of livelihood
for the population:

Agricultural (Agr.) = cultivation, raising of livestock, forestry, fishing.
Manufacture (Manuf.) = manufacture of all goods, mining, printing,
    construction, handicraft production.
Commerce (Com.) = all trade and exchange of goods except credit,
    financial services, and transportation.

---

[4] See the lucid discussion of cluster sampling in Hubert M. Blalock, Jr., *Social
Statistics*, 2nd ed. (New York, 1972), pp. 523-27.

[5] For an excellent description of the statistical tests applicable to indirect sampling,
see Roger Schofield, "Sampling in historical research," in E. A. Wrigley, ed., *Nineteenth-Century Society* (Cambridge, 1972), pp. 177-82.

Banking (Bank.) = credit, financial services, insurance.

Transportation (Trans.) = privately owned transportation services.

State employment (Stat.) = employment in any government agency, public schools, universities, public utilities, religious bodies, and public hospitals.

Free professions (Free) = doctors and lawyers not in the full employ of the state or of a private concern, privately or self-employed teachers and artists, journalists.

Army = active military personnel and their civilian employees, dependents and domestic servants.

Rentiers (Rent.) = those deriving income from the ownership of property, securities, and annuities; pensioners; welfare recipients.

Other = independent persons without stated occupation; individuals in preparation for careers; those confined to medical and penal institutions.

The volumes of *Österreichische Statistik* which include the occupational statistics from each census describe the categories used in full detail.[6] In presenting the data from the sampled parishes in Prague, I have subdivided several of the occupational categories for greater clarity, e.g., manufacture into industry and handicraft production. In addition, I have counted the pensioners and recipients of welfare found in the samples in the "Other" category in order to achieve a more accurate measure of the actual rentier population.

The most succinct definitions of the categories used in the Austrian censuses for status of employment were those published with the 1890 census returns:[7]

Independent (Indep.) = all persons in the position of entrepreneur, i.e., the owners of agricultural, industrial, handicraft, or commercial firms; all those who support themselves by their own work without assuming the status of employee, wage worker, or day-laborer; rentiers, pensioners, recipients of welfare, those in preparation for a career (i.e., students living apart from parents), and those without a given occupation.

Employee (Employ.) = all administrative, supervisorial, and accounting personnel in commercial and advanced technical concerns; all those in agriculture, industry, and commerce, who, while not entrepreneurs,

---

[6] *Öster. Statistik*, V, 3. Heft (1880); XXXIII, 1. Heft (1890); LXVI, 1. Heft (1900); and N. F., III, 1. Heft (1910).

[7] *Öster. Statistik*, XXXIII, 1. Heft, p. III. See also the explanation of the system of ranking provided with the 1900 returns, *Öster. Statistik*, LXVI, 1. Heft, pp. II-XI. The limitations of these categories for analyzing social stratification are discussed in Pavla Horská-Vrbová, "Pokus o využití rakouských statistik pro studium společenského rozvrstvení českých zemí v 2. polovině 19. století," *Československý časopis historický*, XX (1972), pp. 658-59.

direct or supervise production or distribution; all active military; non-independent officials in the free professions; qualified governmental officials and technical personnel.

Worker = all those earning incomes who are not classified as independents or employees and not explicitly reckoned as day-laborers in payrolls; all qualified manual laborers, apprentices; those performing lesser functions in commerce, government, and the free professions in a wage-earning capacity for which the least qualifications are necessary.

Day-laborer = those specifically reckoned as such in the payrolls.

Individuals engaged in domestic cooking, cleaning, washing, and nursing who lived in the households of their employers were considered "servants." All members of households who depended on the head of the household for their support and did not earn any income themselves were counted as "dependents." In 1900 the family members who shared in the work of the head of the household were removed from the category of "workers" and counted separately as "participating family members" (*mithelfende Familienmitglieder*).

The descriptions of the categories for status of employment published with the Austrian censuses always placed all major varieties of state employment in the ranks of "employees" and "workers." Nonetheless, the published statistics for each of the last four censuses before 1918 inexplicably counted a small number of "independents" in the state sector. To maintain consistency between the summary statistics taken from the published returns and the data from the sampled parishes, which report no state employees as "independents," I have wherever possible put the state-employed independents in the category of "employee."

Supplementary Tables

TABLE 1
Sampled Population for the Parishes of Gall, Henry, and Peter, 1890

German Everyday Language

Persons 484	Households 113		R.Cath. 139		Religion	Jew. 321		Evang. 24		Other/no —	

Occupation	TOT.	Ind.	Hand	Bus.	Bank	Trans.	Stat.	Free	Army	Dom. Ind.	Rent	Other/ none
Indep.	107	4	2	38			1	7		4	35	16
Employ.	58	9	1	27	5	1	5	10				
Worker	32		6	19	1	1		2		2	1	
Day-lab.	0											
Part. fam.	10	3		5						1	1	
Servant	27	1		8			2	3			10	3
Depend.	250	29	2	128	4	3	14	21		1	40	8
TOTAL	484	46	11	225	10	5	22	43	0	8	87	27

Birthplace	Prag.	Subu.	Bohem. Morav.	Foreign	Total	Marriages		
Men	105	6	119	19	249	German-German	69	
Women	92	10	113	20	235	German-Czech	4	
TOTAL	197	16	232	39	484			

Czech Everyday Language

Persons 1,171	Households 225		R. Cath. 1,092		Religion	Jew. 50		Evang. 27		Other/no 2	

Occupation	TOT.	Ind.	Hand	Bus.	Bank	Trans.	Stat.	Free	Army	Dom. Ind.	Rent	Other/ none
Indep.	157	7	31	41		2		5		13	25	33
Employ.	74	5	3	18	8	2	33	4	1			
Worker	240	40	75	55	2	15	16	2		34		1
Day-lab.	1		1									
Part. fam.	21	2	3	15						1		
Servant	200	20	12	97	4	2	11	13	1	2	32	6
Depend.	478	54	110	131	22	27	71	17	10	22	7	7
TOTAL	1,171	128	235	357	36	48	131	41	12	72	64	47

Birthplace	Prag.	Subu.	Bohem. Morav.	Foreign	Total
Men	206	39	254	10	509
Women	210	47	393	12	662
TOTAL	416	86	647	22	1,171

TABLE 2

Sampled Population for the Parish of St. Gall, 1890

German Everyday Language

Persons	Households	R. Cath.	Jew.	Evang.	Other/no
75	15	14	60	1	

Religion

Occupation

	TOT.	Ind.	Hand	Bus.	Bank	Trans.	Stat.	Free	Army	Dom. Ind.	Rent	Other/ none
Indep.	15	1	1	6				1		1	3	2
Employ.	9	1		4				4				
Worker	10		4	5				1				
Day-lab.												
Part. fam.	1	1										
Servant	3			3								
Depend.	37	5	2	23				6			1	
TOTAL	75	8	7	41	—	—	—	12	—	1	4	2

Birthplace

	Prag.	Subu.	Bohem. Morav.	Foreign	Total	Marriages	
Men	15	2	22	4	43	German-German	9
Women	12	1	18	1	32	German-Czech	0
TOTAL	27	3	40	5	75		

Czech Everyday Language

Persons	Households	R. Cath.	Jew.	Evang.	Other/no
137	31	131	4	2	

Religion

Occupation

	TOT.	Ind.	Hand	Bus.	Bank	Trans.	Stat.	Free	Army	Dom. Ind.	Rent	Other/ none
Indep.	26	1	2	10				1		3	5	4
Employ.	9	1		2	1		5					
Worker	21	4	4	5	1					7		
Day-lab.												
Part. fam.	9	1		7						1		
Servant	25	2	1	17	1			1			2	1
Depend.	47	9	2	22	8		1	1		3	1	
TOTAL	137	18	9	63	11		6	3		14	8	5

Birthplace

	Prag.	Subu.	Bohem. Morav.	Foreign	Total
Men	23	13	15		51
Women	36	8	42		86
TOTAL	59	21	57	0	137

TABLE 3
Sampled Population for the Parish of St. Henry, 1890

German Everyday Language

Religion				
Persons	Households	R. Cath.	Jew.	Evang.	Other/no
293	66	100	176	17	—

Occupation	TOT.	Ind.	Hand	Bus.	Bank	Trans.	Stat.	Free	Army	Dom. Ind.	Rent	Other/ None
Indep.	65	3	1	23			1	6			22	9
Employ.	31	3		15	3	1	4	5				
Worker	13		1	6	1	1		1		2	1	
Day-lab.	0											
Part. fam.	7	2		3						1	1	
Servant	19			2			2	3			9	3
Depend.	158	20		71	4	3	14	15		1	26	4
TOTAL	293	28	2	120	8	5	21	30	0	4	59	16

Birthplace	Prag.	Subu.	Bohem. Morav.	Foreign	Tot.	Marriages	
Men	70	4	63	9	146	German-German	44
Women	57	8	69	13	147	German-Czech	3
TOTAL	127	12	132	22	293		

Czech Everyday Language

Religion				
Persons	Households	R. Cath.	Jew.	Evang.	Other/no
394	61	366	23	3	2

Occupation	TOT.	Ind.	Hand	Bus.	Bank	Trans.	Stat.	Free	Army	Dom. Ind.	Rent	Other/ None
Indep.	58	4	10	13		1		4		3	3	20
Employ.	22	2		5	4		8	2	1			
Worker	62	11	16	13	1	4	3			14		
Day-lab.	1		1									
Part. fam.	6	1	1	4								
Servant	101	12	3	46	2	1	4	10	1	2	18	2
Depend.	144	10	35	43	9	9	15	4	3	14		2
TOTAL	394	40	66	125	16	15	30	20	5	33	21	24

Birthplace	Prag.	Subu.	Bohem. Morav.	Foreign	Total
Men	67	19	79	3	168
Women	53	21	151	1	226
TOTAL	120	40	230	4	394

TABLE 4
Sampled Population for the Parish of St. Peter, 1890

German Everyday Language

Persons	Households				R. Cath.		Religion Jew.		Evang.		Other/no	
116	32				25		85		6		0	

Occupation

	TOT.	Ind.	Hand	Bus.	Bank	Trans.	Stat.	Free	Army	Dom. Ind.	Rent	Other/ None
Indep.	27			9						3	10	5
Employ.	18	5	1	8	2		1	1				
Worker	9		1	8	0							
Day-lab.												
Part. fam.	2			2								
Servant	5	1		3							1	
Depend.	55	4		34							13	4
TOTAL	116	10	2	64	2	—	1	1	—	3	24	9

Birthplace

	Prag.	Subu.	Bohem. Morav.	Foreign	Tot.	Marriages	
Men	20	0	34	6	60	German-German	16
Women	23	1	26	6	56	German-Czech	1
TOTAL	43	1	60	12	116		

Czech Everyday Langauge

Persons	Households				R. Cath.		Religion Jew.		Evang.		Other/no	
640	133				595		23		22		0	

Occupation

	TOT.	Ind.	Hand	Bus.	Bank	Trans.	Stat.	Free	Army	Dom. Ind.	Rent	Other/ None
Indep.	73	2	19	18		1				7	17	9
Employ.	43	2	3	11	3	2	20	2				
Worker	157	26	55	37		11	13	2		13		
Day-lab.	0											
Part. fam.	6		2	4								
Servant	74	6	8	34	1	1	7	2			12	3
Depend.	287	35	73	66	5	18	55	12	7	5	6	5
TOTAL	640	71	160	170	9	33	95	18	7	25	35	17

Birthplace

	Prag.	Subu.	Bohem. Morav.	Foreign	Total
Men	116	7	160	7	290
Women	121	18	200	11	350
TOTAL	237	25	360	18	640

TABLE 5
Sampled Population for the Parish of St. Nicholas, 1890

German Everyday Language

Persons		Households		R. Cath.		Religion Jew.		Evang.		Other/no	
70		22		61		0		9		0	

Occupation	TOT.	Ind.	Hand	Bus.	Bank	Trans.	Stat.	Free	Army	Dom. Ind.	Rent	Other/ None
Indep.	20	1		3				2			3	11
Employ.	6				1		5					
Worker	3			2			1					
Day-lab.	0											
Part. fam.	0											
Servant	7						1		6			
Depend.	34	1			3		14		9		1	6
TOTAL	70	2	0	5	4	0	21	2	15	0	4	17

Birthplace	Prag.	Subu.	Bohem. Morav.	Foreign	Tot.	Marriages	
Men	11	1	8	7	27	German-German	14
Women	17	1	17	8	43	German-Czech	3
TOTAL	28	2	25	15	70		

Czech Everyday Language

Persons		Households		R. Cath.		Religion Jew.		Evang.		Other/no	
640		153		637		0		3		0	

Occupation	TOT.	Ind.	Hand	Bus.	Bank	Trans.	Stat.	Free	Army	Dom. Ind.	Rent	Other/ None
Indep.	108	2	16	16		1		5		23	13	32
Employ.	33	2		6	1	2	19	2			1	
Worker	142	40	39	25		3	11	1		23		
Day-lab.	5	3					1			1		
Part. fam.	13	3	1	4				3		2		
Servant	50	2	5	13		2	7	2	3		8	8
Depend.	289	40	61	52	3	13	43	14	2	21	8	32
TOTAL	640	92	122	116	4	21	81	27	5	70	30	72

Birthplace	Prag.	Subu.	Bohem. Morav.	Foreign	Total
Men	121	13	134	7	275
Women	151	20	189	5	365
TOTAL	272	33	323	12	640

TABLE 6
Sampled Population for the Parishes of
Gall, Henry, and Peter, 1910

German Everyday Language

			Religion		
Persons	Households	R. Cath.	Jew.	Evang.	Other/no
335	87	92	229	14	—

Occupation

	TOT.	Ind.	Hand	Bus.	Bank	Trans.	Stat.	Free	Army	Dom. Ind.	Rent	Other/ None
Indep.	92	3	5	30				13		1	28	12
Employ.	44	10		19	8		5	2				
Worker	17	2		12				1		2		
Day-lab.	0											
Part. fam.	9		2	5				1			1	
Servant	23	7		5			1	4			4	2
Depend.	150	25	5	61	6		3	28	1		15	6
TOTAL	335	47	12	132	14	0	9	49	1	3	48	20

Birthplace

	Prag.	Subu.	Bohem. Morav.	Foreign	Tot.	Marriages	
Men	62	9	66	15	152	German-German	60
Women	72	7	79	25	183	German-Czech	1
TOTAL	134	16	145	40	335		

Czech Everyday Language

			Religion		
Persons	Households	R. Cath.	Jew.	Evang.	Other/no
1,256	261	1,025	214	14	3

Occupation

	TOT.	Ind.	Hand	Bus.	Bank	Trans.	Stat.	Free	Army	Dom. Ind.	Rent	Other/ None
Indep.	204	14	33	70	1	2		13		18	29	24
Employ.	78	15		35	10	0	11	7				
Worker	244	38	50	86	5	5	31	3		26		
Day-lab.	1						1			1		
Part. fam.	28	4	3	18						2	1	
Servant	227	33	16	102	6	1	11	27			25	6
Depend.	474	54	91	171	14	13	54	25	17	23	4	8
TOTAL	1,256	158	193	482	36	21	107	75	17	70	59	38

Birthplace

	Prag.	Subu.	Bohem. Morav.	Foreign	Total
Men	201	40	255	4	500
Women	252	58	436	10	756
TOTAL	453	98	691	14	1,256

TABLE 7
Occupational Distribution of the Citizen
Residents of Prague I-VIII and Six Suburbs, 1910[a]

	A/Agr-For	B/Mfg.	C/Commerce	D/Govt.-Free-Rent-Other	Total
Germans					
Independ.	35	678	1,228	6,004	7,945
Employee	12	1,502	2,915	2,800	7,299
Worker/day-l.	15	844	1,049	2,692	4,600
Part. fam.	1	23	44	2	70
Servant	15	174	226	658	1,073
All empl.	78	3,221	5,462	12,156	20,917
Dependents	91	3,260	5,432	6,249	15,032
TOTAL	169	6,481	10,894	18,405	35,949
Czechs					
Independ.	361	17,515	20,434	35,927	74,237
Employee	111	6,104	12,344	13,407	31,966
Worker/day.	1,008	80,406	28,665	12,674	122,753
Part. fam.	51	672	1,531	18	2,272
Servant	263	5,435	8,141	10,931	24,770
All empl.	1,794	110,132	71,115	72,957	255,998
Dependents	1,637	99,408	63,246	42,659	206,950
TOTAL	3,431	209,540	134,361	115,616	462,948

[a] From *Österreichische Statistik*, N.F., III, 8. Heft, p. 330.

TABLE 8
Sampled Population for the Parish of St. Henry, 1880

German Everyday Language

Persons	Households	Religion			
		R. Cath.	Jew.	Evang.	Other/no
385	83	197	178	10	—

Occupation	TOT.	Ind.	Hand	Bus.	Bank	Trans.	Stat.	Free	Army	Dom. Ind.	Rent	Other/None
Indep.	63	4	5	21				4			18	11
Employ.	42	1	1	26	2	1	8	3				
Worker	24	7	4	8			2	1		2		
Day-lab.	0											
Part. fam.	7	1	0	6								
Servant	28		4	12			4				7	1
Depend.	221	4	14	134	5		21	9		1	19	14
TOTAL	385	17	28	207	7	1	35	17	—	3	44	26

Birthplace	Prag.	Subu.	Bohem. Morav.	Foreign	Tot.	Marriages	
Men	85	4	94	20	203	German-German	47
Women	76	6	83	17	182	German-Czech	9
TOTAL	161	10	177	37	385		

Czech Everyday Language

Persons	Households	Religion			
		R. Cath.	Jew.	Evang.	Other/no
378	60	329	39	10	—

Occupation	TOT.	Ind.	Hand	Bus.	Bank	Trans.	Stat.	Free	Army	Dom. Ind.	Rent	Other/None
Indep.	42	3	10	10				2		6	1	10
Employ.	16	1		4	2	2	5	2				
Worker	45	3	17	16		1	1			7		
Day-lab.	1						1					
Part. fam.	11	2	3	3				1		2		
Servant	144	9	8	66	1	2	14	12		4	23	5
Depend.	119	11	26	35		6	13	10		12	5	1
TOTAL	378	29	64	134	3	11	34	27	—	31	29	16

Birthplace	Prag.	Subu.	Bohem. Morav.	Foreign	Total
Men	50	10	81	1	142
Women	53	9	171	3	236
TOTAL	103	19	252	4	378

TABLE 9

Directors of the Prague German Casino, 1870-1914

1870

Pres. Franz Schmeykal, lawyer
Dr. Rudolf Haase, rentier
Josef Singer,
F. X. Schmidt, merchant
J. C. Jarsch,
Prof. Dr. Jos. Holzamer, Handelsakad.
Dr. August Hancke, lawyer
Dr. Gustav Herglotz
Johann Stark
Josef Turba
Josef Wesely
Dr. H. Raudnitz (J)[a]
Wilhelm Koch
Johann Krumbholz, text. manufact.
Franz Dörfl
Dr. Karl Claudi, lawyer
J. U. Bencker
Karl Ritter von Wolf-Zdekauer, bank.
A. Schobloch
L. Voss

1887

Pres. Franz Schmeykal, lawyer
V.-P. Otto Forchheimer, commod. merch. (J)
Sec. Dr. Carl Scherks, lawyer
Treas. Carl Thorsch, commodities merch. (J)
Treas. Heinrich Roedl, manufacturer
Dr. Karl K. Claudi, lawyer
Carl Franke, merchant
Julius Fritsche, insur. co. dir.
Dr. Rudolf Haase, rentier

1883

Pres. Franz Schmeykal, lawyer
V.-P. Otto Forchheimer, merchant (J)
Dr. Rudolf Haase, rentier
Dr. Julius Rihl, physician
Hasche, merchant
Reichl
Carl Thorsch, commod. deal. (J)
Julius Ziegler, bank off.
Dr. Karl Scherks, lawyer
Moriz Pfeiffer, rail. insp.
Dr. August Hancke, lawyer
Edmund Eichler, merchant
Johann Krumbholz, manuf.
Prof. Dr. Jos. Holzamer
August Kamm, commod. dealer
Sigmund Mauthner, manuf. (J)
Dr. Karl Claudi, lawyer
Karl R. v. Wolf-Zdekauer
Dr. Heinrich Osborne, lawyer

1892

Pres. Franz Schmeykal, lawyer
V.-P. Otto Forchheimer, merchant (J)
Sec. Dr. August Hancke, lawyer
Treas. Karl R. v. Zdekauer, bank.
Treas. Carl Bencker, manufact.
Adolf Schmidt, agent
Dr. Karl K. Claudi, lawyer
Johann Deistler, rail. off.
Dr. Alfred Goldschmid, lawyer (J)

TABLE 9 (cont.)

1887 (cont.)

Dr. August Hancke, lawyer
Prof. Dr. Jos. Holzamer
August Kamm, commod. dealer
Johann Kluge, candy manufact.
Prof. Dr. Hugo von Kremer-Auenrode
Sigmund Mauthner, text. manuf. (J)
Moriz Pfeiffer, railroad inspect.
Dr. Julius Rihl, physician
Cornelius Russ, railroad official
Wilhelm Spirk, distiller
Stefan Fragl, architect
Karl R. v. Wolf-Zdekauer, banker
Julius Ziegler, merchant
Josef Zink, apothecary

1898

Pres. Otto Forchheimer, commod. merch. (J)
V-P.   Heinrich Rödl, manufacturer
Sec.   Dr. Franz Waldert, lawyer
Treas. Carl Thorsch, banker (J)
Treas. Heinrich Rödl, manufact.
       Carl Bencker, manufact.
       Dr. Karl K. Claudi, lawyer
       Johann Deistler, rail. inspect.
       Philipp Falkowicz, insur. offic. (J)
       Dr. Alfred Goldschmid, lawyer (J)
       Prof. Ferdinand Höhm, girls' lyc.
       August Kamm, merchant
       Dr. Anton Kiemann, lawyer
       Johann Kluge, candy manuf.
       Dr. Ludwig Krieg, lawyer

1892 (cont.)

Heinrich Rödl, manfact.
Sigmund Mauthner, manuf. (J)
Wilhelm Spirk, distill.
Julius Feitoche, insur. dir.
Prof. Ferdinand Höhm, lyceum
August Kamm, merchant
Johann Kluge, manufact.
Moriz Pfeiffer, railroad inspect.
Dr. Julius Rihl, physician
Dr. Carl Scherks, lawyer
Carl Thorsch, merchant (J)
Carl Toekei, merchant
Prof. Dr. Dominick Ullmann, law
Dr. Eduard v. Zahn, lawyer
Julius Ziegler, merchant

1907

Pres. Otto Forchheimer, merchant (J)
V-P.   J. R. Sobitschka, manuf.
Sec.   Dr. Ludwig Krieg, lawyer
Treas. Richard Neumann, manuf.
Treas. August Kamm, merchant
       Dr. Robt. v. Skallheim, judge
       Carl Bencker, manuf.
       Dr. Karl K. Claudi, lawyer
       Philipp Falkowicz, insur.
       Prof. Dr. Joh. Gad, medicine
       Dr. Alfred Goldschmid, lawyer (J)
       Sigmund Kann, com. executive (J)
       Dr. Anton Kiemann, lawyer
       Robert Leonhardt, merchant
       Camill Ludwik, indust. dir.

Moriz Pfeiffer, rail. inspect.
Alexander Richter, manufact.
Dr. Julius Rihl, physician
Dr. Carl Scherks, lawyer
Adolf Schmidt, agent
Philipp Schwarz, architect
J. R. Sobitschka, manufact.
Prof. Dr. Ottokar Weber, phil.
Karl Frh. v. Wolf-Zdekauer, bank
Julius Ziegler

1914
Pres. Univ. Prof. Dr. Adolf Bachmann, phil.
V.-P. August Kamm, merchant
Sec. Dr. Ludwig Krieg, lawyer
Dr. Robert Bauer v. Skallheim, judge
Dr. Hugo Grab, manufacturer
Dr. Alfred Goldschmid, lawyer (J)
Richard Neumann, manuf.
Dr. Viktor von Ottenburg, lawyer, bank dir.
Alexander Richter, manufacturer
Ludwig Hafenbrädl, bank officer
Dr. Eduard Rohn, physician
Dr. Friedrich Elbogen, manufacturer (J)
Max Epler, iron foundry director
August Kamm, merchant
Sigmund Kann, commercial executive (J)
Dr. Anton Kiemann, lawyer
Hans Sobotka, textile manufacturer (J)
Josef Veider, manufacturer
Rudolf Bamberger, insurance co. general agent
Hans Edler von Kreisl, great landowner
Robert Perutz, textile manufacturer (J)

Viktor von Ottenburg, bank.
Anton Pohl, manufact.
Alexander Richter, manuf.
Adolf Schmidt, agent
Hans Sobotka, manufact. (J)
Carl Thorsch, rentier (J)
Josef Veider, manufact.
Prof. Dr. Ottokar Weber, phil.
Karl Frh. v. Wolf-Zdekauer, bank.

Gustav Rulf, bank director
Adolf Schram, manufacturer
Univ. Prof. Ottokar Weber
Karl Frh. von Wolf-Zdekauer, banker

TABLE 10

Directors of the Prague German Club, 1869-1911

1869 - Constitutional Society

Pres. Dr. Franz Schmeykal, lawyer
Otto Forchheimer, commod. merch. (J)[a]
Prof. Dr. Jos. Holzamer, Handels.
Prof. Josef Kaulich, medical fac.
Karl Pickert, newspaper editor
Adolf Schwab, merchant
Dr. Friedr. R. v. Wiener, lawyer (J)
Dr. Alex. Wiechowsky, school dir.
Richard R. v. Dotzauer, merchant

1882

Pres. Dr. Franz Schmeykal, lawyer
Univ. Prof. Karl Czyhlarz, law
Otto Forchheimer, merchant (J)
Prof. Friedrich Kick, tech. col.
Dr. Alfred Klaar, writer
Univ. Prof. Philipp Knoll, med.
Alexander Richter, text. manuf.
Victor Riedl v. Riedenstein, sugar refining
Dr. Johann Urban, lawyer
Dr. Friedr. R. v. Wiener, lawyer (J)

1894

Pres. Otto Forchheimer, merchant (J)
V-P. Julius Lippert, historian, writ.
Sec. Willibald Reichmann, merchant
Dr. Ludwig Bendiener, lawyer (J)
Dr. Alfred Klaar, writer, docent.
Dr. August Rihl, lawyer
Dr. Josef Spindler, lawyer
Dr. Franz Waldert, lawyer
Prof. Carl Broda, Realschule
Univ. Prof. Adolf Bachmann, phil.

1899

Pres. Otto Forchheimer, merchant (J)
V-P. Dr. August Rihl, lawyer
Sec. Dr. Aug. Hackel, school dir.
Dr. Ludwig Bendiener, lawyer (J)
Dr. Josef Eckstein, lawyer (J)
Dr. Johann Kiemann, lawyer
Josef R. Sobitschka, manuf.
Dr. Josef Spindler, lawyer
Dr. Karl Urban, lawyer
Willibald Reichmann, merchant

1903

Pres. Univ. Prof. Adolf Bachmann
V-P. Dr. Ludwig Bendiener, lawyer (J)
Sec. Dr. Josef Eckstein, lawyer (J)
Willibald Reichmann, merchant
Dr. Richard Ausch, lawyer
Dr. Ludwig Krieg, lawyer
Josef Müller, bank officer
Prof. Karl Richter, Gymnasium
Dr. Karl Urban, lawyer

1911

Pres. Dr. Josef Eckstein, lawyer (J)
V-P. Dr. Ludwig Bendiener, lawyer (J)
Sec. Doc. Dr. Bruno Kafka, lawyer (J)
Dr. Richard Ausch, lawyer
Univ. Prof. Adolf Bachmann
August Kamm, merchant
Dr. Ludwig Krieg, lawyer
Josef Müller, bank officer
Willibald Reichmann, merchant
Dr. Franz Wien, lawyer (J)

[a] (J) = Jewish board members.

TABLE 11

Council of the Jewish Religious Community, Prague, 1891

President	Dr. Arnold Rosenbacher, lawyer
Vice-pres.	Dr. Ludwig Bendiener, lawyer
Members	Moritz Austerlitz, partner, textile business
	Sigmund Beer, owner, freight-foward. (*kais. Rat*)
	Josef Bunzel, owner, dry goods bus. (*kais. Rat*)
	Jakob von Dormizer, great landowner
	Dr. Friedrich Duschenes, lawyer
	Seligman Elbogen, owner, sugar refinery
	Sigmund Haurowitz, partner, textile bus.
	Solomon Kohn, writer
	Dr. Koppelmann Lasch, retired lawyer
	Sigmund Mauthner, partner, cotton-spinning factory
	Josef von Portheim, rentier
	Gottlieb Schmelkes, owner, book-printing firm
	Philip Schwab, rentier
	Moritz Ungar, dealer, grain and commodities
	Wilhelm Winterstein, partner, rubber products manuf. (*kais. Rat*)

TABLE 12

Votes for the German Liberal and *Völkisch* Candidates
in Prague in the Reichsrat Election, May 14, 1907[a]

Voting District	Liberal Votes		Völkisch Votes		Ger. Cit. in District as % of Tot. Ger. Pop.
Old Town	723	(14.7%)	87	(10.4%)	12.0%
Lower New Town	886	(18.3)	65	(7.8)	12.3
Upper New Town	650	(13.4)	80	(9.6)	12.0
	2,259	(46.4)	232	(27.8)	36.3
Upper New Town/ Vyšehrad	201	(4.2)	55	(6.6)	3.4
Malá strana/Hradčany	309	(6.4)	72	(8.6)	8.2
Holešovice-Bubny	178	(3.7)	33	(4.0)	4.0
Josefov/Libeň	136	(2.8)	21	(2.5)	3.4
Smíchov (Inner)	510	(10.5)	100	(12.0)	12.0
Vinohrady	789	(16.3)	177	(21.2)	21.3
Outer Žižkov	24	(0.5)	—		
Inner Žižkov	137	(2.8)	75	(9.0)	4.8
Karlín	297	(6.1)	68	(8.2)	7.5
	2,581	(53.6)	601	(72.2)	63.7
TOTAL	4,840	(100%)	833	(100%)	100% (32,332)

[a] From *Bohemia*, 15 May 1907(M).

SOURCES

Archival Collections

PRAGUE

Státní ústřední archiv [SÚA] (Central State Archive)
České místodržitelství [ČM] (Bohemian Governor's Office)
    Documents on voluntary associations
Presidium českého místodržitelství [PM] (Presidium of the Bohemian Governor's Office)
    Police reports on voluntary associations
Tajný spisy Presidia českého místodržitelství [PMT] (Secret Papers of the Presidium of the Bohemian Governor's Office)
    Police intelligence reports
Ministerstvo vnitra/Rakousko [MV/R] (Austrian Ministry of Interior)
    Sect. 22 in genere, in specie: Böhmen, ct. 1757, 1758, reports on civil disorders in Prague
Pozůstalost Karl Urban (personal papers of Dr. Karl Urban)
Pražské policejní ředitelství [PP] (Prague Police Directorate)
    Reports and documents on voluntary associations
    Reports on individuals
Archiv pražského arcibiskupství [APA] (Archive of the Prague Archbishopric)
    Ordinariat, ct. 30-31, papers on the *Los von Rom* movement and Catholic voluntary associations

Archiv hlavního města Prahy [AHMP] (Archive of the Capital City Prague)
Fond společenstev (collection for the craft associations)
    Various documents and registries of masters, members
Fond spolků (collection on voluntary associations)
    spolkový katastr (registry of associations)
    Deutsches Haus (75 cartons)
    Deutsches Landestheater (35 bundles)
    Deutscher Schulpfennig-Verein, various documents
Fond škol (collection on schools)
    Catalogs and registries of students for primary and secondary schools
Sčítací operaty (manuscript census returns)
    1880 (incomplete)
    1890
    1900 (incomplete, unsorted)
    1910

Literarní archiv knihovny Národního muzea (Literary Archive of the Library of the National Museum)
Letters and calling cards of various Prague German figures in the papers of Josef Bayer, Jan Podlipný, Antonín Rezek, František Šubert, and Otakar Winický

Archiv University Karlový [AUK] (Archive of the Charles University)
Matricula Doctorum Universitatis Prag. Germ.
Všestudentský archiv (Archive for all student groups)
Annual reports and various documents for the Lese- und Redehalle der deutschen Studenten and other German student organizations

Státní židovské muzeum [SŽM] (State Jewish Museum)
Židovská náboženská obec, Praha [ŽNOP] (Jewish Religious Community of Prague)
Minutes of the religious community council
Registries of taxpayers for the religious community, 1870, 1891, 1901, 1912
Council minutes and various documents for the Jewish Religious Communities of Karlín, Libeň, and Vinohrady

VIENNA

Österreichisches Staatsarchiv: Allgemeines Verwaltungsarchiv [AVA]
Ministerium des Innern—Praesidium [MI-Praes.]
22 in genere and Böhmen, ct. 843, 853, 2010, 2019, 2020, 2091, 2095
Police and ministerial reports on civil disorders in Prague, 1897-1918
Ministerium für Kultus und Unterricht
53225 - 15 Vereine, Böhmen-Prag
Reports, correspondence for German voluntary associations in Prague
Sozialdemokratische Parteistellen
ct. 134, Böhmen-Organisation, BI-Prag 1910-1913
Annual reports on the German Social Democrats in Prague

Haus-, Hof-, und Staatsarchiv [HHStA]
K. u. K. Ministerium des Äussern
Informationsbüroakten
Intelligence reports on political affairs in Prague and Bohemia
Nachlass Josef M. Baernreither, ct. 33, 34, 36, 47, 50
Nachlass Plener, ct. 18, 19, 29

GERMANY (Filmed in Whaddon Hall by the University of California)

Auswärtiges Amt
Abteilung A, Akten betreffend Böhmen, August 1885-September 1913 (Reels 221, 249, 250, 251, & 252)
Consular reports and news clippings from Prague on local and provincial politics

New York

Leo Baeck Institute, Library and Archive [LBI]
  Unpubl. memoirs of Moritz Austerlitz, Egon Basch, Else Bergmann,
  Richard A. Bermann [pseud. Arnold Höllriegel], Ottilie Bondy.

Contemporary Newspapers and Periodicals

Prague

Bohemia (daily, German liberal)
Deutsche Arbeit (monthly, nonpartisan)
Der Deutsche Volksbote (semimonthly, later weekly, *völkisch*)
Israelitische Gemeindezeitung (semimonthly, independent)
Montagsblatt aus Böhmen (weekly, German liberal)
Národní listy (daily, independent Young Czech)
Politik (daily, Old Czech)
Prager Tagblatt (daily, German liberal)
Právo lidu (daily, Czech Social Democrat)
Selbstwehr (weekly, Jewish nationalist)
Tagesbote aus Böhmen (daily, German liberal)

Vienna

Neue Freie Presse (daily, German liberal)

Leipzig

Deutsches Museum (semimonthly 1851-52, weekly 1852-67)

Published Statistical Sources

Austria. Statistische Central-Commission. *Handbuch der Vereine in den im
  Reichsrate vertretenen Königreichen und Ländern, 1890.* Vienna, 1892.
———. *Österreichisches Städtebuch.* Vienna, 1887 et seq.
———. *Österreichische Statistik.* Vienna, 1882 et seq.
———. *Schematismus der allgemeinen Volksschulen und Bürgerschulen in den im
  Reichsrate vertretenen Königreichen und Ländern auf Grund der stat. Auf-
  nahme vom 15. Mai 1900.* Vienna, 1902.
———. *Statistische Monatsschrift.* Vienna, 1875 et seq.
Bohemia. *Schematismus des Volksschulwesens im Königreich Böhmen.* Prague,
  1889, 1894 et seq.
Bohemia. Statistisches Landesbureau des Kgr. Böhmen/Zemská statistická
  kancelář král. Českého. *Statistisches Handbuch des Königreiches Böhmen/
  Statistická příručka král. Českého.* 1st ed., Prague, 1909; 2d ed., Prague,
  1913.
———. *Zprávy zemského statistického úřadu království Českého* [Reports of the
  Provincial Statistical Bureau of the Kingdom of Bohemia]. Prague,
  1899 et seq.

Czechoslovak Republic. *Statistická příručka republiky Československé* [Statistical Handbook of the Czechoslovak Republic], III. Prague, 1928.

Prague. Statistische Commission der kgl. Hauptstadt Prag und Vororte/ Statistická komise král. hlav. města Prahy. *Ergebnisse der ausserordentlicher Volkszählung in der kgl. Hauptstadt Prag . . . Dez. 1896.* Prague, 1897.

—————. *Die kgl. Hauptstadt Prag mit den Vororten . . . nach den Ergebnissen der Volkszählung vom 31. Dezember 1890.* Prague, 1891.

—————. *Hlavní výsledky popisu obyvatelstva ze dne 31. prosince 1910 v král. hlav. městě Praze* [Main Results of the Census of December 31, 1910 in the Royal Capital Prague]. Prague, 1911.

—————. *Sčítání lidu v král. hlav. městě Praze a obcech sousedních provedené 31. prosince 1900* [Census of the Population in the Royal Capital City Prague and the Neighboring Communities taken on December 31, 1900], Jan Srb, ed., 3 vols. Prague, 1902-08.

—————. *Statistisches Handbüchlein der kgl. Hauptstadt Prag und Vororten/Statistická knížka Prahy a Předměstí.* Prague, 1873 et seq.

—————. *Wohnverhälthnisse in der kgl. Hauptstadt Prag und den Vororten . . . nach den Ergebnissen der Volkszählung vom 31. Dezember 1890,* Josef Erben, ed. Prague, 1895.

Memoirs

Adámek, Karel. *Mé paměty z doby Taaffovy 1879-1893* [Memoirs from the Taaffe Era 1879-1893]. Hlinsko, 1910.

Bondy, Fritz [pseud. N. O. Scarpi]. *Liebes altes Prag: Rückblicke eines gar nicht zornigen alten Mannes.* Zürich and Stuttgart, 1969.

Brod, Max. *Der Prager Kreis.* Stuttgart and Berlin, 1966.

—————. *Streitbares Leben 1884-1968,* rev. ed. Munich, Berlin and Vienna, 1969.

Haas, Willy. *Die literarische Welt.* Munich, 1958.

—————. "Die Prager deutsche Gesellschaft vor dem Weltkrieg." *Prager Montagsblatt,* 27 Dec 1937, 5. Beilage.

Heller, Servác. *Z minulé doby našeho života národního, kulturního a politického* [From the Recent Past of Our National, Cultural, and Political Life]. 5 vols. Prague, 1916-23.

Herrmann, Ignát. *Ze staré Prahy* [From Old Prague]. Prague, 1970.

Kaizl, Josef. *Anmerkungen zur böhmischen Politik.* Vienna, 1906.

—————. *Z mého života* [From My Life], ed. Zdeněk Tobolka. 3 vols. in 4. Prague, 1908-14.

Kiesslich, Anton. *Heitere Erinnerungen aus meinem Turnerleben.* Most, 1922.

Kisch, Egon Erwin. *Marktplatz der Sensationen.* Mexico City, 1942.

Kohn, Hans. *Living in a World Revolution: My Encounters with History.* New York, 1964.

Kopetz, Heinrich Ritter von. *Plaudereien eines alten Pragers.* Prague, 1905.

Kukula, Richard. *Erinnerungen eines Bibliothekars.* Weimar, 1925.

Langer, František. *Byli a bylo* [They were and It was]. Prague, 1971.

Laube, Gustav C. "Jugend Erinnerungen" *Deutsche Arbeit*, III (1903-04), pp. 457-64, 736-42, 893-900.

Malý, Jakub. *Naše znovuzrození: Přehled národního života českého za posledního půlstoletí* [Our Rebirth: A Survey of Czech National Life in the Last Half Century]. Prague, 1880.

Mauthner, Fritz. *Erinnerungen, I: Prager Jugendjahre*. Munich, 1918.

Mayer, Sigmund. *Ein jüdischer Kaufmann 1831 bis 1911*. Leipzig, 1911.

Palacký, Jan. "Palacký doma" [Palacký at Home]. In *Památník Palackého* [Palacký Memorial], ed. Vojtěch Nováček, pp. 126-29. Prague, 1898.

Plener, Ernst von. *Erinnerungen*. 3 vols. Stuttgart and Leipzig, 1911-21.

Pollak, Heinrich. *Dreissig Jahre aus dem Leben eines Journalisten: Erinnerungen und Aufzeichnungen*. 3 vols. Vienna, 1894-98.

Portheim, Gustav von. "Aus meinen Erinnerungen." *Deutsche Arbeit*, VII (1907-08), pp. 714-23.

Stampfer, Friedrich. *Erfahrungen und Erkenntnisse*. Cologne, 1957.

Štech, Václav Vilém. *Vzpomínky, I: V zamlženém zrcadle* [Memoirs, I: In a Dark Glass]. Prague, 1967.

Strobl, Karl Hans. *Heimat im frühen Licht: Jugenderinnerungen aus deutschem Ostland*. České Budějovice and Leipzig, 1942.

Teweles, Heinrich. *Theater und Publikum*. Prague, 1927.

Vondráček, Vladimír. *Lékař vzpomíná 1895-1920* [A Physician Remembers 1895-1920]. Prague, 1973.

Contemporary Publications on Prague and the Czech-German Conflict

Adámek, Karel. *Původ Vídeňských úmluv o navracení s Němcův do sněmu Království Českého* [The Origin of the Vienna Agreement on the Return of the Germans to the Bohemian Diet]. Chrudim, 1890.

―――. *Slovo o židech* [A Word on the Jews]. 2d ed. Chrudim, 1900.

Bachmann, Hermann. *Deutsche Arbeit in Böhmen*. Berlin, 1900.

Bendel, Josef. *Die Deutschen in Böhmen, Mähren, und Schlesien*. 2 vols. Vienna and Těšín, 1884.

Bildungsverein deutscher Arbeiter in Prag. *25 Jahre Arbeiter Vorstellungen*. Prague, 1931.

"Bohemia": Israelitische Humanitätsverein. *Festschrift*. Prague, 1913.

Bolzano, Bernard. *Über das Verhältnis der beiden Volksstämme in Böhmen*. Vienna. 1849.

Brát, Albin. "Příbytečné poměry velkých měst rakouských se zvláštním zřetelem ku Praze a předměstským obcem" [Housing Conditions in the Large Austrian Cities with special reference to Prague and the Suburban Communities]. In *Statistická knížka král. hl. města Prahy za rok 1893*, pp. 6-16. Prague, 1897.

Brechler, Otto. "Das geistige Leben Prags vor hundert Jahren." *Deutsche Arbeit*, X (1910-11), pp. 329-43.

Buber, Martin. *Drei Reden über das Judentum*. Frankfurt a.M., 1911.

Festschrift anlässlich des 30-Jährigen Bestandes der Loge "Bohemia" I.O.B.B. in Prag. Prague, 1923.

Festschrift der Lese- und Redehalle der deutschen Studenten in Prag anlässlich des 150. semestrigen Sitzungsfestes, 1848-1923. Prague, 1923.

Fischel, Alfred. *Materialien zur Sprachenfrage in Österreich.* 2d ed. Brno, 1910.

Fleischner, Ludwig. "Das deutsche Volksbildungswesen in Böhmen." *Deutsche Arbeit,* I (1902), p. 470ff.

Forchheimer, Otto. *Die öffentliche Lage der Deutschen in der Landeshauptstadt Prag.* Prague, 1889.

Frank, Ferdinand. *Die österreichische Volksschule von 1848-1898.* Vienna, 1898.

Geschichte der Prager Burschenschaft "Arminia," 1879-1929. Prague, 1929.

Gluth, Oscar. "Bericht über die Verfassungs- und Verwaltungsorganisation der Stadt Prag." *Verwaltungsorganisation der Städte, VI: Österreich,* pp. 97-135. Leipzig. 1907.

Gruber, Josef. *Die Handels- und Gewerbekammer in Prag in den ersten 50 Jahren ihres Bestandes 1850-1900.* 2 vols. Prague, 1900.

Hackel, Oskar. "Die Geschichte der Burschenschaft 'Carolina,' " *Deutsche Arbeit,* IX (1909-10), pp. 485-501.

Hansl, František, ed. *Smíchovsko a Zbraslavsko.* Smíchov, 1899.

Hauffen, Adolf. "Zur Geschichte der deutschen Universität in Prag." *Mitteilungen des Vereins für Geschichte der Deutschen in Böhmen,* XXVIII (1900), pp. 110-27.

Havlíček-Borovský, Karel. *Politické spisy* [Political Writings]. 3 vols. Prague, 1900-03.

Hecke, Wilhelm. "Die Methode und Technik der österreichischen Volkszählungen." *Statistische Monatsschrift,* N. F., XVII (1912), pp. 466-74.

————. "Volksvermehrung, Binnenwanderung und Umgangssprache in den nördlichen Ländern Österreichs." *Statistische Monatsschrift,* N. F., XIX (1914), pp. 653-723.

Herbst, Eduard. *Das Deutsche Sprachgebiet in Böhmen.* Prague, 1887.

Hermann, Hugo. "Zur Judenfrage." *Deutsche Arbeit,* VII (1908), pp. 277-81.

Herzl, Theodor. "Die Entschwundenen Zeiten" and "Die Jagd in Böhmen." In *Gesammelte Zionistische Werke.* 3d ed. 5 vols. I, pp. 216-22, 249-54. Berlin, 1934-35.

Horáček, Cyril. "Die wirtschaftlichen und sozialen Verhältnisse der Stadt Prag." In *Verfassung und Verwaltungsorganisation der Städte, VI: Österreich,* pp. 39-96. Leipzig, 1907.

Inama-Sternegg, Karl Theodor von. "Die nächste Volkszählung." *Statistische Monatsschrift,* N. F., V, (1900), pp. 453-65.

Jahrbuch für die israel. Cultusgemeinden Böhmens 1894-95. Prague, 1894.

Jesser, Franz. "Der Bund der Deutschen in Böhmen." *Deutsche Arbeit,* X (1911), pp. 463-67.

————. *Zehn Jahre völkische Schutzarbeit: Festschrift anlässlich der Feier des 10-jährigen Bestandes des Bundes der Deutschen in Böhmen.* Prague, 1904.

Ježek, J. *Čtyřicet Let Katolického Spolku Tiskového v Praze* [Forty Years of the Catholic Publication Society in Prague]. Prague, 1911.

Das jüdische Prag: Eine Sammelschrift. Prague, 1917.

Kaloušek, Josef. *České státní právo* [Bohemian State Right]. 2d ed. rev. Prague, 1892.

Karlach, Mikuláš. *Paměti Proboštů vyšehradských z poslední doby a sice od r. 1781 až do 1905* [Recollections of the Priors of Vyšehrad from the most Recent Period, 1781-1905]. Prague, 1905.

Katz, Hermann. *Das neue deutsche Theater in Prague: Ein Gedenkblatt zur Eröffnung.* Prague, 1887.

————. *Klutschaks Führer durch Prag und Umgebung.* 13th ed. Prague, 1887.

Kiemann, Anton. *Die ersten vierzig Jahre des Vereines Deutsches Kasino.* Prague, 1902.

————. *Das fünfte Jahrzehnt des Vereines Deutsches Kasino in Prag 1902-1912.* Prague, 1912.

Klier, Čeněk. *České spořitelnictví v zemích koruny české do roku 1906* [Czech Savings Banks in the Bohemian Crown Lands to 1906]. Prague, 1908.

Klutschak, Franz. *Der Führer durch Prag.* 12th ed. Prague, 1878.

Knoll, Philipp. "Das Deutschtum in Böhmen." Lecture given in Dresden 8 Nov 1885. Dresden, 1885 [Reprinted from the *Dresdner Anzeiger*, Nov 1885].

————. *Beiträge zur heimischen Zeitgeschichte.* Prague, 1900.

Laube, Gustav C. "Die Entstehung der farbentragenden Verbindungen an den Prager Hochschulen." *Deutsche Arbeit*, I (1902), pp. 519-34.

Lippert, Julius. "Der Antisemitismus." *Sammlung Gemeinnütziger Vorträge*, no. 88 (Prague, 1883).

————. "Prag, die deutsche Stadt." *Deutsche Arbeit*, VIII (1908-09), pp. 332-48.

Mathé, Franz, ed. *Geschichte des deutschen Männergesang-Vereins in Prag—vom 25. Feber 1859 bis 1. Oktober 1886.* Prague, 1886.

Meinzingen, Franz v. "Die binnenländische Wanderung und ihre Rückwirkung auf die Umgangssprache nach der letzten Volkszählung." *Statistische Monatsschrift*, N. F., VII (1902), pp. 693-729.

Meyer, Robert. "Die nächste Volkszählung." *Statistische Monatsschrift*, N. F., XV (1910), pp. 661-99.

Müller, Josef and Ferdinand Tallowitz, ed. *Památník vydaný na oslavu dvacetiletého trvání tělocvičné jednoty Sokola pražského* [Album for the Celebration of the Twentieth Anniversary of the Prague Gymnastics Society Sokol]. Prague, 1883.

Neruda, Jan. *Pro strach židovský* [On the Fear of the Jews]. 1869. Reprint. Prague, 1942.

[Palacký, Jan]. *Böhmische Skizzen.* Litomyšl, 1860.

Perko, Franz. "Die Tätigkeit des deutschen Schulvereins in Böhmen." *Deutsche Arbeit*, III (1904), pp. 386-410.

Pfersche, Emil. *Die Parteien der Deutschen in Österreich vor und nach dem Weltkrieg.* Munich and Vienna, 1915.

Plener, Ernst von. *Reden 1873-1911.* Stuttgart and Leipzig, 1911.

"Počet Němců v Praze" [The Number of Germans in Prague]. *Věstník obecní Král. Hlav. Města Prahy,* XVIII (1911), pp. 135-36.

Prager deutsche Worte: Individuelle Meinungsäusserungen deutscher Bewohner Prags über locale Verhältnisse am Ende des 19. Jahrhunderts. Prague, 1900.

"Pravda o poměrech německého obecného školství v Praze" [The Truth about Conditions in the German Public Schools of Prague]. Prague, 1896.

Rauchberg, Heinrich. "Die Bedeutung der Deutschen in Österreich." *Jahrbuch der Gehe-Stiftung zu Dresden,* XIV (1908), pp. 129-70.

———. "Die berufliche und soziale Gliederung der Deutschen und Tschechen in Böhmen." *Deutsche Arbeit,* III (1903-04), pp. 626-45, 709-36.

———. *Die Bevölkerung Österreichs.* Vienna, 1895.

———. *Die deutschen Sparkassen in Böhmen.* Prague, 1906.

———. *Der nationale Besitzstand in Böhmen.* 3 vols. Leipzig, 1905.

———. "Nationale Haushaltungs- und Familienstatistik von Prag." *Deutsche Arbeit,* IV (1904-05), pp. 262-64.

———. "Volkswirtschaft und soziale Arbeit: Die soziale Lage der deutschen Hochschulstudentenschaft Prags." *Deutsche Arbeit,* XII (1912-13), pp. 54-56.

———. "Das Zahlenverhältnis der Deutschen und der Tschechen in Böhmen." *Deutsche Arbeit,* II (1902), pp. 1-33.

Reichenberg in der Zeit der Selbstverwaltung von Jahre 1850 bis 1900. Liberec, 1902.

Rieger, František L. *Průmysl a postup výroby jeho v pusobení svém ke blahobytu a svobodě lidu zvláště pracujícího* [The Effect of Industry and the Advance of its Production on the Welfare of the People, particularly Workers]. Litomyšl, 1860.

Rychnovsky, Ernst. *Der Deutsche Turnverein in Prag 1862-1912.* Prague, 1912.

Sauer, August. *Kulturpolitische Reden und Schriften.* Josef Pfitzner, ed. Liberec, 1928.

Schindler, Josef. *Das Sociale Wirken der katholischen Kirche in der Prager Erzdiözese.* Vienna, 1902.

Schlesinger, Ludwig. "Bemerkungen zur nationalen Abgrenzung in Böhmen." *Mitteilungen des Vereines für Geschichte der Deutschen in Böhmen,* XXVIII (1890), pp. 251-74.

Schnabel, Georg Norbert. *Tafeln zur Statistik von Böhmen.* Prague, 1848.

Schwarzer, Ernst von. *Geld und Gut in Neuösterreich.* Vienna, 1857.

Seifug, A. *Prag und Umgebungen.* 4th ed. Berlin, 1873.

Skedl, Arthur, ed. *Der politische Nachlass des Grafen Eduard Taaffe.* Vienna, Berlin, Leipzig, and Munich, 1922.

Srb, Jan. *Obcovací řeč jako prostředek sesilující národní državu německou v zemích koruny české zvlášť* [Everyday Language as a Means for Strengthening the National Position of Germans particularly in the Bohemian Crown Lands]. Prague, 1909 [Repr. from *Sčítání lidu v Praze a obcech sousedních 1900*, ed. Jan Srb, III].

Starkenstein, E., ed. *Festschrift anlässlich des 30-jährigen Bestandes der Loge "Bohemia" I.O.B.B. in Prag*. Prague, 1923.

Stein, A. et al., ed. *Kalendář česko-židovský* [Czech-Jewish Calendar]. Prague, 1881 et seq.

Stenographischer Bericht über die Verhandlungen der am 28. August in Teplitz im Namen deutscher Städte, Gemeinden und Konstitutioneller Vereine Böhmens zusammengekommenen Vertrauensmänner. Litoměřice, n. d.

Stompfe, Alois. *Devadesát Let Besedy měšťanské v Praze 1846-1936* [Ninety Years of the Burghers' Club in Prague 1846-1936]. Prague, 1936.

Ulbrich, Josef. "Die Nationalitäten- und Verfassungsfrage in Böhmen seit dem Jahre 1848." *Deutsche Arbeit*, IV (1904-05), pp. 1-16.

Die Verhältnisse an den öffentlichen Prager deutschen Volks- und Bürgerschulen. Prague, 1896.

Verhandlungen der Handels- und Gewerbekammer in Prag in den Jahren 1858 bis Ende 1861. Prague, 1862.

Vondruška, Jan E. *Stručný přehled činnosti ústředního spolku Typografická Beseda v Praze 1862-1887* [A Brief Survey of the Activity of the Central Association of the Typographic Club in Prague, 1862-87]. Prague, 1887.

Weber, Ottokar. "Prag." *Deutsche Arbeit*, VIII (1909), pp. 325-26.

Die wichtigsten Volksschulgesetze samt den Lehrplänen für das Königreich Böhmen. Prague, 1907.

Wieser, Friedrich Freiherr von. *Die deutsche Steuerleistung und der öffentliche Haushalt in Böhmen*. Leipzig, 1904.

Winkler, Wilhelm. "Die Bevölkerung Böhmens nach der Nationalität." *Deutsche Arbeit*, XII (1912-13), pp. 221-26, 273-83.

―――. "Schutzarbeit: Deutsch-Prager Vereinsleben." *Deutsche Arbeit*, XIII (1913-14), pp. 527-28.

―――. *Die soziale Lage der Deutschen Hochschulstudentenschaft Prags*. Vienna and Leipzig, 1912.

Wotawa, August Ritter von. *Der Deutsche Schulverein 1880-1905: Eine Gedenkschrift*. Vienna, 1905.

Contemporary Fiction on Prague and the Czech-German Conflict

Brod, Max. *Jüdinnen*. Leipzig, 1915.

―――. *Ein tschechisches Dienstmädchen*. Berlin, 1909.

―――. *Weiberwirtschaft*. Leipzig and Vienna, 1917.

Dyk, Viktor. *Prosinec* [December]. Prague, 1906.

Hauschner, Auguste. *Die Familie Lowositz*. Berlin, 1908.

―――. *Die Familie Lowositz, II: Rudolf und Camilla*. Berlin, 1910.

Hohlbaum, Robert. *Die Prager Studenten*. Berlin, 1936.

Kisch, Egon Erwin. *Die Abenteuer in Prag*. Vienna, Prague, and Leipzig, 1920.

———. *Gesammelte Werke*, II. Berlin and Weimar, 1975.

Kraus, Julius. *Prag: Ein Roman von Völkerzwist und Menschenhader*. Vienna and Leipzig, 1908.

Kraus, Oskar. *Die Meyeriade: Humoristisches Epos aus dem Gymnasialleben*. Leipzig, 1891.

Mauthner, Fritz. *Der letzte Deutsche von Blatna*. Berlin and Vienna, 1913.

Meyrink, Gustav. *Walpurgisnacht: Das Seitenstück zum Golem*. Leipzig, 1917.

Mrštík, Vilém. *Santa Lucia* (1893). Reprint. Prague, 1970.

Rilke, Rainer Maria. "Zwei Prager Geschichten" (1899). In *Erzählungen und Skizzen aus der Frühzeit*, pp. 117-270. Leipzig, 1930.

Šimáček, Matej [Martin Havel]. *Ze zápisků phil. studenta Filipa Kořínka: Pohledy do rodin* [From the Notebooks of Philosophy Student Philip Kořínek: Views of Families]. 4 vols. Prague, 1893-96.

Strobl, Karl Hans. *Der Schipkapass*. Berlin, 1914.

———. *Die Václavbude*. Leipzig, 1902.

Weiskopf, Franz Carl. *Das Slawenlied*. Berlin, 1931.

Werfel, Franz. *Abituriententag*. Berlin, 1928.

———. *Barbara oder die Frömmigkeit*. Berlin, Vienna, and Leipzig, 1929.

Historical Studies of the Habsburg Monarchy

Arkel, Dirk van. *Antisemitism in Austria*. Leiden, 1966.

Boyer, John W. "Church, Economy, and Society in *fin de siècle* Austria: The Origins of the Christian Social Movement, 1875-1897." Ph.D. dissertation, Univ. of Chicago, 1975.

———. "Freud, Marriage, and Late Viennese Liberalism: A Commentary from 1905." *Journal of Modern History*, L(1978), pp. 72-102.

Brügel, Ludwig. *Geschichte der österreichischen Sozialdemokratie*. 5 vols. Vienna, 1922-23.

Burian, Peter. "The State Language Problem in Old Austria." *Austrian History Yearbook*, VI-VII(1970-71), pp. 81-104.

Charmatz, Richard. *Deutschösterreichische Politik*. Leipzig, 1907.

Czeike, Felix. *Liberale, christlichsoziale, und sozialdemokratische Kommunalpolitik (1861-1934)*. Vienna, 1962.

Deak, Istvan. "Comments." *Austrian History Yearbook*, III(1967), pt. 1, pp. 303-08.

Eder, Karl. *Der Liberalismus in Altösterreich*. Vienna and Munich, 1955.

Franz, Georg. *Liberalismus: Die Deutschliberale Bewegung in der habsburgischen Monarchie*. Munich, 1955.

Glettler, Monika. *Sokol und Arbeiterturnvereine der Wiener Tschechen bis 1914*. Munich and Vienna, 1970.

———. *Die Wiener Tschechen um 1900*. Munich and Vienna, 1972.

Good, David F. "Stagnation and 'Take-Off' in Austria 1873-1913." *Economic History Review*, XXVII(1974), pp. 72-87.

Hantsch, Hugo. "Die Beziehungen der Sudetendeutschen zu den Hochschulen Österreichs." *Der Donauraum*, IV (1959), pp. 145-53, 247.

―――. *Die Geschichte Österreichs*, 2nd ed. 2 vols. Graz, 1947.

―――. *Die Nationalitätenfrage im alten Österreich*. Vienna, 1955.

Harrington-Müller, Diethild. *Der Fortschrittsklub im Abgeordnetenhaus des österreichischen Reichsrats 1873-1910*. Vienna, Cologne, and Graz, 1972.

Holotík, L'udovít, ed. *Der österreichisch-ungarische Ausgleich 1867*. Bratislava, 1971.

Hubbard, William H. "Politics and Society in the Central European City: Graz, Austria, 1861-1918." *Canadian Journal of History* V(1970), pp. 25-47.

―――. "A Social History of Graz, Austria, 1861-1914." Ph.D. dissertation, Columbia University, 1973.

Hugelmann, Karl, ed. *Das Nationalitätenrecht des alten Österreich*. Vienna and Leipzig, 1934.

Jenks, William A. *Austria under the Iron Ring*. Charlottesville, Virginia, 1965.

―――. *The Austrian Electoral Reform of 1907*. New York, 1950.

Johnston, William M. *The Austrian Mind: An Intellectual and Social History 1848-1938*. Berkeley and Los Angeles, 1972.

Kann, Robert A. "Ein deutsch-böhmischer Bischof zur Sprachenfrage." In Hugo Hantsch and A. Novotny, ed., *Festschrift für Heinrich Benedikt*. Vienna, 1957.

―――. *Das Nationalitätenproblem der Habsburgermonarchie*. 2nd ed. 2 vols. Graz and Cologne, 1964.

Knoll, Reinhold. *Zur Tradition der christlich-sozialen Partei*. Vienna, Cologne, and Graz, 1973.

Kolmer, Gustav. *Parlament und Verfassung in Österreich*. 8 vols. Vienna and Leipzig, 1902-14.

Kořalka, Jiří. "La Montée du pangermanisme et l'Autriche-Hongrie." *Historica*, X (1965), pp. 213-54.

Křížek, Jurij. "Některé otázky výkladu dějin rozpadu Rakouska-Uherska" [Some Questions on the Interpretation of the History of the Fall of Austria-Hungary]. In Josef Haubelt and Jan Wanner, ed., *Studie z obecných dějin k šedesátinám Oldřicha Říhy* [Studies in General History for the Sixtieth Birthday of Oldřich Říha], pp. 95-112. Prague, 1972.

―――. *Die wirtschaftlichen Grundzüge des österreichisch-ungarischen Imperialismus in der Vorkriegszeit (1900-1914)*. Rozpravy Československé akademie věd: Řada společenských věd, Ročník 73, Sešit 14. Prague, 1963.

Lewis, Gavin. "The Catholic Church and the Christian Social Party in Lower Austria, 1885-1907." Ph.D. dissertation, Princeton University, 1972.

Macartney, C. A. *The Habsburg Empire 1790-1918*. New York, 1969.

Matis, Herbert. *Österreichs Wirtschaft 1848-1913*. Berlin, 1972.

May, Arthur J. *The Hapsburg Monarchy 1867-1914*. Cambridge, Mass., 1951.

McGrath, William J. *Dionysian Art and Populist Politics in Austria*. New Haven, 1974.

Mischler, Ernst and Josef Ulbrich, ed. *Österreichisches Staatswörterbuch.* 2d ed. 4 vols. Vienna, 1905-09.

Molisch, Paul. *Geschichte der deutschnationalen Bewegung in Österreich.* Jena, 1926.

———. *Politische Geschichte der deutschen Hochschulen in Österreich von 1848 bis 1918.* Vienna and Leipzig, 1939.

Mommsen, Hans. *Die Sozialdemokratie und die Nationalitätenfrage im habsburgischen Vielvölkerstaat,* I. Vienna. 1963.

Pichl, Eduard. *Georg Schönerer.* 3rd ed. 6 vols. Oldenburg and Berlin, 1938.

Platz, H. *Das historische Recht und das österreichisch-ungarische Ausgleichsproblem.* Leipzig, 1930.

Prinz, Friedrich. *Prag und Wien 1848.* Munich, 1968.

Redlich, Josef. *Das österreichische Staats- und Reichsproblem.* 2 vols. Leipzig, 1920-26.

Remak, Joachim. "The Healthy Invalid: How Doomed the Habsburg Empire." *Journal of Modern History,* XLI(1969), pp. 127-43.

Rudolph, Richard. *Banking and Industrialization in Austria-Hungary.* Cambridge, 1976.

Schorske, Carl E. "Politics and the Psyche in *fin de siècle* Vienna: Schnitzler and Hofmannsthal." *American Historical Review,* LXVI(1961), pp. 930-46.

———. "Politics in a New Key: An Austrian Triptych." *Journal of Modern History,* XXXIX(1967), pp. 343-86.

———. "The Transformation of the Garden: Ideal and Society in Austrian Literature." *American Historical Review,* LXXII(1966-67), pp. 1283-1320.

Šolle, Zdeněk. *Internacionala a Rakousko* [The International and Austria]. Prague, 1966.

Stourzh, Gerald. "Die Gleichberechtigung der Nationalitäten und die österreichische Dezemberverfassung." In Peter Berger, ed., *Der österreichisch-ungarische Ausgleich von 1867: Vorgeschichte und Wirkungen,* pp. 186-218. Vienna, 1967.

Sutter, Berthold. *Die Badenischen Sprachenverordnungen,* 2 vols. Graz and Cologne, 1960-65.

Taylor, A.J.P. *The Habsburg Monarchy 1809-1918.* (1948). Reprint. New York, 1965.

Urban, Otto. "K problematice rozkladu habsburské monarchie." [On the Problematic of the Disintegration of the Habsburg Monarchy]. In Jaroslav Pátek and Věra Šadová, ed., *Studie z obecných dějin: Sborník k sedmdesátým narozeninám prof. dr. Jaroslava Charváta* [Studies in General History: Collection for the Seventieth Birthday of Prof. Jaroslav Charvát], pp. 169-80. Prague, 1975.

Waber, L. *Die Zahlenmässige Entwicklung der Völker Österreichs 1846-1910.* Brno, 1916.

Wandruszka, Adam. "Österreichs politische Struktur." In Heinrich Benedikt, ed., *Geschichte der Republik Österreich*, pp. 289-486. Munich, 1954.

Wandruszka, Adam and Peter Urbanitsch, ed. *Die Habsburgermonarchie 1848-1918, I: Die wirtschaftliche Entwicklung*. Vienna, 1973.

Whiteside, Andrew G. *Austrian National Socialism before 1918*. The Hague, 1962.

————. "The Germans as an Integrative Force in Imperial Austria: The Dilemma of Dominance." *Austrian History Yearbook*, III(1967), pt. 1, pp. 157-200.

————. *The Socialism of Fools: Georg Ritter von Schönerer and Austrian Pan-Germanism*. Berkeley and Los Angeles, 1975.

Winter, Eduard. *Bernard Bolzano: Ein Denker und Erzieher im österreichischen Vormärz*. Graz, 1967.

————. *Der Josefinismus und seine Geschichte*. Brno, 1943.

————. *Revolution, Neoabsolutismus, und Liberalismus in der Donaumonarchie*. Vienna, 1969.

Zöllner, Erich. "The Germans as an Integrating and Disintegrating Force." *Austrian History Yearbook*, III(1967), pt. 1, pp. 201-33.

Historical Studies of Prague and the Bohemian Lands

Bachmann, Harald. "Der Deutsche Volksrat für Böhmen und die deutschböhmische Parteipolitik." *Zeitschrift für Ostforschung*, XIV(1965), pp. 266-94.

Bianchi, Leonard, ed. *Dějiny štátu a práva na území Československa v období kapitalizmu 1848-1945, I: 1848-1918* [A History of the State and Law in the Lands of Czechoslovakia in the Era of Capitalism 1848-1945, I: 1848-1918]. Bratislava, 1971.

Bittner, Konrad. *Deutsche und Tschechen*. Brno and Leipzig, 1936.

Boháč, Antonín. *Hlavní město Praha: Studie o obyvatelstvu* [The Capital City Prague: A Study of the Population]. Prague, 1923.

Bohmann, Alfred. *Bevölkerungsbewegungen in Böhmen 1847-1947 unter besonderer Berücksichtigung der Entwicklung der nationalen Verhältnisse*. Munich, 1958.

————. *Das Sudetendeutschtum in Zahlen*. Munich, 1959.

Bradley, J.F.N. *Czechoslovakia: A Short History*. Edinburgh, 1971.

Brock, Peter and H. Gordon Skilling, ed. *The Czech Renascence of the Nineteenth Century: Essays presented to Otakar Odložilík*. Toronto, 1970.

Brügel, Johann W. *Czechoslovakia before Munich: The German Minority Problem and British Appeasement Policy*. Cambridge, 1973.

————. *Ludwig Czech: Arbeiterführer und Staatsmann*. Vienna, 1960.

————. *Tschechen und Deutsche 1918-1938*. Berlin, 1967.

Čarek, Jiří, Václav Hlavsa, Josef Janáček, and Václav Lím. *Ulicemi města Prahy od 14. Století do Dneška* [By the Streets of the City of Prague from the Fourteenth Century to Today]. Prague, 1958.

(320) SOURCES

Carter, F. W. "The Industrial Development of Prague 1800-1850." *Slavonic and East European Review*, LI(1973), pp. 243-75.
———. "Public Transport Development in Nineteenth-century Prague." *Transport History*, VI(1973), pp. 205-26.
Václav Čepelák et al. *Dějiny Plzně* [A History of Plzeň], II (1788-1918). Plzeň, 1967.
Červinka, František. *Boje a směry českého studentstva na sklonku minulého a na počátku našeho století* [Struggles and Movements of Czech Students at the End of the Last Century and the Beginning of the Present]. Prague, 1962.
———. *Český nacionalismus v XIX. století* [Czech Nationalism in the 19th Century]. Prague, 1965.
Cesar, Jaroslav and Bohumil Černý. *Politika německých buržoazních stran v Československu v letech 1918-1938* [Politics of the German Bourgeois Parties in Czechoslovakia 1918-38]. 2 vols. Prague, 1962.
Cohen, Gary B. "The Prague Germans 1861-1914: The Problems of Ethnic Survival." Ph.D. dissertation, Princeton University, 1975.
———. "Recent Research on Czech Nation-Building." *Journal of Modern History*, LI(1979), pp. 760-72.
Demetz, Peter. "Noch Einmal: Prager Deutsch." *Literatur und Kritik*, I (1966), pp. 58-59.
Denis, Ernest. *La Bohême depuis la Montagne Blanche*. 2 vols. Paris, 1903.
Diwald, Hellmut. "Bernard Bolzano und der Bohemismus." In Diwald, ed., *Lebendiger Geist: Hans-Joachim Schoeps zum 50. Geburtstag*, pp. 91-115. Leiden, 1959.
———. "Deutschböhmen, die Deutschen Prags und das tschechische Wiedererwachen." *Zeitschrift für Religions- und Geistesgeschichte*, X(1958), pp. 124-41.
Dokoupil, Lumír. "Territorialní a socialní mobilita populace ostravské průmyslové oblasti v období její geneze a počátečního rozvoje" [Geographical and Social Mobility of the Populace of the Ostrava Industrial Region in the Period of its Genesis and Initial Development]. *Československý časopis historický*, XXI(1973), pp. 355-68.
Dřímal, Jaroslav and Václav Peša, ed. *Dějiny města Brna* [History of the City of Brno]. 2 vols. Brno, 1969, 1973.
Epstein, Leo. "Das Wachsen des Prager Deutschtums." *Nation und Stadt*, IV(1930-31), pp. 408-09.
Fleglová, Jana. "Z kulturně vzdělávací činnosti zaměstnanců obchodu na přelomu 19. a 20. století" [On the Educational Activity of Commercial Employees at the Turn of the Century]. *Středočeský sborník historický*, XII(1977), pp. 43-53.
Fochler-Hauke, Gustav. *Deutscher Volksboden und deutsches Volkstum in der Tschechoslowakei*. Heidelberg and Berlin, 1937.
Franzel, Emil. *Sudetendeutsche Geschichte*. 2d ed. Augsburg, 1962.
Freeze, Karen Johnson. "The Young Progressives: The Czech Student

Movement, 1887-1897." Ph.D. dissertation, Columbia University, 1974.

Garver, Bruce M. *The Young Czech Party 1874-1901 and the Emergence of a Multi-Party System.* New Haven and London, 1978.

George, P. and S. Desvignes. "The Greater Prague." *Annals of Geography,* 1948, pp. 249-56.

Glassl, Horst. *Der mährische Ausgleich.* Munich, 1967.

Goldstücker, Eduard. "Über die Prager Deutsche Literatur am Anfang des 20. Jahrhunderts." *Dortmunder Vorträge,* 70(1965).

Goll, Jaroslav. *Rozdělení pražské university Karlo-Ferdinandovy roku 1882 a počátek samostatné university české* [The Division of the Charles-Ferdinand University of Prague in 1882 and the Beginning of the Independent Czech University]. Prague, 1908.

Graus, František. "Die Bildung eines Nationalbewusstseins im Mittelalterlichen Böhmen." *Historica.* XIII(1966), pp. 5-49.

Havránek, Jan. *Boj za všeobecné, přímé a rovné hlasovací právo roku 1893* [The Struggle for Universal, Direct and Equal Suffrage in 1893]. Rozpravy Československé akademie věd, Řada společ. věd, LXXIV, no. 2. Prague, 1964.

————. "Demografický vývoj Prahy v druhé polovině 19. století" [The Demographic Development of Prague in the Second Half of the 19th Century]. *Pražský sborník historický 1969-70,* pp. 70-105.

————. "The Development of Czech Nationalism." *Austrian History Yearbook,* III(1967), pt. 2, pp. 223-60.

————. "Die ökonomische und politische Lage der Bauernschaft in den böhmischen Ländern in den letzten Jahrzehnten des 19. Jahrhunderts." *Jahrbuch für Wirtschaftsgeschichte.* 1966, no. 2, pp. 96-136.

————. "K otázce použíti mikroanalýzy ve studiu demografického vývoje 19. století" [On the Question of the Use of Microanalysis in the Study of Demographic Development in the 19th Century]. In *Z českých dějin: Sborník prací in memoriam Václava Husy* [From Czech History: Collection of Works in Memoriam Václav Husa], pp. 221-35. Prague, 1966.

————. "Social Classes, Nationality Ratios, and Demographic Trends in Prague, 1880-1900." *Historica,* XIII(1966), pp. 171-202.

Herzogenburg, Johanna von. *Prag.* Vienna, 1966.

Heumos, Peter. *Agrarische Interessen und Nationale Politik in Böhmen 1848-1889.* Wiesbaden, 1979.

Hlavsa, Václav. "Pražské territorium v druhé polovině 19. století" [Prague's Territory in the Second Half of the 19th Century]. *Pražský sborník historický 1969-70,* pp. 5-51.

Hohlbaum, Robert, ed. *70 Jahre Akademische Burschenschaft "Carolina" zu Prag.* Karlový Vary, 1930.

Horáček, Cyril. *Počátky českého hnutí dělnického* [The Beginnings of the Czech Workers' Movement]. 2d ed. Prague, 1933.

Horská-Vrbová, Pavla. "Hospodářské a socialní dějiny 1848-1918 v české historiografii uplynulych dvaceti let" [Economic and Social History of the Era 1848-1918 in Czech Historiography of the Last Twenty Years]. *Sborník historický*, XIV(1966), pp. 75-93.

———. "K otázce vzniku české průmyslové buržoazie" [On the Question of the Origins of the Czech Industrial Bourgeoisie]. *Československý časopis historický*, X(1962), pp. 257-84.

———. "Pokus o využíti rakouských statistik pro studium společenského rozvrstvení českých zemí v 2. polovině 19. století" [An Attempt to Use Austrian Statistics for the Study of Social Stratification in the Bohemian Lands in the Second Half of the 19th Century]. *Československý časopis historický*, XX(1972), pp. 648-76.

———. "Pražský průmysl v druhé polovině 19. století" [Prague Industry in the Second Half of the 19th century. *Pražský sborník historický 1969-70*, pp. 52-69.

———. "Ke vzniku a charakteru tak zvaných dělnických besed v šedesátých letech 19. století v Praze" [On the Origin and Character of the so-called Workers' Clubs of Prague in the 1860s]. *Československý časopis historický*, V(1957), pp. 108-36.

Hroch, Miroslav. *Die Vorkämpfer der nationalen Bewegung bei den kleinen Völkern Europas*. Acta Universitatis Carolinae Philosophica et Historia Monographia XXIV. Prague, 1968.

Janáček, Josef, ed. *Dějiny Prahy* [History of Prague]. Prague, 1964.

Jiřík, Karel and Blanka Pitronová, ed. *Dějiny Ostravy* [History of Ostrava]. Ostrava, 1967.

Kádner, Otakar. 'Školství v republice československé" [Education in the Czechoslovak Republic]. In *Československá vlastivěda*, X, pp. 7-222. Prague, 1931.

Karníková, Ludmila. "Ke studiu novodobé průmyslové buržoazie" [On the Study of the Modern Industrial Bourgeoisie]. *Československý časopis historický*, VI(1958), pp. 735-43.

———. *Vývoj obyvatelstva v českých zemích 1754-1914* [The Development of the Population in the Bohemian Lands 1754-1914]. Prague, 1965.

Kazbunda, Karel. *České hnutí roku 1848* [The Czech Movement of 1848]. Prague, 1929.

Kimball, Stanley B. *Czech Nationalism: A Study of the National Theatre Movement 1845-83*. Urbana, 1964.

Klepetař, Harry. *Der Sprachenkampf in den Sudetenländern*. Prague, 1932.

Klier, Richard. *Das Deutschtum Prags in der Vergangenheit*. Karlsbad-Drahowitz and Leipzig, 1936.

Klima, Arnošt. *Revoluce 1848 v českých zemích* [The Revolution of 1848 in the Bohemian Lands]. Prague, 1974.

Kočí, Josef. *Naše národní obrození* [Our National Revival]. Prague, 1960.

Kodedová, Oldřiška. "Die Lohnarbeit auf dem Grossgrundbesitz in Böhmen in der zweiten Hälfte des 19. Jahrhunderts." *Historica*, XIV (1967), pp. 123-74.

Kolejka, Josef. " 'Moravský pakt' z roku 1905" [The Moravian Agreement of 1905]. *Československý časopis historický*, IV(1956), pp. 590-615.

Konirsch, Suzanne G. "Constitutional Aspects of the Struggle between Germans and Czechs in the Austro-Hungarian Monarchy." *Journal of Modern History*, XXVII(1955), pp. 231-61.

Kořalka, Jiří. "Das Nationalitätenproblem in den böhmischen Ländern 1848-1918." *Österreichische Osthefte*, V(1963), pp. 1-12.

———. *Všeněmecký svaz a česká otázka koncem 19. století* [The Pan-German League and the Bohemian Question at the End of the 19th Century]. Rozpravy Československé akademie věd, Řada společ. věd, LXXIII, no. 12. Prague, 1963.

———. *Vznik socialistického dělnického hnutí na liberecku* [The Origin of the Socialist Workers' Movement in the Liberec District]. Liberec, 1956.

Korčák, Jaromír. "The Incidence of suicide among the Sudeten Germans." *The Slavonic and East European Review*, XV(1936), pp. 143-52.

———. "Vzrůst nevýrobních povolání podle národnosti" [The Growth of the Non-productive Occupations according to Nationality]. *Statistický obzor*, XVIII(1937), pp. 169-81.

Kosík, Karel. *Česká radikalní demokracie* [Czech Radical Democracy]. Prague, 1958.

Král, Jiří. *Vznik a vývoj Starého Města Pražského podle zeměpisného vyzkumu* [The Origin and Development of the Old Town of Prague according to Geographic Research]. Prague, 1952.

Kratochvíl, Karel. *Bankéři* [Bankers]. Prague, 1962.

Kratochvíl, Miloš. *O Vývoji městské správy pražské od roku 1848* [On the Development of Municipal Government in Prague since 1848]. Prague, 1936.

Kraus, Vojtěch, ed. *Dějiny obecní správy Král hlav. města Prahy za léta 1860-1880: Díl prvý, Léta 1860-70, prvý svazek* [A History of the Municipal Government of Prague 1860-1880, I: 1860-1870, pt. 1]. Prague, 1903.

Krebs, Hans. *Kampf in Böhmen*. Berlin, 1938.

Kreibich, Karel. *Němci a česká revoluce 1848* [Germans and the Czech Revolution of 1848]. Brno, 1950.

Krejčí, Karel. *Praha: Legend a skutečnosti* [Prague: Legend and Facts]. Prague, 1967.

Krischke, Traugott, ed. *Einladung nach Prag*. Munich and Vienna, 1966.

Krofta, Kamil. *Dějiny československé* [Czechoslovak History]. Prague, 1946.

———. *Das Deutschtum in der tschechoslowakischen Geschichte*. Prague, 1936.

Kubricht, Andrew Paul. "The Czech Agrarian Party, 1899-1914: A Study of National and Political Agitation in the Habsburg Monarchy." Ph.D. dissertation, Ohio State University, 1974.

Lades, Hans. *Die Tschechen und die deutsche Frage*. Erlangen, 1938.

Lehovec, Otto. *Prag: Eine Stadtgeographie und Heimatkunde*. Prague, 1944.

———. "Die Verstädterung der Prager Umgebung." *Zeitschrift für Ostforschung*, I(1952), pp. 440-46.

Lemberg, Eugen, ed. *Der Sudetendeutsche Intellektuelle.* Tagungshefte der Gesellschaft für deutsche Volksbildung in der Tschechoslowakischen Republik, Heft 5. Liberec, 1930.

Líva, Václav. *Pražská města* [The Prague Cities]. Berní rula, 3. Prague, 1949.

Luža, Radomír. *The Transfer of the Sudeten Germans: A Study of Czech-German Relations 1933-1962.* New York, 1964.

Macek, Josef, ed. *Přehled československých dějin, I: Do roku 1848* [A Survey of Czechoslovak History, I: To 1848]. Prague, 1958.

Mamatey, Victor S. and Radomír Luža, ed. *A History of the Czechoslovak Republic 1918-1948.* Princeton, N. J., 1973.

Martínek, Miloslav. "K problému struktury státního úřednictva v Čechach na počátku 20. století" [On the Problem of the Structure of the State Officialdom in Bohemia at the Beginning of the 20th Century]. *Sborník historický,* XXI(1974), pp. 75-119.

Matoušek, Otakar. "Purkyňovská léta spolku a časopisu českých lékařů [The Purkyně Years of the Society and Journal of Czech Physicians]. *Časopis českých lékařů,* XCI(1952), pp. 58-62, 87-93.

Mayer, Theodor. "Zur Geschichte der nationalen Verhältnisse in Prag." In *Aus Sozial- und Wirtschaftsgeschichte: Gedächtnisschrift für Georg von Below,* pp. 254-78. Stuttgart, 1928.

Melniková-Papoušková, Naděžda. *Praha před Sto Lety* [Prague a Hundred Years Ago]. Prague, 1935.

Mendl, Bedřich. *Český průmysl před sto lety a počátky Průmyslové jednoty* [Bohemian Industry a Century Ago and the Beginnings of the Manufacturing Society]. Prague, 1934.

———. *Vývoj řemesel a obchodu v městech pražských* [The Development of the Crafts and Commerce in the Prague Cities]. Prague, 1947.

Míka, Alois. "K národnostním poměrům v Čechach po třicetileté válce" [On National Relations in Bohemia after the Thirty Years' War]. *Československý časopis historický,* XXIV(1976), pp. 535-63.

Míka, Zdeněk. "Průmyslové předměstí Karlín v 19. století a jeho význam pro Prahu" [The Industrial Suburb Karlín in the 19th Century and Its Significance for Prague]. *Pražský sborník historický,* IX(1975), pp. 78-146.

Mommsen, Hans. "Das Problem der internationalen Integration in der böhmischen Arbeiterbewegung." *Bohemia: Jahrbuch des Collegium Carolinum,* II(1961), pp. 193-208.

Moscheles, Julie. "The Demographic, Social and Economic Regions of Greater Prague." *Geographic Review,* XXVII(1937), pp. 414-29.

———. "Prague, a geographical sketch of the Town." *Geographiska Annaler,* II(1920), pp. 67-79.

Münch, Hermann. *Böhmische Tragödie.* Braunschweig, Berlin, and Hamburg, 1949.

Novotný, Karel. "František Palacký a dělnická otázka" [František Palacký and the Workers' Question]. *Československý časopis historický,* XXV (1977), pp. 715-31.

————. "K problematice vytváření manufakturního dělnictva v českých zemích" [On the Problematic of the Formation of the Industrial Working Class in the Bohemian Lands]. *Československý časopis historický*, XXV (1977), pp. 383-407.

Oberdorffer, Kurt. "Der Verein für die Geschichte der Deutschen in Böhmen, 1862-1938." *Bohemia: Jahrbuch des Collegium Carolinum*, III (1962), pp. 9-28.

Obermann, Karl and Josef V. Polišenský, ed. *Aus 500 Jahren deutsch-tschechoslowakischer Geschichte*. Berlin. 1958.

Odložilík, Otakar. *The Caroline University 1348-1948*. Prague, 1948.

Paleček, Antonín. "The Czech Peasant Movement: Its Leader and his Party." *Bohemia: Jahrbuch des Collegium Carolinum*, XVIII(1977), pp. 175-97.

Pech, Stanley Z. *The Czech Revolution of 1848*. Chapel Hill, 1969.

————. "Passive Resistance of the Czechs, 1863-1879." *Slavonic and East European Review*, XXXVI(1958), pp. 434-52.

Pfitzner, Josef. *Das Sudetendeutschtum*. Cologne, 1928.

————. "Die Wahlen in die Frankfurter Nationalversammlung und der Sudetenraum." *Zeitschrift für sudetendeutsche Geschichte*, V(1941-42), pp. 199-240.

————. "Zur nationalen Politik der Sudetendeutschen in den Jahren 1848-1849." *Jahrbuch des Vereines für Geschichte der Deutschen in Böhmen*, III (1930-33), pp. 210-43.

Podlaha, Anton, ed. *Český slovník bohovědný* [Czech Theological Dictionary]. Prague, 1930.

Polišenský, Josef V. *Revoluce a kontrarevoluce v Rakousku 1848*. [Revolution and Counterrevolution in Austria 1848]. Prague, 1975.

Preradovich, Nikolaus. "Die Leistung der Sudetendeutschen in der Donaumonarchie 1848-1918." *Bohemia*, I(1960), pp. 207-20.

Prinz, Friedrich. "Die Böhmischen Länder von 1848 bis 1914." In Karl Bosl, ed., *Handbuch der Geschichte der Böhmischen Länder*, 4 vols., III, pp. 1-235. Stuttgart, 1966-70.

————. "Nation und Gesellschaft in den Böhmischen Ländern im 19. und 20. Jahrhundert." In Prinz, Franz Josef Schmale, and Ferdinand Seibt, ed., *Geschichte in der Gesellschaft: Festschrift für Karl Bosl zum 65. Geburtstag*, pp. 333-49. Stuttgart, 1974.

————. "Das Schulwesen der Böhmischen Länder von 1848-1939. Ein Überblick." In Karl Bosl, ed., *Aktuelle Forschungsprobleme um die Erste Tschechoslowakische Republik*, pp. 49-66. Munich and Vienna, 1969.

Purš, Jaroslav. *Dělnické hnutí v českých zemích 1849-1867* [The Working-Class Movement in the Bohemian Lands 1849-1867]. Rozpravy Československé akademie věd, Řada společ. věd, LXXI. Prague, 1961.

————. "Die Entwicklung des Kapitalismus in der Landwirtschaft der böhmischen Länder in der Zeit von 1849-1879." *Jahrbuch für Wirtschaftsgeschichte*, III(1963), pp. 31-97.

Purš, Jaroslav. "The Industrial Revolution in the Czech Lands." *Historica*, II(1960), pp. 183-272.

———. "The Situation of the Working Class in the Czech Lands in the Phase of the Expansion and Completion of the Industrial Revolution 1849-1873." *Historica*, VI(1963), pp. 145-237.

———. "Tábory v českých zemích v letech 1868-1871" [Camp Meetings in the Bohemian Lands 1868-71]. *Československý časopis historický*, VI (1958), pp. 234-65, 446-69, 661-89.

———. "The Working-Class Movement in the Czech Lands in the Expansive Phase of the Industrial Revolution." *Historica*, X(1965), pp. 67-157.

Rádl, Emanuel. *Der Kampf zwischen Tschechen und Deutschen*. Liberec, 1928.

Říha, Oldřich. "O národním hnutí a národnostní otázce 1848-1918" [On the National Movement and the Nationality Question 1848-1918]. *Československý časopis historický*, II(1954), pp. 47-68.

——— and Július Mésároš, ed. *Přehled československých dějin, II: 1848-1918* [A Survey of Czechoslovak History, II: 1848-1918]. 2 vols. Prague, 1960.

Ritschel, Augustin. "Das Prager Deutsch." *Phonetische Studien*, VI (1893), pp. 129-33.

Rosenheim, Richard. *Die Geschichte der deutschen Bühnen in Prag*. Prague, 1938.

Roucek, Joseph S. "Socio-graphic Aspects of the Minorities Problem of Czechoslovakia." *Journal of Central European Affairs*, III(1944), pp. 183-97.

Šafránek, Jan. *Školy české: Obraz jejich Vývoje a Osudů* [Czech Schools: A Portrait of their Development and Trials]. 2 vols. Prague, 1913-18.

Schmid-Egger, Barbara. *Klerus und Politik in Böhmen um 1900*. Munich, 1974.

Seibt, Ferdinand. *Bohemica: Probleme und Literatur seit 1945. Historische Zeitschrift*, Sonderheft 4. Munich, 1970.

———. "Die Deutschen in der tschechischen Historiographie 1945-1965." *Bohemia: Jahrbuch des Collegium Carolinum*, IX(1968), pp. 288-306.

———. *Deutschland und die Tschechen*. Munich. 1974.

Seton-Watson, R. W. *A History of the Czechs and Slovaks*. London, 1943.

Skála, Emil. "Das Prager Deutsch." In Eduard Goldstücker, ed., *Weltfreunde*, pp. 119-25. Neuwied, 1967.

Skilling, H. Gordon. "The Czech-German Conflict in Bohemia 1867-1914." Unpubl. revision (1967) of Ph.D. dissertation, University of London, 1940.

———. "The Partition of the University of Prague." *Slavonic Review*, XXVII (1949), pp. 430-49.

Slavíček, Antonín. "Dějiny a archiv spolku Lese- und Redehalle der deutschen Studenten in Prag" [The History and Archive of the Association Lese- und Redehalle der deutschen Studenten in Prag]. Unpubl. diploma essay, Philosophical Faculty, Charles University, 1973.

Šmahel, František. "The Idea of the Czech Nation in Hussite Bohemia." *Historica*, XVI(1969), pp. 143-248; XVII(1970), pp. 93-198.

Šolle, Zdeněk. *Dělnické hnutí v českých zemích koncem minulého století* [The Working-Class Movement in the Bohemian Lands at the End of the Last Century]. Prague, 1951.

———. "Kontinuität und Wandel in der sozialen Entwicklung der böhmischen Länder 1872-1930." In Karl Bosl, ed., *Aktuelle Forschungsprobleme um die Erste Tschechoslowakische Republik*, pp. 23-48. Munich and Vienna, 1969.

———. "K počátkům dělnického hnutí v Praze" [On the Beginnings of the Working-Class Movement in Prague]. *Československý časopis historický*, V(1957), pp. 664-87; VI(1958), pp. 266-310; VII(1959), pp. 49-70.

———. *Ke vzniku první dělnické strany v naší zemi* [On the Origin of the First Workers' Party in Our Land]. Prague, 1953.

Srb, Vladimír and Milan Kučera. "Vývoj obyvatelstva českých zemí v 19. století" [The Development of the Population of the Bohemian Lands in the 19th Century]. *Statistika a demografie*, I(1959), pp. 109-52.

Stölzl, Christoph. *Die Ära Bach in Böhmen*. Munich and Vienna, 1971.

Strauss, Emil. *Die Entstehung der deutschböhmischen Arbeiterbewegung Geschichte der deutschen Sozialdemokratie Böhmens bis 1888*. Prague, 1925.

———. *Von Hainfeld bis zum Weltkriege: Geschichte der deutschen Sozialdemokratie Böhmens, II: 1889-1914*. Prague, 1926.

Thomson, S. Harrison. "Czech and German: Action, Reaction, and Interaction." *Journal of Central European Affairs*, I(1941), pp. 306-23.

———. *Czechoslovakia in European History*. 1st ed., Princeton, N. J., 1943; 2d ed. rev., Princeton, 1953.

———. "The Czechs as Integrating and Disintegrating Factors in the Habsburg Empire." *Austrian History Yearbook*, III(1967), pt. 2, pp. 203-22.

———. "Germans in Bohemia from Maria Theresa to 1918." *Journal of Central European Affairs*, II(1942), pp. 161-80.

Tobolka, Zdeněk. *Politické dějiny Československého národa od r. 1848 až do Dnešní Doby* [Political History of the Czechoslovak Nation from 1848 to Today]. 4 vols. in 5. Prague, 1932-37.

Tramer, Hans. "Prague—City of Three Peoples." *Leo Baeck Institute Year Book*, IX(1964), pp. 305-39.

Trost, Pavel. "Franz Kafka und das Prager Deutsch." *Germanistica Pragensia*, III(1964), pp. 29-37.

———. "Das späte Prager Deutsch." *Germanistica Pragensia*, II(1962), pp. 30-39.

———. "Und wiederum: Prager Deutsch." *Literatur und Kritik*, I(1966), pp. 107-08.

Ulbrich, Zdeněk, ed. *Soziologische Studien zur Verstädterung der Prager Umgebung*. Prague, 1938.

O úloze bývalé Národní socialistické strany [On the Work of the Former National Socialist Party]. Prague, 1959.

Urfus, Valentin. "Průmyslový liberalismus a české měšťanstvo v období národního obrození" [Industrial Liberalism and the Czech Middle Class in the Period of the National Revival]. *Právněhistorické studie*, X (1964), pp. 5-32.

Vojtěch, Tomáš. "Organizační vývoj mladočeské strany do roku 1891" [Organizational Development of the Young Czech Party to 1891]. *Československý časopis historický*, XXV(1977), pp. 554-84.

Vomáčková, Věra. "K národnostní otázce v buržoasní revoluce 1848 v českých zemích" [On the Nationality Question in the Bourgeois Revolution of 1848 in the Bohemian Lands]. *Československý časopis historický*, IX(1961), pp. 1-16.

Votrubec, Ctibor. *Praha zeměpis velkoměsta* [Prague: Geography of a Great City]. Prague, 1965.

Wechsberg, Joseph. *Prague: The Mystical City*. New York, 1971.

Werner, Arthur. *Die Studentenlegionen der Prager Universität vom 30-jährigen Krieg bis 1848*. Prague, 1934.

Winkler, Erwin. *Prags Bevölkerung in der Statistik*. Prague, 1938.

Winters, Stanley B. "Austro-Slavism, Panslavism and Russophilism in Czech Political Thought, 1870-1900." In Winters and Joseph Held, ed., *Intellectual and Social Developments in the Habsburg Empire from Maria Theresa to World War I*, pp. 175-202. New York and London, 1975.

————. "The Young Czech Party (1874-1914): An Appraisal." *Slavic Review*, XXVIII(1969), pp. 426-44.

Wiskemann, Elizabeth. *Czechs and Germans*. 1st ed., New York, 1938; 2d ed., New York, 1967.

Wolfgramm, Eberhard. "Deutsche und tschechische Demokraten im Jahre 1850. Die Korrespondentenberichte aus Prag in der 'Deutschen Monatsschrift.' " In Hans H. Bielfeldt, ed., *Deutsch-slawische Wechselseitigkeit in sieben Jahrhunderten*, pp. 436-510. Berlin, 1956.

Wolmar, Wolfgang W. von. *Prag und das Reich: 600 Jahre Kampf deutscher Studenten*. Dresden, 1943.

Wünsch, Franz J. *Deutsche Archive und Archivpflege in den Sudetenländern*. Wissenschaftliche Materialien zur Landeskunde der Böhmischen Länder, Heft 2. Munich, 1958.

Začek, Joseph F. "Nationalism in Czechoslovakia." In Ivo J. Lederer and Peter Sugar, ed., *Nationalism in Eastern Europe*, pp. 166-205. Seattle, 1969.

25 Jahre Arbeiter Vorstellungen des Bildungsvereins deutscher Arbeiter in Prag. Prague, 1931.

70 Jahre akad. Burschenschaft Carolina zu Prag. Karlový Vary, 1930.

Studies of the Jews of Prague and Central Europe

Barany, George. " 'Magyar Jew or: Jewish Magyar' ? (To the Question of Jewish Assimilation in Hungary)." *Canadian-American Slavic Studies*, VIII(1974), pp. 1-44.

Borman, Stuart. "The Prague Student Zionist Movement, 1896-1914." Ph.D. dissertation, University of Chicago, 1972.

Červinka, František. "The Hilsner Affair." *Leo Baeck Institute Year Book*, XIII(1968), pp. 142-57.

Cohen, Gary B. "Jews in German Society: Prague, 1860-1914." *Central European History*, X(1977), pp. 28-54.

Dějiny českožidovského hnutí [A History of the Czech-Jewish Movement]. Prague, 1932.

Fraenkel, Josef, ed. *The Jews of Austria*. London, 1967.

Gold, Hugo, ed. *Die Juden und Judengemeinden Böhmens in Vergangenheit und Gegenwart*. Brno, 1934.

Goldman, Nachum. *Deutsche und Juden*. Frankfurt, 1967.

Goldstücker, Eduard. "Jews between Czechs and Germans around 1848." *Leo Baeck Institute Year Book*, XVII(1972), pp. 61-71.

Jenks, William A. "The Jews in the Habsburg Empire 1879-1918." *Leo Baeck Institute Year Book*, XVI(1971), pp. 155-62.

———. *The Jews in Austria*. New York, 1960.

The Jews of Czechoslovakia. 2 vols. Philadelphia and New York, 1968-71.

Kann, Robert A. "Assimilation and Antisemitism in the German-French Orbit in the Nineteenth and Early Twentieth Century." *Leo Baeck Institute Year Book*, XIV(1969), pp. 92-115.

———. "German-speaking Jewry during Austria-Hungary's Constitutional Era (1867-1918)." *Jewish Social Studies*, X(1948), pp. 239-56.

———. "Hungarian Jewry during Austria-Hungary's Constitutional Period 1867-1918." *Jewish Social Studies* VII(1945), pp. 357-86.

Karady, Victor and Istvan Kemeny. "Les Juifs dans la Structure des classes en Hongrie." *Actes de la Recherche en sciences sociales*, no. 22(June 1978), pp. 25-60.

Kestenberg-Gladstein, Ruth. *Neuere Geschichte der Juden in den böhmischen Ländern, I: Das Zeitalter der Aufklärung*. Tübingen, 1969.

Kisch, Guido. "Linguistic Conditions among Czechoslovak Jewry." In Miroslav Rechcigl, Jr., ed., *Czechoslovakia Past and Present*, II, pp. 1451-62. The Hague, 1968.

Lador-Lederer, J. J. "Jews in Austrian Law." *East European Quarterly*, XII (1978), pp. 25-41, 129-42.

Mayer, Sigmund. *Die Wiener Juden: Kommerz, Kultur, Politik 1700-1900*. 2d ed. Vienna and Berlin, 1918.

McCagg, William O., Jr. "Hungary's 'Feudalized' Bourgeoisie." *Journal of Modern History*, XLIV(1972), pp. 65-78.

———. *Jewish Nobles and Geniuses in Modern Hungary*. Boulder, 1972.

Muneles, Otto. *Bibliografický přehled židovské Prahy* [Bibliographical Survey of Jewish Prague]. Prague, 1952.

Oelsner, Toni, "Three Jewish Families in Modern Germany." *Jewish Social Studies*, IV(1942), pp. 241-68, 349-98.

Pulzer, Peter G. J. *The Rise of Political Anti-Semitism in Germany and Austria*. New York, 1964.

Rachmuth, M. "Zur Wirtschaftsgeschichte der Prager Juden." *Jahrbuch der Gesellschaft für Geschichte der Juden in der Č.S.R.*, V(1933), pp. 9-78.

Riff, Michael A. "The Assimilation of the Jews of Bohemia and the Rise of Political Anti-Semitism, 1848-1918." Ph.D. dissertation, University of London, 1974.

Roubík, František. "Drei Beiträge zur Entwicklung der Judenemanzipation in Böhmen." *Jahrbuch der Gesellschaft für Geschichte der Juden in der Č.S.R.*, V(1933), pp. 373-84.

Rürup, Reinhard. *Emanzipation und Antisemitismus.* Kritische Studien zur Geschichtswissenschaft, XV. Göttingen, 1975.

Ruppin, Arthur. *Soziologie der Juden.* 2 vols. Berlin, 1930-31.

Rychnovsky, Ernst, ed. *Thomas G. Masaryk and the Jews.* New York, 1941.

Segall, Jacob. *Die beruflichen und sozialen Verhältnisse der Juden in Deutschland.* Berlin, 1912.

Simon, Walter B. "The Jewish Vote in Austria." *Leo Baeck Institute Year Book*, XVI(1971), pp. 97-121.

Stein, Adolf. *Die Geschichte der Juden in Böhmen.* Brno, 1904.

Steinherz, Samuel, ed. *Die Juden in Prag: Bilder aus ihrer tausendjährigen Geschichte.* Prague, 1927.

Stern-Täubler, S. "The First Generation of Emancipated Jews." In *Leo Baeck Institute Year Book*, XV(1970), pp. 3-40.

Stölzl, Christoph. "Zur Geschichte der böhmischen Juden in der Epoche des modernen Nationalismus." *Bohemia: Jahrbuch des Collegium Carolinum*, XIV(1973), pp. 179-221; XV(1974), pp. 129-57.

Stoffers, Wilhelm. *Juden und Ghetto in der deutschen Literatur bis zum Ausgang des Weltkrieges.* Nymwegen, 1939.

Straus, Raphael. *Die Juden in Wirtschaft und Gesellschaft.* Frankfurt, 1964.

Tietze, Hans. *Die Juden Wiens: Geschichte-Wirtschaft-Kultur.* Leipzig, 1933.

Vyskočil, Josef. "Die Tschechisch-Jüdische Bewegung." *Judaica Bohemiae*, III(1968).

Weinryb, Bernard D. "Jews in Central Europe." *Journal of Central European Affairs*, VI(1946), pp. 43-77.

Biographies

Allmayer-Beck, Johann Christoph. *Ministerpräsident Baron Beck.* Munich, 1956.

Arndt, Franziska. *F. C. Weiskopf.* Leipzig, 1965.

Bachmann, Adolf. "Ludwig Schlesinger." *Mitteilungen des Vereines für Geschichte der Deutschen in Böhmen*, XXXVIII(1900), pp. 345-52.

Bachmann, Harald. *Adolf Bachmann: Ein österreichischer Historiker und Politiker.* Munich, 1962.

Bartoš, Josef. *Miroslav Tyrš.* 2d ed. rev. Prague, 1930.

Binder, Hartmut. "Franz Kafka and the Weekly Paper *Selbstwehr*." *Leo Baeck Institute Year Book*, XII(1967), pp. 135-48.

Brod, Max. *Franz Kafka: A Biography.* 2d ed. rev. New York, 1960.

Demetz, Peter. *René Rilkes Prager Jahre.* Düsseldorf, 1953.

Eisner, Pavel. *Franz Kafka and Prague.* New York, 1950.

Frank, Philipp. *Einstein: His Life and Times.* New York, 1947.

Haas, Willy. "Werfels erster Lehrmeister." *Witiko,* II(1929), pp. 137-39.

Heller, K. D. *Ernst Mach: Wegbereiter der modernen Physik.* Vienna, 1964.

Hermsdorf, Klaus. *Franz Kafka.* Berlin, 1961.

Illy, Jozsef. "Albert Einstein in Prague." *Isis,* CXX, no. 251 (1979), pp. 76-84.

Jodl, Margarete. *Friedrich Jodl: Sein Leben und Werk.* Stuttgart and Berlin, 1920.

Kisch, Guido. *Alexander Kisch 1848-1917.* Halle-Saale, 1934.

[Klaar, Alfred]. *Franz Schmeykal.* Prague, 1894.

Mrázek, Karel, ed. *Tyršův Sborník* [Collection of Works on Tyrš]. Prague, 1932.

Novotný, Jan. *František Cyril Kampelík.* Prague, 1975.

Politzer, Heinz. "Prague and the Origins of Rainer Maria Rilke, Franz Kafka, and Franz Werfel." *Modern Language Quarterly,* XVI(1955), pp. 49-63.

Schebek, Edmund. *Richard Ritter von Dotzauer.* Prague, 1895.

Stewart, Desmond S. *Theodor Herzl.* New York, 1974.

Stölzl, Christoph. *Kafkas böses Böhmen: Zur Sozialgeschichte eines Prager Juden.* Munich, 1975.

Teweles, Heinrich. "David Kuh." *Mitteilungen des Vereins für Geschichte der Deutschen in Böhmen,* XVII(1879), pp. 309-15.

Treixler, Gustav. "Richard Ritter von Dotzauer." In Erich Gierach, ed., *Sudetendeutsche Lebensbilder,* II, pp. 303-11. Liberec, 1930.

Urzidil, Johannes. *There Goes Kafka.* Detroit, 1968.

Utitz, Emil. *Egon Erwin Kisch: Der klassische Journalist.* Berlin, 1956.

Wagenbach, Klaus. *Franz Kafka: Eines Biographie seiner Jugend, 1883-1912.* Bern, 1958.

Weber, Ottokar. "Franz Schmeykal." In Erich Gierach, ed., *Sudetendeutsche Lebensbilder,* III, pp. 310-16. Liberec, 1934.

Weltsch, Felix. "The Rise and Fall of the Jewish-German Symbiosis—The Case of Franz Kafka." *Leo Baeck Institute Year Book,* I(1956), pp. 255-78.

Weltsch, Robert. "Max Brod and His Age." *Leo Baeck Memorial Lecture,* no. 13. New York, 1970.

Wolfsgruber, Coelestin. *Friedrich Kardinal Schwarzenberg.* 3 vols. Vienna, 1906-17.

Studies of Urban Social Structures, Ethnicity, and Ethnic Conflict

Anderson, Eugene N. and Pauline R. Anderson. *Political Institutions and Social Change in Continental Europe in the Nineteenth Century.* Berkeley and Los Angeles, 1967.

Arendt, Hannah, *The Origins of Totalitarianism.* 2d ed. New York, 1958.

Armstrong, John A. "Mobilized Diaspora in Tsarist Russia: The Case of the Baltic Germans." In Jeremy Azrael, ed., *Soviet Nationality Policies and Practices,* pp. 63-104. New York and London, 1978.

Balser, Frolinde. *Die Anfänge der Erwachsenenbildung in Deutschland in der ersten Hälfte des 19. Jahrhunderts.* Stuttgart, 1959.

Banks, J. A. *Prosperity and Parenthood.* London, 1954.

Barth, Fredrik, ed. *Ethnic Groups and Boundaries.* Boston, 1969.

Basham, Richard D. *Crisis in Blanc and White: Urbanization and Ethnic Identity in French Canada.* Cambridge, Mass., 1978.

Beutin, Ludwig. *Gesammelte Schriften zur Wirtschafts- und Sozialgeschichte.* Cologne and Graz, 1963.

Beveridge, W.H.B. *Voluntary Action: A Report on Methods of Social Advance.* New York, 1948.

Birker, Karl. *Die Deutschen Arbeiterbildungsvereine 1840-1870.* Berlin, 1973.

Born, Karl Erich. "Der soziale und wirtschaftliche Strukturwandel Deutschlands am Ende des 19. Jahrhunderts." *Vierteljahrschrift für Sozial- und Wirtschaftsgeschichte,* L(1963), pp. 361-76.

Bottomore, Thomas. "Social Stratification in Voluntary Organizations." In D. V. Glass, ed., *Social Mobility in Britain,* pp. 349-82. London, 1954.

Bourdieu, Pierre. *The Algerians.* Rev. ed. Boston, 1962.

Bramsted, Ernest K. *Aristocracy and the Middle Classes in Germany.* Rev. ed. Chicago, 1964.

Connor, Walker. "Nation-Building or Nation-Destroying" *World Politics,* XXIV(1972), pp. 319-55.

Conze, Werner and Dieter Groh. *Die Arbeiterbewegung in der nationalen Bewegung.* Stuttgart, 1966.

Croon, Helmut. "Bürgertum und Verwaltung in den Städten des Ruhrgebiets im 19. Jahrhundert." *Tradition,* IX(1964), pp. 23-41.

————. "Die Stadtvertretungen in Krefeld und Bochum in 19. Jahrhundert." In *Forschungen zu Staat und Verfassung: Festgabe für Fritz Hartung,* pp. 289-306. Berlin, 1958.

————. "Das Vordringen der politischen Parteien im Bereich der kommunalen Selbstverwaltung." In Croon, ed., *Kommunale Selbstverwaltung im Zeitalter der Industrialisierung,* pp. 23-37. Stuttgart, Berlin, Cologne, and Mainz, 1971.

Deutsch, Karl W. *Nationalism and Social Communication.* 2d ed. Cambridge, Mass., 1966.

Enloe, Cynthia H. *Ethnic Conflict and Political Development.* Boston, 1973.

Esman, Milton J., ed. *Ethnic Conflict in the Western World.* Ithaca and London, 1977.

Freudenthal, Herbert. *Vereine in Hamburg.* Hamburg, 1968.

Geertz, Clifford. "The Integrative Revolution: Primordial Sentiments and Civil Politics in the New States." In Geertz, ed., *Old Societies and New States: The Quest for Modernity in Asia and Africa,* pp. 105-57. New York and London, 1963.

————. *The Interpretation of Cultures*. New York, 1973.

Gillis, John R. *Youth and History: Tradition and Change in European Age Relations 1770-present*. New York and London, 1974.

Glazer, Nathan and Daniel P. Moynihan. *Beyond the Melting Pot*. Cambridge, Mass., 1963.

————, ed. *Ethnicity: Theory and Experience*. Cambridge, Mass., 1975.

Gordon, Milton M. *Assimilation in American Life*. New York, 1964.

————. "Social Structure and Goals in Group Relations." In Morroe Berger, Theodore Abel, and Charles H. Page, ed., *Freedom and Control in Modern Society*, pp. 141-57. New York, 1954.

Habermas, Jürgen. *Strukturwandel der Öffentlichkeit*. Neuwied, 1972.

Hagen, William. "National Solidarity and Organic Work in Prussian Poland." *Journal of Modern History*, XLIV(1972), pp. 38-64.

Hah, Chong-Do and Jeffrey Martin. "Toward a Synthesis of Conflict Integration Theories of Nationalism." *World Politics*, XXVII(1975), pp. 361-86.

Hechter, Michael. "The Political Economy of Ethnic Change." *American Journal of Sociology*, LXXIX(1974), pp. 1151-78.

————. "Towards a Theory of Ethnic Change." *Politics and Society*, II(1971), pp. 21-45.

Henriksson, Anders H. "The Riga German Community: Social Change and the Nationality Question, 1860-1905." Ph.D. dissertation, University of Toronto, 1978.

Hofmann, Wolfgang. *Die Bielefelder Stadtverordneten 1850-1914*. Lübeck and Hamburg, 1964.

Hroch, Miroslav. "K problematice formování buržoazního národa v Evropě" [On the Problematic of Forming a Bourgeois Nation in Europe]. *Československý časopis historický*, IX(1961), pp. 374-95.

Huggett, Frank E. *Modern Belgium*. New York and Washington, 1969.

Hunt, Chester L. and Lewis Walker. *Ethnic Dynamics: Patterns of Intergroup Relations in Various Societies*. Homewood, Ill., 1974.

Iggers, Georg G. "The Political Theory of Voluntary Associations in Early Nineteenth-century German Liberal Thought." In D. B. Robertson, ed., *Voluntary Associations: A Study of Groups in Free Societies*, pp. 141-58. Richmond, 1966.

Kocka, Jürgen. *Unternehmensverwaltung und Angestelltenschaft am Beispiel Siemens 1847-1914*. Stuttgart, 1967.

Köllmann, Wolfgang. *Sozialgeschichte der Stadt Barmen im 19. Jahrhundert*. Tübingen, 1960.

Kroeger, Gert. "Zur Situation der baltischen Deutschen." *Zeitschrift für Ostforschung*, XVII(1968), pp. 601-32.

Mallinson, Vernon. *Belgium*. New York and Washington, 1970.

Meyer, Wolfgang. *Das Vereinswesen der Stadt Nürnberg im 19. Jahrhundert*. Nürnberg, 1970.

Milner, Henry and Sheilagh H. Milner. *The Decolonization of Quebec*. Toronto, 1973.

Nipperdey, Thomas. *Die Organisation der deutschen Parteien vor 1918.* Düsseldorf, 1961.

———. "Verein als soziale Struktur im späten 18. und frühen 19. Jahrhundert." In Hartmut Boockmann et al., *Geschichtswissenschaft und Vereinswesen im 19. Jahrhundert,* pp. 1-44. Göttingen, 1972.

Pred, A. R. *The Spatial Dynamics of United States Urban-Industrial Growth.* Cambridge, Mass., 1966.

Puhle, Hans-Jürgen. "Parlament, Parteien, und Interessenverbände 1890-1914." In Michael Stürmer, ed., *Das Kaiserliche Deutschland,* pp. 340-77. Düsseldorf, 1970.

Rosenberg, Hans. *Grosse Depression und Bismarckzeit.* Berlin, 1967.

———. "Political and Social Consequences of the Great Depression of 1873-1896 in Central Europe." *Economic History Review,* XIII(1943), pp. 58-73.

———. *Die Weltwirtschaftskrisis von 1857-1859. Vierteljahrschrift für Social- und Wirtschaftsgeschichte,* Beiheft 30. Stuttgart and Berlin, 1934.

Rothman, J. *Minority Group Identification and Intergroup Relations.* New York, 1967.

Schermerhorn, R. A. *Comparative Ethnic Relations: A Framework for Theory and Research.* New York, 1970.

Schmitt, Heinz. *Das Vereinsleben Weinheim.* Weinheim, 1963.

Shafer, Boyd C. *Nationalism: Myth and Reality.* New York, 1955.

Sheehan, James J. *German Liberalism in the Nineteenth Century.* Chicago, 1978.

———. "Liberalism and the City in Nineteenth Century Germany." *Past and Present,* LI(1971), pp. 116-37.

———. "Liberalism and Society in Germany, 1815-48." *Journal of Modern History,* XLV(1973), pp. 583-604.

Shils, Edward. "Primordial, Personal, Sacred, and Civil Ties." *British Journal of Sociology,* VIII(1957), pp. 130-45.

Simpson, George E. and J. Milton Yinger. *Racial and Cultural Minorities.* 4th ed. New York, 1972.

Smith, Constance E. and Anne Freedman. *Voluntary Associations: Perspectives on the Literature.* Cambridge, Mass., 1972.

Sombart, Werner. *Der Bourgeois.* Munich, 1913.

Stein, Maurice R. *The Eclipse of Community.* Princeton, N. J., 1960.

Stephens, Meic. *Linguistic Minorities in Western Europe.* Llandysul, 1976.

Sugar, Peter F. "External and Domestic Roots of Eastern European Nationalism." In Ivo J. Lederer and Sugar, ed., *Nationalism in Eastern Europe,* pp. 3-54. Seattle, 1969.

Thernstrom, Stephan. *The Other Bostonians.* Cambridge, Mass., 1973.

———. *Poverty and Progress: Social Mobility in a 19th Century City.* Cambridge, Mass., 1964.

Thomas, Dorothy S. *Research Memorandum on Migration Differentials.* New York, 1938.

——— and Simon Kuznets, ed. *Population Redistribution and Economic Growth*. 3 vols. Philadelphia, 1957-64.

Wäntig, H. *Gewerbliche Mittelstandspolitik*. Leipzig, 1897.

Wagner, Gustav. *Die Deutschen in Litauen: Ihre Kulturellen und Wirtschaftlichen Gemeinschaften zwischen den beiden Weltkriegen*. Marburg a. d. Lahn, 1959.

Weber, Adna Ferrin. *The Growth of Cities in the Nineteenth Century*. 1899. Reprint. Ithaca, 1963.

Weber, Max. "Class, Status, and Party." In Hans Gerth and C. Wright Mills, ed., *From Max Weber: Essays in Sociology*, pp. 180-95. New York, 1946.

Wehler, Hans-Ulrich. *Das Deutsche Kaiserreich 1871-1918*. Göttingen, 1973.

Windisch, E. V. "Die Entstehung der Voraussetzungen für die Nationalitätenbewegung in Ungarn in der zweiten Hälfte des 19. Jahrhunderts." *Acta Historica Academie Scientarum Hungaricae*, XI(1965), pp. 3-56.

Wittram, Reinhard. *Baltische Geschichte: Die Ostseelande Livland, Estland, Kurland 1180-1918*. Munich, 1954.

Wrigley, E. A. *Population and History*. New York and Toronto, 1969.

———, ed. *Nineteenth-Century Society: Essays in the use of Quantitative Methods for the Study of Social Data*. Cambridge, 1972.

Wuorinen, John H. *A History of Finland*. New York and London, 1965.

———. *Nationalism in Modern Finland*. New York, 1931.

Yeo, Stephen. *Religion and Voluntary Organisations in Crisis*. London, 1976.

Zolberg, Aristide R. "The Making of Flemings and Walloons: Belgium, 1830-1914." *Journal of Interdisciplinary History*, V(1974-75), pp. 179-236.

Library of Congress Cataloging in Publication Data

Cohen, Gary B., 1948-
　The politics of ethnic survival.

　Originally presented as the author's thesis (Ph.D.)
—Princeton, 1975.
　Bibliography: p.
　Includes index.
　1.　Germans—Czechoslovakia—Prague—History.
2.　Prague (Czechoslovakia)—History.　　I.　Title.
II.　Title: Germans in Prague, 1861-1914.
DB2624.G4C63　　1981　　　943.7'1200431　　　81-47119
ISBN 0-691-05332-4　　　　　　　　　　　　AACR2